1.1:969-76/V.1

2146834849

Jx
33
3
09-76
v.1

D0539184

WITHDRAWN

Foreign Relations of the
United States, 1969–1976

Volume I

Foundations of
Foreign Policy,
1969–1972

Editors	Louis J. Smith
	David H. Herschler
General Editor	David S. Patterson

United States Government Printing Office
Washington
2003

DEPARTMENT OF STATE PUBLICATION 11017

Office of the Historian

Bureau of Public Affairs

For sale by the Superintendent of Documents, U.S. Government Printing Office
Internet: bookstore.gpo.gov   Phone: Toll Free (866) 512-1800;   DC area (202) 512-1800
Fax: (202) 512-2250 Mail: Stop SSOP, Washington, DC 20402-0001
ISBN 0-16-051282-4

Preface

The *Foreign Relations of the United States* series presents the official documentary historical record of major foreign policy decisions and significant diplomatic activity of the United States Government. The Historian of the Department of State is charged with the responsibility for the preparation of the *Foreign Relations* series. The staff of the Office of the Historian, Bureau of Public Affairs, plans, researches, compiles, and edits the volumes in the series. Official regulations codifying specific standards for the selection and editing of documents for the series were first promulgated by Secretary of State Frank B. Kellogg on March 26, 1925. These regulations, with minor modifications, guided the series through 1991.

A new statutory charter for the preparation of the series was established by Public Law 102–138, the Foreign Relations Authorization Act, Fiscal Years 1992 and 1993, which was signed by President George Bush on October 28, 1991. Section 198 of P.L. 102–138 added a new Title IV to the Department of State's Basic Authorities Act of 1956 (22 USC 4351, et seq.).

The statute requires that the *Foreign Relations* series be a thorough, accurate, and reliable record of major United States foreign policy decisions and significant United States diplomatic activity. The volumes of the series should include all records needed to provide comprehensive documentation of major foreign policy decisions and actions of the United States Government. The statute also confirms the editing principles established by Secretary Kellogg: the *Foreign Relations* series is guided by the principles of historical objectivity and accuracy; records should not be altered or deletions made without indicating in the published text that a deletion has been made; the published record should omit no facts that were of major importance in reaching a decision; and nothing should be omitted for the purposes of concealing a defect in policy. The statute also requires that the *Foreign Relations* series be published not more than 30 years after the events recorded.

Structure and Scope of the Foreign Relations Series

This volume is part of a subseries of volumes of the *Foreign Relations* series that documents the most important issues in the foreign policy of the administration of Richard M. Nixon. The subseries will present a documentary record of major foreign policy decisions and actions of President Nixon's administration. This volume documents the intellectual assumptions underlying the foreign policy decisions made by the administration.

Focus of Research and Principles of Selection for Foreign Relations, 1969–1976, Volume I

The purpose of this volume, which is a departure from previous volumes published in the *Foreign Relations* series, is to document the intellectual foundations of the foreign policy of the first Nixon administration. Previous volumes have been compiled to meet the legislatively mandated standard that the *Foreign Relations* series shall be "a thorough, accurate, and reliable documentary record of major United States foreign policy decisions and significant diplomatic activity." This volume is unique in that it explores the collective mind-set of the Nixon administration on foreign policy issues rather than documenting foreign policy decisions or diplomatic exchanges. It takes as its canvas the entire record of the first Nixon administration. Therefore the documents selected are necessarily a sampling chosen to illustrate policy perspectives and themes, rather than a thorough record of a bilateral relationship or of a major issue. A measure of the departure of this volume from previous volumes in the *Foreign Relations* series is the extent to which it draws upon the published record of speeches, press releases, press conferences and briefings, interviews, and testimony before Congressional committees to document policy positions and the assumptions of administration officials on the foreign policy process.

President Nixon had a strong interest in foreign policy and he and his assistant for National Security Affairs, Henry Kissinger managed many of the more important aspects of foreign policy from the White House. Nixon and Kissinger shared a well-defined general perception of world affairs. The editors of the volume sought to present a representative selection of documents chosen to develop the primary intellectual themes that ran through and animated the administration's foreign policy. The documents selected focus heavily upon the perspectives of Nixon and Kissinger but also include those of Secretary of State Rogers, Secretary of Defense Laird, Under Secretary of State Richardson and others.

In a volume that explores the administration's intellectual assumptions on a variety of issues, three principal themes emerge. During a stop on Guam in July 1969, President Nixon articulated what would become known as the Nixon doctrine. Conditioned by the experience of Vietnam, Nixon defined a more limited role for the United States in potential future conflicts. He stated "that as far as the problems of military defense, except for the threat of a major power involving nuclear weapons, the United States is going to encourage and has the right to expect that this problem will be handled by, and responsibility for it taken by, Asian nations themselves." The Nixon doctrine was subsequently expanded to apply to all allies of the United States. A second foreign policy theme that runs through the record of the first Nixon administration is that of linkage, the concept of linking progress on foreign policy issues in dealing with the Soviet Union. Triangular diplomacy, the third theme developed in the volume, involved balancing relations with the Soviet Union and the People's Republic of China. Triangular diplomacy embraced the assumptions underlying the diplomatic opening to China and the Moscow summit in 1972.

Editorial Methodology

The documents are presented chronologically according to Washington time. Memoranda of conversation are placed according to the time and date of the conversation, rather than the date the memorandum was drafted.

Editorial treatment of the documents published in the *Foreign Relations* series follows Office style guidelines, supplemented by guidance from the General Editor and the chief technical editor. The source text is reproduced as exactly as possible, including marginalia or other notations, which are described in the footnotes. Texts are transcribed and printed according to accepted conventions for the publication of historical documents within the limitations of modern typography. A heading has been supplied by the editors for each document included in the volume. Spelling, capitalization, and punctuation are retained as found in the source text, except that obvious typographical errors are silently corrected. Other mistakes and omissions in the source text are corrected by bracketed insertions: a correction is set in italic type; an addition in roman type. Words or phrases underlined in the source text are printed in italics. Abbreviations and contractions are preserved as found in the source text, and a list of abbreviations is included in the front matter of each volume.

Bracketed insertions are also used to indicate omitted text that deals with an unrelated subject (in roman type) or that remains classified after declassification review (in italic type). The amount of material not declassified has been noted by indicating the number of lines or pages of source text that were omitted. Entire documents withheld for declassification purposes have been accounted for and are listed with headings, source notes, and number of pages not declassified in their chronological place. All brackets that appear in the source text are so identified by footnotes.

The first footnote to each document indicates the source of the document, original classification, distribution, and drafting information. This note also provides the background of important documents and policies and indicates whether the President or his major policy advisers read the document.

Editorial notes and additional annotation summarize pertinent material not printed in the volume, indicate the location of additional documentary sources, provide references to important related documents printed in other volumes, describe key events, and provide summaries of and citations to public statements that supplement and elucidate the printed documents. Information derived from memoirs and other first-hand accounts has been used when appropriate to supplement or explicate the official record.

The numbers in the index refer to document numbers rather than to page numbers.

Advisory Committee on Historical Diplomatic Documentation

The Advisory Committee on Historical Diplomatic Documentation, established under the Foreign Relations statute, reviews records, advises, and makes recommendations concerning the *Foreign Relations* series. The Advisory Committee monitors the overall compilation and editorial process of the series and advises on all aspects of the preparation and declassification of the series. The Advisory Committee does not necessarily review the contents of individual volumes in the series, but it makes recommendations on issues that come to its attention and reviews volumes as it deems necessary to fulfill its advisory and statutory obligations.

The Advisory Committee encouraged the addition of this volume to the *Foreign Relations* series and reviewed and endorsed the compilation.

Presidential Recordings and Materials Preservation Act Review

Under the terms of the Presidential Recordings and Materials Preservation Act (PRMPA) of 1974 (44 USC 2111 note), the National Archives and Records Administration (NARA) has custody of the Nixon Presidential historical materials. The requirements of the PRMPA and implementing regulations govern access to the Nixon Presidential historical materials. The PRMPA and implementing public access regulations require NARA to review for additional restrictions in order to ensure the protection of the privacy rights of former Nixon White House officials, since these officials were not given the opportunity to separate their personal materials from public papers. Thus, the PRMPA and implementing public access regulations require NARA formally to notify the Nixon estate and former Nixon White House staff members that the agency is scheduling for public release Nixon White House historical materials. The Nixon estate and former White House staff members have 30 days to contest the release of Nixon historical materials in which they were a participant or are mentioned. Further, the PRMPA and implementing regulations require NARA to segregate and return to the creator of files private and personal materials. All *Foreign Relations* volumes that include materials from NARA's Nixon Presidential Materials Staff are processed and released in accordance with the PRMPA.

Declassification Review

The Information Response Branch of the Office of IRM Programs and Services, Bureau of Administration, Department of State, conducted the declassification review for the State Department of the documents published in this volume. The review was conducted in accordance with the standards set forth in Executive Order 12958 on Classified National Security Information and applicable laws.

The principle guiding declassification review is to release all information, subject only to the current requirements of national security as embodied in law and regulation. Declassification decisions entailed concurrence of the appropriate geographic and functional bureaus in the Department of State, other concerned agencies of the U.S. Government, and the appropriate foreign governments regarding specific documents of those governments.

The final declassification review of this volume, which began in 2001 and was completed in 2002, resulted in the decision to withhold minor excisions in two documents; no documents were withheld in full. The editors are confident, on the basis of the research conducted in preparing this volume and as a result of the declassification review process described above, that the documentation and editorial notes presented here provide an undiluted record of the intellectual foundations of the foreign policy of the first Nixon administration.

Acknowledgments

The editor wishes to acknowledge the assistance of officials at the Nixon Presidential Materials Project of the National Archives and Records Administration (Archives II), at College Park, Maryland.

Paul Claussen, Evan Duncan, David Goldman, David Herschler, Joseph Hilts, Susan Holly, Douglas Keene, Daniel Lawler, Sidney Ploss, and Louis Smith collected the documentation for this volume. David Herschler and Louis Smith selected and edited it, under the supervision of David S. Patterson, the then General Editor of the *Foreign Relations* series. Rita M. Baker did the copy and technical editing, and Susan C. Weetman coordinated the final declassification review. Juniee Oneida prepared the index.

Marc J. Susser
The Historian
Bureau of Public Affairs

March 2003

Contents

Sources

Sources for the Foreign Relations Series

The Foreign Relations statute requires that the published record in the *Foreign Relations* series include all records needed to provide comprehensive documentation on major U.S. foreign policy decisions and significant U.S. diplomatic activity. It further requires that government agencies, departments, and other entities of the U.S. Government engaged in foreign policy formulation, execution, or support cooperate with the Department of State Historian by providing full and complete access to records pertinent to foreign policy decisions and actions and by providing copies of selected records. Many of the sources consulted in the preparation of this volume have been declassified and are available for review at the National Archives and Records Administration.

The editors of the *Foreign Relations* series have complete access to all the retired records and papers of the Department of State: the central files of the Department; the special decentralized files ("lot files") of the Department at the bureau, office, and division levels; the files of the Department's Executive Secretariat, which contain the records of international conferences and high-level official visits, correspondence with foreign leaders by the President and Secretary of State, and memoranda of conversations between the President and Secretary of State and foreign officials; and the files of overseas diplomatic posts. All the Department's indexed central files through July 1973 have been permanently transferred to the National Archives and Records Administration at College Park, Maryland (Archives II). Many of the Department's decentralized office (or lot) files covering the 1969–1976 period, which the National Archives deems worthy of permanent retention, have been transferred or are in the process of being transferred from the Department's custody to Archives II.

The editors of the *Foreign Relations* series also have full access to the papers of President Nixon and other White House foreign policy records, including tape recordings of conversations with key U.S. and foreign officials. Presidential papers maintained and preserved at the Presidential libraries and the Nixon Presidential Materials Project at Archives II include some of the most significant foreign affairs-related documentation from the Department of State and other Federal agencies including the National Security Council, the Central Intelligence Agency, the Department of Defense, and the Joint Chiefs of Staff.

Access to the Nixon White House tape recordings is governed by the terms of the Presidential Recordings and Materials Preservation Act (P.L. 93–526; 88 Stat. 1695) and an access agreement with the Office of Presidential Libraries of the National Archives and Records Administration and the Nixon estate. In February 1971 President Nixon initiated a voice activated taping system in the Oval Office of the White House and, subsequently, in the President's Office in the Executive Office Building, Camp David, the Cabinet Room, and White House and Camp David telephones. The audiotapes include conversations of President Nixon with his Assistant for National Security Affairs Henry Kissinger, other White House aides, Secretary of State Rogers, other Cabinet officers, members of Congress, and key foreign officials. The clarity of the voices on the tape recordings is often very poor, but the editors made every effort to verify the accuracy of the transcripts that they prepared of the recorded conversations. Readers are urged to consult the recordings for a full appreciation of those aspects of the discussions that cannot be fully captured in a transcription, such as the speakers' inflections and emphases that may convey nuances of meaning, as well as the larger context of the discussion.

Research for this volume was completed through special access to restricted documents at the Nixon Presidential Materials Project. While all the material printed in this volume has been declassified, some of it is extracted from still-classified documents. The Nixon Presidential Materials Staff is processing and declassifying many of the documents used in this volume, but they may not be available in their entirety at the time of publication.

Sources for Foreign Relations, 1969–1976, Volume I

Research for this volume was undertaken by a team of ten historians, two of whom compiled the volume from the collective research. The experience of the team in researching other *Foreign Relations* volumes governed the decisions made concerning the collections and specific files searched for the volume. Research into the full foreign policy record of the Nixon administration was necessarily selective.

Much of the record included in the volume was drawn from public sources. Speeches and policy statements were garnered from a number of sources, the most important of which were the *Public Papers of the Presidents of the United States* and the Department of State *Bulletin*. A very useful source of information on the intellectual assumptions underlying foreign policy proved to be the background briefings that Kissinger provided periodically to the press. Kissinger sometimes provided these briefings in conjunction with other senior officials, such as Joseph Sisco, and Nixon very occasionally provided a background briefing as well. These documents were not classified but they were not made public in order to protect the identities of those giving the briefings.   The background briefings can be found in the Library of Congress, Manuscript Division, Kissinger Papers, Subject File, Boxes CL 425–426.

Among the classified sources consulted, the most useful were found in the Presidential papers and other White House records maintained by the Nixon Presidential Materials Project. In the White House Special Files, the President's Office Files contain many of the records used in the volume of Nixon's meetings with foreign leaders.   The Office Files also include Patrick Buchanan's summaries of Nixon's meetings with leaders of Congress on foreign policy issues.   In the National Security Council Files, the Agency Files, the Subject Files, the President's Trip Files, and the Presidential/HAK Memcons were particularly useful. The agency files for the National Security Council and the Department of State contain thoughtful assessments of the foreign policy process.   The Subject Files include memoranda from Kissinger to Nixon as well as memoranda of conversation involving Kissinger and the President.   The President's Trip Files contain the very valuable memoranda of Kissinger's conversations with Soviet Ambassador Anatoly Dobrynin. Among the most productive of the files researched of those maintained by the Nixon Presidential Materials Project were the National Security Council Secretariat Files pertaining to the annual reports on foreign policy that President Nixon submitted to Congress beginning on February 18, 1970. The reports grew out of wide-ranging conceptual analysis, only some of which could be included in the volume. These files can be found in boxes 1303–1309 of the Nixon Project's NSC collection. Boxes 325–328 contain NSC Files, Subject Files, which also include material on The President's Annual Review of Foreign Policy, 1970–1972.

Of the files of the Department of State's Secretariat, the most useful for the purposes of this volume were the conference files and the Head of State correspondence. The Senior Review Group of the National Security Council conducted reviews of major foreign policy issues. The records of the Senior Review Group were consulted at the National Security Council before they were transferred to the National Archives. They are now housed in the Nixon Presidential Materials, NSC Institutional Files (H-Files).

The Kissinger Papers at the Library of Congress include records of Kissinger's telephone conversations. Boxes 359–375 contain a chronological file of transcripts of conversations covering the period 1969–1972. Boxes 394–395 comprise the Dobrynin file of telephone conversations, including Kissinger's conversations with Soviet Ambassador Dobrynin and Chargé Vorontsov. Boxes 396–397 contain transcripts of conversations tape-recorded at Kissinger's residence. The entire collection is invaluable for the light it sheds on the full range of foreign policy issues dealt with by the Nixon administration. There are few instances in the collection, however, of broad, conceptual exchanges.

Much of the documentation used in the volume has been made available for use in the *Foreign Relations* series thanks to the consent of the agencies mentioned, the assistance of their staffs, and especially the cooperation and support of the National Archives and Records Administration.

The following list identifies the particular files and collections used in the preparation of this volume. The declassification and transfer to the National Archives of the Department of State records is in process, and many of these records are already available for public review at the National Archives. The declassification review of other records is going forward in accordance with the provisions of Executive Orders 12958 and 13142, under which all records over 25 years old, except file series exemptions requested by agencies and approved by the President.

Unpublished Sources

Richard Nixon Library and Birthplace, Yorba Linda, California

Nixon Papers

National Archives and Records Administration, College Park, Maryland

Record Group 59, General Records of the Department of State

Lot Files

S/S Files: Lot 70 D 387
    Conference Files, January 1969–February 1970

S/S Files: Lot 70 D 419
    Visit Files, 1968–1969

S/S Files: Lot 71 D 227
    Conference Files

S/S Files: Lot 71 D 228
    Transition books for the Nixon administration, December 1968

S/S Files: Lot 71 D 243
    Visit Files, January–December 1970

S/S Files: Lot 72 D 319
    Presidential Correspondence with United States Ambassadors, July 1969–April 1971

S/S Files: Lot 72 D 320
    Head of State correspondence, January 1969–May 1971

S/S Files: Lot 72 D 373
  Miscellaneous trip and visit files, 1970–1972

S/S Files: Lot 73 D 288
  NSC/Cabinet files, 1970–1972

S/S Files: Lot 73 D 323
  Conference Files, 1971–1972

S/S Files: Lot 74 D 164
  President's Evening Reading, 1964–1973; Kissinger–Irwin meetings, 1970–1972

S/S Files: Lot 76 D 435
  Records of US-USSR conversations, 1961–1970

S/S–I Files: Lot 79 D 245
  International conferences attended by the President, Secretary of State, and others, 1949–1970

S/S–NSC Files: Lot 80 D 212
  National Security Study Memoranda (NSSMs), January 1969–May 1980

S/S–NSC Files: Lot 81 D 309
  National Security Council Under Secretaries Committee, Study Memoranda, 1969–1976

S/S–NSC Files: Lot 83 D 276
  National Security Council Under Secretaries Committee, 1969–1977

S/S–I Files: 86 D 183
  National Security Council files, 1969–1977

Nixon Presidential Materials Project

National Security Council Secretariat Files
  Richard M. Nixon Annual Review 1970–1974

National Security Council Files
  Agency Files
  President's Trip Files
  Kissinger Office Files
  Subject Files
  Presidential/HAK Memcons
  Staff Files
  VIP Visits

National Security Council Institutional Files
  Senior Review Group Minutes
  National Security Council Meeting Minutes

White House Special Files
  President's Office Files

White House Central Files
  Staff Members and Office Files, Office of Presidential Papers and Archives, Daily Diary

White House Tapes

Washington National Records Center, Suitland, Maryland

Department of Defense

OSD Files: FRC 330 76–0028
  Secretary of Defense staff meetings, 1969–1972

Library of Congress, Washington, D.C.

Manuscript Division
  Kissinger Papers
  Richardson Papers

United States Senate

Records of the Senate Foreign Relations Committee

Published Sources

U.S. Government Documentary Collections

U.S. Department of State, Department of State *Bulletin*, 1969–1972

U.S. Foreign Assistance in the 1970's: Report to the President of the United States From the Task Force on International Development (Washington:, D.C., Government Printing Office, 1970)

U.S. National Archives and Records Administration, *Public Papers of the Presidents of the United States: Richard Nixon, 1969, 1970, 1971, 1972* (Washington, D.C.: Government Printing Office, 1970, 1971, 1972, 1973)

U.S. *Weekly Compilation of Presidential Documents, 1969, 1970, 1971, 1972* (Washington, D.C.: Government Printing Office, 1970, 1971, 1972, 1973)

Memoirs

Kissinger, Henry A., *American Foreign Policy: Three Essays* (New York: W.W. Norton & Company, 1969)

Kissinger, Henry A., *White House Years* (Boston: Little, Brown and Company, 1979)

Nixon, Richard, *RN: The Memoirs of Richard Nixon* (New York: Grosset & Dunlap, 1978)

Nixon–Agnew Campaign Committee, *Nixon on the Issues* (New York: 1968)

Abbreviations

ABC, American Broadcasting Company
ABM, anti-ballistic missile
ADB, Asian Development Bank
AID, Agency for International Development
ANZUS, Australia, New Zealand, United States (security treaty)
ASEAN, Association of South East Asian Nations
ASPAC, Asian and Pacific Council

CBS, Columbia Broadcasting System
CBW, chemical and biological weapons
CENTO, Central Treaty Organization
CIA, Central Intelligence Agency
CIAP, Comite Interamericana de la Alianza para el Progreso (Inter-American Committee on the Alliance for Progress)
CIEP, Council on International Economic Policy

DPRC, Defense Program Review Committee

FRG, Federal Republic of Germany (West Germany)
FY, Fiscal Year

GATT, General Agreement on Tariffs and Trade
GDR, German Democratic Republic (East Germany)
GNP, Gross National Product
GVN, Government of Vietnam

HR, designation for legislation introduced in the House of Representatives

IBRD, International Bank for Reconstruction and Development (World Bank)
ICBM, inter-continental ballistic missile
IMF, International Monetary Fund

LDC, less developed countries

MACV, Military Assistance Command, Vietnam
MIRV, multiple individually targeted reentry vehicles

NATO, North Atlantic Treaty Organization
NBC, National Broadcasting Company
NLF, National Liberation Front
NPT, Non-Proliferation Treaty
NSC, National Security Council
NSDM, National Security Decision Memorandum
NSSM, National Security Study Memorandum

POW, prisoner of war
PRC, People's Republic of China

RG, Record Group
ROC, Republic of China

SALT, Strategic Arms Limitation Talks
SDS, Students for a Democratic Society
SEATO, Southeast Asia Treaty Organization
SIOP, Single Integrated Operational Plan
SLBM, submarine-launched ballistic missile
SST, supersonic transport

TV, television

UAR, United Arab Republic
UK, United Kingdom
UN, United Nations
US, United States
USSR, Union of Soviet Socialist Republics

WEU, West European Union
WW, World War

Persons

Brezhnev, Leonid, General Secretary of the Communist Party of the Soviet Union

Buchanan, Patrick, Special Assistant to the President

Butterfield, Alexander P., Deputy Assistant to the President

Ceausescu, Nicolae, President of Romania

Chiang Kai-shek, President of the Republic of China

Chou En-lai, Premier of the State Council of the People's Republic of China

Dayan, Moshe, Defense Minister of Israel

De Gaulle, Charles, President of France

Dobrynin, Anatoly F., Soviet Ambassador to the United States

Ehrlichman, John D., Counsel to the President, January–November 1969; thereafter Assistant to the President for Domestic Affairs

Flanigan, Peter, Assistant to the President

Gromyko, Andrei A., Soviet Foreign Minister

Haig, Alexander M., Jr., Senior Military Assistant to the President for National Security Affairs, January 1969–June 1970; Deputy Assistant to the President for National Security Affairs, June 1970–January 1973

Haldeman, H. R., Assistant to the President

Heath, Edward, Prime Minister of the United Kingdom after June 1970

Kennedy, Richard, member of the National Security Council Staff from January 1970

Keogh, James, Special Assistant to the President, January 1969–December 1971

Kissinger, Henry A., Assistant to the President for National Security Affairs

Klein, Herbert G., White House Director of Communications

Kosygin, Alexei N., Chairman of the Council of Ministers of the Soviet Union

Laird, Melvin R., Secretary of Defense

Lord, Winston, member of the National Security Council Staff, 1969–1970; thereafter staff member Office of the Assistant to the President for National Security Affairs

Mao Tse-tung, Chairman of the Chinese Communist Party and of the Politburo of the People's Republic of China

Moynihan, Daniel P., Assistant to the President for Urban Affairs, January–December 1969; Counselor to the President, January 1970–January 1971

Nixon, Richard M., President of the United States

Packard, David, Deputy Secretary of Defense, January 1969–December 1971

Price, Raymond, Special Assistant to the President

Richardson, Elliot L., Under Secretary of State, January 1969–June 1970; Secretary of Health, Education and Welfare, June 1970–January 1973
Rogers, William P., Secretary of State

Safire, William, Special Assistant to the President
Sato, Eisaku, Prime Minister of Japan
Scali, John, Special Consultant to the President
Shultz, George P., Secretary of Labor, January 1969–June 1970; Director of the Office of Management and Budget, June 1970–May 1972; thereafter Secretary of the Treasury
Sisco, Joseph J., Assistant Secretary of State for International Organization Affairs until February 1969, thereafter Assistant Secretary of State for Near Eastern and South Asian Affairs
Smith, Gerard, Director of the Arms Control and Disarmament Agency
Stans, Maurice, Secretary of Commerce

Tito, Josip Broz, President of Yugoslavia

Wilson, Harold, Prime Minister of the United Kingdom until June 1970
Wright, W. Marshall, member of the National Security Council Staff, June 1970–April 1972; Deputy Assistant Secretary of State for Congressional Relations, April–December 1972

Ziegler, Ronald, White House Press Secretary

Foundations of Foreign Policy, 1969–1972

1. Editorial Note

The intellectual assumptions on which the foreign policy of the Nixon administration was based were established, in large measure, by President Nixon and his Assistant for National Security Affairs, Henry Kissinger. Nixon assumed office in 1969 as an established practitioner of foreign policy and Kissinger was a recognized authority on the foreign policy process. Both men came to their new responsibilities with well-developed views on foreign policy. A selection of speeches and writings by Nixon and Kissinger during the 2-year period prior to the assumption of office in 1969 is presented at the beginning of the volume to provide a background for the views developed during the initial 4 years of the administration.

In July 1967 Nixon outlined his views on the role the United States should play in the world in a speech given to the members of the exclusive Bohemian men's club in San Francisco. In his memoirs, Nixon described the speech as the one that gave him the most pleasure and satisfaction of his political career. (See Document 2) Nixon narrowed his focus in the *Foreign Affairs* article he published in October 1967 to "Asia After Vietnam." The article, which stresses a continuing role for the United States as an Asian power, presages the diplomatic opening to China and contains the germ of what would become the Nixon Doctrine. (See Document 3) Nixon's determination to limit the role of the United States in combating Communist aggression in light of the experience in Vietnam is more explicit in an excerpt from a campaign speech he gave in May 1968. (See Document 5) A logical concomitant of the Nixon Doctrine was the perception that the burden of the fighting in South Vietnam would have to shift from United States to South Vietnamese forces. Nixon pointed to the need to "Vietnamize" the war in a campaign speech in October 1968. (See Document 7) Kissinger published an essay in 1968 entitled "Central Issues of American Foreign Policy" which provides an overview of his perspective on foreign policy at that point. (See Document 4)

1

2.   Address by Richard M. Nixon to the Bohemian Club[1]

San Francisco, July 29, 1967.

My fellow Bohemians and our guests: In my years of making speeches, I have never appeared on an occasion where more of the audience was behind me!

After four months of travel to four continents, I can't tell you how good it is to be back at Bohemia. It is dangerous to be dogmatic about any issue in the world today. But of this one thing I am sure—it's much more pleasant to get stoned in Bohemia than in Caracas.

It was Mr. Hoover's custom on this occasion to put into perspective some of the great issues of the day. In that tradition, I would like to discuss American foreign policy.

I do not intend to dwell on current issues like Vietnam and the Mid-East which are the subject of such constant attention in the daily press. Rather, I suggest we do what we Americans seldom have the time and patience to do: Let us take the long view. Let us evaluate the great forces at work in the world and see what America's role should be if we are to realize our destiny of preserving peace and freedom in the world in this last third of the twentieth century.

One striking impression stands out after months of travel to major countries: We live in a new world. Never in human history have more changes taken place in the world in one generation.

It is a world of new leaders. True, De Gaulle, Mao Tse-tung and Chiang Kai-shek are still with us; but Churchill, Adenauer, Stalin, Khrushchev, Nehru, Sukarno—the other giants of the post-war period have all left the world stage.

It is a world of new people. One-half of the people now living in the world were born since World War II. This presents at once a problem and an opportunity for peace. Because, as one Asian Prime Minister puts it, the new generation has neither the old fears nor the old guilts of the old generation.

It is a world of new ideas. Communism, Marxism, Socialism, anti-colonialism—the great ideas which stirred men to revolution after

---

[1] Source: The Richard Nixon Library, Nixon Papers. Unclassified; Off-the-Record; Not for Publication. Printed by permission of the Richard Nixon Library and Birthplace, Yorba Linda, California. The speech was delivered in the Bohemian Grove, on the shore of a small lake near San Francisco, site of the annual retreat of the Bohemian men's club. Nixon notes in his memoirs that former President Herbert Hoover had regularly delivered the featured Lakeside address at the retreat, and after Hoover's death in 1964, Nixon was invited to deliver the 1967 address in Hoover's honor. (*RN: The Memoirs of Richard Nixon*, p. 284)

World War II have lost their pulling power. As the Shah of Iran says—"the new generation is not imprisoned by any ism." The young people in all countries on both sides of the Iron Curtain are groping for a new cause—a new religion. If any idea "turns them on" it is a new sense of pragmatism—"what will work."

Because we live in a new world, many of the old institutions are obsolete and inadequate. The UN, NATO, foreign aid, USIA were set up to deal with the world of twenty years ago. A quick trip around the world will show how different the problems are today.

Twenty years ago Western Europe was weak economically and dependent on the United States. It was united by a common fear of the threat of Communist aggression. Today Western Europe is strong economically and economic independence has inevitably led to more political independence. The winds of détente have blown so strongly from East to West that except for Germany most Europeans no longer fear the threat from the East. The consequences of this change are enormous as far as NATO is concerned. As Harold Macmillan puts it, "Alliances are kept together by fear, not by love." Even without De Gaulle, the European Alliance would be in deep trouble.

Let us look at the Communist world. Twenty years ago the Soviet Union dominated a monolithic Communist empire. Today, the Soviet Union and Communist China are in a bitter struggle for leadership of the Communist world. Eastern Europe turns West, though we must recognize that the differences in Eastern Europe still cause less trouble to the Soviet Union than the differences in Western Europe cause to the United States. The Soviet economic system is turning away from the enforced equality of Marxism to the incentives of capitalism.

Let us look at Latin America:

Twenty years ago Castro was a nobody. Cuba and all the other Latin republics were considered to be solidly, permanently, and docilely on the side of the United States. Today Castro has the strongest military force in the Western Hemisphere next to the United States and he is exporting revolution all over the continent. But even if Castro did not exist, Latin America would have to be considered a major trouble spot. Despite the Alliance for Progress, Latin America is barely holding its own in the race between production and population. As it continues to fall further behind the rest of the world, it becomes a tinder box for revolution.

Let us turn to Africa:

Just ten years ago Ethiopia and Liberia were the only independent countries in Black Africa. Today there are thirty independent countries in Black Africa. Fifteen of these countries have populations less than the State of Maryland, and each has a vote in the UN Assembly equal to that of the United States. There were twelve coups in Black Africa in the last year. No one of the thirty countries has a representative government by our standards and the prospects that any will have such a government in a generation or even a half-century are remote.

Ironically, non-Communist Asia, except for Vietnam, is the area which has experienced the most hopeful change. Japan has recovered from the devastation of World War II to the point that its one hundred million people produce as much as Communist China's seven hundred million. Korea, Taiwan, Singapore, Malaysia, and Thailand are all dramatic economic success stories.

There are grey areas:

As General Romulo might put it, the Philippines suffer from too much American style democracy. Indonesia is recovering from too much Sukarno. India suffers from too many people and a host of other problems too numerous to enumerate. But over-all, it can be said without fear of contradiction that the prospects for progress in non-Communist Asia are better than those in Communist Asia.

Let us look at the balance of power in the world:

Twenty years ago the United States had a monopoly on the atomic bomb and our military superiority was unquestioned. Even five years ago our advantage was still decisive. Today the Soviet Union may be ahead of us in megaton capacity and will have missile parity with the United States by 1970. Communist China within five years will have a significant deliverable nuclear capability.

Finally, let us look at American prestige:

Twenty years ago, after our great World War II victory, we were respected throughout the world. Today, hardly a day goes by when our flag is not spit upon, a library burned, an embassy stoned some place in the world. In fact, you don't have to leave the United States to find examples.

This is a gloomy picture; but there is a much brighter side as well.

Communism is losing the ideological battle with freedom in Asia, Africa, Latin America as well as in Europe. In Africa, the Communist appeal was against colonialism. Now that the colonialists are gone, they must base their case on being for Communism. But African tribalism and rebellious individualism are simply incompatible with the rigid discipline a Communist system imposes.

In Latin America, the utter failure of Communism in Cuba has drastically weakened the appeal of the Communist ideology in the rest of Latin America.

In Asia, the remarkable success of private enterprise oriented economies in Japan, Korea, Taiwan, Malaysia and Thailand, as con-

trasted to the failure of Communism in China and the failure of socialism in Burma and Indonesia, makes it possible to state unequivocally
that the only way for the Communists to win in Vietnam, or anywhere
else in Asia, is by force and terror; they will never win by persuasion.

All over the world, whether from East Germany to West, from
Communist China to free China, from Communist Cuba to the free
American republics, the traffic is all one way—from Communism to
freedom.

Let us reappraise U.S. policy in the light of the new world in which
we live.

In Western Europe we must recognize that clearly apart from De
Gaulle's actions the new economic independence of European countries
and the lack of fear of Soviet aggression have contributed to a situation
where it is not possible to keep the old alliance together on its former
basis.

Yet, whatever changes may have occurred as far as the Soviet threat
is concerned, one factor has not changed: A major reason for setting up
the alliance was to provide a military, political and economic home for
the most powerful people in Europe—the Germans. If the alliance is
allowed to continue to disintegrate, Germany, denied the right to develop nuclear weapons, will be left defenseless in the heart of Europe and
the Soviet Union, holding the pawn of East Germany, will have a tempting diplomatic target.

The highest priority American foreign policy objective must be to
set up a new alliance, multilateral, if possible, bilateral, if necessary,
which will keep Germany solidly on the Western side.

Let us look at the third world—Africa, Asia, Latin America. We
reach one inescapable conclusion—foreign aid needs a complete overhaul.

More money alone is not the answer. Latin America is a case in
point. Nine billion dollars has been spent on the Alliance for Progress in
the last six years with these results: The growth rate in Latin America
was less than in the previous five years. The growth rate in Latin
America was less than that of non-Communist Asia and of Communist
Eastern Europe. Latin America will become a permanent international
depressed area unless revolutionary changes are made in its economic,
educational and governmental institutions.

Krieger of Argentina, probably the ablest of Latin America's economic ministers, puts the case this way: "You Americans should be
more blunt in attaching conditions to your aid programs. Of course, the
recipients aren't going to like it. But the United States does us no favor
when you aid an unsound economic and social institution. All you do
is to help perpetuate a system that should be changed."

In that spirit, let us use our aid programs to work toward such objectives as the following:

The Latin American educational system is the most obsolete and inadequate in the world in terms of preparing students for contributions to a modern industrial state. It must be modernized and brought into the twentieth century.

In Latin America, Africa, as well as in countries like India, there should be more emphasis on agriculture, less on industrialization.

In every area of the world private, rather than government, enterprise should be encouraged, not because we are trying to impose our ideas but because one works and the other doesn't.

The United States should use its aid programs to reward our friends and discourage our enemies. Before the recent Mid-East crisis, the fact that the U.S. had continued its aid programs to countries like the U.A.R., Algeria and Guinea when their leaders never missed a chance to condemn the United States in world forums had the effect of discouraging our friends, confusing the neutrals and bringing contempt from our enemies.

I would like to illustrate my last point with an example. Four of the most dramatic economic success stories are Thailand, Iran, Taiwan and Mexico.

Thailand has a limited monarchy.

Iran has a strong monarchy.

Taiwan has a strong President with an oligarchy.

Mexico has one-party government.

Not one of these countries has a representative democracy by Western standards. But it happens that in each case their system has worked for them.

It is time for us to recognize that much as we like our own political system, American style democracy is not necessarily the best form of government for people in Asia, Africa and Latin America with entirely different backgrounds.

Let us turn now to the most fundamental question—why continue foreign aid at all? We must recognize that frustration over Vietnam, disillusionment with our European allies who, despite our immense post-World War II aid to them, more often than not refused to cooperate with us in our foreign policy objectives, and the shocking mismanagement and waste in many of the aid programs have all combined to create a new spirit of isolationism in the United States which is becoming stronger in both political parties.

But, let us take a longer view. With the advance of transportation and communications so vividly described by other Lakeside speakers, the world by the end of this century will be a great city. As the world becomes smaller, the differences between rich and poor will appear much larger. The three billion people living in the less advanced areas of the world will not tolerate permanent second class economic status. For example, at that time the people of the United States will have a per capita income ten times as large as that of our closest friends and neighbors in Latin America. The time to defuse this potentially explosive situation is now.

Let us turn now to subject A, the Soviet Union.

This Spring a great debate raged in the chanceries of Europe and among foreign policy experts in the United States as to how much Soviet policy had changed under its new leaders. Some Soviet experts on both sides of the Atlantic saw the new Soviet leaders turning 180 degrees from past policies and seeking permanent peace with the United States and Europe as well as using their influence to end the war in Vietnam.

The record of the Soviets in the Middle East war has caused a sober reassessment of this point of view. At a time that they were talking peace and détente in Europe, the Soviet leaders were spending 4 billion dollars arming Nasser and his colleagues. They encouraged the Arab leaders in their aggressive actions. They blocked diplomatic moves to avoid the war. They supported a cease-fire only when it became necessary for them to do so to save their Arab clients from further losses.

Then came the Glassboro conference. Kosygin was a gentleman. He did not bang his shoe on the table at the United Nations. Many hoped that the Soviet leaders had learned their lesson and the spirit of Hollybush swept over the land. But it soon became apparent that, while the music was different, the words were the same.

More revealing have been the actions of the Soviet leaders since Glassboro. Kosygin stopped to see Castro on his way back to Moscow. The Soviet Union is sending millions of dollars in arms to build the shattered Arab armies. The Soviet Union is still providing 100 per cent of the oil and 85 per cent of all sophisticated military equipment for the armies of North Vietnam. The Soviet line against West Germany has perceptively hardened. The Soviet Union continues to build both offensive and defensive missiles.

This does not mean that the Soviet leaders have not changed. But what we must recognize is that the change is one of the head and not of the heart—of necessity, not choice.

These are some of the facts which forced the change: Communist China is a threat in the East; the Soviet Union needs friends in the West. The military and economic strength of Western Europe thwarted their progressive designs on that area. They faced increased demand for consumer goods from the Russian people. They looked down the nuclear gunbarrel in the Cuban confrontation.

The Soviet leaders today have three major foreign policy objectives:

They are still Communists and they are committed to the goal of a Communist world; they are battling the Chinese for leadership of that world. They want to achieve that goal without war. At the same time they want more economic progress at home. They will work with us only when doing so serves one or more of these three objectives.

In the light of this analysis, the policy America should follow becomes clear.

Militarily, we must recognize that we have not had a world war for twenty years because of America's clear military superiority. That superiority is now threatened, both because of Soviet progress in missile development and because of an attitude in U.S. policy circles that nuclear parity with the Soviets is enough. Because the primary Soviet goal is still victory rather than peace, we must never let the day come in a confrontation like Cuba and the Mid-East where they, rather than we, have military superiority. The cost of maintaining that superiority, including the development of an ABM capability, is a necessary investment in peace.

Economically, we should have a policy which encourages more trade with the Soviet Union and Eastern European countries. We must recognize, however, that to them trade is a political weapon. I believe in building bridges but we should build only our end of the bridge. For example, there should be no extension of long term credits or trade in strategic items with any nation, including the Soviet Union, which aids the enemy in North Vietnam.

Diplomatically we should have discussions with the Soviet leaders at all levels to reduce the possibility of miscalculation and to explore the areas where bilateral agreements would reduce tensions. But we must always remember in such negotiations that our goal is different from theirs: We seek peace as an end in itself. They seek victory with peace being at this time a means toward that end.

In sum, we can live in peace with the Soviet Union but until they give up their goal for world conquest it will be for them a peace of necessity and not of choice.

As we enter this last third of the twentieth century the hopes of the world rest with America. Whether peace and freedom survive in the world depends on American leadership.

Never has a nation had more advantages to lead. Our economic superiority is enormous; our military superiority can be whatever we choose to make it. Most important, it happens that we are on the right side—the side of freedom and peace and progress against the forces of totalitarianism, reaction and war.

There is only one area where there is any question—that is whether America has the national character and moral stamina to see us through this long and difficult struggle.

In this context, the tragic events in Detroit take on a new meaning. This was more than just another Negro riot. The looters were white as well as black. We are reaping the whirlwind for a decade of growing disrespect for law, decency and principle in America.

Without sanctimonious moralizing, let's look at some hard facts. Our judges have gone too far in weakening the peace forces as against the criminal forces in this country. Our opinion-makers have gone too far in promoting the doctrine that when a law is broken—blame society, not the criminal. Our teachers, preachers and politicians have gone too far in advocating the idea that each individual should determine what laws are good and what laws are bad and that he then should obey the law he likes and disobey the law he dislikes.

In the aftermath of these tragic events everyone will have a solution. Some will say we need more laws. Others will say we need more law enforcement. Others will say we need more money for cities, housing, education and welfare. Each of these approaches deserves consideration and some should be adopted.

But in the final analysis there could be no progress without respect for law. There will be no respect for law in a nation whose people lack character. We need a national crusade to build American character in home, church and school. Above all, we need examples of character from our great men.

We in Bohemia were privileged to know such a man.

I could describe Herbert Hoover as a great statesman. I could describe him as a great businessman. I could describe him as a great humanitarian. But, above all, he will be remembered as a man of great character.

No leader in our history was more viciously vilified. Deserted by his friends, maligned by his enemies, he triumphed over adversity. In the twilight of his life he stood tall above his detractors. His triumph was a triumph of character. We can be thankful that he was one of those rare men who lived to hear the overwhelmingly favorable verdict of history on his career.

Two thousand years ago when these great trees were saplings—the poet Sophocles wrote, "One must wait until the evening to see how splendid the day has been."

Herbert Hoover's life was eloquent proof of those words.

And as we near the evening of another Bohemian Encampment, we, too, can look back and say, "How splendid the day has been."

---

3.   **Article by Richard M. Nixon**[1]

ASIA AFTER VIET NAM

The war in Viet Nam has for so long dominated our field of vision that it has distorted our picture of Asia. A small country on the rim of the continent has filled the screen of our minds; but it does not fill the map. Sometimes dramatically, but more often quietly, the rest of Asia has been undergoing a profound, an exciting and on balance an extraordinarily promising transformation. One key to this transformation is the emergence of Asian regionalism; another is the development of a number of the Asian economies; another is gathering disaffection with all the old isms that have so long imprisoned so many minds and so many governments. By and large the non-communist Asian governments are looking for solutions that work, rather than solutions that fit a preconceived set of doctrines and dogmas.

Most of them also recognize a common danger, and see its source as Peking. Taken together, these developments present an extraordinary set of opportunities for a U.S. policy which must begin to look beyond Viet Nam. In looking toward the future, however, we should not ignore the vital role Viet Nam has played in making these developments possible. Whatever one may think of the "domino" theory, it is beyond question that without the American commitment in Viet Nam Asia would be a far different place today.

The U.S. presence has provided tangible and highly visible proof that communism is not necessarily the wave of Asia's future. This was a vital factor in the turnaround in Indonesia, where a tendency toward fatalism is a national characteristic. It provided a shield behind which the anti-communist forces found the courage and the capacity to stage their counter-coup and, at the final moment, to rescue their country from the Chinese orbit. And, with its 100 million people, and its 3,000-

---

[1] Source: *Foreign Affairs*, Vol. 46, No. 1, October 1967, pp. 113–125. Reprinted by permission of *Foreign Affairs*, 2002. Copyright 1967 by the Council on Foreign Relations, Inc.

mile arc of islands containing the region's richest hoard of natural resources, Indonesia constitutes by far the greatest prize in the Southeast Asian area.

Beyond this, Viet Nam has diverted Peking from such other potential targets as India, Thailand and Malaysia. It has bought vitally needed time for governments that were weak or unstable or leaning toward Peking as a hedge against the future—time has imposed severe strains on the United States, not only militarily and economically but socially and politically as well. Bitter dissension has torn the fabric of American intellectual life, and whatever the outcome of the war the tear may be a long time mending. If another friendly country should be faced with an externally supported communist insurrection—whether in Asia, or in Africa or even Latin America—there is serious question whether the American public or the American Congress would now support a unilateral American intervention, even at the request of the host government. This makes it vitally in their own interest that the nations in the path of China's ambitions move quickly to establish an indigenous Asian framework for their own future security.

In doing so, they need to fashion arrangements able to deal both with old-style wars and with new—with traditional wars, in which armies cross over national boundaries, and with the so-called "wars of national liberation," in which they burrow under national boundaries.

I am not arguing that the day is past when the United States would respond militarily to communist threats in the less stable parts of the world, or that a unilateral response to a unilateral request for help is out of the question. But other nations must recognize that the role of the United States as world policeman is likely to be limited in the future. To ensure that a U.S. response will be forthcoming if needed, machinery must be created that is capable of meeting two conditions: (a) a collective effort by the nations of the region to contain the threat by themselves; and, if that effort fails, (b) a collective request to the United States for assistance. This is important not only from the respective national standpoints, but also from the standpoint of avoiding nuclear collision.

Nations not possessing great power can indulge in the luxury of criticism of others; those possessing it have the responsibility of decision. Faced with a clear challenge, the decision not to use one's power must be as deliberate as the decision to use it. The consequences can be fully as far-reaching and fully as irrevocable.

If another world war is to be prevented, every step possible must be taken to avert direct confrontations between the nuclear powers. To achieve this, it is essential to minimize the number of occasions on which the great powers have to decide whether or not to commit their forces. These choices cannot be eliminated, but they can be reduced by the development of regional defense pacts, in which nations undertake, among themselves, to attempt to contain aggression in their own areas.

If the initial response to a threatened aggression, of whichever type—whether across the border or under it—can be made by lesser powers in the immediate area and thus within the path of aggression, one of two things can be achieved: either they can in fact contain it by themselves, in which case the United States is spared involvement and thus the world is spared the consequences of great-power action; or, if they cannot, the ultimate choice can be presented to the United States in clear-cut terms, by nations which would automatically become allies in whatever response might prove necessary. To put it another way, the regional pact becomes a buffer separating the distant great power from the immediate threat. Only if the buffer proves insufficient does the great power become involved, and then in terms that make victory more attainable and the enterprise more palatable.

This is particularly important when the threat takes the form of an externally supported guerrilla action, as we have faced in Viet Nam, as is even now being mounted in Thailand, and as could be launched in any of a half-dozen other spots in the Chinese shadow. Viet Nam has shown how difficult it is to make clear the distinction between this and an ordinary factional civil war, and how subject the assisting power is to charges of having intervened in an internal matter. Viet Nam's neighbors know that the war there is not internal, but our own allies in Europe have difficulty grasping the fact.

The fragmenting of the communist world has lent credence to the frequently heard argument that a communist advance by proxy, as we have seen attempted in Viet Nam, is of only peripheral importance; that with the weakening of rigid central control of the communist world, local fights between communist and non-communist factions are a local matter. This ignores, however, the fact that with the decentralization of communist control has come an appropriately tailored shift in communist tactics. National communism poses a different kind of threat than did the old-style international communism, but by being subtler it is in some ways more dangerous.

SEATO was useful and appropriate to its time, but it was Western in origin and drew its strength from the United States and Europe. It has weakened to the point at which it is little more than an institutional embodiment of an American commitment, and a somewhat anachronistic relic of the days when France and Britain were active members. Asia today needs its own security undertakings, reflecting the new realities of Asian independence and Asian needs.

Thus far, despite a pattern of rapidly increasing cooperation in cultural and economic affairs, the Asian nations have been unwilling to form a military grouping designed to forestall the Chinese threat, even though several have bilateral arrangements with the United States. But an appropriate foundation-stone exists on which to build: the Asian and Pacific Council. ASPAC held its first ministerial-level meeting in Seoul in June 1966, and its second in Bangkok in July 1967. It has carefully limited itself to strengthening regional cooperation in economic, cultural and social matters, and its members have voiced strong feelings that, as Japan's Foreign Minister Takeo Miki put it at the Bankok meeting, it should not be made "a body to promote anti-communist campaigns."

Despite ASPAC's present cultural and economic orientation, however, the solidifying awareness of China's threat should make it possible—if the need for a regional alliance is put in sufficiently compelling terms—to develop it into an alliance actively dedicated to concerting whatever efforts might be necessary to maintain the security of the region. And ASPAC is peculiarly well situated to play such a role. Its members (South Korea, Japan, Taiwan, Thailand, Malaysia, South Viet Nam, the Philippines, Australia and New Zealand, with Laos as an observer) all are acutely conscious of the Chinese threat. All except Malaysia have military ties with the United States. It has the distinct advantage of including Australia and New Zealand, which share the danger and would be able to contribute substantially to its strength, without an unbalancing great-power presence.

I do not mean to minimize the difficulties of winning acceptance of such a concept. In Japan, public opinion still lags behind official awareness of military needs. The avowedly neutralist nations under China's cloud would be reluctant, at present, to join any such grouping. But looking further down the road we can project either an erosion of their neutralism or the formation of their own loose association or associations, which might be tied into a militarily oriented ASPAC on an interlocking or cooperative basis. One can hope that even India might finally be persuaded to give its support, having itself been the target of overt Chinese aggression, and still cherishing as it does a desire to play a substantial role beyond its own borders.

III[2]

Military security has to rest, ultimately, on economic and political stability. One of the effects of the rapidity of change in the world today is that there can no longer be static stability; there can only be dynamic stability. A nation or society that fails to keep pace with change is in danger of flying apart. It is important that we recognize this, but equal-

---

[2] There are no sections marked I or II.

ly important that in trying to maintain a dynamic stability we remember that the stability is as important as the dynamism.

If a given set of ends is deemed desirable, then from the standpoint of those dedicated to peace and an essential stability in world order the desideratum is to reach those ends by evolutionary rather than revolutionary means. Looking at the pattern of change in non-communist Asia, we find that the professed aims of the revolutionaries are in fact being achieved by an evolutionary process. This offers a dramatic opportunity to draw the distinction between the fact of a revolutionary *result* and the *process* of revolutionary change. The Asian nations are showing that evolutionary change can be as exciting as revolutionary change. Having revolutionized the aims of their societies, they are showing what can be achieved within a framework of dynamic stability.

The "people," in the broadest sense, have become an entity to be served rather than used. In much of Asia, this change represents a revolution of no less magnitude than the revolution that created the industrial West, or that in the years following World War II transformed empires into new and struggling nations. It is precisely the promise of this reversal that has been at the heart of communist rhetoric, and at the heart of the popular and intellectual appeal which that rhetoric achieved.

Not all the governments of non-communist Asia fit the Western ideal of parliamentary democracy—far from it. But Americans must recognize that a highly sophisticated, highly advanced political system, which required many centuries to develop in the West, may not be best for other nations which have far different traditions and are still in an earlier stage of development. What matters is that these governments are consciously, deliberately and programmatically developing in the direction of greater liberty, greater abundance, broader choice and increased popular involvement in the processes of government.

Poverty that was accepted for centuries as the norm is accepted no longer. In a sense it could be said that a new chapter is being written in the winning of the West: in this case, a winning of the promise of Western technology and Western organization by the nations of the East. The cultural clash has had its cost and produced its strains, but out of it is coming a modernization of ancient civilizations that promises to leap the centuries.

The process produces transitional anomalies—such as the Indian woman squatting in the mud, forming cow-dung patties with her hands and laying them out to dry, while a transistor radio in her lap plays music from a Delhi station. It takes a long time to bring visions of the future to the far villages—but time is needed to make those visions credible, and make them achievable. Too wide a gap between reality and expectation always produces an explosive situation, and the fact that what the leaders know is possible is unknown to the great mass of the peasantry helps buy time to make the possible achievable. But the important thing is that the leaders do know what is possible, and by and large they are determined to make it happen.

Whether that process is going to proceed at a pace fast enough to keep one step ahead of the pressure of rising expectations is one of the great questions and challenges of the years ahead. But there is solid ground for hope. The successful Asian nations have been writing extra-ordinary records. To call their performance an economic miracle would be something of a semantic imprecision; it would also be a disservice. Precisely because the origins and ingredients of that success are not miraculous, it offers hope to those which have not yet turned the corner.

India still is a staggering giant, Burma flirts with economic chaos, and the Philippines, caught in a conflict of cultures and in search of an identity, lives in a precarious economic and social balance. But the most exciting trends in economic development today are being recorded by those Asian nations that have accepted the keys of progress and used them. Japan, Hong Kong, Taiwan, Thailand, Korea, Singapore and Malaysia all have been recording sustained economic growth rates of 7 percent a year or more; Japan has sustained a remarkable average of 9 percent a year since 1950, and an average 16.7 percent per year increase in exports over the same period. Thailand shifted into a period of rapid growth in 1958 and has averaged 7 percent a year since. South Korea, despite the unflattering estimates of its people's abilities by the average G.I. during the Korean War, is shooting ahead at a growth rate that has averaged 8 percent a year since 1963, with an average 42 percent a year increase in its exports.

These rapidly advancing countries vary widely in their social traditions and political systems, but their methods of economic management have certain traits in common: a prime reliance on private enterprise and on the pricing mechanisms of the market as the chief determinant of business decisions; a pacing of monetary expansion to match growth in output; receptivity to private capital investment, both domestic and foreign, including such incentives as tax advantages and quick government clearance of proposed projects; imaginative national programs for dealing with social problems; and, not least, a generally restrained posture in government planning, with the government's role suggestive rather than coercive. These nations have, in short, discovered and applied the lessons of America's own economic success.

IV

Any discussion of Asia's future must ultimately focus on the respective roles of four giants: India, the world's most populous non-communist nation; Japan, Asia's principal industrial and economic power; China, the world's most populous nation and Asia's most immediate threat; and the United States, the greatest Pacific power. (Although the U.S.S.R. occupies much of the land map of Asia, its principal focus is toward the West and its vast Asian lands are an appendage of European Russia.)

India is both challenging and frustrating: challenging because of its promise, frustrating because of its performance. It suffers from escalating overpopulation, from too much emphasis on industrialization and not enough on agriculture, and from too doctrinaire a reliance on government enterprise instead of private enterprise. Many are deeply pessimistic about its future. One has to remember, however, that in the past five years India has fought two wars and faced two catastrophic droughts. On both the population and the agricultural fronts, India's present leaders at least are trying. And the essential factor, from the standpoint of U.S. policy, is that a nation of nearly half a billion people is seeking ways to wrench itself forward without a sacrifice of basic freedoms; in exceedingly difficult circumstances, the ideal of evolutionary change is being tested. For the most populous representative democracy in the world to fail, while Communist China—surmounting its troubles—succeeded, would be a disaster of worldwide proportions. Thus the United States must do two things: (1) continue its aid and support for Indian economic objectives; and (2) do its best to persuade the Indian Government to shift its means and adjust its institutions so that those objectives can be more quickly and more effectively secured, drawing from the lessons not only of the United States but also of India's more successful neighbors, including Pakistan.

Japan has been edging cautiously and discreetly toward a wider leadership role, acutely conscious at every step that bitter memories of the Greater East Asia Co-Prosperity Sphere might rise to haunt her if she pressed too hard or too eagerly. But what would not have been possible ten, or even five, years ago is becoming possible today. Half the people now living in Asia have been born since World War II, and the new generation has neither the old guilts (in the case of the Japanese themselves) nor the old fears born of conquest.

The natural momentum of Japan's growth, the industry of her people and the advanced state of her society must inevitably propel Japan into a more conspicuous position of leadership. Japan's industrial complex, expanding by 14 percent annually since 1950, already is comparable to that of West Germany or the United Kingdom. Japan's gross national product ($95 billion) is substantially greater than that of mainland China, with seven times the population. Japan is expected soon to rank as the world's third-strongest economic power, trailing only the

United States and the Soviet Union. Along with this dramatic economic surge, Japan will surely want to play a greater role both diplomatically and militarily in maintaining the balance in Asia. As the Prime Minister of one neighboring country put it: "The Japanese are a great people, and no great people will accept as their destiny making better transistor radios and teaching the underdeveloped how to grow better rice."

This greater role will entail, among other things, a modification of the present terms of the Japanese Constitution, which specifically provides that "land, sea and air forces, as well as other war potential, will never be maintained." (Japan's 275,000 men presently under arms are called "Self-Defense Forces.") Twenty years ago it was considered unthinkable that Japan should acquire even a conventional military capability. Five years ago, while some Japanese thought about it, they did not talk about it. Today a substantial majority of Japanese still oppose the idea, but it is openly discussed and debated. Looking toward the future, one must recognize that it simply is not realistic to expect a nation moving into the first rank of major powers to be totally dependent for its own security on another nation, however close the ties. Japan's whole society has been restructured since World War II. While there still are traces of fanaticism, its politics at least conform to the democratic ideal. Not to trust Japan today with its own armed forces and with responsibility for its own defense would be to place its people and its government under a disability which, whatever its roots in painful recent history, ill accords with the role Japan must play in helping secure the common safety of non-communist Asia.

Any American policy toward Asia must come urgently to grips with the reality of China. This does not mean, as many would simplistically have it, rushing to grant recognition to Peking, to admit it to the United Nations and to ply it with offers of trade—all of which would serve to confirm its rulers in their present course. It does mean recognizing the present and potential danger from Communist China, and taking measures designed to meet that danger. It also means distinguishing carefully between long-range and short-range policies, and fashioning short-range programs so as to advance our long-range goals.

Taking the long view, we simply cannot afford to leave China forever outside the family of nations, there to nurture its fantasies, cherish its hates and threaten its neighbors. There is no place on this small planet for a billion of its potentially most able people to live in angry isolation. But we could go disastrously wrong if, in pursuing this long-range goal, we failed in the short range to read the lessons of history.

The world cannot be safe until China changes. Thus our aim, to the extent that we can influence events, should be to induce change. The way to do this is to persuade China that it *must* change: that it cannot satisfy its imperial ambitions, and that its own national interest requires a turning away from foreign adventuring and a turning inward toward the solution of its own domestic problems.

If the challenge posed by the Soviet Union after World War II was not precisely similar, it was sufficiently so to offer a valid precedent and a valuable lesson. Moscow finally changed when it, too, found that change was necessary. This was essentially a change of the head, not of the heart. Internal evolution played a role, to be sure, but the key factor was that the West was able to create conditions—notably in the shoring up of European defenses, the rapid restoration of European economies and the cementing of the Atlantic Alliance—that forced Moscow to look to the wisdom of reaching some measure of accommodation with the West. We are still far from reaching a full détente, but at least substantial progress has been made.

During the next decade the West faces two prospects which, together, could create a crisis of the first order: (1) that the Soviets may reach nuclear parity with the United States; and (2) that China, within three to five years, will have a significant deliverable nuclear capability—and that this same China will be outside any nonproliferation treaty that might be signed, free, if it chooses, to scatter its weapons among "liberation" forces anywhere in the world.

This heightens the urgency of building buffers that can keep the major nuclear powers apart in the case of "wars of national liberation," supported by Moscow or Peking but fought by proxy. It also requires that we now assign to the strengthening of non-communist Asia a priority comparable to that which we gave to the strengthening of Western Europe after World War II.

Some counsel conceding to China a "sphere of influence" embracing much of the Asian mainland and extending even to the island nations beyond; others urge that we eliminate the threat by preemptive war. Clearly, neither of these courses would be acceptable to the United States or to its Asian allies. Others argue that we should seek an anti-Chinese alliance with European powers, even including the Soviet Union. Quite apart from the obvious problems involved in Soviet participation, such a course would inevitably carry connotations of Europe vs. Asia, white vs. non-white, which could have catastrophic repercussions throughout the rest of the non-white world in general and Asia in particular. If our long-range aim is to pull China back in to the family of nations, we must avoid the impression that the great powers or the European powers are "ganging up;" the response should clearly be one of active defense rather than potential offense, and must be untainted with any suspicion of racism.

For the United States to go it alone in containing China would not only place an unconscionable burden on our own country, but also would heighten the chances of nuclear war while undercutting the independent development of the nations of Asia. The primary restraint on China's Asian ambitions should be exercised by the Asian nations in the path of those ambitions, backed by the ultimate power of the United States. This is sound strategically, sound psychologically and sound in terms of the dynamics of Asian development. Only as the nations of non-communist Asia become so strong—economically, politically and militarily—that they no longer furnish tempting targets for Chinese aggression, will the leaders in Peking be persuaded to turn their energies inward rather than outward. And that will be the time when the dialogue with mainland China can begin.

For the short run, then, this means a policy of firm restraint, of no reward, of a creative counterpressure designed to persuade Peking that its interests can be served only by accepting the basic rules of international civility. For the long run, it means pulling China back into the world community—but as a great and progressing nation, not as the epicenter of world revolution.

"Containment without isolation" is a good phrase and a sound concept, as far as it goes. But it covers only half the problem. Along with it, we need a positive policy of pressure and persuasion, of dynamic detoxification, a marshaling of Asian forces both to keep the peace and to help draw off the poison from the Thoughts of Mao.

Dealing with Red China is something like trying to cope with the more explosive ghetto elements in our own country. In each case a potentially destructive force has to be curbed; in each case an outlaw element has to be brought within the law; in each case dialogues have to be opened; in each case aggression has to be restrained while education proceeds; and, not least, in neither case can we afford to let those now self-exiled from society stay exiled forever. We have to proceed with both an urgency born of necessity and a patience born of realism, moving step by calculated step toward the final goal.

V

And finally, the role of the United States.

Weary with war, disheartened with allies, disillusioned with aid, dismayed at domestic crises, many Americans are heeding the call of the new isolationism. And they are not alone; there is a tendency in the whole Western world to turn inward, to become parochial and isolationist—dangerously so. But there can be neither peace nor security a generation hence unless we recognize now the massiveness of the forces at work in Asia, where more than half the world's people live and where the greatest explosive potential is lodged.

Out of the wreckage of two world wars we forged a concept of an Atlantic community, within which a ravaged Europe was rebuilt and the westward advance of the Soviets contained. If tensions now strain that community, these are themselves a byproduct of success. But history has its rhythms, and now the focus of both crisis and change is shifting. Without turning our backs on Europe, we have now to reach out westward to the East, and to fashion the sinews of a Pacific community.

This has to be a community in the fullest sense: a community of purpose, of understanding and of mutual assistance, in which military defenses are coordinated while economies are strengthened; a community embracing a concert of Asian strengths as a counterforce to the designs of China; one in which Japan will play an increasing role, as befits its commanding position as a world economic power; and one in which U.S. leadership is exercised with restraint, with respect for our partners and with a sophisticated discretion that ensures a genuinely Asian idiom and Asian origin for whatever new Asian institutions are developed.

In a design for Asia's future, there is no room for heavy-handed American pressures; there is need for subtle encouragement of the kind of Asian initiatives that help bring the design to reality. The distinction may seem superficial, but in fact it is central both to the kind of Asia we want and to the effectiveness of the means of achieving it. The central pattern of the future in U.S.-Asian relations must be American support for Asian initiatives.

The industrial revolution has shown that mass abundance is possible, and as the United States moves into the post-industrial world—the age of computers and cybernetics—we have to find ways to engineer an escape from privation for those now living in mass poverty. There can be no security, whatever our nuclear stockpiles, in a world of boiling resentment and magnified envy. The oceans provide no sanctuary for the rich, no barrier behind which we can hide our abundance.

The struggle for influence in the Third World is a three-way race among Moscow, Peking and the West. The West has offered both idealism and example, but the idealism has often been unconvincing and the example non-idiomatic. However, an industrialized Japan demonstrates the economically possible in Asian terms, while an advancing Asia tied into a Pacific community offers a bridge to the underdeveloped elsewhere. During this final third of the twentieth century, the great race will be between man and change: the race to control change, rather than be controlled by it. In this race we cannot afford to wait for others to act, and then merely react. And the race in Asia is already under way.

4.   **Essay by Henry A. Kissinger**[1]

CENTRAL ISSUES OF AMERICAN FOREIGN POLICY

The twentieth century has known little repose. Since the turn of the century, international crises have been increasing in both frequency and severity. The contemporary unrest, although less apocalyptic than the two world wars which spawned it, is even more profoundly revolutionary in nature.

The essence of a revolution is that it appears to contemporaries as a series of more or less unrelated upheavals. The temptation is great to treat each issue as an immediate and isolated problem which once surmounted will permit the fundamental stability of the international order to reassert itself. But the crises which form the headlines of the day are symptoms of deep-seated structural problems. The international system which produced stability for a century collapsed under the impact of two world wars. The age of the superpowers, which temporarily replaced it, is nearing its end. The current international environment is in turmoil because its essential elements are all in flux simultaneously. This essay will concentrate on structural and conceptual problems rather than specific policy issues.

I. The Structural Problem

For the first time, foreign policy has become global. In the past, the various continents conducted their foreign policy essentially in isolation. Throughout much of history, the foreign policy of Europe was scarcely affected by events in Asia. When, in the late eighteenth and nineteenth

---

[1] Source: From *American Foreign Policy: Three Essays* by Henry Kissinger. (New York: W. W. Norton, 1969), pp. 51–97. © Copyright 1977, 1974, 1969 by Henry Kissinger. Used by permission of W.W. Norton & Company, Inc. The other two essays in the book are entitled "Domestic Structure and Foreign Policy" and "The Vietnam Negotiations." The latter was also published in January 1969 in *Foreign Affairs* (Vol. 47, No. 2). The essay printed here was first published in *Agenda for a Nation* (Washington, D.C.: The Brookings Institution, 1968)

centuries, the European powers were extending their influence through-out the world, the effective decisions continued to be made in only a few great European capitals. Today, statesmen face the unprecedented prob-lem of formulating policy for well over a hundred countries. Every nation, no matter how insignificant, participates in international affairs. Ideas are transmitted almost instantaneously. What used to be consid-ered domestic events can now have world-wide consequences.

The revolutionary character of our age can be summed up in three general statements: (a) the number of participants in the international order has increased and their nature has altered; (b) their technical abil-ity to affect each other has vastly grown; (c) the scope of their purposes has expanded.

Whenever the participants in the international system change, a peri-od of profound dislocation is inevitable. They can change because new states enter the political system, or because there is a change in values as to what constitutes legitimate rule, or, finally, because of the reduction in influence of some traditional units. In our period, all of these factors have combined. Since the end of the Second World War, several score of new states have come into being. In the nineteenth century the emergence of even a few new nations produced decades of adjustment, and after the First World War, the successor states of the Austro-Hungarian Empire were never assimilated. Our age has yet to find a structure which match-es the responsibilities of the new nations to their aspirations.

As the number of participants has increased, technology has multi-plied the resources available for the conduct of foreign policy. A scien-tific revolution has, for all practical purposes, removed technical limits from the exercise of power in foreign policy. It has magnified insecuri-ties because it has made survival seem to depend on the accidents of a technological breakthrough.

This trend has been compounded by the nature of contemporary domestic structures. As long as the states' ability to mobilize resources was limited, the severity of their conflicts had definite bounds. In the eighteenth century, custom restricted the demands rulers by "divine right" could make upon their subjects; a philosophy of minimum gov-ernment performed the same role through much of the nineteenth cen-tury. Our period has seen the culmination of a process started by the French Revolution: the basing of governmental legitimacy on popular support. Even totalitarian regimes are aberrations of a democratic legit-imacy; they depend on popular consensus even when they manufacture it through propaganda and pressure. In such a situation, the consensus is decisive; limitations of tradition are essentially irrelevant. It is an iron-ic result of the democratization of politics that it has enabled states to marshal ever more resources for their competition.

Ideological conflict compounds these instabilities. In the great periods of cabinet diplomacy, diplomats spoke the same language, not only in the sense that French was the lingua franca, but more importantly because they tended to understand intangibles in the same manner. A similar outlook about aims and methods eases the tasks of diplomacy—it may even be a precondition for it. In the absence of such a consensus, diplomats can still meet, but they lose the ability to persuade. More time is spent on defining contending positions than in resolving them. What seems most reasonable to one side will appear most problematical to the other.

When there is ideological conflict, political loyalties no longer coincide with political boundaries. Conflicts among states merge with divisions within nations; the dividing line between domestic and foreign policy begins to disappear. At least some states feel threatened not only by the foreign policy of other countries but also, and perhaps especially, by domestic transformations. A liberalized Communist regime in Prague—which had in no way challenged Soviet preeminence in foreign policy—caused the Kremlin to believe that its vital interests were threatened and to respond by occupying the country without even the pretext of legality.

The tensions produced by ideological conflict are exacerbated by the reduction in influence of the states that were considered great powers before the First World War. The world has become militarily bipolar. Only two powers—the United States and the Union of Soviet Socialist Republics—possess the full panoply of military might. Over the next decade, no other country or group of countries will be capable of challenging their physical preeminence. Indeed, the gap in military strength between the two giant nuclear countries and the rest of the world is likely to increase rather than diminish over that period.

Military bipolarity is a source of rigidity in foreign policy. The guardians of the equilibrium of the nineteenth century were prepared to respond to change with counteradjustment; the policy-makers of the superpowers in the second half of the twentieth century have much less confidence in the ability of the equilibrium to right itself after disturbance. Whatever "balance" there is between the superpowers is regarded as both precarious and inflexible. A bipolar world loses the perspective for nuance; a gain for one side appears as an absolute loss for the other. Every issue seems to involve a question of survival. The smaller countries are torn between a desire for protection and a wish to escape big-power dominance. Each of the superpowers is beset by the desire to maintain its preeminence among its allies, to increase its influence among the uncommitted, and to enhance its security vis-à-vis its opponent. The fact that some of these objectives may well prove incompatible adds to the strain on the international system.

But the age of the superpowers is now drawing to an end. Military bipolarity has not only failed to prevent, it has actually encouraged political multipolarity. Weaker allies have good reason to believe that their defense is in the overwhelming interest of their senior partner. Hence, they see no need to purchase its support by acquiescence in its policies. The new nations feel protected by the rivalry of the superpowers, and their nationalism leads to ever bolder assertions of self-will. Traditional uses of power have become less feasible, and new forms of pressure have emerged as a result of transitional loyalties and weak domestic structures.

This political multipolarity does not necessarily guarantee stability. Rigidity is diminished, but so is manageability. Nationalism may succeed in curbing the preeminence of the superpowers; it remains to be seen whether it can supply an integrating concept more successfully in this century than in the last. Few countries have the interest and only the superpowers have the resources to become informed about global issues. As a result, diplomacy is often geared to domestic politics and more concerned with striking a pose than contributing to international order. Equilibrium is difficult to achieve among states widely divergent in values, goals, expectations, and previous experience.

The greatest need of the contemporary international system is an agreed concept of order. In its absence, the awesome available power is unrestrained by any consensus as to legitimacy; ideology and nationalism, in their different ways, deepen international schisms. Many of the elements of stability which characterized the international system in the nineteenth century cannot be re-created in the modern age. The stable technology, the multiplicity of major powers, the limited domestic claims, and the frontiers which permitted adjustments are gone forever. A new concept of international order is essential; without it stability will prove elusive.

This problem is particularly serious for the United States. Whatever our intentions or policies, the fact that the United States disposes of the greatest single aggregate of material power in the world is inescapable. A new international order is inconceivable without a significant American contribution. But the nature of this contribution has altered. For the two decades after 1945, our international activities were based on the assumption that technology plus managerial skills gave us the ability to reshape the international system and to bring about domestic transformations in "emerging countries." This direct "operational" concept of international order has proved too simple. Political multipolarity makes it impossible to impose an American design. Our deepest challenge will be to evoke the creativity of a pluralistic world, to base order on political multipolarity even though overwhelming military strength will remain with the two superpowers.

II. The Limits of Bipolarity:
The Nature of Power in the Modern Period

Throughout history, military power was considered the final recourse. Statesmen treated the acquisition of additional power as an obvious and paramount objective. As recently as twenty-five years ago, it would have been inconceivable that a country could possess *too much* strength for effective political use; every increment of power was—at least theoretically—politically effective. The minimum aim was to assure the impermeability of the territory. Until the Second World War, a state's strength could be measured by its ability to protect its population from attack.

The nuclear age has destroyed this traditional measure. Increasing strength no longer necessarily confers the ability to protect the population. No foreseeable force level—not even full-scale ballistic missile defenses—can prevent levels of damage eclipsing those of the two world wars. In these conditions, the major problem is to discipline power so that it bears a rational relationship to the objectives likely to be in dispute. The paradox of contemporary military strength is that a gargantuan increase in power has eroded its relationship to policy. The major nuclear powers are capable of devastating each other. But they have great difficulty translating this capability into policy except to prevent direct challenges to their own survival—and this condition is interpreted with increasing strictness. The capacity to destroy is difficult to translate into a plausible threat even against countries with no capacity for retaliation. The margin of superiority of the superpowers over the other states is widening; yet other nations have an unprecedented scope for autonomous action. In relations with many domestically weak countries, a radio transmitter can be a more effective form of pressure than a squadron of B-52s. In other words, power no longer translates automatically into influence. This does not mean that impotence increases influence, only that power does not automatically confer it.

This state of affairs has profound consequences for traditional notions of balance of power. In the past, stability has always presupposed the existence of an equilibrium of power which prevented one state from imposing its will on the others.

The traditional criteria for the balance of power were territorial. A state could gain overwhelming superiority only by conquest; hence, as long as territorial expansion was foreclosed, or severely limited, the equilibrium was likely to be preserved. In the contemporary period, this is no longer true. Some conquests add little to effective military strength; major increases in power are possible entirely through developments within the territory of a sovereign state. China gained more in real military power through the acquisition of nuclear weapons than if it had conquered all of Southeast Asia. If the Soviet Union had occupied Western Europe but had remained without nuclear weapons, it would be less powerful than it is now with its existing nuclear arsenal within its present borders. In other words, the really fundamental changes in the balance of power have all occurred *within* the territorial limits of sovereign states. Clearly, there is an urgent need to analyze just what is understood by power—as well as by balance of power—in the nuclear age.

This would be difficult enough were technology stable. It becomes enormously complicated when a scientific revolution produces an upheaval in weapons technology at five-year intervals. Slogans like "superiority," "parity," "assured destruction," compete unencumbered by clear definitions of their operational military significance, much less a consensus on their political implications. The gap between experts and decision-makers is widening.

In short, as power has grown more awesome, it has also turned abstract, intangible, elusive. Deterrence has become the dominant military policy. But deterrence depends above all on psychological criteria. It seeks to keep an opponent from a given course by posing unacceptable risks. For purposes of deterrence, the opponent's calculations are decisive. A bluff taken seriously is more useful than a serious threat interpreted as a bluff. For political purposes, the meaningful measurement of military strength is the assessment of it by the other side. Psychological criteria vie in importance with strategic doctrine.

The abstract nature of modern power affects domestic disputes profoundly. Deterrence is tested negatively by things which do *not* happen. But it is never possible to demonstrate *why* something has not occurred. Is it because we are pursuing the best possible policy or only a marginally effective one? Bitter debate even among those who believe in the necessity of defense policy is inevitable and bound to be inconclusive. Moreover, the longer peace is maintained—or the more successful deterrence is—the more it furnishes arguments for those who are opposed to the very premises of defense policy. Perhaps there was no need for preparedness in the first place because the opponent never meant to attack. In the modern state, national security is likely to be a highly divisive domestic issue.

The enormity of modern power has destroyed its cumulative impact to a considerable extent. Throughout history the use of force set a precedent; it demonstrated a capacity to use power for national ends. In the twentieth century any use of force sets up inhibitions against resorting to it again. Whatever the outcome of the war in Vietnam, it is clear that it has greatly diminished American willingness to become involved in this form of warfare elsewhere. Its utility as a precedent has therefore been importantly undermined.

The difficulty of forming a conception of power is paralleled by the problem of how to use it diplomatically. In the past, measures to increase readiness signaled the mounting seriousness with which an issue was viewed.[2] But such measures have become less obvious and more dangerous when weapons are always at a high state of readiness—solid-fuel missiles require less than ten minutes to be fired—and are hidden either under the ground or under the oceans. With respect to nuclear weapons, signaling increased readiness has to take place in a narrow range between the danger of failure and the risk of a preemptive strike.

Even when only conventional weapons are involved, the question of what constitutes a politically meaningful threat is increasingly complicated. After the capture of the *Pueblo*, the United States called up thirteen thousand reservists and moved an aircraft carrier into the waters off the shores of Korea. Did the fact that we had to call up reserves when challenged by a fifth-rate military power convey that we meant to act or that we were overextended? Did the move of the aircraft carrier indicate a decision to retaliate or was it intended primarily to strike a pose?

The problem is illustrated dramatically by the war in Vietnam. A massive breakdown of communication occurred not only within the policy-making machinery in the United States but also between the United States and Hanoi. Over the past five years, the U.S. government has found it difficult, if not impossible, to define what it understood by victory. President Johnson extended an open-ended offer for unconditional negotiations. Yet our troops were deployed as if this offer had not been made. The deployment was based on purely military considerations; it did not take into account the possibility that our troops might have to support a negotiation—the timing of which we had, in effect, left to the opponent. Strategy divorced from foreign policy proved sterile.

These perplexities have spurred new interest in arms-control negotiations, especially those dealing with strategic missiles. These negotiations can be important for the peace and security of the world. But to be effective, they require an intellectual resolution of the issues which have bedeviled the formulation of military policy. Unless we are able to give an operational meaning to terms such as "superiority" or "stability," negotiations will lack criteria by which to judge progress.

---

[2] Sometimes these measures got out of control; the mobilization schedules were one of the principal reasons for the outbreak of the First World War. [Footnote in the source text.]

Thus, whatever the course—a continuation of the arms race or arms control—a new look at American national security policy is essential. Over ten years have passed since the last comprehensive, bipartisan, high-level reevaluation of all aspects of national security: the Gaither Committee. A new administration should move quickly to bring about such a review. It should deal with some of the following problems: (a) a definition of the national interest and national security over the next decade; (b) the nature of military power in that period; (c) the relationship of military power to political influence; (d) implications and feasibility (both military and political) of various postures—superiority, parity, and so on; (e) the implications (both political and military) of new developments such as MIRV (multiple individually targeted reentry vehicles) and ballistic missile defenses; (f) the prospects for arms control, including specific measures to moderate the arms race.

III. Political Multipolarity: The Changed Nature of Alliances

No area of policy illustrates more dramatically the tensions between political multipolarity and military bipolarity than the field of alliance policy. For a decade and a half after the Second World War, the United States identified security with alliances. A global network of relationships grew up based on the proposition that deterrence of aggression required the largest possible grouping of powers.

This system of alliances was always in difficulty outside the Atlantic area because it tried to apply principles drawn from the multipolar world of the eighteenth and nineteenth centuries when several major powers of roughly equal strength existed. Then, indeed, it was impossible for one country to achieve dominance if several others combined to prevent it. But this was not the case in the era of the superpowers of the forties and fifties. Outside Europe, our allies added to our strength only marginally; they were in no position to reinforce each other's capabilities.

Alliances, to be effective, must meet four conditions: (1) a common objective—usually defense against a common danger; (2) a degree of joint policy at least sufficient to define the casus belli; (3) some technical means of cooperation in case common action is decided upon; (4) a penalty for noncooperation—that is, the possibility of being refused assistance must exist—otherwise protection will be taken for granted and the mutuality of obligation will break down.

In the system of alliances developed by the United States after the Second World War, these conditions have never been met outside the North Atlantic Treaty Organization (NATO). In the Southeast Asia Treaty Organization (SEATO) and the Central Treaty Organization (CENTO), to which we belong in all but name, there has been no consensus as to the danger. Pakistan's motive for obtaining U.S. arms was not security against a Communist attack but protection against India. The Arab members of CENTO armed not against the U.S.S.R. but against Israel. Lacking a conception of common interests, the members of these alliances have never been able to develop common policies with respect to issues of war and peace. Had they been able to do so, such policies might well have been stillborn anyway, because the technical means of cooperation have been lacking. Most allies have neither the resources nor the will to render mutual support. A state which finds it difficult to maintain order or coherence of policy at home does not increase its strength by combining with states suffering similar disabilities.

In these circumstances, SEATO and CENTO have grown moribund as instruments of collective action. Because the United States has often seemed more eager to engage in the defense of its SEATO and CENTO allies than they themselves, they have become convinced that non-cooperation will have no cost. In fact, they have been able to give the impression that it would be worse for us than for them if they fell to Communism. SEATO and CENTO have become, in effect, unilateral American guarantees. At best, they provide a legal basis for bilateral U.S. aid.

The case is different with NATO. Here we are united with countries of similar traditions and domestic structures. At the start, there was a common conception of the threat. The technical means for cooperation existed. Mechanisms for developing common policies came into being—especially in the military field. Thus in its first decade and a half, NATO was a dynamic and creative institution.

Today, however, NATO is in disarray as well. Actions by the United States—above all, frequent unilateral changes of policy—are partially responsible. But the most important cause is the transformation of the international environment, specifically the decline in the preeminence of the superpowers and the emergence of political multipolarity. Where the alliances outside of Europe have never been vital because they failed to take into account the military bipolarity of the fifties, NATO is in difficulties because it has yet to adjust to the political multipolarity of the late sixties.

When NATO was founded in 1949, Europeans had a dual fear: the danger of an imminent Soviet attack and the prospect of eventual U.S. withdrawal. In the late 1960s, however, the fear of Soviet invasion has declined. Even the attack on Czechoslovakia is likely to restore anxiety about Soviet military aggression only temporarily. At the same time, two decades of American military presence in Europe coupled with American predominance in NATO planning have sharply reduced the fear that America might wash its hands of European concerns.

When NATO was formed, moreover, the principal threat to world peace seemed to lie in a Soviet attack on Europe. In recent years, the view has grown that equally grave risks are likely to arise in trouble spots outside Europe. To most Europeans, these do not appear as immediate threats to their independence or security. The irony here is striking. In the fifties, Europeans were asking for American assistance in Asia and the Middle East with the argument that they were defending the greater interests of freedom. The United States replied that these very interests required American aloofness. Today, the roles are precisely reversed. It is Europe that evades our entreaties to play a global role; that is to say, Europeans do not consider their interests at stake in America's extra-European involvement.

These are symptoms of deeper, structural problems, however. One problem, paradoxically, is the growth of European economic strength and political self-confidence. At the end of the Second World War, Europe was dependent on the United States for economic assistance, political stability, and military protection. As long as Europe needed the shelter of a superpower, American predominance was inevitable. In relations with the United States, European statesmen acted as lobbyists rather than as diplomats. Their influence depended less on the weight of their countries than on the impact of their personalities. A form of consultation evolved whereby Europeans sought to influence American actions by giving us a reputation to uphold or—to put it more crudely—by oscillating between flattery and almost plaintive appeals for reassurance. The United States, secure in its predominance, in turn concentrated on soothing occasional European outbreaks of insecurity rather than on analyzing their causes.

Tutelage is a comfortable relationship for the senior partner, but it is demoralizing in the long run. It breeds illusions of omniscience on one side and attitudes of impotent irresponsibility on the other. In any event, the United States could not expect to perpetuate the accident of Europe's postwar exhaustion into a permanent pattern of international relations. Europe's economic recovery inevitably led to a return to more traditional political pressures.

These changes in Europe were bound to lead to a difficult transitional period. They could have resulted in a new partnership between the United States and an economically resurgent and politically united Europe, as had been envisaged by many of the early advocates of Atlantic unity. However, the European situation has not resolved itself in that way. Thoughtful Europeans know that Europe must unite in some form if it is to play a major role in the long run. They are aware, too, that Europe does not make even approximately the defense effort of which it is capable. But European unity is stymied, and domestic politics has almost everywhere dominated security policy. The result is a massive frustration which expresses itself in special testiness toward the United States.

These strains have been complicated by the growth of Soviet nuclear power. The changed nature of power in the modern period has affected NATO profoundly. As the risks of nuclear war have become enormous, the credibility of traditional pledges of support has inevitably been reduced. In the past, a country would carry out a commitment because, it could plausibly be argued, the consequences of not doing so were worse than those of coming to the ally's assistance. This is no longer self-evident. In each of the last three annual statements by the Secretary of Defense on the U.S. defense posture, the estimate of *dead* in a general nuclear war ranged from 40 to 120 million. This figure will, if anything, increase. It will become more and more difficult to demonstrate that *anything* is worse than the elimination of over half of a society in a matter of days. The more NATO relies on strategic nuclear war as a counter to all forms of attack, the less credible its pledges will be.

The consciousness of nuclear threat by the two superpowers has undermined allied relationships in yet another way. For understandable reasons, the superpowers have sought to make the nuclear environment more predictable—witness the nuclear test ban treaty and the nonproliferation treaty. But the blind spot in our policy has been the failure to understand that, in the absence of full consultation, our allies see in these talks the possible forerunner of a more comprehensive arrangement affecting their vital interests negotiated without them. Strategic arms talks thus emphasize the need of political understanding in acute form. The pattern of negotiating an agreement first and then giving our allies an opportunity—even a full one—to comment is intolerable in the long run. It puts the onus of failure on them, and it prevents them from doing more than quibble about a framework with which they may disagree. Strains have been reinforced by the uncertain American response to the Soviet invasion of Czechoslovakia—especially the reluctance to give up the prospect of a summit meeting. Atlantic relations, for all their seemingly normalcy, thus face a profound crisis.

This state of affairs has been especially difficult for those Americans who deserve most credit for forging existing Atlantic relations. Two decades of hegemony have produced the illusion that present Atlantic arrangements are "natural," that wise policy consists of making the existing framework more tolerable. "Leadership" and "partnership" are invoked, but the content given to these words is usually that which will support the existing pattern. European unity is advocated to enable Europeans to share burdens on a world-wide scale.

Such a view fails to take into account the realities of political multipolarity. The aim of returning to the "great days of the Marshall Plan" is impossible. Nothing would sunder Atlantic relationships so surely as the attempt to reassert the notions of leadership appropriate to the early days of NATO. In the bipolar world of the forties and fifties, order could be equated with military security; integrated command arrangements sufficed as the principal bond of unity. In the sixties, security, while still important, has not been enough. Every crisis from Berlin to Czechoslovakia has seen the call for "strengthening NATO" confined to military dispositions. Within months a malaise has become obvious again because the overriding need for a common political conception has not been recognized. The challenge of the seventies will be to forge unity with political measures.

It is not "natural" that the major decisions about the defense of an area so potentially powerful as Western Europe should be made three thousand miles away. It is not "normal" that Atlantic policies should be geared to American conceptions. In the forties and fifties, practicing unity—through formal resolutions and periodic reassurances—was profoundly important as a symbol of the end of our isolationism. In the decade ahead, we cannot aim at unity as an end in itself; it must emerge from common conceptions and new structures.

"Burden-sharing" will not supply that impetus. Countries do not assume burdens because it is fair, only because it is necessary. While there are strong arguments for Atlantic partnership and European unity, enabling Europe to play a global role is not one of them. A nation assumes responsibilities not only because it has resources but because it has a certain view of its own destiny. Through the greater part of its history—until the Second World War—the United States possessed the resources but not the philosophy for a global role. Today, the poorest Western European country—Portugal—has the widest commitments outside Europe because its historic image of itself has become bound up with its overseas possessions. This condition is unlikely to be met by any other European country—with the possible exception of Great Britain—no matter what its increase in power. Partially as the result of decolonization, Europeans are unlikely to conduct a significant global policy whatever their resources or their degree of unity. Cooperation between the United States and Europe must concentrate on issues within the Atlantic area rather than global partnership.

Even within the Atlantic area, a more equitable distribution of responsibilities has two prerequisites: there must be some consensus in the analysis of the international situation, at least as it affects Europe; there must be a conviction that the United States cannot or will not carry all the burdens alone. Neither condition is met today. The traditional notion of American leadership tends to stifle European incentives for autonomy. Improved consultation—the remedy usually proposed—can only alleviate, not remove, the difficulty.

The problem of consultation is complex, of course. No doubt unilateral American action has compounded the uneasiness produced by American predominance and European weakness. The shift in emphasis of American policy, from the NATO multilateral force to the nonproliferation treaty, and frequent unilateral changes in strategic doctrine, have all tended to produce disquiet and to undermine the domestic position of ministers who had staked their futures on supporting the American viewpoint.

It is far from self-evident, however, that more extensive consultation within the existing framework can be more than a palliative. One problem concerns technical competence. In any large bureaucracy—and an international consultative process has many similarities to domestic administrative procedures—the weight given to advice bears some relation to the competence it reflects. If one partner possesses all the technical competence, the process of consultation is likely to remain barren. The minimum requirement for effective consultation is that each ally have enough knowledge to give meaningful advice.

But there are even more important limits to the process of consultation. The losing party in a domestic dispute has three choices: (a) it can accept the setback with the expectation of winning another battle later on—this is the usual bureaucratic attitude and it is based on the assurance of another hearing; (b) if advice is consistently ignored, it can resign and go into opposition; (c) as the opposition party, it can have the purpose either of inducing the existing government to change its course or of replacing it. If all these avenues are closed, violence or mounting frustration are the consequences.

Only the first option is open to sovereign states bound together by an alliance, since they obviously cannot resign or go into opposition without wrecking the alliance. They cannot affect the process by which their partners' decision-makers are chosen despite the fact that this may be crucial for their fate. Indeed, as long as the need to maintain the alliance overrides all other concerns, disagreement is likely to be stifled. Advice without responsibility and disagreement without an outlet can turn consultation into a frustrating exercise which compounds rather than alleviates discord.

Consultation is especially difficult when it lacks an integrating over-all framework. The consultation about the nonproliferation treaty concerned specific provisions but not the underlying general philosophy which was of the deepest concern to many of our allies, especially Italy and the Federal Republic of Germany. During periods of détente, each ally makes its own approach to Eastern Europe or the U.S.S.R. without attempting to further a coherent Western enterprise. During periods of crisis, there is pressure for American reassurance but not for a clearly defined common philosophy. In these circumstances, consultation runs the risk of being irrelevant. The issues it "solves" are peripheral; the central issues are inadequately articulated. It deals haphazardly in answers to undefined questions.

Such a relationship is not healthy in the long run. Even with the best will, the present structure encourages American unilateralism and European irresponsibility. This is a serious problem for the United States. If the United States remains the trustee of every non-Communist area, it will exhaust its psychological resources. No country can act wisely simultaneously in every part of the globe at every moment of time. A more pluralistic world—especially in relationships with friends—is profoundly in our long-term interest. Political multipolarity, while difficult to get used to, is the precondition for a new period of creativity. Painful as it may be to admit, we could benefit from a counterweight that would discipline our occasional impetuosity and, by supplying historical perspective, modify our penchant for abstract and "final" solutions.

All of this suggests that there is no alternative to European unity either for the United States or for Europe. In its absence, the malaise can only be alleviated, not ended. Ultimately, this is a problem primarily for the Europeans. In the recent past, the United States has often defeated its purposes by committing itself to one particular form of European unity—that of federalism. It has also complicated British membership in the Common Market by making it a direct objective of American policy.

In the next decade the architectonic approach to Atlantic policy will no longer be possible. The American contribution must be more philosophical; it will have to consist more of understanding and quiet, behind-the-scenes encouragement than of the propagation of formal institutional structures. Involved here is the American conception of how nations cooperate. A tradition of legalism and habits of predominance have produced a tendency to multiply formal arrangements.

But growing European autonomy forces us to learn that nations cooperate less because they have a legal obligation to do so than because they have common purposes. Command arrangements cannot substitute for common interests. Coordinated strategy will be empty unless it reflects shared political concepts. The chance of disagreements on peripheral issues may be the price for unity on issues that really matter. The memory of European impotence and American tutelage should not delude us into believing that we understand Europe's problems better than it does itself. Third-force dangers are not avoided by legal formulas, and, more important, they have been overdrawn. It is hard to visualize a "deal" between the Soviet Union and Europe which would jeopardize our interests without jeopardizing European interests first. In any event, a sense of responsibility in Europe will be a much better counter to Soviet efforts to undermine unity than American tutelage.

In short, our relations with Europeans are better founded on developing a community of interests than on the elaboration of formal legal obligations. No precise blueprint for such an arrangement is possible because different fields of activity have different needs. In the military sphere, for example, modern technology will impose a greater degree of integration than is necessary in other areas. Whatever their formal autonomy, it is almost inconceivable that our allies would prefer to go to war without the support of the United States, given the relatively small nuclear forces in prospect for them. Close coordination between Europe and the United States in the military sphere is dictated by self-interest, and Europe has more to gain from it than the United States.

For this very reason, it is in our interest that Europeans should assume much greater responsibility for developing doctrine and force levels in NATO, perhaps by vitalizing such institutions as the West European Union (WEU), perhaps by alternative arrangements. The Supreme Allied Commander should in time be a European.

Military arrangements are not enough, however. Under current conditions, no statesman will risk a cataclysm simply to fulfill a legal obligation. He will do so only if a degree of *political* cooperation has been established which links the fate of each partner with the survival of all the others. This requires an entirely new order of political creativity.

Coordination is especially necessary in East-West relations. The conventional view is that NATO can be as useful an instrument for détente as for defense. This is doubtful—at least in NATO's present form. A military alliance, one of the chief cohesive links of which is its integrated command arrangement, is not the best instrument for flexible diplomacy. Turning NATO into an instrument of détente might reduce its security contribution without achieving a relaxation of tensions. A diplomatic confrontation of NATO and the Warsaw Pact would have all the rigidities of the bipolar military world. It would raise fears in Western Europe of an American-Soviet condominium, and it would tend to legitimize the Soviet hegemonical position in Eastern Europe. Above all, it would fail to take advantage of the flexibility afforded by greater Western European unity and autonomy. As Europe gains structure, its attraction for Eastern Europe is bound to increase. The major initiatives to improve relations between Western and Eastern Europe should originate in Europe with the United States in a reserve position.

Such an approach can work only if there is a real consensus as to objectives. Philosophical agreement can make possible flexibility of method. This will require a form of consultation much more substantial than that which now exists and a far more effective and coherent European contribution.

To be sure, events in Czechoslovakia demonstrate the limits of Eastern European autonomy that the Soviet Union is now prepared to tolerate. But the Soviet Union may not be willing indefinitely to use the Red Army primarily against allies as it has done three times in a decade and a half. In any event, no Western policy can guarantee a more favorable evolution in Central Europe; all it can do is to take advantage of an opportunity if it arises.

Policy outside Europe is likely to be divergent. Given the changed European perspective, an effort to bring about global burden-sharing might only produce stagnation. The allies would be able to agree primarily on doing nothing. Any crisis occurring anywhere would turn automatically and organically world-wide. American acceptance of European autonomy implies also European acceptance of a degree of American autonomy with respect to areas in which, for understandable reasons, European concern has lessened.

There may be opportunities for cooperation in hitherto purely national efforts—for example, our space program. European participation in it could help to remedy the "technological gap."

Finally, under present circumstances, an especially meaningful community of interests can be developed in the social sphere. All modern states face problems of bureaucratization, pollution, environmental control, urban growth. These problems know no national considerations. If the nations of the Atlantic work together on these issues—through either private or governmental channels or both—a new generation habituated to cooperative efforts could develop similar to that spawned in different circumstances by the Marshall Plan.

It is high time that the nations bordering the Atlantic deal—formally, systematically, and at the highest level—with questions such as these: (a) What are the relative roles of Europe and the United States in East-West contacts? (b) Is a division of functions conceivable in which Western Europe plays the principal role in relation to Eastern Europe while the United States concentrates on relationships with the U.S.S.R.? (c) What forms of political consultation does this require? (d) In what areas of the world is common action possible? Where are divergent courses indicated? How are differences to be handled?

Thus, we face the root questions of a multipolar world. How much unity should we want? How much diversity can we stand? These questions never have a final answer within a pluralistic society. Adjusting the balance between integration and autonomy will be the key challenge of emerging Atlantic relations.

IV. Bipolarity and Multipolarity: The Conceptual Problem

In the years ahead, the most profound challenge to American policy will be philosophical: to develop some concept of order in a world which is bipolar militarily but multipolar politically. But a philosophical deepening will not come easily to those brought up in the American tradition of foreign policy.

Our political society was one of the few which was *consciously* created at a point in time. At least until the emergence of the race problem, we were blessed by the absence of conflicts between classes and over ultimate ends. These factors produced the characteristic aspects of American foreign policy: a certain manipulativeness and pragmatism, a conviction that the normal pattern of international relations was harmonious, a reluctance to think in structural terms, a belief in final answers—all qualities which reflect a sense of self-sufficiency not far removed from a sense of omnipotence. Yet the contemporary dilemma is that there are no total solutions; we live in a world gripped by revolutions in technology, values, and institutions. We are immersed in an unending process, not in a quest for a final destination. The deepest problems of equilibrium are not physical but psychological or moral. The shape of the future will depend ultimately on convictions which far transcend the physical balance of power.

The New Nations and Political Legitimacy. This challenge is especially crucial with respect to the new nations. Future historians are likely to class the confusion and torment in the emerging countries with the great movements of religious awakening. Continents which had been dormant for centuries suddenly develop political consciousness. Regions which for scores of years had considered foreign rule as natural struggle for independence. Yet it is a curious nationalism which defines itself not as in Europe by common language or culture but often primarily by the common experience of foreign rule. Boundaries—especially in Africa—have tended to follow the administrative convenience of the colonial powers rather than linguistic or tribal lines. The new nations have faced problems both of identity and of political authority. They often lack social cohesiveness entirely, or they are split into competing groups, each with a highly developed sense of identity.

It is no accident that between the Berlin crisis and the invasion of Czechoslovakia, the principal threats to peace came from the emerging areas. Domestic weakness encourages foreign intervention. The temptation to deflect domestic dissatisfactions into foreign adventures is ever present. Leaders feel little sense of responsibility to an over-all international equilibrium; they are much more conscious of their local grievances. The rivalry of the superpowers offers many opportunities for blackmail.

Yet their relations with other countries are not the most significant aspect of the turmoil of the new countries. It is in the new countries that questions of the purpose of political life and the meaning of political legitimacy—key issues also in the modern state—pose themselves in their most acute form. The new nations weigh little in the physical balance of power. But the forces unleashed in the emergence of so many new states may well affect the moral balance of the world—the convictions which form the structure for the world of tomorrow. This adds a new dimension to the problem of multipolarity.

Almost all of the new countries suffer from a revolutionary malaise: revolutions succeed through the coming together of all resentments. But the elimination of existing structures compounds the difficulty of establishing political consensus. A successful revolution leaves as its legacy a profound dislocation. In the new countries, contrary to all revolutionary expectations, the task of construction emerges as less glamorous and more complex than the struggle for freedom; the exaltation of the quest for independence cannot be perpetuated. Sooner or later, positive goals must replace resentment of the former colonial power as a motive force. In the absence of autonomous social forces, this unifying role tends to be performed by the state.

But the assumption of this role by the state does not produce stability. When social cohesiveness is slight, the struggle for control of authority is correspondingly more bitter. When government is the principal, sometimes the sole, expression of national identity, opposition comes to be considered treason. The profound social or religious schisms of many of the new nations turn the control of political authority quite literally into a matter of life and death. Where political obligation follows racial, religious, or tribal lines, self-restraint breaks down. Domestic conflicts assume the character of civil war. Such traditional authority as exists is personal or feudal. The problem is to make it "legitimate"—to develop a notion of political obligation which depends on legal norms rather than on coercive power or personal loyalty.

This process took centuries in Europe. It must be accomplished in decades in the new nations, where preconditions of success are less favorable than at comparable periods in Europe. The new countries are subject to outside pressures; there is a premium on foreign adventures to bring about domestic cohesiveness. Their lack of domestic structure compounds the already great international instabilities.

The American role in the new nations' efforts to build legitimate authority is in need of serious reexamination. The dominant American view about political structure has been that it will follow more or less automatically upon economic progress and that it will take the form of constitutional democracy.

Both assumptions are subject to serious questions. In every advanced country, political stability preceded rather than emerged from the process of industrialization. Where the rudiments of popular institutions did not exist at the beginning of the Industrial Revolution, they did not receive their impetus from it. To be sure, representative institutions were broadened and elaborated as the countries prospered, but their significant features antedated economic development and are not attributable to it. In fact, the system of government which brought about industrialization—whether popular or authoritarian—has tended to be confirmed rather than radically changed by this achievement.

Nor is democracy a natural evolution of nationalism. In the last century, democracy was accepted by a ruling class whose estimate of itself was founded outside the political process. It was buttressed by a middle class, holding a political philosophy in which the state was considered to be a referee of the ultimately important social forces rather than the principal focus of national consciousness. Professional revolutionaries were rarely involved; their bias is seldom democratic.

The pluralism of the West had many causes which cannot be duplicated elsewhere. These included a church organization outside the control of the state and therefore symbolizing the limitation of government power; the Greco-Roman philosophical tradition of justice based on human dignity, reinforced later by the Christian ethic; an emerging bourgeoisie; a stalemate in religious wars imposing tolerance as a practical necessity and a multiplicity of states. Industrialization was by no means the most significant of these factors. Had any of the others been missing, the Western political evolution could have been quite different.

This is why Communism has never succeeded in the industrialized Western countries for which its theory was devised; its greatest successes have been in developing societies. This is no accident. Industrialization—in its early phases—multiplies dislocations. It smashes the traditional framework. It requires a system of values which makes the sacrifices involved in capital formation tolerable and which furnishes some integrating principles to contain psychological frustrations.

Communism is able to supply legitimacy for the sacrifices inseparably connected with capital formation in an age when the maxims of laissez faire are no longer acceptable. And Leninism has the attraction of providing a rationale for holding on to power. Many of the leaders of the new countries are revolutionaries who sustained themselves through the struggle for independence by visions of the transformations to be brought about after victory. They are not predisposed even to admit the possibility of giving up power in their hour of triumph. Since they usually began their struggle for independence while in a small minority and sustained it against heavy odds, they are not likely to be repelled by the notion that it is possible to "force men to be free."

The ironic feature of the current situation is that Marxism, professing a materialistic philosophy, is accepted only where it does not exist: in some new countries and among protest movements of the advanced democratic countries. Its appeal is its idealistic component and not its economic theory. It offers a doctrine of substantive change and an explanation of final purposes. Its philosophy has totally failed to inspire the younger generation in Communist countries, where its bureaucratic reality is obvious.

On the other hand, the United States, professing an idealistic philosophy, often fails to gain acceptance for democratic values because of its heavy reliance on economic factors. It has answers to technical dislocations but has not been able to contribute much to building a political and moral consensus. It offers a procedure for change but little content for it.

The problem of political legitimacy is the key to political stability in regions containing two-thirds of the world's population. A stable domestic system in the new countries will not automatically produce international order, but international order is impossible without it. An American agenda must include some conception of what we understand by political legitimacy. In an age of instantaneous communication, we cannot pretend that what happens to over two-thirds of humanity is of no concern or interest to the United States. This does not mean that our goal should be to transfer American institutions to the new nations—even less that we should impose them. Nor should we define the problem as how to prevent the spread of Communism. Our goal should be to build a moral consensus which can make a pluralistic world creative rather than destructive.

Irrelevance to one of the great revolutions of our time will mean that we will ultimately be engulfed by it—if not physically, then psychologically. Already some of the protest movements have made heroes of leaders in repressive new countries. The absurdity of founding a claim for freedom on protagonists of the totalitarian state—such as Guevara or Ho or Mao—underlines the impact of the travail of the new countries on older societies which share none of their technical but some of their spiritual problems, especially the problem of the nature of authority in the modern world. To a young generation in rebellion against bureaucracy and bored with material comfort, these societies offer at least the challenge of unlimited opportunity (and occasionally unlimited manipulativness) in the quest for justice.

A world which is bipolar militarily and multipolar politically thus confronts an additional problem. Side by side with the physical balance of power, there exists a psychological balance based on intangibles of value and belief. The presuppositions of the physical equilibrium have changed drastically; those of the psychological balance remain to be discovered.

The Problem of Soviet Intentions. Nothing has been more difficult for Americans to assimilate in the nuclear age than the fact that even enmity is complex. In the Soviet Union, we confront an opponent whose public pronouncements are insistently hostile. Yet the nuclear age imposes a degree of cooperation and an absolute limit to conflicts.

The military relationship with the Soviet Union is difficult enough; the political one confronts us with a profound conceptual problem. A society which regards peace as the normal condition tends to ascribe tension not to structural causes but to wicked or shortsighted individuals. Peace is thought to result either from the automatic operation of economic forces or from the emergence of a more benign leadership abroad.

The debate about Soviet trends between "hard-liners" and "soft-liners" illustrates this problem. Both sides tend to agree that the purpose of American policy is to encourage a more benign evolution of Soviet society—the original purpose of containment was, after all, to bring about the *domestic* transformation of the U.S.S.R. They are at one that a settlement presupposes a change in the Soviet system. Both groups imply that the nature of a possible settlement is perfectly obvious. But the apostles of containment have never specified the American negotiating program to be undertaken from the position of strength their policy was designed to achieve. The advocates of relaxation of tensions have been no more precise; they have been more concerned with atmosphere than with the substance of talks.

In fact, the difference between the "hawks" and "doves" has usually concerned timing: the hawks have maintained that a Soviet change of heart, while inevitable, was still in the future, whereas the doves have argued that it has already taken place. Many of the hawks tend to consider all negotiations as fruitless. Many of the doves argue—or did before Czechoslovakia—that the biggest step toward peace has already been accomplished by a Soviet change of heart about the cold war; negotiations need only remove some essentially technical obstacles.

The difference affects—and sometimes poisons—the entire American debate about foreign policy. Left-wing critics of American foreign policy seem incapable of attacking U.S. actions without elevating our opponent (whether it happens to be Mao or Castro or Ho) to a pedestal. If they discern some stupidity or self-interest on our side, they assume that the other side must be virtuous. They then criticize the United States for opposing the other side. The right follows the same logic in reverse: they presuppose *our* good intentions and conclude that the other side must be perverse in opposing us. Both the left and the right judge largely in terms of intentions. In the process, whatever the issue—whether Berlin or Vietnam—more attention is paid to whether to get to the conference room than what to do once we arrive there. The dispute over Communist intentions has diverted attention from elaborating our own purposes. In some quarters, the test of dedication to peace has been whether one interprets Soviet intentions in the most favorable manner.

It should be obvious, however, that the Soviet domestic situation is complex and its relationship to foreign policy far from obvious. It is true that the risks of general nuclear war should be as unacceptable to Moscow as to Washington; but this truism does not automatically produce détente. It also seems to lessen the risks involved in local intervention. No doubt the current generation of Communist leaders lacks the ideological dynamism of their predecessors who made the revolution; at the same time, they have at their disposal a military machine of unprecedented strength, and they must deal with a bureaucracy of formidable vested interests. Unquestionably, Soviet consumers press their leaders to satisfy their demands; but it is equally true that an expanding modern economy is able to supply *both* guns and butter. Some Soviet leaders may have become more pragmatic; but in an elaborated Communist state, the results of pragmatism are complex. Once power is seized and industrialization is largely accomplished, the Communist Party faces a difficult situation. It is not needed to conduct the government, and it has no real function in running the economy (though it tries to do both). In order to justify its continued existence and command, it may develop a vested interest in vigilance against outside danger and thus in perpetuating a fairly high level of tension.

It is beyond the scope of this essay to go into detail on the issue of internal Communist evolution. But it may be appropriate to inquire why, in the past, every period of détente has proved stillborn. There have been at least five periods of peaceful coexistence since the Bolshevik seizure of power, one in each decade of the Soviet state. Each was hailed in the West as ushering in a new era of reconciliation and as signifying the long-awaited final change in Soviet purposes. Each ended abruptly with a new period of intransigence, which was generally ascribed to a victory of Soviet hard-liners rather than to the dynamics of the system. There were undoubtedly many reasons for this. But the tendency of many in the West to be content with changes of Soviet tone and to confuse atmosphere with substance surely did not help matters. It has enabled the Communist leaders to postpone the choice which they must make sooner or later: whether to use détente as a device to lull the West or whether to move toward a resolution of the outstanding differences. As long as this choice is postponed, the possibility exists that latent crises may run away with the principal protagonists, as happened in the Middle East and perhaps even in Czechoslovakia.

The eagerness of many in the West to emphasize the liberalizing implications of Soviet economic trends and to make favorable interpretation of Soviet intentions a test of good faith may have the paradoxical consequence of strengthening the Soviet hard-liners. Soviet troops had hardly arrived in Prague when some Western leaders began to insist that the invasion would not affect the quest for détente while others continued to indicate a nostalgia for high-level meetings. Such an attitude hardly serves the cause of peace. The risk is great that if there is no penalty for intransigence there is no incentive for conciliation. The Kremlin may use negotiations—including arms control—as a safety valve to dissipate Western suspicions rather than as a serious endeavor to resolve concrete disputes or to remove the scourge of nuclear war.

If we focus our policy discussions on Soviet purposes, we confuse the debate in two ways: Soviet trends are too ambiguous to offer a reliable guide—it is possible that not even Soviet leaders fully understand the dynamics of their system; it deflects us from articulating the purposes we should pursue, whatever Soviet intentions. Peace will not, in any event, result from one grand settlement but from a long diplomatic process, and this process requires some clarity as to our destination. Confusing foreign policy with psychotherapy deprives us of criteria by which to judge the political foundations of international order.

The obsession with Soviet intentions causes the West to be smug during periods of détente and panicky during crises. A benign Soviet tone is equated with the achievement of peace; Soviet hostility is considered to be the signal for a new period of tension and usually evokes purely military countermeasures. The West is thus never ready for a Soviet change of course; it has been equally unprepared for détente and intransigence.

These lines are being written while outrage at the Soviet invasion of Czechoslovakia is still strong. There is a tendency to focus on military implications or to speak of strengthening unity in the abstract. But if history is a guide, there will be a new Soviet peace offensive sooner or later. Thus, reflecting about the nature of détente seems most important while its achievement appears most problematical. If we are not to be doomed to repeat the past, it may be well to learn some of its lessons: we should not again confuse a change of tone with a change of heart. We should not pose false inconsistencies between allied unity and détente; indeed, a true relaxation of tensions presupposes Western unity. We should concentrate negotiations on the concrete issues that threaten peace, such as intervention in the third world. Moderating the arms race must also be high on the agenda. None of this is possible without a concrete idea of what we understand by peace and a creative world order.

V. An Inquiry Into the American National Interest

Wherever we turn, then, the central task of American foreign policy is to analyze anew the current international environment and to develop some concepts which will enable us to contribute to the emergence of a stable order.

First, we must recognize the existence of profound structural problems that are to a considerable extent independent of the intentions of the principal protagonists and that cannot be solved merely by good will. The vacuum in Central Europe and the decline of the Western European countries would have disturbed the world equilibrium regardless of the domestic structure of the Soviet Union. A strong China has historically tended to establish suzerainty over its neighbors; in fact, one special problem of dealing with China—Communism apart—is that it has had no experience in conducting foreign policy with equals. China has been either dominant or subjected.

To understand the structural issue, it is necessary to undertake an inquiry, from which we have historically shied away, into the essence of our national interest and into the premises of our foreign policy. It is part of American folklore that, while other nations have interests, we have responsibilities; while other nations are concerned with equilibrium, we are concerned with the legal requirements of peace. We have a tendency to offer our altruism as a guarantee of our reliability: "We have no quarrel with the Communists," Secretary of State Rusk said on one occasion; "all our quarrels are on behalf of other people."

Such an attitude makes it difficult to develop a conception of our role in the world. It inhibits other nations from gearing their policy to ours in a confident way—a "disinterested" policy is likely to be considered "unreliable." A mature conception of our interest in the world would obviously have to take into account the widespread interest in stability and peaceful change. It would deal with two fundamental questions: What is it in our interest to prevent? What should we seek to accomplish?

The answer to the first question is complicated by an often-repeated proposition that we must resist aggression anywhere it occurs since peace is indivisible. A corollary is the argument that we do not oppose the fact of particular changes but the method by which they are brought about. We find it hard to articulate a truly vital interest which we would defend however "legal" the challenge. This leads to an undifferentiated globalism and confusion about our purposes. The abstract concept of aggression causes us to multiply our commitments. But the denial that our interests are involved diminishes our staying power when we try to carry out these commitments.

Part of the reason for our difficulties is our reluctance to think in terms of power and equilibrium. In 1949, for example, a State Department memorandum justified NATO as follows: "[The treaty][3] obligates the parties to defend the purposes and principles of the United Nations, the freedom, common heritage and civilization of the parties and their free institutions based upon the principles of democracy, individual liberty and the role of law. It obligates them to act in defense of peace and security. It is directed against no one; it is directed solely against aggression. It seeks not to influence any shifting balance of power but to strengthen a balance of principle."

But principle, however lofty, must at some point be related to practice; historically, stability has always coincided with an equilibrium that made physical domination difficult. Interest is not necessarily amoral; moral consequences can spring from interested acts. Britain did not contribute any the less to international order for having a clear-cut concept of its interest which required it to prevent the domination of the Continent by a single power (no matter in what way it was threatened) and the control of the seas by anybody (even if the immediate intentions were not hostile). A new American administration confronts the challenge of relating our commitments to our interests and our obligations to our purposes.

The task of defining positive goals is more difficult but even more important. The first two decades after the end of the Second World War posed problems well suited to the American approach to international relations. Wherever we turned, massive dislocations required attention. Our pragmatic, ad hoc tendency was an advantage in a world clamoring for technical remedies. Our legal bent contributed to the development of many instruments of stability.

In the late sixties, the situation is more complex. The United States is no longer in a position to operate programs globally; it has to encourage them. It can no longer impose its preferred solution; it must seek to evoke it. In the forties and fifties, we offered remedies; in the late sixties and in the seventies our role will have to be to contribute to a structure that will foster the initiative of others. We are a superpower physically, but our designs can be meaningful only if they generate willing coop-

---

[3] All brackets in the source text.

eration. We can continue to contribute to defense and positive programs, but we must seek to encourage and not stifle a sense of local responsibility. Our contribution should not be the sole or principal effort, but it should make the difference between success and failure.

This task requires a different kind of creativity and another form of patience than we have displayed in the past. Enthusiasm, belief in progress, and the invincible conviction that American remedies can work everywhere must give way to an understanding of historical trends, an ordering of our preferences, and above all an understanding of the difference our preferences can in fact make.

The dilemma is that there can be no stability without equilibrium but, equally, equilibrium is not a purpose with which we can respond to the travail of our world. A sense of mission is clearly a legacy of American history; to most Americans, America has always stood for something other than its own grandeur. But a clearer understanding of America's interests and of the requirements of equilibrium can give perspective to our idealism and lead to humane and moderate objectives, especially in relation to political and social change. Thus our conception of world order must have deeper purposes than stability but greater restraints on our behavior than would result if it were approached only in a fit of enthusiasm.

Whether such a leap of the imagination is possible in the modern bureaucratic state remains to be seen. New administrations come to power convinced of the need for goals and for comprehensive concepts. Sooner, rather than later, they find themselves subjected to the pressures of the immediate and the particular. Part of the reason is the pragmatic, issue-oriented bias of our decision-makers. But the fundamental reason may be the persuasiveness of modern bureaucracy. What started out as an aid to decision-making has developed a momentum of its own. Increasingly, the policy-maker is more conscious of the pressures and the morale of his staff than of the purpose this staff is supposed to serve. The policy-maker becomes a referee among quasi-autonomous bureaucratic bodies. Success consists of moving the administrative machinery to the point of decision, leaving relatively little energy for analyzing the decision's merit. The modern bureaucratic state widens the range of technical choices while limiting the capacity to make them.

An even more serious problem is posed by the change of ethic of precisely the most idealistic element of American youth. The idealism of the fifties during the Kennedy era expressed itself in self-confident, often zealous, institution building. Today, however, many in the younger generation consider the management of power irrelevant, perhaps even immoral. While the idea of service retains a potent influence, it does so largely with respect to problems which are clearly *not* connected with the strategic aspects of American foreign policy; the Peace Corps is a good example. The new ethic of freedom is not "civic"; it is indifferent or even hostile to systems and notions of order. Management is equated with manipulation. Structural designs are perceived as systems of "domination"—not of order. The generation which has come of age after the fifties has had Vietnam as its introduction to world politics. It has no memory of occasions when American-supported structural innovations were successful or of the motivations which prompted these enterprises.

Partly as a result of the generation gap, the American mood oscillates dangerously between being ashamed of power and expecting too much of it. The former attitude deprecates the use or possession of force; the latter is overly receptive to the possibilities of absolute action and overly indifferent to the likely consequences. The danger of a rejection of power is that it may result in a nihilistic perfectionism which disdains the gradual and seeks to destroy what does not conform to its notion of utopia. The danger of an overconcern with force is that policy-makers may respond to clamor by a series of spasmodic gestures and stylistic maneuvers and then recoil before their implications.

These essentially psychological problems cannot be overemphasized. It is the essence of a satisfied, advanced society that it puts a premium on operating within familiar procedures and concepts. It draws its motivation from the present, and it defines excellence by the ability to manipulate an established framework. But for the major part of humanity, the present becomes endurable only through a vision of the future. To most Americans—including most American leaders—the significant reality is what they see around them. But for most of the world—including many of the leaders of the new nations—the significant reality is what they wish to bring about. If we remain nothing but the managers of our physical patrimony, we will grow increasingly irrelevant. And since there can be no stability without us, the prospects of world order will decline.

We require a new burst of creativity, however, not so much for the sake of other countries as for our own people, especially the youth. The contemporary unrest is no doubt exploited by some whose purposes are all too clear. But that it is there to exploit is proof of a profound dissatisfaction with the merely managerial and consumer-oriented qualities of the modern state and with a world which seems to generate crises by inertia. The modern bureaucratic state, for all its panoply of strength, often finds itself shaken to its foundations by seemingly trivial causes. Its brittleness and the world-wide revolution of youth—especially in advanced countries and among the relatively affluent—suggest a spiritual void, an almost metaphysical boredom with a political environment that increasingly emphasizes bureaucratic challenges and is dedicated to no deeper purpose than material comfort.

Our unrest has no easy remedy. Nor is the solution to be found primarily in the realm of foreign policy. Yet a deeper nontechnical challenge would surely help us regain a sense of direction. The best and most prideful expressions of American purposes in the world have been those in which we acted in concert with others. Our influence in these situations has depended on achieving a reputation as a member of such a concert. To act consistently abroad we must be able to generate coalitions of shared purposes. Regional groupings supported by the United States will have to take over major responsibility for their immediate areas, with the United States being concerned more with the over-all framework of order than with the management of every regional enterprise.

In the best of circumstances, the next administration will be beset by crises. In almost every area of the world, we have been living off capital—warding off the immediate, rarely dealing with underlying problems. These difficulties are likely to multiply when it becomes apparent that one of the legacies of the war in Vietnam will be a strong American reluctance to risk overseas involvements.

A new administration has the right to ask for compassion and understanding from the American people. But it must found its claim not on pat technical answers to difficult issues; it must above all ask the right questions. It must recognize that, in the field of foreign policy, we will never be able to contribute to building a stable and creative world order unless we first form some conception of it.

---

5.   **Editorial Note**

In a campaign speech delivered in Omaha, Nebraska, on May 6, 1968, Richard Nixon proposed a "new diplomacy" to deal with future aggression:

"Since World War II ended, the United States has been actively involved in two major wars to defend the freedom of other lands from Communist aggression. We fought in Korea and we are fighting in Vietnam. In these conflicts, America has taken more than a quarter of a million casualties, and fifty thousand dead. In both wars, the United

States provided most of the money, most of the arms and most of the men to defend these countries. The efforts that were made were right in my view, but I believe it is time now for a new diplomacy.

"While we are the richest nation and the most powerful nation in the non-Communist world, we must remember that we are only two hundred million Americans, and there are two billion people in the non-Communist world. It is time to develop a new diplomacy for the United States, a diplomacy to deal with future aggression—so that when the freedom of friendly nations is threatened by aggression, we help them with our money and help them with our arms; but we let them fight the war and don't fight the war for them. This should be the goal of a new diplomacy for America." (Nixon–Agnew Campaign Committee, *Nixon on the Issues*, New York, 1968, pages 1–2)

6.   Editorial Note

Richard Nixon offered his perspective on prospects for détente with the Soviet Union in his acceptance speech at the Republican convention in Miami Beach, Florida, on August 8, 1968:

"And now to the leaders of the Communist world, we say: After an era of confrontation, the time has come for an era of negotiation.

"Where the world's super powers are concerned, there is no acceptable alternative to peaceful negotiation.

"Because this will be a period of negotiation, we shall restore the strength of America so that we shall always negotiate from strength and never from weakness.

"So we begin with the proposition that if we are to have peace we must negotiate. If we are to negotiate we must negotiate from strength. If we are to have strength we must restore the strength of the United States and also we must restore the strength of the Western Alliance.

"Despite the recent setbacks, the years just ahead can bring a breakthrough for peace, they must be a time of careful probing, of intensive negotiations, of a determined search for those areas of accommodation between East and West on which a climate of mutual trust can eventually be built. But this can only succeed if Western strength is sufficient to back up our diplomacy. As one of Europe's leading statesmen has phrased it: 'genuine détente presupposes security; it does not replace it'.

"First, the United States must be strong. We've got to make sure that our president will always be able to negotiate from strength. He must negotiate with the leaders of the Soviet because in today's nuclear world there is no alternative to negotiation. The Soviet Union knows it and we know it. And that is why I will re-establish the strength of the United States, not only here, but re-establish also the strength of our NATO Alliance which has been allowed to crumble and go to pieces during this Administration." (*Nixon on the Issues*, pages 29–30)

The full text of the speech was published in *The New York Times* on August 9.

7.   Editorial Note

On October 7, 1968, Richard Nixon addressed a conference organized by United Press International in Washington. In the course of his remarks, he argued for shifting the burden of fighting in Vietnam to the South Vietnamese forces:

"I would put far greater emphasis, as the present command in Vietnam is now beginning to do, on the training of the South Vietnamese to fight their own battles and on giving the South Vietnamese people other than the military something to fight for rather than something simply to be against.

"It is a cruel irony that the American effort to safeguard the *independence* of South Vietnam has produced an ever-increasing dependency in our ally. If South Vietnam's future is to be secure, this process must now be reversed.

"At the same time, we need far greater and more urgent attention to training the South Vietnamese themselves, and equipping them with the best of modern weapons. As they are phased in, American troops can be phased out. This phasing-out will save American lives and cut American costs. Further, it is essential if South Vietnam is to develop both the military strength and the strength of spirit to survive now and in the future." (*Nixon on the Issues*, pages 9–10)

8.   **Editorial Note**

Secretary of State-designate William Rogers testified on January 15, 1969, before the Senate Foreign Relations Committee, which was meeting in executive session to consider Rogers' qualifications to be Secretary of State. The confirmation hearing was chaired by Senator J. William Fulbright of Arkansas. Fulbright began by questioning Rogers about his views on a variety of issues he might deal with as Secretary, and in the process asked him to assess the prospects for achieving détente with the Soviet Union:

"The Chairman. What I really think I am driving at is, there is this different view, one is that any kind of co-existence with Russia over a long period is impossible. This is what you seem to gather from previous views of the Secretary of Defense, at least according to some of the press. I don't take any responsibility of knowing what it is, but this has been in the press and in quotes in his book.

"We know that gentleman in the past, and I am sure in the future, is extremely important in foreign policy. And here you are and there they are. I mean the reconciliation of these views and they are different, if you feel there is a possibility of co-existence and gradual mellowness, mellowing of the relations between the Russians and ourselves or do you feel it is hopeless and there is no way of having a compromise with the devil?

"Mr. Rogers. Well, I wouldn't want to agree with what may be your premise about what Mr. Laird thinks.

"The Chairman. I don't state that as an affirmative matter.

"Mr. Rogers. I am not sure.

"The Chairman. I state that as having been said in the press.

"Mr. Rogers. But I would be glad to comment on my own attitude on it. I think that we have to have hope in that regard. If we don't, conflict is inevitable, and I think that the Soviet Union is going to some day come to the conclusion that they have to get along with the rest of the world and with us in particular, and I think that there are many hopeful signs now, aside from what they say, which may make that possible.

"First I think the Sino-Soviet split is probably one of the most important things that has happened in international relations since the takeover of mainland China, and they are obviously tremendously concerned about that.

"Secondly, I think they are having difficulty, obviously they are having difficulty, in the socialist countries, and I think that the justification that they advance for the invasion of Czechoslovakia is going to be one of the most difficult things for them to live with in the future that I can imagine. I mean if you listen to what they say in the United Nations about self-determination, the right of sovereignty and the right of people to solve their own problems and all these things, and then look at what they said as a justification of Czechoslovakia you know they are in an impossible position when it gets down to thoughtful people, and some of these nations in the world are watching very carefully.

"So I think that it is a good time probably, as soon as the impact of Czechoslovakia wears off a little bit, it is a good thing to try to probe for initiatives toward peace. So I have hope in that regard."

Later in the hearing, the discussion turned to a similar concern when Senator Jacob Javits of New York asked for Rogers' views on the possibility of reconciliation with China:

"The other thing I wanted to ask you, Mr. Rogers, is also a matter of basic philosophy because it epitomizes whether this must result in war or is there a way out, is what do you think about the possibilities with Communist China? Do you see the possibility of any way that we have of bringing about some reconciliation with this enormous body of people or must it just be fought out with one or the other really [*finally*?] yielding?

"Mr. Rogers. Well, Senator, I don't suppose anybody can answer that question with any degree of certainty. I would not want anything that I say to reflect on past decisions. I think it is important to develop channels of communications with Red China, if it is possible and as soon as it is possible, and I think to a large extent that depends on their attitude. Certainly we should be willing to, and I think the President-elect has indicated a very strong desire in that direction. And as you know there has—the Red Chinese have proposed a meeting in Warsaw in February sometime, and we obviously will pursue that initiative. But in answer to your question what they intend to do I don't believe I can do that.

"You know, I think in the long run you can't have a billion people outside the world community. It just doesn't make any sense. What we can do to further their becoming peaceful and constructive factors in world affairs is I think beyond anybody's ability to predict. But I certainly think we should try, in every way we can but we should be sensible about it and recognize the practicalities as they exist."

Senator Javits concluded his questioning by asking how Rogers perceived his prospective role as Secretary of State:

"Senator Javits. That brings me to my last question. I think you misunderstood. You thought I was asking you what you thought they felt. My last question is do you conceive of your role as Secretary of State to be an activist role or a protected role? In other words, do you conceive of your role as being solely to safeguard the interests of the United States throughout the world or do you conceive of your role also as being an active force for peace in the world on the theory that if there is peace in the world this is to the great satisfaction of our country and that we must have initiatives and be leaders and really try to move the world toward peace even though it involves risk on our part.

"Mr. Rogers. Well, as you know the Constitution is silent on the Secretary of State. The duties of the Secretary of State are spelled out in an Act of 1789 which would say that he will perform such activities that are enjoined and entrusted to him by the President.

"Now, I would hesitate to characterize my attitude except to say, whether I am an activist or protector or whatever, but I think that the role has to be assumed, and I have assumed it with this in mind, to do everything possible to make the world more secure, safer for people, and to hopefully bring about peace and I think the Secretary of State should advise the President actively to achieve this end. If I didn't think so I wouldn't have taken the job." (Nomination of William P. Rogers to be Secretary of State; Hearing held before the Committee on Foreign Relations, United States Senate, January 15, 1969; Records of the Senate Foreign Relations Committee)

The reference by Fulbright to a book written by Secretary of Defense-designate Laird is apparently a reference to Melvin R. Laird (ed.), *Republican Papers* (New York: Frederick A. Praeger, 1968).

9.   **Editorial Note**

The theme that ran through the world view President Nixon offered in his inaugural address on January 20, 1969, was the search for peace:

"As we learn to go forward together at home, let us also seek to go forward together with all mankind.

"Let us take as our goal: Where peace is unknown, make it welcome; where peace is fragile, make it strong; where peace is temporary, make it permanent.

"After a period of confrontation, we are entering an era of negotiation.

"Let all nations know that during this administration our lines of communication will be open.

"We seek an open world—open to ideas, open to the exchange of goods and people—a world in which no people, great or small, will live in angry isolation.

"We cannot expect to make everyone our friend, but we can try to make no one our enemy.

"Those who would be our adversaries, we invite to a peaceful competition—not in conquering territory or extending dominion, but in enriching the life of man.

"As we explore the reaches of space, let us go to the new worlds together—not as new worlds to be conquered, but as a new adventure to be shared.

"With those who are willing to join, let us cooperate to reduce the burden of arms, to strengthen the structure of peace, to lift up the poor and the hungry.

"But to all those who would be tempted by weakness, let us leave no doubt that we will be as strong as we need to be for as long as we need to be.

"Over the past 20 years, since I first came to this Capital as a freshman Congressman, I have visited most of the nations of the world. I have come to know the leaders of the world and the great forces, the hatreds, the fears that divide the world.

"I know that peace does not come through wishing for it—that there is no substitute for days and even years of patient and prolonged diplomacy.

"I also know the people of the world.

"I have seen the hunger of a homeless child, the pain of a man wounded in battle, the grief of a mother who has lost her son. I know these have no ideology, no race.

"I know America. I know the heart of America is good.

"I speak from my own heart, and the heart of my country, the deep concern we have for those who suffer and those who sorrow.

"I have taken an oath today in the presence of God and my countrymen to uphold and defend the Constitution of the United States. To that oath I now add this sacred commitment: I shall consecrate my Office, my energies, and all the wisdom I can summon to the cause of peace among nations.

"Let this message be heard by strong and weak alike:

"The peace we seek—the peace we seek to win—is not victory over any other people, but the peace that comes 'with healing in its wings';

with compassion for those who have suffered; with understanding for those who have opposed us; with the opportunity for all the peoples of this earth to choose their own destiny.

"Only a few short weeks ago we shared the glory of man's first sight of the world as God sees it, as a single sphere reflecting light in the darkness.

"As the Apollo astronauts flew over the moon's gray surface on Christmas Eve, they spoke to us of the beauty of earth—and in that voice so clear across the lunar distance, we heard them invoke God's blessing on its goodness.

"In that moment, their view from the moon moved poet Archibald MacLeish to write: 'To see the earth as it truly is, small and blue and beautiful in that eternal silence where it floats, is to see ourselves as riders on the earth together, brothers on that bright loveliness in the eternal cold—brothers who know now they are truly brothers.'

"In that moment of surpassing technological triumph, men turned their thoughts toward home and humanity—seeing in that far perspective that man's destiny on earth is not divisible; telling us that however far we reach into the cosmos, our destiny lies not in the stars but on earth itself, in our own hands, in our own hearts.

"We have endured a long night of the American spirit. But as our eyes catch the dimness of the first rays of dawn, let us not curse the remaining dark. Let us gather the light.

"Our destiny offers not the cup of despair, but the chalice of opportunity. So let us seize it not in fear, but in gladness—and 'riders on the earth together,' let us go forward, firm in our faith, steadfast in our purpose, cautious of the dangers, but sustained by our confidence in the will of God and the promise of man." (*Public Papers of the Presidents of the United States: Richard Nixon, 1969*, pages 3–4)

President Nixon spoke at 12:16 p.m. from the east front of the Capitol. The address was broadcast on radio and television.

10.   Letter From President Nixon to Secretary of Defense Laird[1]

Washington, February 4, 1969.

Dear Mel:

I have been giving much thought to our relations with the Soviet Union and would like to give you, informally, my ideas on this central security problem. My purpose in doing so is not to prejudge the scheduled systematic review by the National Security Council of our policy options with respect to the USSR, but rather to set out the general approach which I believe should guide us in our conduct as we move from confrontation to negotiation.

1. I believe that the tone of our public and private discourse about and with the Soviet Union should be calm, courteous and non-polemical. This will not prevent us from stating our views clearly and, if need be, firmly; nor will it preclude us from candidly affirming our attitude—negatively if warranted—toward the policies and actions of the Soviet Union. But what I said in my Inaugural address concerning the tone and character of our domestic debates should also govern the tone and character of our statements in the international arena, most especially in respect of the Soviet Union.[2]

2. I believe that the basis for a viable settlement is a mutual recognition of our vital interests. We must recognize that the Soviet Union has interests; in the present circumstances we cannot but take account of them in defining our own. We should leave the Soviet leadership in no doubt that we expect them to adopt a similar approach toward us. This applies also to the concerns and interests of our allies and indeed of all nations. They, too, are entitled to the safeguarding of their legitimate interests. In the past we have often attempted to settle things in a fit of enthusiasm, relying on personal diplomacy. But the "spirit" that permeated various meetings lacked a solid basis of mutual interest and, therefore, every summit meeting was followed by a crisis in less than a year.

3. I am convinced that the great issues are fundamentally interrelated. I do not mean by this to establish artificial linkages between spe-

---

[1] Source: National Archives, Nixon Presidential Materials, NSC Files, Box 220, Agency Files, Department of Defense, Vol. I, 1/12/69. Secret. President Nixon sent an identical letter on February 4 to Secretary of State Rogers. (Ibid., Box 279, Agency Files, Department of State, Vol. I, 1/17/69)

[2] In his inaugural address, Nixon said: "We cannot learn from each other until we stop shouting at one another—until we speak quietly enough so that our words can be heard as well as our voices." (*Public Papers of the Presidents of the United States: Richard Nixon, 1969*, p. 2)

cific elements of one or another issue or between tactical steps that we may elect to take. But I do believe that crisis or confrontation in one place and real cooperation in another cannot long be sustained simultaneously. I recognize that the previous Administration took the view that when we perceive a mutual interest on an issue with the USSR, we should pursue agreement and attempt to insulate it as much as possible from the ups and downs of conflicts elsewhere. This may well be sound on numerous bilateral and practical matters such as cultural or scientific exchanges. But, on the crucial issues of our day, I believe we must seek to advance on a front at least broad enough to make clear that we see some relationship between political and military issues. I believe that the Soviet leaders should be brought to understand that they cannot expect to reap the benefits of cooperation in one area while seeking to take advantage of tension or confrontation elsewhere. Such a course involves the danger that the Soviets will use talks on arms as a safety valve on intransigence elsewhere. I note, for example, that the invasion of Hungary was followed by abortive disarmament talks within nine months. The invasion of Czechoslovakia was preceded by the explorations of a summit conference (in fact, when Ambassador Dobrynin informed President Johnson of the invasion of Czechoslovakia, he received the appointment so quickly because the President thought his purpose was to fix the date of a summit meeting). Negotiation and the search for agreement carry their own burdens; the Soviets—no less than we—must be ready to bear them.

4. I recognize the problem of giving practical substance to the propositions set forth in the previous paragraph. Without attempting to lay down inflexible prescriptions about how various matters at issue between ourselves and the USSR should be connected, I would like to illustrate what I have in mind in one case of immediate and widespread interest—the proposed talks on strategic weapons. I believe our decision on when and how to proceed does not depend exclusively on our review of the purely military and technical issues, although these are of key importance. This decision should also be taken in the light of the prevailing political context and, in particular, in light of progress toward stabilizing the explosive Middle East situation, and in light of the Paris talks. I believe I should retain the freedom to ensure, to the extent that we have control over it, that the timing of talks with the Soviet Union on strategic weapons is optimal. This may, in fact, mean delay beyond that required for our review of the technical issues. Indeed, it means that we should—at least in our public position—keep open the option that there may be no talks at all.

5. I am of course aware that the Soviets are seeking to press us to agree to talks and I know also of the strong views held by many in this country. But I think it is important to establish with the Soviets early in

the Administration that our commitment to negotiation applies to a range of major issues so that the "structure of peace" to which I referred in the Inaugural will have a sound base.

Sincerely,

RN

---

11.   **Editorial Note**

Henry Kissinger discussed the Nixon administration's perception of the linkage between political and strategic issues during a background briefing for the press at the White House on February 6, 1969:

"Q. Can you tell us more about why the President wants to have strategic negotiations and political negotiations going forward on separately different facts [*tracks?*]?

"Dr. Kissinger. I was lured here because I was told you all could hardly wait to hear me expound on the National Security Council system and my exerted influence on it.

"To take the question of the linkage between the political and the strategic environment. We have come through two phases. In the 1950's, it used to be said that a political settlement had to precede an arms settlement. It was said that the arms race is the result of political tensions, not the cause of them, and, therefore, the way to deal with the problems of arms was to solve first all the political problems and then the arms would take care of themselves.

"In reaction to that, they developed an arms control school in which you and I participated in various stages as colleagues in which the argument used to be that the arms race portion was essentially autonomous with producing tension and in which the level of political tension was more or less irrelevant to what could be done in the arms field.

"This led to about ten years of negotiations in the arms field which have had some successes, of which the Non-Proliferation Treaty is one, but during which, I think it is fair to say, that the level of arms has increased substantially, both quantitatively and qualitatively and the level of tension has also increased substantially.

"Now, if you review the last 20 years and look at the incidents that significantly increase the dangers of war, I think it would be difficult to think of one that was caused by the general balance of arms. But it is possible to think of very many that were caused by the general balance of political relationships.

"Therefore, the President's view is not that there must be a settlement of all political issues. He has emphatically rejected that in his press conference before this. His view is, if I understand it correctly, that there is a danger, that if arms control and political issues become too much disassociated that arms control may be used as a safety valve to make political conflict safer rather than eliminate political conflict.

"He has, therefore, suggested that there be enough movement in the political field to indicate that the arms control negotiations do not unwittingly, instead of reducing the danger of war, offer a means by which political conflict can be intensified and yet managed. He is asking for enough movement, not to produce a final settlement, but to indicate that there is enough good faith in the direction of trying to reduce the intensity of political conflict.

"In short, he would like to deal with the problem of peace on the entire front in which peace is challenged and not only on the military one." (Library of Congress, Manuscript Division, Kissinger Papers, Box CL 425, Subject File, Background Briefings, Feb–May 1969)

For the record of Nixon's press conference on February 6, see *Public Papers of the Presidents of the United States: Richard Nixon, 1969*, pages 66–76.

---

12.   **Memorandum From the President's Special Assistant (Buchanan) to President Nixon**[1]

Washington, February 19, 1969.

(One Observer's notes on the President's first meeting with the bipartisan leadership of Capitol Hill.)[2]

---

[1] Source: National Archives, Nixon Presidential Materials, White House Special Files, President's Office Files, Box 77, Memoranda for the President, Jan 21–Apr 6, 1969. Confidential.

[2] The President's briefing of the Congressional leadership took place at 8:35 a.m. in the Cabinet Room of the White House. Eight Senators and ten Representatives attended. Agnew, Helms, Kissinger, and Ehrlichman also attended from the Executive branch. (Ibid., White House Central Files, Staff Members and Office Files, Office of Presidential Papers and Archives, Daily Diary)

With Rogers on his right and Laird to the left, the President opened the meeting with a fifteen-minute discourse on the purposes of these bipartisan meetings, and the objectives of his forthcoming visit to Europe.[3] Speaking slowly and deliberately, the President expressed the hope that the meetings could be used for both the traditional end of "briefing" the leadership, and a secondary end of providing a channel through which the Administration might receive the views of the men of power on the Hill.

On Europe, and the coming trip, the President said he was under no illusions that grand tours or "abrazos" or a "new spirit" would resolve basic differences between adversaries, or even allies. He was going, he said, because several basic problems of NATO require immediate attention, because he believed that past administrations had not paid adequate "attention" to Europe, because the views of these Western partners had not been given adequate consideration in the past, even in negotiating the NPT. There was a need for "more consultation in advance."

Secondly, the President had the feeling that perhaps American leadership in the past had been looking "too much to collateral areas" and not enough to what, "some still call the blue chip."

Third, there were very great substantive differences between the allies and the President's trip might establish a basis for "continuing consultation" on such issues as the Mideast. Fourth, going there has a "symbolic importance." We will be "prepared to discuss anything," the President noted, adding that some fifty hours of discussions are currently scheduled in the eight-day trip.

At the close of his monologue, the President cautioned against unjustifiable optimism. We have to recognize, he said, that basic disagreements are not going to be solved by meetings, with these meetings, however, we can reduce to a minimum those disagreements which result from a lack of communication or consultation.

[Omitted here is discussion of the possibility of adding a stop in Malta to the President's European agenda, and a discussion of how to handle the question of ratification of the Nuclear Non-Proliferation Treaty with the West German Government.]

Arms Control

The President now gave his detailed views on reports in the press—from his first press conference—that he had irrevocably linked progress

---

[3] From February 23 to March 2, President Nixon visited London, Bonn, Rome, Paris, and NATO Headquarters in Brussels to consult with European allies. (Ibid.)

in arms talks with progress on political problems—so tightly as to make progress in one a "condition" of progress with the other.

Not so, the President said. Certainly, we want to move on them both at the same time, since the history of wars shows that arms races are occasionally a cause of conflict, but in far more instances, it is a political problem that produces the war, and not the level of armaments.

The President wanted progress in both at the same time, but he wanted to emphasize that progress in one is not "a condition" of progress in the other.

With regard to the Soviets, the President pointed out quite clearly that if Soviet aid to North Vietnam were halted, or Soviet assistance to the "more aggressive neighbors" of Israel were halted, the problems would be reduced to a level where they would not require any American intervention. Thus the Soviets did have the "big stroke" in helping to resolve these political problems.

[Omitted here is discussion of other foreign policy issues.]

---

13.   Editorial Note

On February 28, 1969, President Nixon arrived in Paris on the fifth stop of his European trip and met with President Charles de Gaulle. In the course of a wide-ranging conversation, Nixon discussed with de Gaulle prospects for détente with the Soviet Union and asked de Gaulle's opinion on the efficacy of linking negotiations on strategic and political issues:

"The President said that he would like to indicate his reasons for announcing his policy up to this point. When he was inaugurated six weeks ago if he had announced that on the next day he was going to meet Kosygin and Brezhnev at the summit, the US press and the world would have applauded and said that now progress was really being made. He had not done this because he felt it was necessary to have very careful planning for a meeting at the summit, there had been the spirit of Glassboro, of Vienna and of Camp David and these hopes had been dashed. It was different when we were meeting with our friends and people who were basically like us. He felt that it would be a mistake for the President of the United States to go to a meeting without knowing what we were going to talk about or where we were going.

This would simply raise hopes that would subsequently be dashed. Consequently he believed that we should have talks first with our friends and allies including France. The Soviets had interest in talks on the limitation of strategic weapons. This was a matter that could affect the capability of the US forces in Europe. Another reason for not rushing into arms talks was that it was generally claimed that an arms race increased the risk of war. He thought it was clear that both the USSR and the US would like to reduce the financial burden on themselves. He wished to make clear that on this matter he would not make the decision in this matter on a financial basis, the US had to be able to afford whatever security required. One had to recognize a historic fact that wars also were caused by political tensions. If a freeze on strategic arms were to take place an explosion would still occur in the Middle East, at Berlin or in Vietnam and this could lead to war. He felt that this opportunity should be seized by the new administration and he shared the General's view that détente was desirable. However we should be hard and pragmatic in dealing with the Soviets. They knew what they wanted and we must know what we want. While we would not make talks on Middle East and other matters a condition for talks on limitation of strategic weapons, we did feel that it was proper to suggest at Ambassadorial level as indeed we had that we felt that we should try and make progress on all fronts to achieve a détente. We should talk in the UN in the framework of the Four Powers on the Middle East and discuss later what could be done there. We would like the Soviets' help on solving the Vietnamese problem, we realized that their situation in this matter was delicate with the Chinese but the Soviets did have great influence on the North Vietnamese. After all 85 percent of their weapons came from the Soviet Union. Perhaps we could also make some progress in the Central [Europe?] area on Berlin. Not of course a solution as neither side could give enough to settle the matter; we could perhaps make some progress. The President said he would like to know the General's opinion whether he thought we were correct in proceeding cautiously in asking the Soviets to talk on several areas rather than discussing only limitation of strategic weapons with them. The reason why the President was opposed to an agreement on arms limitation only without progress on political issues such as the Middle East, Europe and Vietnam was because such an agreement would create a sort of euphoria of peace.

"General de Gaulle said he felt that the President was quite right. A détente was the only acceptable policy. One must be cautious and not speak of everything at once, nor should one be overly polite and make concessions to them. The French who had started the policy of détente with them had never made any concessions even on Germany and they certainly had reasons to do so but had not. Now France was on much better terms with the Soviets and had made no concessions to them. Practically if the US were to start conversations on political subjects as well as on strategic missiles—ABM's and so forth—and if contact could be made with them on other subjects such as Vietnam and the Middle East he felt that the US could do this with all prudence and dignity. He believed that the President should not rush to Moscow and lay out the red carpet before Brezhnev but that the President was quite right in seeking to have adequate preparations made in advance." (Memorandum of conversation; National Archives, Nixon Presidential Materials, NSC Files, Box 447, President's Trip Files, Memcons–Europe, Feb 23–March 2, 1969)

The meeting was held in de Gaulle's office in the Elysée Palace at 3:42 p.m. (Ibid., White House Central Files, Staff Members and Office Files, Office of Presidential Papers and Archives, Daily Diary) The full text of the memorandum of conversation is scheduled to be published in the Supplement to *Foreign Relations*, 1969–1976, China, 1969–1972.

14.   Editorial Note

President Nixon met again with President de Gaulle on March 1, 1969, at the Grand Trianon Palace in Versailles. Among the topics discussed was Nixon's desire to develop "parallel relationships" with China and the Soviet Union:

"The President said that if the General agreed they might talk for an hour on Sunday [March 2]. He would like to have the General's views at that time on Vietnam and Southeast Asia. By that time the President would have been briefed by Lodge and his team. There was one other matter about which they might talk if time permitted. In 1963 when he had talked to the General, and he was talking privately now, not for public announcements that might embarrass the Soviet Union, whether it might not be wise to develop lines of communications with the Soviets and the Chinese and so to speak not put all of our eggs in one basket. There was considerable sentiment in the U.S. State Dept, not only in favor of a Soviet-U.S. détente but also for a lineup of the Soviets, Europe and the U.S. against Chinese. His own view was that while this might be a good short-range policy, he felt that for the longer range it was more important to recognize that our interests might perhaps best be served by recognizing that China and the USSR were two great powers and it might be better to develop parallel relationships with them. This was of course in some measure largely theoretical as it was difficult to have relations with the Chinese."

After a digression on developments in Vietnam, de Gaulle and Nixon returned to a discussion of the possibility of improving relations with China without adversely affecting relations with the Soviet Union:

"General de Gaulle then said that they had been talking about China. What about the possibility of relations with China and how would this affect relationships with the Soviets? Some said that one should try and play the Chinese off against the Soviets and try to divide them. Others felt that it was worth trying to improve relations with both. The French had relations with the Chinese and it had not brought them much advantage except perhaps economically and a bit culturally, but mostly economically and in some cases some exchanges. They had some and might perhaps have more. The Chinese had great economic requirements and diplomatic relations facilitated economic relations. The French had renewed relations with China but had not expected much of it as the Chinese had appeared to be in a state of ebullition. The Cultural Revolution had been accompanied by great agitation and they had done nothing else except agitate. This was not satisfactory for political relations with them. They now appeared to be calming down and returning to a more normal situation. He believed that there was advantage in having relations with them. They were a huge entity and certainly had great resources. They were working and making progress in industry, in technology, in nuclear matters. They had ambitions and actions everywhere, even in Paris, in Africa and in Asia. As time passed they would have more political weight. What attitude should we adopt—that of isolating them and letting them cook in their own juice— of having no opening or contacts with them? He had no illusions but did not feel that we should isolate them in their own rage. We should have exchanges at all levels and we might eventually see the beginnings of a détente. How this would affect the Soviets was difficult to know. The Soviets usually recommended that one should have normal relations with the Chinese. They had such relations themselves even though these were not always easy. That, however, was their business. The West should try to get to know China, to have contacts and to penetrate it. We should try to get them to sit at the table with us and offer them openings. The French felt that this was the best policy and we could see what conclusions could be drawn. If the U.S. began to have relations with China this would mean that China would probably get into the UN. This would have much effect and a lot of dust would be stirred up but he did not believe that the overall results would be bad. The Prime Minister queried on this but the General agreed with him.

"The President said that he had talked to [André] Malraux on the previous evening. He had seen Mao on the eve of the Cultural Revolution and Mao had said that he had to stir up everything otherwise China would go to sleep.

"The President said that as he saw it, there were two policies which might be followed, a short range policy and a long range policy. In the short range policy there could be no changes for a number of reasons relating to their impact on Asia. On a long range policy he felt that it would be detrimental to the interests of the U.S. in 10 years for it to appear that the West was ganging up with the Soviet Union against China. He felt that it was important for the French to extend their communications and keep a line open into China and in looking down the road towards talks with the Soviet Union we might keep an anchor to windward with respect to China. This did not mean that we would do anything so crude as to suggest we play China off against the Soviet Union. The Soviets would resent this bitterly. In 10 years when China had made significant nuclear progress we would have to have more communications than we had today.

"General de Gaulle said that the French already had relations with the Chinese and it would be better for the U.S. to recognize China before they were obliged to do it by the growth of China. He felt that this would be better and that was why the French had chosen to do it earlier." (Memorandum of conversation; National Archives, Nixon Presidential Materials, NSC Files, Box 447, President's Trip Files, Memcons–Europe, Feb 23–Mar 2, 1969)

The meeting was held at 10 a.m. (Ibid., White House Central Files, Staff Members and Office Files, Office of Presidential Papers and Archives, Daily Diary)

---

15.   **Editorial Note**

On March 4, 1969, President Nixon invited Congressional leaders to the White House to brief them on the results of his trip to Western Europe. In the course of the briefing, Nixon discussed the defense of the Western alliance and his inclination to rely upon a "flexible response."

"The President now discussed two different theories of Western strategy, which have been adopted at one time or another by Western leaders.

"The first is the theory that any conflict in Europe between East and West will inevitably result in a nuclear exchange, and thus all that is needed in the way of American forces there is a 'trip wire,' a 'few battalions.' This has some strong proponents, the President said (although using the argument he did not refer it as 'massive retaliation'). However, 'would an American President' deliver a nuclear strike on the Soviets if they moved into West Berlin, he said. Let's assume they did move in and occupy Berlin. We may want a 'flexible response.' The existence of conventional ground forces could have some military effect there, for us—but an 'enormous political effect.' There is even a question of whether we need to have more options available to us militarily in Europe than we now have, the President said.

"(To sum up briefly, it appeared to this observer that the President quite clearly had rejected the notion of massive retaliation, even should the Soviets move in force into West Berlin. He had opted instead for a 'flexible response' for a range of weapons which we might employ. One of the advantages of having our troops in Germany was thus military options, but more important was the enormous political effect they provided.)

"However, the President noted, it was simply a hard fact that the American military commitment of five-and-a-third or six divisions or whatever it is cannot continue ad infinitum. We did not threaten the Europeans with any withdrawal, but we did make clear the above fact." (Notes on the meeting prepared as a March 4 memorandum to the President by the President's Special Assistant Patrick J. Buchanan; National Archives, Nixon Presidential Materials, White House Special Files, President's Office Files, Box 77, Memoranda for the President, Jan 21–Apr 6, 1969)

According to the President's Daily Diary, eight Senators and nine Representatives attended the bipartisan briefing. Agnew, Laird, Rogers, and Helms also attended, as did Kissinger, Ehrlichman, Harlow, and Klein of the White House staff. (Ibid., White House Central Files, Staff Members and Office Files, Office of Presidential Papers and Archives, Daily Diary)

16.   Letter From President Nixon to the Head of the Delegation
         to the Eighteen-Nation Disarmament Conference (Smith)[1]

Washington, March 15, 1969.

Dear Ambassador Smith:

In view of the great importance which I attach to the work of the Eighteen Nation Disarmament Conference in Geneva, I wish to address directly to you, as the new Director of the Arms Control and Disarmament Agency and the head of our delegation, my instructions regarding the participation of the United States in this conference.

The fundamental objective of the United States is a world of enduring peace and justice, in which the differences that separate nations can be resolved without resort to war.

Our immediate objective is to leave behind the period of confrontation and to enter an era of negotiation.

The task of the Delegation of the United States to the disarmament conference is to serve these objectives by pursuing negotiations to achieve concrete measures which will enhance the security of our own country and all countries.

The new Administration has now considered the policies which will help us to make progress in this endeavor.

I have decided that the Delegation of the United States should take these positions at the Conference.

First, in order to assure that the seabed, man's latest frontier, remains free from the nuclear arms race, the United States delegation should indicate that the United States is interested in working out an international agreement that would prohibit the implacement or fixing of nuclear weapons or other weapons of mass destruction on the seabed. To this end, the United States Delegation should seek discussion of the factors necessary for such an international agreement. Such an agreement would, like the Antarctic Treaty and the Treaty on Outer Space[2] which are already in effect, prevent an arms race before it had a chance to start. It would ensure that this potentially useful area of the world remained available for peaceful purposes.

---

[1] Source: *Public Papers of the Presidents of the United States: Richard Nixon, 1969*, pp. 227–229. Nixon sent the letter to Gerard Smith, Director of the Arms Control and Disarmament Agency, in Geneva, where the Eighteen-Nation Disarmament Conference convened on March 18. The letter was released that day. Smith held the personal rank of Ambassador as head of the U.S. delegation.

[2] The Antarctic Treaty was signed December 1, 1959 (12 UST; TIAS 4780) and the Treaty on Outer Space was signed January 27, 1967 (18 UST; TIAS 6347).

Second, the United States supports the conclusion of a comprehensive test ban adequately verified. In view of the fact that differences regarding verification have not permitted achievement of this key arms control measure, efforts must be made towards greater understanding of the verification issue.

Third, the United States Delegation will continue to press for an agreement to cut off the production of fissionable materials for weapons purposes and to transfer such materials to peaceful purposes.

Fourth, while awaiting the United Nations Secretary General's study on the effects of chemical and biological warfare, the United States Delegation should join with other delegations in exploring any proposals or ideas that could contribute to sound and effective arms control relating to these weapons.

Fifth, regarding more extensive measures of disarmament, both nuclear and conventional, the United States Delegation should be guided by the understanding that actual reduction of armaments, and not merely limiting their growth or spread, remains our goal.

Sixth, regarding the question of talks between the United States and the Soviet Union on the limitation of strategic arms, the United States hopes that the international political situation will evolve in a way which will permit such talks to begin in the near future.

In carrying out these instructions, the United States Delegation should keep in mind my view that efforts toward peace by all nations must be comprehensive. We cannot have realistic hopes for significant progress in the control of arms if the policies of confrontation prevail throughout the world as the rule of international conduct. On the other hand, we must attempt to exploit every opportunity to build a world of peace—to find areas of accord—to bind countries together in cooperative endeavors.

A major part of the work of peace is done by the Eighteen-Nation Disarmament Committee. I expect that all members of the United States Delegation will devote that extra measure of determination, skill, and judgment which this high task merits.

I shall follow closely the progress that is made and give my personal consideration to any problems that arise whenever it would be helpful for me to do so.

Please convey to all your colleagues my sincere wishes for success in our common endeavor. Over the years, their achievements at the Eighteen-Nation Disarmament Conference have been outstanding. I am confident that in the future our efforts, in cooperation with theirs, will be equal to any challenge and will result in progress for the benefit of all.

Sincerely,

Richard Nixon

17.   Editorial Note

In a meeting with Australian Prime Minister John Gorton at the White House on April 1, 1969, President Nixon cited the domino theory in expressing his concern about the possible effects of a precipitate United States withdrawal from Vietnam:

"The President said the so-called domino theory is spoken of disparagingly these days, but in fact our posture in Viet-Nam affects the countries of Southeast Asia; countries such as Japan, which would not wish to see a solution in Viet-Nam that encouraged the 'hawks' of the Communist world, and in fact our whole relationship with the Communist powers on the world scene. The Viet-Nam war poisons our relations with certain European countries, the President said; they are not interested in it and do not care about it. The Latin American countries tend to feel the same way. Domestic opposition is substantial. Nevertheless we must persevere in our effort to achieve a workable peace, orchestrating the diplomatic and military instruments we have at hand for the purpose. He said one point that bears emphasis is that we cannot achieve an effective peace without the cooperation of the South-Vietnamese. President Thieu is coming along well and is quite reasonable, but he cannot be rushed unduly." (Memorandum of conversation; National Archives, Nixon Presidential Materials, White House Special Files, President's Office Files, B Series documents withheld in Box 7 from documents originally filed in folder 7 of Box 57)

18.   Address by President Nixon to the North Atlantic Council[1]

Washington, April 10, 1969.

Mr. Secretary, Mr. President, Mr. Secretary General,[2] Your Excellencies, and our distinguished guests:

---

[1] Source: *Public Papers of the Presidents of the United States: Richard Nixon, 1969*, p. 272–276. Nixon spoke at 2:26 p.m. in the Departmental Auditorium of the State Department.

[2] Reference is to Secretary of State Rogers; Honorary President of the North Atlantic Council Willy Brandt, Vice Chancellor of the Federal Republic of Germany; and Secretary General of the North Atlantic Treaty Organization Manlio Brosio.

As we gather here today, we celebrate a momentous anniversary.

We celebrate one of the great successes of the postwar world.

Twenty years ago, as has already been mentioned, a few dedicated men gathered in Washington to cement an Atlantic partnership between the older nations of Europe and their offspring in the New World—and in this very room the North Atlantic Treaty was signed. Some of the men who were here then are here today—and I would like to suggest that those who were here then and who are here today stand for a moment. [Applause][3]

Gentlemen, with our hindsight, we now have saluted your foresight at that time. In referring to that event, I thought I should share with you the conversation that I had with some of the founders in the room prior to coming to this meeting.

Secretary Acheson[4] recalled that before the signing of the treaty the Marine Band played "We've Got Plenty of Nothing" and "It Ain't Necessarily So."

Certainly what has happened in those 20 years proved that as far as the music was concerned, it was not prophetic.

As we sit here today we also look back on those 20 years, what has happened, and we think, as the previous speakers have indicated, of all of those who have contributed to the Alliance and particularly to the one who commanded the armies that liberated Europe, the first Supreme Commander of the forces of NATO, the American President who did so much to bring NATO to its strength and to give life to its principles—to Dwight David Eisenhower.

His life demonstrated that there is a moral force in the world which can move men and nations. There is a spiritual force lodged in the very roots of man's being.

As for NATO, it is precisely because it has always been more than a military alliance that its strength has been greater than the strength of arms. This Alliance represents a moral force which, if we marshal it, will ennoble our efforts.

Dwight Eisenhower was a great humanist. He was also a great realist. If he were with us today, he would have recognized that together, as men of the Old World and of the New World, we must find ways of living in the real world.

As we know too well, that real world today includes men driven by suspicion, men who would take advantage of their neighbors, men who confuse the pursuit of happiness with the pursuit of power.

---

[3] Brackets in the source text. The North Atlantic Treaty was signed in Washington on April 4, 1949.

[4] Dean Acheson, Secretary of State, 1949–1953.

It also is peopled with men of good will, with men of peace and with men of hope and with men of vision.

No nation, and no community of nations, is made up entirely of one group of men or another. No part of the world has a monopoly on wisdom or virtue.

Those who think simply in terms of "good" nations and "bad" nations—of a world of staunch allies and sworn enemies—live in a world of their own. Imprisoned by stereotypes, they do not live in the real world.

On the other hand, those who believe that all it takes to submerge national self-interest is a little better communication, those who think that all that stands in the way of international brotherhood is stubborn leadership—they, too, live in a world of their own. Misled by wishful thinking, they do not live in the real world.

Two decades ago, the men who founded NATO faced the truth of their times; as a result, the Western world prospers today in freedom. We must follow their example by once again facing the truth—not of earlier times, but of our own times.

Living in the real world of today means recognizing the sometimes differing interests of the Western nations, while never losing sight of our great common purposes.

Living in the real world of today means understanding old concepts of East versus West, understanding and unfreezing those concepts, but never losing sight of great ideological differences that still remain.

We can afford neither to blind our eyes with hatred nor to distort our vision with rose-colored glasses. The real world is too much with us to permit either stereotyped reacting or wishful thinking to lay waste our powers.

Let us then count ourselves today among the hopeful realists.

In this same spirit of hopeful realism, let us look at NATO today.

We find it strong but we find it challenged. We find disputes about its structure, political divisions among its members, and reluctance to meet prescribed force quotas. Many people on both sides of the Atlantic today find NATO anachronistic, something quaint and familiar and even a bit old-fashioned.

As the Alliance begins its third decade, therefore, there are certain fundamentals to be reaffirmed:

First, NATO is needed; and the American commitment to NATO will remain in force and it will remain strong. We in America continue to consider Europe's security to be our own.

Second, having succeeded in its original purpose, the Alliance must adapt to the conditions of success. With less of the original cement of fear, we must forge new bonds to maintain our unity.

Third, when NATO was founded, the mere fact of cooperation among the Western nations was of tremendous significance, both symbolically and substantively. Now the symbol is not enough; we need substance. The Alliance today will be judged by the content of its cooperation, not merely by its form.

Fourth, the allies have learned to harmonize their military forces; now, in the light of the vast military, economic, and political changes of two decades, we must devise better means of harmonizing our policies.

Fifth, by its nature, ours is more than a military alliance; and the time has come to turn a part of our attention to those nonmilitary areas in which we all could benefit from increased collaboration.

Now, what does all this mean for the future of the Western Alliance?

To deal with the real world, we cannot respond to changing conditions merely by changing our words. We have to adapt our actions.

It is not enough to talk of flexible response, if at the same time we reduce our flexibility by cutting back on conventional forces.

It is not enough to talk of relaxing tension, unless we keep in mind the fact that 20 years of tension were not caused by superficial misunderstandings. A change of mood is useful only if it reflects some change of mind about political purpose.

It is not enough to talk of European security in the abstract. We must know the elements of insecurity and how to remove them. Conferences are useful if they deal with concrete issues which means they must, of course, be carefully prepared.

It is not enough to talk of détente, unless at the same time we anticipate the need for giving it the genuine political content that would prevent détente from becoming delusion.

To take one example, a number of America's Western partners have actively supported the idea of strategic arms control talks with the Soviet Union. I support that idea. When such talks are held, we shall work diligently for their success.

But within our Alliance we must recognize that this would imply a military relationship far different from the one that existed when NATO was founded. Let's put it in plain words. The West does not today have the massive nuclear predominance that it once had, and any sort of broad-based arms agreement with the Soviets would codify the present balance.

How would progress towards arms control affect the nature of consultation within our Alliance?

Up to now, our discussions have mainly had to do with tactics—ways and means of carrying out the provisions of a treaty drawn a generation ago. We have discussed clauses in proposed treaties; in the negotiations to come, we must go beyond these to the processes which these future treaties will set in motion. We must shake off our preoccupation with formal structure to bring into focus a common world view.

Of course, there is a diversity of policies and interests among the Western nations; and, of course, those differences must be respected. But in shaping the strategies of peace, these differences need not block the way—not if we break through to a new and deeper form of political consultation.

To be specific, the forthcoming arms talks will be a test of the ability of the Western nations to shape a common strategy.

The United States fully intends to undertake deep and genuine consultation with its allies, both before and during any negotiations directly affecting their interests. That is a pledge I shall honor—and I expect to consult at length on the implications of anything that might affect the pattern of East-West relations.

In passing that test together, this Alliance will give new meaning to the principle of mutual consultation.

To seize the moment that this opportunity presents, we would do well to create new machinery for Western political consultation, as well as to make greater use of the machinery that we have.

First, I suggest that deputy foreign ministers meet periodically for a high-level review of major, long-range problems before the Alliance.

Second, I suggest creation of a special political planning group, not to duplicate the work now being done by the Council or by the senior political advisers, but to address itself specifically and continually to the longer-range problems we face.

This would by no means preclude efforts to develop a fuller European cooperation. On the contrary, we in the United States would welcome that cooperation. What ties us to Europe is not weakness or division among our partners but community of interest with them.

Third, I strongly urge that we create a committee on the challenges of modern society, responsible to the deputy ministers, to explore ways in which the experience and resources of the Western nations could most effectively be marshaled toward improving the quality of life of our peoples.

That new goal is provided for in Article II of our treaty, but it has never been the center of our concerns. Let me put my proposal in concrete terms and in personal terms. On my recent trip to Europe I met with world leaders and private citizens alike. I was struck by the fact that our discussions were not limited to military or political matters. More often than not our talks turned to those matters deeply relevant to our societies—the legitimate unrest of young people, the frustration of the gap between generations, the need for a new sense of idealism and purpose in coping with an automating world.

These were not subjects apart from the concerns of NATO; indeed they went to the very heart of the real world we live in. We are not allies because we are bound by treaty; we bind ourselves by treaty because we are allied in meeting common purposes and common concerns.

For 20 years, our nations have provided for the military defense of Western Europe. For 20 years we have held political consultations.

Now the alliance of the West needs a third dimension.

It needs not only a strong military dimension to provide for the common defense, and not only a more profound political dimension to shape a strategy of peace, but it also needs a social dimension to deal with our concern for the quality of life in this last third of the 20th century.

This concern is manifested in many ways, culturally and technologically, through the humanities and the sciences.

The Western nations share common ideals and a common heritage. We are all advanced societies, sharing the benefits and the gathering torments of a rapidly advancing industrial technology. The industrial nations share no challenge more urgent than that of bringing 20th century man and his environment to terms with one another—of making the world fit for man, and helping man to learn how to remain in harmony with the rapidly changing world.

We in the United States have much to learn from the experiences of our Atlantic allies in their handling of internal matters: for example, the care of infant children in West Germany, the "new towns" policy of Great Britain, the development of depressed areas programs in Italy, the great skill of the Dutch in dealing with high density areas, the effectiveness of urban planning by local governments in Norway, the experience of the French in metropolitan planning.

Having forced a working partnership, we all have a unique opportunity to pool our skills, our intellects, and our inventiveness in finding new ways to use technology to enhance our environments, and not to destroy them.

The work of this committee would not be competitive with any now being carried on by other international agencies. Neither would it be our purpose to limit this cooperation and the benefits that flow from it to our own countries. Quite the opposite; our purpose would be to share both ideas and benefits, recognizing that these problems have no national or regional boundaries. This could become the most positive dimension of the Alliance, opening creative new channels to all the rest of the world.

When I visited the North Atlantic Council in Brussels I posed the question: "In today's world, what kind of an alliance shall we strive to build?"

Today I have sketched out some of the approaches that I believe the Alliance should take.

I believe we must build an Alliance strong enough to deter those who might threaten war, close enough to provide for continuous and far-reaching consultation, trusting enough to accept the diversity of views, realistic enough to deal with the world as it is, and flexible enough to explore new channels of constructive cooperation.

Ten years ago, addressing the North Atlantic Council in this same room, President Eisenhower spoke of the need for unity. Listen to his words: There is not much strength in the finger of one hand, he said, but when five fingers are balled into a fist, you have a considerable instrument of defense.

We need such an instrument of defense and the United States will bear its fair share in keeping NATO strong.

All of us are also ready, as conditions change, to turn that fist into a hand of friendship.

NATO means more than arms, troop levels, consultative bodies, and treaty commitments. All of these are necessary. But what makes them relevant to the future is what the Alliance stands for. To discover what this Western Alliance means today, we have to reach back, not across two decades, but through the centuries to the very roots of the Western experience.

When we do, we find that we touch a set of elemental ideals, eloquent in their simplicity, majestic in their humanity, ideals of decency and justice and liberty and respect for the rights of our fellow men. Simple, yes; and to us they seem obvious. But our forebears struggled for centuries to win them and in our own lifetimes we have had to fight to defend them.

These ideals are what NATO was created to protect. It is to these ideals, on this proud anniversary, that we are privileged to consecrate the Alliance anew. These ideals—and the firmness of our dedication to them—give NATO's concept its nobility, and NATO's backbone its steel.

19. Report on Meeting of the Cabinet Committee on Economic Policy[1]

Washington, April 10, 1969.

[Omitted here is discussion of trade issues, particularly as they bore on agricultural exports. The focus of the discussion was Secretary Stans' upcoming trip to Europe.]

Mr. Samuels suggested that Secretary Stans stress "outwardness" rather than "inwardness" in trade policy. "Americans and Europeans have had some protectionist problems in the short run, but we have to make clear that this policy cannot be permanent." The President added, "Our mid-western friends here in America will stick with us on NATO but if we start fooling around with their soy beans, their votes are gone. Maury [Stans], if I were you, I would point out the growing isolationism in America. There's Vietnam, there are the obvious failures in foreign aid—overlooking the places it succeeded—and also there is the concern here with our own cities.

"There is no question about what the new leadership stands for," the President continued, "but we face a political problem at home. If the American people get the impression that the European economy is turning inward, the Europeans can forget about political cooperation; no administration could survive supporting their case.

"This isolationism is a troublesome trend," the President went on. "The people are saying now 'Why don't we cut the military budget? Why not bring home the divisions in Europe?' The next step could be 'Let the rest of the world go hang.' Of course, that would be a disastrous policy in the long run, but the Europeans and the Japanese have to understand that the string is running out. Maury, you have to use great discretion on this and not refer to it publicly at all. But tell them our problem. They don't hesitate to tell us theirs."

[Omitted here is discussion of a broad range of economic issues.]

---

[1] Source: National Archives, Nixon Presidential Materials, White House Special Files, President's Office Files, Box 77, Memoranda for the President, Jan 21–Apr 6, 1969. No classification marking. No drafting information provided. The meeting was held in the Cabinet Room. Among those present were President Nixon, Vice President Agnew, Secretary of Agriculture Hardin, Secretary of Commerce Stans, Budget Director Mayo, Counselor to the President Arthur Burns, and Deputy Under Secretary of State for Economic Affairs Nathaniel Samuels.

20.   Memorandum From the President's Deputy Assistant
       (Butterfield) to the President's Assistant for National
       Security Affairs (Kissinger)[1]

Washington, April 12, 1969.

SUBJECT

   Notes from the President (Action Item)

The following item concerning "U.S. Power" appeared in the President's April 10th News Summary: "The U.S. has lost 'the desire and ability' to be the dominant power in the world, Britain's Institute for Strategic Studies said. In the past year Russia has become the 'full equal' of the United States in military and political terms and is likely to overtake America in Inter Continental Ballistic Missiles by mid-1969. It said, however, that with its great stock of submarines and planes the United States will nevertheless retain a lead in total number of nuclear weapons. The survey predicted the possibility of a less active American role in the world in the 1970s—maybe the smallest U.S. international role since before World War II. 'It was largely accidental that the end of the American desire and ability to be the universal and dominant power should coincide with the end of eight years of Democrat rule,' the survey said. This course is not due to a choice of Americans of 'isolation for its own sake, but because their recent experience at home and abroad, had exhausted their confident sense of purpose and ability.'"

With reference to the content of this paragraph, the President addressed these comments to you:

   "Henry—
   (1) Very important and accurate.
   (2) We need to get this broadly circulated.

Alexander P. Butterfield[2]

---

[1]   Source: National Archives, Nixon Presidential Materials, NSC Files, Box 341, Subject Files, HAK/President Memoranda 1969–1970. No classification marking. A copy was sent to Keogh.

[2]   Printed from a copy that bears this typed signature.

21.   Editorial Note

On April 21, 1969, Secretary of State Rogers defined administration policy objectives in Asia in an address at the annual luncheon of the Associated Press in New York City. He used the address to send another signal of the administration's desire for improved relations with China:

"One cannot speak of a future Pacific community without reference to China.

"The United States Government understands perfectly well that the Republic of China on the island of Taiwan and Communist China on the mainland are both facts of life.

"We know that by virtue of its size, population, and the talents of its people, mainland China is bound to play an important role in East Asian and Pacific affairs.

"We have attempted to maintain a dialogue with the leaders of Communist China through periodic meetings in Warsaw; and we were disappointed 2 months ago when those leaders saw fit to cancel at the last moment a continuation of those talks.

"We have made a number of specific suggestions—an exchange of journalists, a relaxation of travel restrictions, the sale of grain and pharmaceuticals—in the hope that such steps would lead to a better climate between us. We regret that these overtures have been rejected—and that the leaders of Communist China have elected instead to attack the Nixon administration public pronouncements.

"Of course we recognize and have treaty relations with the Republic of China, which plays a responsible and constructive role in the international community. Whatever may be the ultimate resolution of the dispute between the Republic of China on Taiwan and the People's Republic of China on the mainland, we believe strongly it must be brought about by peaceful means.

"As things stand now, Communist China is in trouble domestically and externally. The present leaders look with enmity or suspicion upon their neighbors. They are hostile toward the United Nations; hostile toward the United States; hostile toward the Soviet Union; and have shown little interest in normal diplomatic relations with other countries. They still preach violence as a permanent way of life.

"We can expect all this to change with time. Not even a nation as large as mainland China can live forever in isolation from a world of interdependent states.

"Meanwhile, we shall take initiatives to reestablish more normal relations with Communist China and we shall remain responsive to any indications of less hostile attitudes from their side."

In the course of his address, Rogers also summarized the administration's objective of shifting the burden of combat in Vietnam to South Vietnam forces:

"The United States is committed to achieving a peace in Viet-Nam which will permit the people of South Viet-Nam to determine their own future, free from outside interference by anyone.

"That is our objective. It has been stated many times. It is known to all concerned. It is not subject to change.

"The South Vietnamese, together with the five allies who responded to their appeal for help, have denied the North Vietnamese Communists the military victory they were seeking. Together we have safeguarded the right of the people in the South to make their own decisions.

"The leaders in Hanoi know that they cannot win by military means.

"That is why there is a new sense of self-confidence in South Viet-Nam.

"And that is why we can now be deeply engaged, as we are, in an intensive program of upgrading the equipment and combat capability of the armed forces of the Republic of Viet-Nam so they are able to take over an ever larger measure of their own defense.

"I want to emphasize that this is something that the leaders of South Viet-Nam very much want—and have so stated publicly and privately.

"This, of course, is what we want, too.

"The readiness of replacement forces, the level of offensive actions by the enemy, or progress in the Paris peace talks will determine the scope and timing of actual transfers of responsibility—and the consequent release of our forces.

"In Paris we have put forward concrete proposals for bringing an end to armed conflict in Viet-Nam. These proposals have been drawn up on the assumption that the leaders of North Viet-Nam are, in fact, now prepared to negotiate an end to the war. On this assumption, we seek to negotiate the withdrawal of all outside combat forces from the territory of South Viet-Nam. This process of troop withdrawal cannot get started by postulating abstract propositions. It cannot get started by taking last things first. It must begin at the beginning." (Department of State *Bulletin*, May 12, 1969, pages 397–400)

22.   **Editorial Note**

On April 28, 1969, Secretary of Commerce Maurice Stans reported to President Nixon on the results of a mission he had just led to consult with the economic and trade ministers of Western European nations. Stans reported the trip a success, with the European officials reacting favorably to the administration's efforts to improve relations with Europe by consulting on matters of mutual concern before policy decisions were made in Washington. He also reported positive reactions to his emphasis on four economic freedoms as the basis for dealing with international economic problems:

"In my public speeches and meetings with the American and European business leaders, I expressed the basis of the Administration's approach to international economic problems in terms of four economic freedoms expressed as ideals:

"1. Freedom to trade
"2. Freedom to travel
"3. Freedom to invest
"4. Freedom to exchange technology

"The response was positive and favorable." (Memorandum from Secretary Stans to President Nixon, April 28, 1969; National Archives, Nixon Presidential Materials, NSC Files, Box 213, Agency Files, Commerce, 1970, Vol. I)

_____

23.   **Editorial Note**

The Nixon administration's determination to "Vietnamize" the combat in Vietnam was balanced by President Nixon's concern that a rapid withdrawal of U.S. forces from Vietnam would lead to an isolationist reaction. In a conversation on May 12, 1969, with Singapore Prime Minister Lee Kwan Yew at the White House, Nixon expressed his concern:

"The President said that he is personally quite familiar with the high stakes in Asia. A pull-out of the American forces precipitously would be disastrous for Asia, including countries like Japan and India. Europe would be affected. But, the most serious effect would be in the

United States. When a great power fails, it deeply affects the will of the people. While the public would welcome peace initially, they would soon be asking why we pulled out and this would in turn lead an attack on the leadership and establishment and the U.S. role in the war. Isolation could easily be the consequence.

"The President assured Lee that we are going to hold the line in Vietnam. We would make reasonable proposals for peace but never agree to a disguised defeat." (Memorandum of conversation; National Archives, Nixon Presidential Materials, White House Special Files, President's Office Files, B Series documents withheld in Box 7 from documents originally filed in folder 11 of Box 57)

---

24.   Editorial Note

On May 15, 1969, the National Security Council's Senior Review Group, chaired by Henry Kissinger, met to consider U.S. China policy. The discussion addressed the question of how to balance relations with China and the Soviet Union. Kissinger "wondered whether we really wanted China to be a world power like the Soviet Union, competing with us, rather than their present role which is limited to aiding certain insurgencies."

"Nutter mentioned Sino-Soviet difficulties and Kissinger suggested that this was a key issue. What is our view of the evolution of Sino-Soviet relations, how much can we influence them, should we favor one or the other, etc. Brown noted that China thinks that we favor the Soviet Union, while Unger suggested that present policy gives us the flexibility to take advantage of Sino-Soviet developments. Kissinger noted that the Soviets and Chinese each think we are playing with the other."

Kissinger added: "Some Kremlinologists believe that any attempt to better our relations with China will ruin those with the Soviet Union. History suggested to him that it is better to align yourself with the weaker, not the stronger of two antagonistic partners. It is not clear to him that you achieve better relations with the Soviets necessarily because of a hard policy toward China and vice versa. Everyone agrees that we wish to reduce the risk of war with 700 million people, but the question is whether alignment with the Soviets, more conciliatory posture toward China or some combination would best achieve this end."

(Minutes of Senior Review Group Meeting; National Security Council, Secretariat Files, Senior Review Group Minutes, May 15, 1969 Meeting) The meeting was held at 2:10 p.m. in the White House Situation Room. The other members of the group cited in the discussion are Assistant Secretary of Defense for International Security Affairs G. Warren Nutter, Deputy Assistant Secretary of State for East Asian and Pacific Affairs Winthrop Brown, and Lieutenant General Frederick T. Unger, Director for Plans and Policy on the Joint Staff of the Joint Chiefs of Staff. The full text of the minutes is scheduled for publication in *Foreign Relations, 1969–1976, China, 1969–1972.*

25.   **Editorial Note**

President Nixon briefed a joint meeting of the National Security Council and the Cabinet on May 15, 1969, on the televised speech on Vietnam he had delivered the previous evening. During the briefing, Nixon summarized his objectives and strategy in pursuing a settlement to the conflict:

"In a summary statement, the President began by pointing out that the end of World War II was delayed by the insistence on unconditional surrender. If the enemy knows there is no way out but military defeat, he has nothing to gain by offering a settlement. What we have provided is a way out. On the other side of the coin, some people feel that it is only necessary to put out a proposal to get peace. What must be realized is that we are talking to an enemy whose first objective is not peace. They want South Vietnam. So if we are going to get genuine negotiations, just putting out a proposal is not enough. We needed to threaten that if they don't talk they will suffer.

"The President listed four principal factors in the U.S. position. One, we are for peace—we are reasonable. Two, we aim to convince the enemy that if there is no settlement, we have an option which is military action not only at the present level but at an expanded level. Three, we want to make clear that they can't win by sitting us out. Four, we want to convince them that they aren't going to get what they want by erosion of the will of the U.S. So, said the President, we have offered them a way out. We have tried to indicate that we will not tolerate a continuation of their fight-talk strategy. We have tried to convince them that the time is coming when South Vietnam will be strong enough to handle a major part of the load. Beyond all this, said the President, it was necessary to give the impression to the enemy that the people of the U.S. are going to support a sound peace proposal and not accept peace at any price. Then and only then will the enemy realize that the war must be ended." (Memorandum of National Security Council/Cabinet Meeting, drafted by the President's Special Assistant James Keogh; National Archives, Nixon Presidential Materials, White House Special Files, President's Office Files, Box 1, Memoranda for the President 1969–1970, Beginning May 11, 1969)

Members of the National Security Council, the Cabinet, and 24 sub-Cabinet and White House officials attended the meeting, which lasted from 10:08 to 11:44 a.m. (Ibid., White House Central Files, Staff Memoranda and Office Files, Office of Presidential Papers and Archives, Daily Diary) The full text of the memorandum is scheduled for publication in *Foreign Relations, 1969–1976, Southeast Asia, 1969–1972*. In his speech to the nation on May 14, President Nixon outlined a proposal for mutual withdrawal in Vietnam over a period of 12 months. The text of the speech is printed in *Public Papers of the Presidents of the United States: Richard Nixon, 1969*, pages 369–375.

---

26.   Special Message From President Nixon to the Congress[1]

Washington, May 28, 1969.

Americans have for many years debated the issues of foreign aid largely in terms of our own national self-interest.

Certainly our efforts to help nations feed millions of their poor help avert violence and upheaval that would be dangerous to peace.

Certainly our military assistance to allies helps maintain a world in which we ourselves are more secure.

Certainly our economic aid to developing nations helps develop our own potential markets overseas.

And certainly our technical assistance puts down roots of respect and friendship for the United States in the court of world opinion.

---

[1] Source: *Public Papers of the Presidents of the United States: Richard Nixon, 1969*, pp. 411–417.

These are all sound, practical reasons for our foreign aid programs.

But they do not do justice to our fundamental character and purpose. There is a moral quality in this Nation that will not permit us to close our eyes to the want in this world, or to remain indifferent when the freedom and security of others are in danger.

We should not be self-conscious about this. Our record of generosity and concern for our fellow men, expressed in concrete terms unparalleled in the world's history, has helped make the American experience unique. We have shown the world that a great nation must also be a good nation. We are doing what is right to do.

A Fresh Approach

This Administration has intensively examined our programs of foreign aid. We have measured them against the goals of our policy and the goad of our conscience. Our review is continuing, but we have come to this central conclusion:

U.S. assistance is essential to express and achieve our national goals in the international community—a world order of peace and justice.

But no single government, no matter how wealthy or well-intentioned, can by itself hope to cope with the challenge of raising the standard of living of two-thirds of the world's people. This reality must not cause us to retreat into helpless, sullen isolation. On the contrary, this reality must cause us to redirect our efforts in four main ways:

We must enlist the energies of private enterprise, here and abroad, in the cause of economic development. We must do so by stimulating additional investment through businesslike channels, rather than offering ringing exhortations.

We must emphasize innovative technical assistance, to ensure that our dollars for all forms of aid go further, and to plant the seeds that will enable other nations to grow their own capabilities for the future.

We must induce other advanced nations to join in bearing their fair share—by contributing jointly to multilateral banks and the United Nations, by consultation and by the force of our example, and by effective coordination of national and multilateral programs in individual countries.

We must build on recent successes in furthering food production and family planning.

To accomplish these goals, this Administration's foreign aid proposals will be submitted to the Congress today. [Omitted here are elaboration of the four points listed above, an outline of the administration's budget requests for foreign assistance, and notice of the President's intention to appoint a non-governmental task force to review and make recommendations on foreign assistance programs.]

Toward a World of Order

Foreign aid cannot be viewed in isolation. That is a statement with a double meaning, each side of which is true.

If we turn inward, if we adopt an attitude of letting the underdeveloped nations shift for themselves, we would soon see them shift away from the values so necessary to international stability. Moreover, we would lose the traditional concern for humanity which is so vital a part of the American spirit.

In another sense, foreign aid must be viewed as an integral part of our overall effort to achieve a world order of peace and justice. That order combines our sense of responsibility for helping those determined to defend their freedom; our sensible understanding of the mutual benefits that flow from cooperation between nations; and our sensitivity to the desires of our fellow men to improve their lot in the world.

In this time of stringent budgetary restraint, we must stimulate private investment and the cooperation of other governments to share with us in meeting the most urgent needs of those just beginning to climb the economic ladder. And we must continue to minimize the immediate impact on our balance of payments.

This request for foreign economic and military assistance is the lowest proposed since the program began. But it is about 900 million dollars more than was appropriated last year. I consider it necessary to meet essential requirements now, and to maintain a base for future action.

The support by the Congress of these programs will help enable us to press forward in new ways toward the building of respect for the United States, security for our people and dignity for human beings in every corner of the globe.

Richard Nixon

27.   Address by President Nixon[1]

Colorado Springs, Colorado, June 4, 1969.

[Omitted here are the President's introductory remarks in which he warned the graduating class that they were beginning their military careers at a difficult time. He told them that they would have to be prepared to risk their lives in a limited war while facing those at home who questioned the need for a strong national defense and saw a danger in the power of the military.]

This paradox of military power is a symptom of something far deeper that is stirring in our body politic. It goes beyond the dissent about the war in Vietnam. It goes beyond the fear of the "military-industrial complex."

The underlying questions are really these: What is America's role in the world? What are the responsibilities of a great nation toward protecting freedom beyond its shores? Can we ever be left in peace if we do not actively assume the burden of keeping the peace?

When great questions are posed, fundamental differences of opinion come into focus. It serves no purpose to gloss over these differences, or to try to pretend that they are mere matters of degree. Because there is one school of thought that holds that the road to understanding with the Soviet Union and Communist China lies through a downgrading of our own alliances and what amounts to a unilateral reduction of our arms in order to demonstrate our "good faith."

They believe that we can be conciliatory and accommodating only if we do not have the strength to be otherwise. They believe that America will be able to deal with the possibility of peace only when we are unable to cope with the threat of war.

Those who think that way have grown weary of the weight of free world leadership that fell upon us in the wake of World War II. They argue that we—that the United States is as much responsible for the tensions in the world as the adversaries we face.

They assert that the United States is blocking the road to peace by maintaining its military strength at home and its defenses abroad. If we would only reduce our forces, they contend, tensions would disappear and the chances for peace would brighten.

America's powerful military presence on the world scene, they believe, makes peace abroad improbable and peace at home impossible.

---

[1] Source: *Public Papers of the Presidents of the United States: Richard Nixon, 1969,* 432–437. The President was speaking at the Air Force Academy Commencement Exercises.

Now we should never underestimate the appeal of the isolationist school of thought. Their slogans are simplistic and powerful: "Charity begins at home. Let's first solve our problems at home and then we can deal with the problems of the world."

This simple formula touches a responsive chord with many an overburdened taxpayer. It would be easy, easy for a President of the United States to buy some popularity by going along with the new isolationists. But I submit to you that it would be disastrous for our Nation and the world.

I hold a totally different view of the world, and I come to a different conclusion about the direction America must take.

Imagine for a moment, if you will, what would happen to this world if America were to become a dropout in assuming the responsibility for defending peace and freedom in the world. As every world leader knows, and as even the most outspoken critics of America would admit, the rest of the world would live in terror.

Because if America were to turn its back on the world, there would be peace that would settle over this planet, but it would be the kind of peace that suffocated freedom in Czechoslovakia.

The danger to us has changed, but it has not vanished. We must revitalize our alliances, not abandon them.

We must rule out unilateral disarmament, because in the real world it wouldn't work. If we pursue arms control as an end in itself, we will not achieve our end. The adversaries in the world are not in conflict because they are armed. They are armed because they are in conflict, and have not yet learned peaceful ways to resolve their conflicting national interests.

The aggressors of this world are not going to give the United States a period of grace in which to put our domestic house in order—just as the crises within our society cannot be put on a back burner until we resolve the problem of Vietnam.

The most successful solutions that we can possibly imagine for our domestic programs will be meaningless if we are not around to enjoy them. Nor can we conduct a successful peace policy abroad if our society is at war with itself at home.

There is no advancement for Americans at home in a retreat from the problems of the world. I say that America has a vital national interest in world stability, and no other nation can uphold that interest for us.

We stand at a crossroad in our history. We shall reaffirm our destiny for greatness or we shall choose instead to withdraw into ourselves. The choice will affect far more than our foreign policy; it will determine the quality of our lives.

A nation needs many qualities, but it needs faith and confidence above all. Skeptics do not build societies; the idealists are the builders. Only societies that believe in themselves can rise to their challenges. Let us not, then, pose a false choice between meeting our responsibilities abroad and meeting the needs of our people at home. We shall meet both or we shall meet neither.

That is why my disagreement with the skeptics and the isolationists is fundamental. They have lost the vision indispensable to great leadership. They observe the problems that confront us; they measure our resources and then they despair. When the first vessels set out from Europe for the New World these men would have weighed the risks and they would have stayed behind. When the colonists on the eastern seaboard started across the Appalachians to the unknown reaches of the Ohio Valley, these men would have counted the costs and they would have stayed behind.

Our current exploration of space makes the point vividly; here is testimony to man's vision and to man's courage. The journey of the astronauts is more than a technical achievement; it is a reaching-out of the human spirit. It lifts our sights; it demonstrates that magnificent conceptions can be made real.

They inspire us and at the same time they teach us true humility. What could bring home to us more the limitations of the human scale than the hauntingly beautiful picture of our earth seen from the moon?

When the first man stands on the moon next month every American will stand taller because of what he has done, and we should be proud of this magnificent achievement.

We will know then that every man achieves his own greatness by reaching out beyond himself, and so it is with nations. When a nation believes in itself—as Athenians did in their Golden Age, as Italians did in the Renaissance—that nation can perform miracles. Only when a nation means something to itself can it mean something to others.

That is why I believe a resurgence of American idealism can bring about a modern miracle, and that modern miracle is a world order of peace and justice.

[Omitted here are Nixon's concluding remarks, in which he argued for sufficient defense expenditures to maintain a strong military establishment.]

**28.   Letter From President Nixon to the Director of the Arms
Control and Disarmament Agency (Smith)[1]**

Washington, July 21, 1969.

Dear Gerry:

Following our discussion today, I wish to convey to you my thoughts on the forthcoming talks with the Soviet Union on strategic arms. You and your associates will be dealing with a subject of crucial significance to the safety of this country. My purpose in these talks is to determine whether it is feasible to make arrangements with the Soviet Government that will contribute to the preservation and, if possible, the improvement of this country's security. Any arrangement with the Soviet Union, especially if it is to be in the form of explicit and formal commitments, must meet this test to my own full satisfaction.

When I speak of this country's security, I fully realize that we cannot expect to return to an era when our country was literally immune to physical threat. Neither our military programs nor any negotiation with our potential adversaries can achieve that. But I am speaking of a situation in which I, as President and Commander-in-Chief, have at my disposal military forces that will provide me with the best assurance attainable in present and foreseeable circumstances that no opponent can rationally expect to derive benefit from attacking, or threatening to attack us or our allies. I am determined, moreover, to pass on to my successor that same sense of assurance.

If the Soviet leaders operate on similar premises (which we do not know and which their current military programs give some reason to doubt), there could be, I believe, a prospect of reaching an understanding with them whereby, in the first instance, limits would be placed on the quantitative and qualitative growth of strategic forces. It will be your task to obtain evidence that will assist me in making a determination whether such a prospect is real and what the elements of such an understanding could be.

Any understanding, whatever the form, that places limitations on Soviet forces will obviously involve limitations on ours. I will judge the resulting relationship of US-Soviet strategic forces in terms of the criteria for strategic sufficiency that I have established.

---

[1]   Source: National Archives, Nixon Presidential Materials, NSC Files, Box 197, Agency Flies, ACDA, 1/20/69–12/31/69. Secret; Nodis. Drafted in the NSC Staff by Helmut Sonnenfeldt, and revised by Kissinger and Nixon.

Moreover, I will accept limitations on our forces only after I have assured myself of our ability to detect Soviet failure to implement limitations on their own forces in sufficient time to protect our security interests. In this latter connection, you should know that I am determined to avoid, within the Government and in the country at large, divisive disputes regarding Soviet compliance or non-compliance with an understanding or agreement. Nor will I bequeath to a future President the seeds of such disputes. In our open society and political system it is my duty to provide persuasive public evidence not only of any Soviet non-compliance with an agreement but also of Soviet compliance with it. Any agreed limitations must therefore meet the test of verifiability. I recognize that this may not be obtainable with 100 percent assurance; but the margin of uncertainty must be reasonable. I will make this judgement.

I have carefully examined the possible alternative arrangements that might be entered into with the Soviet Union, as developed through our National Security Council process. In the absence of any indications from the Soviet Union of the direction they propose to take, I do not find it possible to make a clear selection among them. I do not, therefore, desire to propose to the Soviet Government a specific set of measures corresponding to the five alternatives analyzed in NSSM 62.[2] You should outline to the Soviet representatives the various approaches we have studied, as reflected in Alternatives I, II and III of NSSM 62 and indicate our readiness to examine jointly with them these and any others they might advance. You may state that we are prepared to consider limitations on all strategic offensive and defensive weapons systems, that our suggestions are not exhaustive but that we wish to hear their views before advancing any additional ones ourselves. Upon completion of the work of the MIRV verification panel, I may authorize presenting aspects of Alternative IV.

In short, your task in the initial phases of the talks is to explore Soviet intentions without yourself placing on the table the full range of alternative arrangements that we might consider. In the light of the progress of the explorations, and other relevant factors, I will determine the timing and contents of any specific limitation proposal that we might make to the Soviet Union.

Let me, in conclusion, outline my general approach to our relations with the USSR so that you and your associates will be guided thereby in

---

[2] NSSM 62 was addressed on July 2 to the Secretaries of State and Defense, the Director of Central Intelligence, the Director of the Arms Control and Disarmament Agency, the Chairman of the Atomic Energy Commission, and the President's Science Adviser. In this memorandum, Kissinger, on behalf of the President, directed the preparation of negotiating positions for the strategic arms control talks. (National Archives, Nixon Presidential Materials, NSC Files, Box 365, Subject Files, National Security Study Memoranda (NSSMs), Nos. 43–103)

your talks. I have conveyed to the Soviet leaders my view that our relations should be based on a recognition by each side of the legitimate security interests of the other; I have conveyed to them also my readiness to engage in bona fide negotiations on concrete issues. I have told them that I have no interest either in polemical exchanges or in the mere atmospherics of détente. Having propounded these principles and acted on them in practice since entering office, I believe the seriousness of this Administration in pursuing the path of equitable accommodation with the Soviet Union is being demonstrated. I consider that the approach to the arms limitation talks outlined above will serve to provide further such demonstration. The other side has the opportunity to respond to the same spirit. If it does so, arrangements to restrain the pace of competition in the field of strategic armaments should be within our reach.

Sincerely,

Richard Nixon[3]

---

[3] Printed from a copy that indicates Nixon signed the original.

---

29. Editorial Note

On July 25, 1969, during a tour of Asia, President Nixon met with reporters in Guam. His remarks were on a background basis, for attribution but not direct quotation. Nixon was in Guam after witnessing the splashdown in the Pacific Ocean of the Apollo astronauts following their return from the first landing on the moon. Speaking at 6:30 p.m. in the Top O' the Mar Officers Club, Nixon outlined what was first called the Guam Doctrine and later the Nixon Doctrine. Looking to the future, Nixon said that Asia "poses, in my view, over the long haul, looking down to the end of the century, the greatest threat to the peace of the world, and, for that reason, the United States should continue to play a significant role." But he qualified the scope of that role:

"Asians will say in every country that we visit that they do not want be dictated to from outside, Asia for Asians. And that is what we want, and that is the role we should play. We should assist but we should not dictate.

"At this time the political and economic plans that they are developing are very hopeful. We will give assistance to those plans. We, of course, will keep the treaty commitments that we have.

"But as far as our role is concerned, we must avoid the kind of policy that will make countries in Asia so dependent upon us that we are dragged into conflicts such as the one we have in Vietnam."

In response to a question, the President reiterated that the United States would honor its treaty commitments, but added "that as far as the problems of military defense, except for the threat of a major power involving nuclear weapons, that the United States is going to encourage and has a right to expect that this problem will be handled by, and responsibility for it taken by, the Asian nations themselves."

The full text of the President's remarks was subsequently released and is printed in *Public Papers of the Presidents of the United States: Richard Nixon, 1969*, pages 544–556.

President Nixon's remarks stirred great interest among the press and the public in both Asia and the United States. The doctrine was refined and restated repeatedly and became one of the principal foreign policy themes of the Nixon administration. As to its origins, Henry Kissinger recalls that in preparing for the Asian trip he and Nixon had discussed redefining the parameters of U.S. commitments in the region in light of U.S. experience in Vietnam, but he was surprised by Nixon's informal remarks in Guam. According to Kissinger, the original intention was to make a speech along similar lines later in the summer. (Kissinger, *White House Years*, pages 222–225)

In his memoirs, Nixon notes that the doctrine he announced on Guam was misinterpreted by some as signaling a U.S. withdrawal from Asia, as well as other parts of the world. In his view, "the Nixon Doctrine was not a formula for getting America out of Asia, but one that provided the only sound basis for America's staying in and continuing to play a responsible role in helping non-communist nations and neutrals as well as our Asian allies to defend their independence." (Nixon, *RN, The Memoirs of Richard Nixon*, page 395)

---

30.   **Editorial Note**

In a background briefing for reporters in Bangkok, Thailand, on July 29, 1969, Henry Kissinger amplified on the doctrine articulated by President Nixon in Guam 4 days earlier (see Document 29). In response to a question as to how the Asian nations consulted on the President's tour had responded to the President's remarks in Guam, Kissinger said:

"I would prefer to answer how the Asian nations have taken to the President's general position, because the text of the Guam conference isn't available and we haven't presented the Guam conference as such, although of course, we stand fully behind it.

"We have had full and detailed conversations with the Asian nations about the general philosophy that the President expressed at Guam and repeated at Manila.

"The Asian nations that we have talked to have agreed with us that the future of Asia must be, in the first instance, shaped by Asians and cannot be developed on the basis of prescriptions devised in Washington. They have also agreed with our general philosophy that the United States will, of course, fully live up to all of its commitments in this area, and that it will, of course, remain a Pacific power.

"However, it is clear that in the new period, in the period ahead, it becomes important to understand the various dangers that the Asian nations may face. As against military aggression from the outside, the President has repeated at every stop our intention to live up to those commitments that we have made, as well as to those commitments that are implied in the general United Nations Charter and the inherent importance of various countries.

"As regards internal subversion, we have stated that the primary responsibility for combating internal subversion has to be borne by the countries concerned with respect to manpower, with American material and technical help where that is indicated and thought appropriate.

"I am happy to report to you that this view has been shared by the heads of Government of every country in which we have spoken, and I have been particularly authorized by the heads of Government of Thailand to express to you their complete agreement with our philosophy, that the manpower to fight internal subversion has to be supplied by the countries concerned, with American material and technical help where indicated.

"Q. Does that mean that the United States now has decided not to supply any combat troops where a country is faced with internal subversion?

"Dr. Kissinger: The general policy is that internal subversion has to be the primary responsibility of the threatened country. In an overwhelming majority of the cases, to which it is hard to think of an exception, the numbers involved are not tremendous. We are talking now of internal subversion.

"Q. The numbers of what?

"Dr. Kissinger: The numbers of guerrillas involved are not tremendous. Therefore, local manpower should have the predominant responsibility for meeting this.

"The United States stands ready to supply material assistance, advice and technical assistance where that is requested and where our interests so dictate. But the general policy is as I have indicated.

"You understand, of course, that it is never possible to be absolutely categorical about every last case, but this is the general policy as it now stands." (Library of Congress, Manuscript Division, Kissinger Papers, Box CL 425, Subject File, Background Briefings, June–Dec 1969)

---

31.   Memorandum of Conversation[1]

Bangkok, July 29, 1969, 4 p.m.

PARTICIPANTS

The President
Ellsworth Bunker, Ambassador to South Vietnam
Robert S. Lindquist, Chargé in Malaysia
William H. Burns, Chargé in Singapore
G. McMurtrie Godley, Ambassador to Laos
Arthur W. Hummel, Ambassador to Burma
Carol Laise, Ambassador to Nepal
Andrew V. Corry, Ambassador to Ceylon
Leonard Unger, Ambassador to Thailand
Norman Hannah, DCM in Thailand
Robert G. Neumann, Ambassador to Afghanistan
Henry A. Kissinger, Assistant to the President
Ronald Ziegler, Assistant to the President
Harold H. Saunders, NSC Staff

President: Thanks for coming. Time precludes visiting some countries. On the other hand, being in area provides opportunity to hear your countries' reactions to our policies generally—everything from foreign assistance over. What I have tried to get across on trip so far:

I have general belief that Asia is where the action is and ought to be—in spite of Vietnam. Other areas naturally important too. US/Soviet

---

[1] Source: National Archives, Nixon Presidential Materials, NSC Files, Box 1023, Presidential/HAK Memcons, President's Asian and European Trip, July–Aug 1969. No classification marking. The meeting, held in the Embassy in Bangkok, was a gathering of regional Chiefs of Mission held during Nixon's trip to several Asian countries and Romania, which he took in July and August 1969. Additional documentation on the trip is ibid., President's Trip Files, Boxes 452–454. For the full text of the memorandum of conversation, see *Foreign Relations*, 1969–1976, Southeast Asia, 1969–1972.

relations will be taken care of at highest level. Latin America will not change much. Africa will not govern itself for 200 years. But in terms of conflict involving us, likeliest place is Asia. Mid-East possibly, but there less likely because that would be between US and USSR. But in Asia, countries on edge of China ripe for export of revolution.

As I see it, the way we end Vietnam war will determine whether we can have viable policy in Asia—a settlement that will not be seen as US defeat and will not lead to Communist takeover in a few years. Don't have to put this in domino terms.

One could conclude that getting out of Vietnam any way would be best thing we could do. But—though everyone wants peace—the most detrimental effect of a Vietnam settlement would be a settlement that produced Communist victory in a few years. US people would throw up hands on further active Asian involvement. We are going through critical phase for US world leadership—American people never wanted to be world leaders in first place and maybe that's why we have never had a world policy.

[Omitted here are reports by Chiefs of Mission Godley, Hummel, Lindquist, Burns, Neumann, Corry, Laise, and Bunker on developments in their respective areas of responsibility.]

President: Let me sum up.

On Mid-East, no progress of significance. I anticipate none. May only come only at a very high level only when Soviets realize they may be drawn in. Arabs they support in shaky positions. Very pessimistic situation at this time.

On Vietnam, no significant progress in Paris on public talks—don't talk about private contacts. Soviets have played minimal role; expect none unless they can get something because they can't get caught at it. Escalation that would involve US and USSR remote. Ties us down. One factor in other direction is that they have their troubles. As long as Vietnam going on, difficult to make progress in other fields with us. If USSR needs or wants better relations with US, moving on Vietnam would open door. If I were where they sit, I would keep "giving it to the US" in Vietnam.

Chinese-Soviet and US attitude. I don't think we should rush quickly into embrace with USSR to contain China. Best US stance is to play each—not publicly. US–USSR–Europe lined up against rest of Asia not a pretty prospect. US–USSR security pact would invite Soviet adventurism in area; can let people talk about it but not do anything about.

What really rides on Vietnam, is whether US people are going to play big role in world or not. That question is [in] very serious doubt. Mass of people usually think right but intellectuals oppose all but passive US role. How can we conduct policies in Asia so that we can play role we should:

1. Viable Vietnamese government for at least five years.
2. Where problem is internal subversion, countries must deal with problem themselves. We will help—but not American ground forces. Even when there is foreign exported revolution. Not talking about invasion by conventional troops.
3. I feel that with all criticism of US, Asia leaders realize worst thing for them would be for US to bug out of Vietnam because that would leave vacuum. Collective security is a good theme—but not real for five years (even Japan).
4. We have to conduct policy so we can sell it in US.

---

32.   **Editorial Note**

The final stop in Asia on the tour undertaken by President Nixon in July and August 1969 was in Pakistan. Henry Kissinger used the occasion of a background briefing for the press in Lahore on August 1 to expand the definition of the doctrine established by Nixon in Guam on July 25:

"We came to Asia to put before the countries we visited our general approach to Asian policy, which I perhaps can sum up briefly as follows:

"One, that we will honor all commitments which we have made; two, that we will not undertake any new formal commitments; three, that the best defense against the insurrection is to prevent it from happening, by removing the conditions that give rise to it. If insurrection reaches the form, or if subversion reaches the form of insurrection, the American role should be confined, essentially, to technical and military assistance and not to the supply of ground forces in those cases in which we feel our interest is sufficiently involved to engage ourselves at all.

"Five, that peace in Asia is a pre-condition to peace in the world, and that peace in Asia cannot result primarily from American conceptions, but has to involve Asian initiatives, and a structure developed by Asians.

"Therefore, we would look favorably upon regional and subregional arrangements that have an Asian origin, and we would be prepared to give our support, especially in the economic field, where it is asked for and where our view of the necessities coincides with that of the countries concerned.

"I believe that while when we started out there was a fear in many of the countries that we visited that the United States might withdraw from Asia altogether, or might withdraw too precipitously from Vietnam, that there is an understanding that we are moving into a new phase, that we are looking for more permanent relationships and not the essentially emergency measures that were inevitable in the immediate post-war period.

"I believe also that there is a general recognition that the way the war in Vietnam ends will affect the American posture towards international affairs and towards a role in Asia, and I think we have laid the basis for a relationship which, over a longer period of time, will be more viable than the existing one." (Library of Congress, Manuscript Division, Kissinger Papers, Box CL 425, Subject File, Background Briefings, June–Dec 1969)

---

33. Editorial Note

During his visit to Lahore, Pakistan, on August 1, 1969, President Nixon discussed with President Yahya Khan the importance of ending the diplomatic isolation of China:

"President Nixon stated it as his personal view—not completely shared by the rest of his government or by many Americans—that Asia cannot move forward if a nation as large as China remains isolated. He further said that the US should not be party to any arrangements designed to isolate China. He asked President Yahya to convey his feeling to the Chinese at the highest level."

Nixon met privately with Yahya; no U.S. record of the meeting has been found. Pakistan's Ambassador to the United States, Agha Hilaly, subsequently shared the Pakistani record of the meeting with Harold Saunders of the NSC Staff. That record, dated August 28, is in the National Archives, Nixon Presidential Materials, NSC Files, Box 1032, Files for the President, China Materials, Cookies II, Chronology of Exchanges with the PRC.

This closely-held initiative, which led to Nixon's trip to China in 1972 and to the ultimate re-establishment of relations between the

United States and China, contrasted with the view Nixon expressed in a conversation in San Francisco on August 21 with President Pak of the Republic of Korea. Nixon described China as aggressive and unsuitable for membership in the United Nations:

"We have relaxed our travel restrictions and purchases with regard to Communist China, but we regard Communist China as an aggressive nation. U.S. policy toward China has not changed, and we will not admit the country into the U.N." (Memorandum of conversation; ibid., White House Special Files, President's Office Files, Box 79, Memoranda for the President, Aug 3–Dec 28, 1969)

34.   Editorial Note

When he returned from his trip to Asia and Romania, President Nixon briefed Congressional leaders on August 4, 1969, on the new policy he had outlined in Guam. In the process, he drew the broader implications of the policy:

"The centerpiece of the meeting was a monologue by the President on his just completed trip to Southeast Asia, South Asia and Romania. The President began the meeting with a discussion of American policy in Asia. He said that if you gentlemen are somewhat confused by the seeming contradiction between my statements in various Asian countries, this is quite deliberate. American policy in Asia is in a transition stage. We have to realize that these are different countries requiring different approaches; the U.S. must move away from a monolithic approach to a country-by-country approach in the area. However, that approach will work only if we have some general operative principles. The President then reverted to his own background; I came from the 'era of pacts,' he said. I supported this approach in the past, but now 25 years after World War II, we have to revise our policy to meet the new situation. It is important this be done subtly and gradually.

"The President said that his visits with Yahya Khan in Pakistan and Ceausescu in Romania were worth going half way around the world to see. He said their reports were extremely helpful regarding the Sino-Soviet problem, and that we have difficulty getting hard intelligence on this because we simply have no agents in some of those areas. The policy we should begin to follow now, he indicated, is this.

The U.S. must keep the commitments it has made thus far, the treaties it has made, because a failure here would bring drastic repercussions both in terms of what would happen to the people and in terms of American credibility in the area. However, we should not expand any treaty; the time has come to examine our commitments on a country by country basis. In some areas, he said, it is not in our interest to have an agreement. I don't believe we should become involved in some of these areas if we can possibly avoid it. However, he reiterated that he felt that history would vindicate the decisions in Vietnam and that the war there is in the basic interest of peace in the Pacific. The President reaffirmed his conviction that were it not for the U.S. keeping the cork in the bottle in Vietnam, the 115 million people in Indonesia would now be under Communist rule. These then were the basics of the new policy:

"To maintain the credibility of America's existing commitments and to make no new commitments in the area. However, if a major power should move across a border openly, this would be a different ball game, but since that would involve a confrontation of some kind with the U.S., the President felt the likelihood of that kind of activity to be small. Our policy in the future, he said, will be to help them fight the war and not fight the war for them. This referred to other non-Communist Asian nations.

"In the event that the difficulties in an Asian country arise from an internal threat, these countries will be called upon to handle it entirely on their own. In the event that the aggression within is subsidized from the outside, we will provide them with American assistance in the form of arms and material, but we will not provide the troops. This is the new approach: we will help them in a material way and not a manpower way, he said." (Notes drafted by Patrick J. Buchanan and submitted to the President in a memorandum dated August 5; National Archives, Nixon Presidential Materials, White House Special Files, President's Office Files, Box 79, Memoranda for the President, Aug 3–Dec 28, 1969)

According to the President's Daily Diary, the meeting was held at 8:35 a.m. in the Cabinet Room of the White House. Eleven Senators and eleven Members of the House of Representatives attended the bipartisan leadership meeting. (Ibid., White House Central Files, Staff Members and Office Files, Office of Presidential Papers and Archives, Daily Diary)

35.   Memorandum of Conversation[1]

San Clemente, California, September 2, 1969, 11:45 a.m.

SUBJECT

President's Task Force on Foreign Aid[2]

PARTICIPANTS

The President
Rudolph Peterson, Chairman of the President's Task Force on International
    Development
Dr. Henry A. Kissinger, Assistant to the President for National Security Affairs
C. Fred Bergsten, Senior Staff, NSC

The President began the meeting by speaking bluntly about the objectives of the Task Force. It would not be like the earlier Task Forces on aid chaired by General Clay and others. This group must come up with a truly new approach to foreign aid or the U.S. aid program will die.

AID's presentation to the National Security Council was the worst it had had this year. (This is not due to Dr. Hannah, who was new at the time and had not yet been able to effect any changes.) The State Department wants to give aid to every country in the world and the result is lots of "Mickey Mouse programs." The President does not believe in this approach.

Foreign aid is not an abject failure, the President continued. There are numerous success stories. In all of them, however, there were additional key factors beyond aid, such as U.S. military expenditures or impressive natural resources.

Mr. Peterson can expect to hear from the State Department that government-to-government aid is best because State likes to use aid to stroke its clients. They believe in aid to socialist countries and enter-

---

[1] Source: National Archives, Nixon Presidential Materials, NSC Files, Box 1026, Presidential/HAK Memcons, June–Dec 1969. No classification marking. The meeting was held in the President's office in the Western White House. No drafting information is provided but the memorandum was apparently drafted by C. Fred Bergsten of the NSC Staff.

[2] On September 2 the White House Press Secretary announced the appointment of Rudolph Peterson, President of the Bank of America, as chairman of the President's Task Force on International Development. President Nixon had announced his intention to appoint such a task force of private citizens to review the entire range of U.S. foreign assistance activities in his May 28 message to Congress on foreign assistance (see Document 26). On September 24 the White House Press Office announced the membership of the task force. (National Archives, Nixon Presidential Materials, NSC Files, Box 193, Agency Files, AID, Task Forces on AID) In an October 6 memorandum to Peterson, Kissinger noted the high priority the President attached to the task force and his instruction that the agencies cooperate fully with it. (Ibid.) For documentation on the Peterson Task Force, see *Foreign Relations*, 1969–1976, vol. IV, Documents 119 ff.

prises and are not worried by such events as India's nationalization of the banking system. The President asserted that we need to get away from government-to-government aid and from aiding countries who are headed toward adoption of totalitarian socialist systems. This is not because of ideology.

It is because aid simply will not be effective in such environments. The success stories to date have occurred mainly in environments where the private sector played a major role. He had told Mrs. Gandhi, for example, that public aid was not expandable—only private investment was.

Latin America is a disaster, the President continued. State and AID like to provide aid to consumer/social enterprises for purposes such as health and housing. This is wrong. We must help countries help themselves through supporting industries which have multiplier effects throughout the economy. We must help them increase their GNP's so they can build the needed infrastructure themselves. The way to help poor people is to help increase the size of the pie from which they can get a slice.

The President stated that there has been no really new thought in the foreign aid field in twenty years. There are always references to "trade and aid" and increasing private investment but we have added nothing really new. Everybody is caught in the Marshall Plan syndrome, which unfortunately could not work outside Europe and Japan.

The President did not pretend to have the answer himself. He did feel, however, that our program was far too fragmented. We do not need to aid every country. For example, some of the former metropoles should bear the responsibility for their ex-colonies. The U.S. should only aid countries where there is a major U.S. interest. We should not attempt to dictate the type of political system maintained in foreign countries, although many of the Task Force members will probably espouse socialist approaches and repeat many of the old tired ideas.

The President concluded that Congress will not provide money to do what is needed in the aid field unless we have a new name and a new approach to the program. He stressed the importance of getting an exceptionally able staff for the Task Force and that the group must not be on the defensive about the aid effort.

Dr. Kissinger, at the President's request, added that the whole U.S. approach to aid has been exceedingly defensive because of the lack of a new concept. The bias has been that foreign aid is good and the only job is to sell it. Another problem is that aid has fallen into the hands of economists, which was all right in Europe where the need was essentially technical and the requisite private energy and political structures existed, but which will not work where political structures do not exist as is the case in many LDCs.

There is no necessary progression from economic growth to political stability, Dr. Kissinger continued. In fact, there must be a political structure or else economic growth will not occur. We therefore need an explicit consideration of the link between political and economic frameworks in particular countries.

Dr. Kissinger added that Mr. Peterson will hear that leftist totalitarian approaches are completely acceptable but that the U.S. should oppose rightist approaches. This is particularly strange because we do not know what democracy means in a less developed country. This is another conceptual problem which must be tackled. He was afraid that his academic colleagues were not very fertile in answering it.

The President suggested that our effort should appear publicly as aid without strings but that in practice it, of course, could not be. On the issue of bilateral versus multilateral aid, he noted that many foreigners prefer bilateral assistance from the U.S. Indonesia, for example, was uneasy about multilateral aid because they felt it let the Japanese get additional leverage through the use of U.S. money—they feel it is not truly multilateral. The President also noted that Indonesia was very high on his list—the State Department disagreed, but the President thought Indonesia was one country which could make it. The President stressed that Japan and Western Europe must increase their aid efforts, however.

The President continued that the U.S. should use its aid for humanitarian purposes in particular circumstances. Furthermore, we should not simply help those who meet our ideas of proper political organization. The key is to help those who follow economic approaches, particularly reliance on the private sector, which we consider feasible in leading to real development. He would not be worried about the politics of the leaders of particular countries but rather about the climate for investment and other major economic approaches.

The President further stressed that population control is a must. He urged Mr. Peterson to read his message to the Congress on population[3] and to work closely with the White House staff involved in this effort. Population control must go hand in hand with aid. The U.S. has finally bitten the bullet on this issue and made it a top priority national policy.

Trade is another key area, and he urged Mr. Peterson to speak with Ambassador Gilbert,[4] Secretary Stans and others involved in U.S. trade policy. We will probably want to try some new initiatives in this area. Linkage among trade, aid and population control may be the necessary new approach.

---

[3] For text of the President's July 18 message to Congress on problems of population growth, see *Public Papers of the Presidents of the United States: Richard Nixon, 1969*, pp. 521–530.

[4] Carl J. Gilbert, Special Representative for Trade Negotiations.

On military aid, the President warned that many of the panelists will probably oppose it completely. He agrees that we should not supply exotic weapons to countries which do not need them. However, State/AID is wrong to not want to help Indonesia militarily; they must have sufficient military assistance to maintain internal security. More broadly, the military may be the most stable force in most countries. He would therefore hope that Mr. Peterson would have no preconceptions that the military or rightist leaders are villains. Mr. Peterson agreed that there is a new breed of military men around the world, especially in Latin America.

The President summarized that we should follow an aid approach that will work. Otherwise we should forget it. A banker's approach, especially that of the Bank of America with its record of innovative financing, is good for this problem.

In response to Mr. Peterson's question about the thrust of overall U.S. foreign policy, the President said that Congress will not buy any aid program not directly related to U.S. foreign policy objectives, except perhaps for a few clear humanitarian cases. He felt that our long term foreign policy interests will be well served by broad, generous foreign assistance programs. Because of the growing gulf between our wealth and that of most countries, and the shrinking of the world through modern communications, people in the LDCs will not stand for continuation of the status quo. It will develop like our own urban problems.

For the next five years, however, our efforts will be limited by budgetary restrictions. We must thus bore in where it really counts with what we have. In the longer term, we must think of broader approaches.

The President stated his strong conviction that aid won't work unless and until recipient countries develop political stability. He agrees with Dr. Kissinger that aid does not necessarily lead to political stability. He would use our limited resources in areas where some stability already exists.

We need some success stories. In the Pakistan/India situation, for example, Pakistan comes out way ahead in terms of likely progress, partly because India is headed down the road toward becoming a socialist state. Latin America is an exceptionally difficult case and we will send Mr. Peterson a copy of the Rockefeller report when it is received.[5]

---

[5] At the request of President Nixon, New York Governor Nelson Rockefeller undertook a mission to survey the quality of life in the other nations of the Western Hemisphere. Rockefeller's report, including policy recommendations, was released by Nixon on November 10, and is printed in Department of State *Bulletin*, December 8, 1969, pp. 493–540.

Dr. Kissinger added that individual success stories in given regions could spread out through the region by galvanizing others into action. We need to move toward greater self-reliance on the part of other countries. This is the thrust of our overall foreign policy—to get others to shoulder a greater share of the burden.

Dr. Kissinger continued that we must get away from abstract notions. Our policy must relate to concrete objectives of mutual interest between the U.S. and other countries. Earlier U.S. aid efforts were relatively easy technical problems. We now have the problem of developing a world order in which the U.S. does not have to carry the entire burden. This means relating individual countries to others in their regions and then relating them to the U.S. We are in for some troubled years ahead, especially in Latin America.

The President reiterated that his foreign policy approach is based on pragmatism. The test of a particular policy is how well it will work. We must get away from ideological battles. In response to a question from Mr. Peterson, he affirmed that he was not terribly concerned with electoral systems in other countries. Dr. Kissinger added that we must look at their foreign policy as it affects us.

Concerning the plethora of small U.S. programs in Africa, the President said he was not impressed by the argument that the Communists will pour in aid if we don't. We need not react every time to such a threat. The question is whether U.S. interests in the particular countries are vital. We must not let other countries shake us down, even though some of our friends are among those who do so.

The President reiterated that we should not pour money down ratholes. We should test a specific program by asking whether it will work. The Task Force should look into all the international lending organizations and the trade area, where we must consider preferential arrangements. In general, the Task Force should take a broad view of its mandate.

Mr. Peterson asked who would be his main point of contact with the Administration. The President replied that Dr. Kissinger, or anyone he might designate, would be that point. The Task Force should of course get input from Dr. Hannah, who is very able and will be developing some new ideas as he gets new people.

The President also noted that we probably have too many Americans abroad, a point on which he probably differs with Dr. Hannah. Point IV was great in its time, but the U.S. generally has the wrong people overseas. We should not assume that the best possible world is one in which many Americans are helping out overseas. In fact, the Task Force must assume that our present aid program is not full of good administrators. Many of our people are dedicated but many are incompetent, partly because AID is short of money and is a resting place for persons nearing retirement.

American businessmen abroad are not so good either, because the best businessmen do not view foreign assignments as the road to success. However, the President suggested that Mr. Peterson seek the views of a thousand U.S. businessmen overseas on our aid program, perhaps through getting the top 25–30 companies to canvass their people and pass their ideas on to us.

The President concluded that Mr. Peterson faced an extremely difficult job. The effort had been tried before and failed. In addition, many people disagreed with the views that the President had been spelling out. What he did know, however, was that the effort of the past will not sell even if it is right. And Dr. Kissinger added that with the loss of purpose in aid the annual appropriation process had become an end in itself.

The President instructed Mr. Peterson to take both a short-term and a long-term look at the problem. What kind of a world do we want in the future? How much can and will others do?

He did not have an answer to these questions. He did know that it was ridiculous to simply compare the percentages of different countries' GNPs which are spent on aid, in view of the burden assumed by the U.S. in the military area. Dr. Kissinger added that it was also irrelevant to compare percentages when the magnitudes differed so sharply. The President also instructed Mr. Peterson to look at the personnel and organization of our aid effort.

Mr. Peterson concluded that his effort must be to decide upon a new approach and also recommend how to implement it. The President concurred and stressed that the whole program must be reorganized.

---

36.   Editorial Note

Henry Kissinger sent a memorandum to President Nixon on September 10, 1969, in which he expressed his reservations about prospects for "Vietnamization" of the conflict in Vietnam:

"Three elements on the Vietnam front must be considered—(1) our efforts to 'win the war' through military operations and pacification, (2) 'Vietnamization,' and (3) the political position of the GVN.

"(1) I do not believe that with our current plans we can win the war within two years, although our success or failure in hurting the enemy remains very important.

"(2) 'Vietnamization' must be considered both with regard to its prospects for allowing us to turn the war over to the Vietnamese, and with regard to its effect on Hanoi and U.S. public opinion. I am not optimistic about the ability of the South Vietnamese armed forces to assume a larger part of the burden than current MACV plans allow. These plans, however, call for a thirty-month period in which to turn the burden of the war over to the GVN. I do not believe we have this much time.

"In addition, 'Vietnamization' will run into increasingly serious problems as we proceed down its path.

"—Withdrawal of U.S. troops will become like salted peanuts to the American public: The more U.S. troops come home, the more will be demanded. This could eventually result, in effect, in demands for unilateral withdrawal—perhaps within a year.

"—The more troops are withdrawn, the more Hanoi will be encouraged—they are the last people we will be able to fool about the ability of the South Vietnamese to take over from us. They have the option of attacking GVN forces to embarrass us throughout the process or of waiting until we have largely withdrawn before doing so (probably after a period of higher infiltration).

"—Each U.S. soldier that is withdrawn will be relatively more important to the effort in the south, as he will represent a higher percentage of U.S. forces than did his predecessor. (We need not, of course, continue to withdraw combat troops but can emphasize support troops in the next increments withdrawn. Sooner or later, however, we must be getting at the guts of our operations there.)

"—It will become harder and harder to maintain the morale of those who remain, not to speak of their mothers.

"—'Vietnamization' may not lead to reduction in U.S. casualties until its final stages, as our casualty rate may be unrelated to the total number of American troops in South Vietnam. To kill about 150 U.S. soldiers a week, the enemy needs to attack only a small portion of our forces.

"—'Vietnamization' depends on broadening the GVN, and Thieu's new government is not 'significantly broader than the old (see below). The best way to broaden the GVN would be to create the impression that the Saigon government is winning or at least permanent. The more uncertainty there is about the outcome of the war, the less the prospect for 'Vietnamization.'

"(3) We face a dilemma with the GVN: The present GVN cannot go much farther towards a political settlement without seriously endangering its own existence; but at the same time, it has not gone far enough to make such a settlement likely.

"Thieu's failure to 'broaden' his government is disturbing, but not because he failed to include a greater variety of Saigon's Tea House politicians. It is disturbing because the politicians clearly do not believe that Thieu and his government represent much hope for future power, and because the new government does not offer much of a bridge to neutralist figures who could play a role in future settlement. This is not to mention his general failure to build up political strength in non-Catholic villages. In addition, as U.S. troops are withdrawn, Thieu becomes more dependent on the political support of the South Vietnamese military." (National Security Council, Special NSC Meeting Folder, 9/12/69 Vietnam)

The full text of the memorandum is scheduled for publication in *Foreign Relations*, 1969–1976, Vietnam, 1969–1970. It is also printed in Kissinger, *White House Years*, pages 1480–1482.

---

37.   **Editorial Note**

President Nixon addressed the United Nations General Assembly on September 18, 1969, and expressed the determination of the United States to remain fully engaged as a world power:

"I am well aware that many nations have questions about the world role of the United States in the years ahead—about the nature and extent of our future contribution to the structure of peace.

"Let me address those doubts and address them quite candidly before this organization.

"In recent years, there has been mounting criticism here in the United States of the scope and the results of our international commitments.

"This trend, however, has not been confined to the United States alone. In many countries we find a tendency to withdraw from responsibilities, to leave the world's often frustrating problems to the other fellow and just to hope for the best.

"As for the United States, I can state here today without qualification: We have not turned away from the world.

"We know that with power goes responsibility.

"We are neither boastful of our power, nor apologetic about it. We recognize that it exists, and that, as well as conferring certain advantages, it also imposes upon us certain obligations.

"As the world changes, the pattern of those obligations and responsibilities changes.

"At the end of World War II, the United States for the first time in history assumed the major responsibility for world peace.

"We were left in 1945 as the one nation with sufficient strength to contain the new threats of aggression, and with sufficient wealth to help the injured nations back to their feet.

"For much of the world, those first difficult postwar years were a time of dependency.

"The next step was toward independence, as new nations were born and old nations revived.

"Now we are maturing together into a new pattern of interdependence.

"It is against this background that we have been urging other nations to assume a greater share of responsibility for their own security, both individually and together with their neighbors. The great challenge now is to enlist the cooperation of many nations in preserving peace and in enriching life. This cannot be done by American edict, or by the edict of any other nation. It must reflect the concepts and the wishes of the people of those nations themselves.

"The history of the postwar period teaches that nationalism can be dangerously disruptive—or powerfully creative.

"Our aim is to encourage the creative forms of nationalism; to join as partners where our partnership is appropriate, and where it is wanted, but not to let a U.S. presence substitute for independent national effort or infringe on national dignity and national pride.

"It is not my belief that the way to peace is by giving up our friends or letting down our allies. On the contrary our aim is to place America's international commitments on a sustainable, long term basis, to encourage local and regional initiatives, to foster national independence and self-sufficiency, and by so doing to strengthen the total fabric of peace.

"It would be dishonest, particularly before this sophisticated audience, to pretend that the United States has no national interests of its own, or no special concern for its own interests.

"However, our most fundamental national interest is in maintaining that structure of international stability on which peace depends, and which makes orderly progress possible."

The full text of the speech is printed in *Public Papers of the Presidents of the United States: Richard Nixon, 1969*, pages 724–725.

---

38.   **Editorial Note**

On September 27, 1969, President Nixon met at Camp David, Maryland, with the political team he had selected to help prepare for the 1970 Congressional elections. When the discussion turned to Vietnam, the President melded his concern over what he saw as the dangers inherent in an effort to disengage from the war in Southeast Asia with his determination not to be the "first American President to lose a war."

"The President turned briefly to Vietnam. If for one month he said everybody would 'shut up' about the war, we would be a long way toward getting it over.

"The President noted again that he did not intend to be the 'first American President to lose a war' that he 'had three years and three months left in office' that we have 'turned it around' as far as world opinion is concerned on the Vietnam thing, that if we lost the war in Vietnam or pulled an elegant bug-out the United States would 'retreat from the world.' This *'first defeat in American history'* he said *would 'destroy the confidence of the American people in themselves.'*

"By 1970 elections, the President said, one way or the other, it is going to be over with; we are going to be able by then to 'see the light at the end of the tunnel.'" (Notes drafted on September 29 as a memorandum for the President's file by Patrick J. Buchanan; National Archives, Nixon Presidential Materials, White House Special Files, President's Office Files, Box 79, Memoranda for the President, Aug 3–Dec 28, 1969)

According to the President's Daily Diary, the meeting was held at 2:15 p.m. The group the President met with included Senators Hugh Scott, Robert Griffin, and John Tower; Congressmen Gerald Ford, Leslie Arends, Bob Wilson, and Rogers Morton; and H.R. Haldeman, Bryce Harlow, Donald Rumsfeld, Harry Dent, Lyn Nofziger, and Patrick Buchanan from the Office of the President. (Ibid., White House Central Files, Staff Members and Office Files, Office of Presidential Papers and Archives, Daily Diary)

39.   Memorandum From the President's Assistant for National Security Affairs (Kissinger) to President Nixon[1]

Washington, undated.

SUBJECT

　A Strategic Overview

　　Attached is a memorandum written by an acquaintance of mine which provides a rather comprehensive assessment of the United States' position in the world. Although I do not agree with its every last word, it does define the problem we face—the generally deteriorating strategic position of the United States during the past decade.

　　Many analysts have written about the problems faced by the Communists. But I do not believe that the world situation, *as viewed from Moscow,* provides great cause for Communist pessimism.

　　Andrei Zhdanov's "two-camp" speech in September 1947 referred only to Bulgaria, Poland and Romania as relatively secure Communist states and allies. He saw no real possibility in the Middle East and no hope in Latin America. He considered China to be imperialist. But Zhdanov's pessimistic outlook has not been justified by subsequent events—certainly during the last decade.

　　—In the Middle East, Russian influence is spreading and moderate Arab governments are under increasing pressure.

　　—In Latin America, the potential for guerrilla warfare grows, and the outlook for future Nasser-type (if not Communist), anti-American governments improves.

　　—In Europe, NATO is in a state of malaise, accentuated by our shifting policies over the last 10 years. Europeans are increasingly concerned about isolationist currents within the U.S. (particularly within the liberal community).

　　—In Asia, as you saw on your trip, leaders are concerned about the future U.S. role there.

　　You inherited this legacy of the past decade. The lesson one can draw from it is not that we can fight this trend on every issue. But foreign policy depends on an accumulation of nuances, and no opponent

---

[1]　Source: National Archives, Nixon Presidential Materials, NSC Files, Box 397, Subject Files, A Strategic Overview. Confidential. An attached memorandum to Kissinger from Kenneth Cole, Executive Director of the Domestic Council, is dated October 14. Cole stated that the President was returning Kissinger's memorandum and its attachment and wanted them sent to Secretaries Rogers and Laird and Attorney General Mitchell for their comments. (Ibid.)

of ours can have much reason to believe that we will stick to our position on the issues which divide us. When Hanoi compares our negotiating position on Vietnam now with that of 18 months ago, it must conclude that it can achieve its goals simply by waiting. Moscow must reach the same conclusion.

These are dangerous conclusions for an enemy to draw, and I believe that we therefore face the prospect of major confrontations.

Hence, my concern about the gravity of the situation, of which I thought I should let you know.

Attachment

Washington, September 29, 1969.

THE MODERN WORLD, A SINGLE "STRATEGIC THEATER"

Section A

1. It is one of the truisms of our time that because of the sensational development of communications and transportation, the globe has shrunk with distances between formerly far-away countries having been reduced to mere hours of flight time. We all pay continuous lip service to the axiom that the hallmark, today, of relations among States, even among continents, is *inter*dependence rather than independence. But while every political writer and speaker belabors this point ad nauseum, we actually deal with the Mideast, Latin America, the Atlantic Region, Eastern Europe, NE Asia, and SE Asia as if we were still living in the WW-II era when it was realistic and feasible to speak of a European, an India–Burma–China, a Pacific "Strategic Theater" as essentially separate and autonomous.

2. In theory, people may understand the phenomenon of interdependence rather well and be quite aware of the fact that the whole globe, by now, has become a single strategic theater. In practice, however, near-unavoidable bureaucratic compartmentalization has led to specialization among experts and decision-makers: Those who are knowledgeable regarding the strategically more and more important Trucial Oman, know little or nothing about Canada, and those who are experts on Berlin have no eyes for, or interest in, the issue of Okinawa. The man who daily struggles with the agonizing problem of Vietnam can hardly be expected to pay special attention to the latest coup in Libya, and the person concerned with US aid to Latin America has little time or inclination to consider recent political developments in Czechoslovakia.

3. Since, by chance, it has become my specialty to be a generalist, let me draw for you a sketch of how seemingly isolated developments in specific areas are deeply interconnected in fact, how the single stones of the mosaic actually form a clearly recognizable overall tableau.

Section B

I

1. It might be helpful to start out with a remarkable, largely unnoticed, passage in Senator Mansfield's Report to the President, on his recent Pacific tour. Having stated that the leaders of the Asian countries visited by him "agree" that the role of the US in Asian affairs should shrink, the Senator remarked that there was also "some uneasiness" among those leaders "that the pendulum will swing too far from [US][2] over-involvement to non-involvement." Mansfield is not a "pessimist," because—as you may remember—he had on the very eve of the invasion of Czechoslovakia reported to President Johnson that, on the basis of his analysis of the situation in East Europe, he considered a reduction of US forces in Germany not only appropriate but even desirable. Actually, the Senator's wording—"some uneasiness" in non-Communist Asia about the US moving toward a stance of non-involvement—constitutes a "diplomatic" understatement which barely hints at, but does not really reflect at all, the overwhelming fear of such countries as S. Vietnam, Cambodia, Laos, Thailand, Malaysia, Singapore—and even Indonesia, the Philippines and Australia—to have to face potential future aggressors essentially with their *own* military forces.

2. Your country specialists will tell you, if you ask them, that the Indonesian leaders—despite the size and relative geographic protectedness of their island nation—have informed us of a need for the US to "stay" for at least 3 more years in Vietnam, so that they might peacefully consolidate their country without fear of Communist direct or indirect aggression.

3. It also deserves to be noted that Gen Romulo—unwaveringly pro-US and anti-Communist—nevertheless remarked in a public speech, some time ago, when he took over the position of Foreign Minister at Manila, that in view of the impossibility to rely henceforth on US protection it would be necessary to "adjust" Philippine Foreign Policy. He remarked, in this connection, that, as of that day, Philippine Foreign Office references to China would no longer be to the "Chinese Mainland" but to the People's Republic of China, the country's official designation adopted by the Mao regime. In an interview given by Romulo at the UN in N.Y. he expressed a wish (see *NY Times* of

---

[2] All brackets in the source text.

September 22, 1969) "that the UN, in its peace-keeping efforts would consider [General] MacArthur's suggestion that borders threatened by guerrilla infiltration or possible enemy invasion be sealed off with a belt of radioactive materials." The suggestion of so strong, and innately unpopular, a measure by a SE Asian Foreign Minister does reveal more than mere "uneasiness" in the face of coming dangers.

4. The Prime Minister of Singapore, Mr. Lee, who proudly calls himself an Asian Socialist, shocked the anti-Vietnam War Swedish Social Democrats last year, when he declared in an address to that party's annual Congress, that the US was fighting in Vietnam for the independence of Singapore and that this independence was predicated on US willingness to continue the fight.

5. You also remember that Sihanouk of Cambodia—certainly not a friend and even less a tool of the US—has explained again and again over many years that he had no choice but to accommodate to China the powerful, because one day, regardless of US protestations to the contrary, Washington would move its forces out of SE Asia and he, as a convinced Cambodian nationalist, deemed it his task to establish such relations with the Communist victors of tomorrow that, at least, the Communist takeover would be "peaceful."[3] In a very dramatic, typically Sihanoukian letter to the editors of the NYT the Cambodian Chief of State asked his US readers not to consider him naive regarding Communist intentions. I know very well, he wrote, that, although they [Communists] are friendly to me now, "they will say 'Sihanouk down on your knees,' once they are victorious and oust me without ceremony." I do not have to point out to you that, by now, the Cambodians are actually trying to cooperate, tacitly and secretly, with the hated S. Vietnamese in a not very successful attempt to prevent expansion of de facto Communist control over still further areas of their small country.

6. You are also, I believe, fully aware of what Souvanna Phouma of Laos, the leaders of Thailand and those of Malaysia—to say nothing of Chiang Kai-shek in Taiwan—tell us in confidence as regards their true feelings; i.e., naked fear, concerning a US military withdrawal from SE Asia.

II

1. The preceding paragraphs have been devoted to SE Asia not only because—by chance, or due to some inherent geopolitical necessity—that region of the world happens to be at the moment our most obviously active area of preoccupation, but also because, for that very reason, it must be these days the center of your own attention and deepest

---

[3] Nixon underscored this sentence, beginning at "he had no choice."

worries. The world, too, focuses its attention on Vietnam, as an indicator of the direction in which US policy and strategy in general are likely to move. You know more, of course, about US future plans and intentions than anyone else, except the President of the US and his Secretary of State, but I venture the assertion that *any* objective analyst—be he in Peking or Bonn, Moscow or Paris, Ottawa or Cairo—simply cannot help reaching the conclusion that, so far, *all* the indicators point in one direction only: an ultimate pull-out, a radical reduction of military commitments, a withdrawal of US military power not simply in hotly contested Vietnam but on a worldwide scale.

2. It can hardly be questioned by now that we are on the verge of restoring the Ryukyus, our great stronghold in the NE Asia region, to Japan. And even such bases as we may retain on those islands will be, more likely than not, under the same restrictive regime now applying to our troops and military installations in the Japanese homeland (in accordance with the US/Japan Status of Forces Agreement). That South Korea—already shaken and frightened by the meek US reaction to the capture of the "Pueblo" and to the shooting down of our EC-121—is deeply worried by this development is well known and more than natural, especially since Seoul is afraid, not entirely without justification, that in the "post-Vietnam" period we might thin out, or even reduce greatly, the US forces now stationed in that country. Less well known is the fact that the Japanese themselves—although Tokyo, for obvious reasons, cannot publicly admit it—feel less well protected with the US military strength on Okinawa diminished or newly restricted. It is generally, and somewhat superficially, assumed that this heightened sense of insecurity may have the salutary effect of spurring Japan into making a greater defense effort of its own. But one must ask, whether it would really be in the US interest, if the Japanese followed this line of thought to its logical conclusion; i.e., to the establishment of a purely Japanese nuclear weapons arsenal. Moreover, the leftist opposition, and pacifism in general, are sufficiently powerful within Japan to create such internal upheaval, if the government were actually to embark on any large-scale rearmament, that there would be a lengthy period of instability and weakness in the country, before it could actually become militarily more self-reliant. In the meantime Japan could hardly fail to seek an accommodation with Red China or the USSR or, "ideally," both. In any event: The simultaneous US trend to reduce its power position in North *as well as* in South East Asia, is bound to have a profound effect on the political and strategic thinking and planning of *any* Asian country which in the ultimate analysis—willingly or reluctantly—has to rely on the US as a protective shield against the potential super power: China. New Delhi, for example, cannot very well assume that the US is prepared to come to its rescue, when it observes Washington's eagerness to move

out and away in regard to Pacific areas (such as Indochina and Okinawa/Japan) in which the US has long had an infinitely more pronounced and direct interest than in India. The Indian leaders, in addition, would have to be influenced by the stark military fact that, in the event of a Communist takeover in SE Asia, their country would be outflanked in the East, with a pro-Chinese Pakistan constituting at the same time a (real or imagined) threat in the West.

III

1. As regards the Mid East, it is customary to think, to the exclusion of almost any other consideration, of the Arab/Israeli conflict. No doubt, the present Administration is engaged in a superhuman effort to make the two sides see reason and prevent a "fourth round," but in view of earlier US performances, it must be decidedly difficult for Arabs or Israelis to rely on anything but their own brute strength. A US role as an effective guarantor of any future compromise solution is simply not credible, because of our obvious past and present reluctance (with the one exception of Lebanon in 1958) to back up diplomatic agreements or political friendships with a US military presence.

2. Cynics used to believe that, because of the Jewish vote in the US, Washington would necessarily have to intervene in Israel's favor in any "real emergency." Actually, the historical record proves otherwise. In 1956, we turned against our French and British allies *and* our Israeli protégés and impelled the latter to evacuate the Sinai peninsula; while in 1967, when Nasser threatened war with remarkable frankness, we tried in every way to dissuade Tel Aviv from reacting to the Egyptian blockade of the Straits of Tiran by non-peaceful means. Israel then started military action on her own, strictly against our wish and will, and won so quickly and overwhelmingly that our readiness to come to its rescue no longer had to be tested. I do not, as you know, consider it an a priori US task and mission to protect Israel, but it so happens that in the eyes of the world that small Western enclave in a non-Western environment is considered our "client," and conclusions must be drawn, of needs, everywhere (not only in Moscow and Tel Aviv but in other capitals as well) from the fact that the US is obviously disinclined to support even its own client, *if* that would mean military involvement.

3. Those Arab regimes, on the other hand, which have struggled to stay relatively pro-West can be even *less* trustful as regards our active help than the Israelis, since there is no Arab constituency in this country.

4. We have in the past been unable to protect the pro-US royal regime in Iraq. We did not help Saudi Arabia against the Nasser-supported Republican Yemen. We tolerated the establishment of a radical-

ly leftist, pro-Peking rather than pro-Moscow, Republic of South Yemen, when the British withdrew from Aden and the Aden Protectorates. We showed no interest, when the moderate government in the Sudan was overthrown by revolutionary radicals; and we obviously will do nothing, if after complete withdrawal of the British from the Persian Gulf area, the present rulers of the various Sheikdoms there should be thrown out by wild-eyed Arab nationalists with Marxist leanings. From the point of view of the moderate Arab leaders it must appear that friendship with the US does not offer protection and does not pay.[4] Only a few weeks ago, King Idris of Libya was ousted by a group of officers leaning toward the Iraqi type of Baathism, one of the most fanatic and anti-Western forms of Arab radicalism. We seemed grateful that, for the time being, the new rulers declared their willingness to tolerate our base at Wheelus and promised not to nationalize the US and other Western oil companies. For King Idris, however, we were either unwilling or unable to do anything. One of the results of the Libyan coup—apart from the fact that roughly one billion $ in annual oil revenues has now passed into the hands of avowed Revolutionaries—is the ominous deterioration of Tunisia's position. Long one of the "most reasonable" and most enlightened among Arab countries, Tunisia, still led by the distinctly pro-Western Bourguiba, suddenly finds herself surrounded by *two* hostile neighbors: Libya and Algeria. Bourguiba can hardly help feeling that with his moderation he has betted on the wrong horse. Small moderate Lebanon, too—which in 1958 was still able to call on US military help—is currently being forced to abandon its traditional policy of neutrality and to tolerate, despite surprisingly courageous counter-efforts by its President Helou, the takeover of its southernmost border areas by Arab Commando groups composed almost exclusively of non-Lebanese. Considering the lack of any physical outside support for Helou, it seems only a question of time, when he, too, will be replaced by regimes of the kind now governing neighboring Syria and Iraq.

5. Under the circumstances, even those Arabs who used to maintain a degree of friendship with the US cannot possibly place great trust in Washington's declarations of amity. It may be a paradox, but must nevertheless be understood, that, precisely because we have shown ourselves so peaceful and patient, so obviously unwilling to intervene with force anywhere or against anyone, it will now be virtually impossible for *either* Arab *or* Jew to see in the United States the great power that would actually protect one side against the other and maintain any

---

[4] Nixon highlighted the first five sentences of paragraph 4 and added the following note in the margin: "K—a deadly accurate *analysis.*"

agreed upon peaceful order by forceful means, should that prove necessary. If a country is so clearly shying away from physical involvement, it is difficult to believe that it will ever permit itself to become so involved.

6. It has widely been assumed that the USSR would restrain the Arabs, as we might restrain the Israelis, out of a fear of a direct US/USSR confrontation. It should be observed, however, that the Soviet interest to exercise such restraining influence is bound to decrease to more or less the same degree to which Moscow's fear of a direct confrontation of the two super powers diminishes. The more the Soviets—looking at US actions and inactions around the world—become convinced that the US remains unbendingly resolved to negotiate rather than to confront, the smaller their incentive to restrain *their* clients; i.e., in the Mid East case, the Arabs.

IV

1. In Latin America, too, the US has demonstrated such extreme unwillingness recently to use "power" that we actually seem to have placed a premium on hotheaded and undesirable ventures by extremists. We have let Ecuador, Peru, and others, arrogate to themselves exclusive fishing rights in a zone of 200 miles from their coastlines, and we have permitted US fishing boats found in those zones to be shelled or brought to port by foreign naval vessels, whence they have been released only against payment of arbitrary "fines." We leaned over backwards not to apply the Hickenlooper Amendment[5] as a sanction against Peru for uncompensated expropriation, by a revolutionary Officers Junta, of hundreds of millions worth of US property. The example was quickly followed by Bolivia where a few days ago, another revolutionary group likewise led by a general, enacted certain measures, on the very first day of its existence, foreshadowing expropriation of US oil companies in that country.[6]

2. The Latin temperament is rather volatile by nature and the colossus to the North is not necessarily popular among Latinos. It is dangerous, therefore, and does not promote peaceful developments, if the impression is created that irresponsible—or even normally quite

---

[5] The Hickenlooper Amendment to the Foreign Assistance Act of 1961, proposed by Senator Bourke Hickenlooper (R.–Iowa), was adopted by the Congress on August 1, 1962, as one of the amendments that constituted the Foreign Assistance Act of 1962. The Hickenlooper Amendment provided for the suspension of foreign aid to any country that expropriated U.S. property without prompt and adequate compensation. (P.L. 87–565, 76 Stat. 260–261)

[6] Nixon highlighted the final sentence of this paragraph and added the following comment in the margin: "K—note—what does State advise on this?"

responsible—elements, can act wildly and illegally without having to fear any serious reaction on our part. We certainly could not hold the Brazilian government responsible for the recent unprecedented kidnapping of the US Ambassador in full daylight. But it is doubtful whether our concern for a single diplomat's life, our clearly manifested "hope" that all the kidnappers' demands be fulfilled speedily to save one man, was as humane as it seemed: Since it has become all too clear now that the host country of a US representative can be blackmailed with such surprising ease, it must be feared that there will be further kidnappings of US diplomats in the foreseeable future.[7]

3. It is no longer seriously doubted today that the Balaguer regime in the Dominican Republic with all its deficiencies, is, nevertheless, the best administration that country has ever had since 1865 (when Santo Domingo gained its final independence from Spain). The regime was established after order had been restored in the Republic by US military intervention, which at the time was bitterly criticized by many, even well-meaning people as an act of US "imperialism." No US President, of course, would like to repeat a similar venture. Yet, it is not desirable, in the very interest of peace, to let everybody assume, as appears to be the case today, that the US will no longer intervene anywhere in Latin America at any time.[8]

V

1. When Czechoslovakia was invaded in August 1968, the experts, and large segments of public opinion, found *one* consolation in the mournful event: It would re-awaken the Western World to the danger from the East and revive the somewhat lethargic NATO. The prediction (which, as you may recall, I contradicted at the time) was wrong. The lasting impression that finally resulted was that of NATO's and the US' virtually total non-reaction, except in words, and the capability of brute force (applied in this case by the Soviets) to impose its will.

2. The Germans, as you know only too well from frequent and direct observation, have—after two World Wars lost, with five totally different regimes following each other within 50 years, and with their country still divided—by no means regained their self-confidence. I

---

[7] Nixon underscored the second sentence of this paragraph, highlighted the final sentence, and wrote the following marginal comment: "K—*I agree*—We dropped *this one.*"

[8] Nixon underscored and highlighted the final sentence of this paragraph and added the following marginal comment: "K—I agree—Be sure our Latin speech makes this clear." The reference is apparently to the speech Nixon delivered to the annual meeting of the Inter-American Press Association on October 31. For text, see *Public Papers of the Presidents of the United States: Richard Nixon, 1969*, pp. 893–901.

transmitted to you the other day a report containing the remarks of a German leader[9] who, upon his return from an official visit to Moscow, while admitting that the Soviets had remained totally rigid and offered absolutely nothing, concluded nevertheless that W. Germany had no choice but to come to terms with Moscow "because," he said, "I have twice recently been in Washington and found there such a trend toward isolationism that I am certain the Americans will sooner or later pull their forces out of Germany." The individual in question may have been objectively wrong, but the fear he expressed is actually shared by virtually *all* Germans who do have opinions on foreign and world affairs.

3. After having visited Washington and signed the Offset Agreement,[10] Chancellor Kiesinger thought he had obtained a US undertaking that current US force strength in Germany would be fully maintained during, at least, the two years covered by said Agreement. You are far better aware of the fact than I am that his impressions were overoptimistic.

4. It is sometimes asserted that the very threat of US troop reductions would bring about a greater defense effort by the united Europeans themselves. In actual fact, however, Europe—though united it *would* be a Great Power—is *not* yet united, and Italians, Germans, Frenchmen, Beneluxers, and Scandinavians think of themselves as small, in terms of military strength, and in need of protection by the only super power that happens to exist in the non-Communist world: the US. When big brother even appears to falter, the little brethren will not move forward courageously—as we seem to think—but, on the contrary, they will anxiously take several steps backwards.

5. By coincidence, I happened to be in Italy at the end of August, when the fact leaked out that our very small garrison there (in the Verona/Vicenza area with a logistic base at Leghorn) would be cut in half for "economy reasons." The Italians guessed, more or less correctly, that no more than a total of about 1,500 men would be involved. Not a single Italian, whom I heard discuss the matter— regardless of whether he stood politically on the right, left or center— accepted that explanation. Everybody assumed, as a matter of course, that this was simply the first installment of a total US military pullout from Italy.

---

[9] Nixon's marginal comment at this point reads: "K—who is this?"

[10] An agreement between the United States and the Federal Republic of Germany to offset the costs of the U.S. forces stationed in Germany was signed in Washington on July 9. For text of the joint statement announcing the agreement, see Department of State *Bulletin,* August 4, 1969, p. 92. When Chancellor Kurt Kiesinger visited Washington in August, he confirmed the agreement.

6. The Canadians, incidentally, encounter the same disbelief throughout Europe, when they adduce economic motives for withdrawing roughly one-half of *their* small European garrison. Unaware of Trudeau's marked sense of independence, many Europeans actually believe that Canada could not very well take such a measure without the, at least tacit, approval of Washington. This, then, leads to the further conclusion that the entire North American continent is beginning to turn inward and intent on ultimately withdrawing *all* its forces still stationed on foreign soil.

VI

1. You will not expect in this sketch any analysis of the complex issue of US/USSR relations. But one comment deserves to be made in the general context I have chosen: The Soviets are developing some genuine fear of Red China and its intractable leaders. They might, therefore, feel impelled by self-interest to seek a *genuine* Kremlin/Washington détente, and even make certain concessions to the US as a conceivable future ally, semi-ally or at least friendly "neutral" in a Soviet-Chinese confrontation. The entire Soviet assessment, however, of the weight and value of the United States as a friend or foe, will depend very largely on their considering us either strong-willed or else weak in purpose and resolve. The realists in the Kremlin may now be "taking our measure," and a US yielding, and reluctant to act on all fronts, will appear less interesting and important to them as a factor in the international power struggle than a super power obviously able *and* willing to use its strength.[11]

VII

1. This then is the overall image of the US as a reluctant giant: seeking peace and reconciliation almost feverishly, withdrawing forces not in one but in many parts of the world, tired of using its physical power and firmly resolved to cut existing commitments and keep out, for a very long time to come, of any confrontation that might lead to any military involvement.[12]

2. This picture appears to be confirmed by a flow of US governmental statements on military budget cuts, temporary suspension of the draft, overall reduction of forces, deactivation of units, and mothballing of naval vessels. Although in reality these various measures, so far, are not earth-shaking in themselves, they do produce the impres-

---

[11] Nixon highlighted the final sentence of this paragraph and added the following marginal note: "good analysis."

[12] Nixon underscored this paragraph and wrote in the margin: "Sad but true!"

sion of an irreversible trend, of deliberate first steps on the road toward a liquidation of very many long-held power positions, of a systematic retreat into an inner shell. Even though we do not want it, we do appear to friendly as well as hostile observers as intent upon descending from a stage to make room for new actors whom nobody can fully see as yet, but who cannot fail to appear to take the spaces we are leaving empty.

VIII

1. Anyone with a sense of history will grasp the tragic elements in this situation. The President by training and instinct knows, of course, exactly what is at stake. So do you, a historian and a man with a pronounced sense of power realities. The policy on which we seem embarked is very obviously dictated by a conviction that "public opinion" demands it and that, accordingly, the government is essentially helpless to act otherwise. This pessimism about the public might be unwarranted. Results of a Gallup poll, published in today's *NYT* (see Annex)[13] indicate that 3 out of 5 persons polled consider US intervention in Vietnam justified. The votes lie not with those professors, students, and other particularly visible and audible protesters, nor with the writers and readers of our few great (or perhaps only big) newspapers.

2. The votes lie with the masses, and I have the truly frightening suspicion that these very masses—which today do not even care very much about foreign affairs and foreign problems—will be the first ones to yell for retribution and stampede forward over our bodies, howling that we have betrayed them, when a year or two from now it becomes clear that our well meant policy, allegedly attuned to public opinion, will have led to defeat, and to crises infinitely more terrible than that Vietnam war we have to face now. Lincoln used artillery in the streets of New York against rebellious "copperheads;" about 1100 people were killed in two days as a result. He was considered, however, not only a great man but a great humanitarian, when it turned out, subsequently, that he had been "right." "The people" are not very just, they forgive the victor, but always make scapegoats of their own leaders who are not victorious.[14] The Dolchstosslegende (the propaganda tale of the "stab in the back" of the fighting troops) unfortunately can be invented in any country and at any time.

---

[13] Not printed.

[14] Nixon underscored this sentence.

40. Editorial Note

On October 20, 1969, President Nixon and Henry Kissinger met in the Oval Office of the White House with Soviet Ambassador Anatoly Dobrynin to discuss relations between the United States and the Soviet Union. Nixon used the occasion to put into practice his concept of linkage:

"President Nixon said he did not believe much in personal diplomacy, and he recognized that the Ambassador was a strong defender of the interests of his own country. The President pointed out that if the Soviet Union found it possible to do something in Vietnam, and the Vietnam war ended, the U.S. might do something dramatic to improve Soviet-U.S. relations, indeed something more dramatic than they could now imagine. But until then, real progress would be difficult.

"Ambassador Dobrynin asked whether this meant that there could be no progress. The President replied that progress was possible, but it would have to be confined essentially to what was attainable in diplomatic channels. He said that he was very happy to have Ambassador Dobrynin use the channel through Dr. Kissinger, and he would be prepared to talk to the Ambassador personally. He reiterated that the war could drag on, in which case the U.S. would find its own way to bring it to an end. There was no sense repeating the proposals of the last six months. However, he said, in the meantime, while the situation continued, we could all keep our tone down and talk correctly to each other. It would help, and would lay the basis for further progress, perhaps later on when conditions were more propitious.

"The President said that the whole world wanted us to get together. He too wanted nothing so much as to have his Administration remembered as a watershed in U.S.-Soviet relations, but we would not hold still for being 'diddled' to death in Vietnam." (National Archives, Nixon Presidential Materials, NSC Files, Box 489, President's Trip Files, Dobrynin/HAK, 1969, [Part 1])

41.   Memorandum From the President's Assistant for National Security Affairs (Kissinger) to President Nixon[1]

Washington, October 20, 1969.

SUBJECT

Analysis of changes in international politics since World War II and their implications for our basic assumptions about U.S. foreign policy

In your meeting with the NSC Staff on October 2 you expressed the view that many basic aspects of international politics have changed during the past two decades, and you suggested that we ought to have an analysis of the implications of these changes for the underlying premises of U.S. foreign policy.

One of the first studies the Staff undertook was a comprehensive review of major trends in international politics. Part of that rather long review was a summary of these trends in the context of the postwar evolution of American foreign policy and the current mood of reassessment. I have attached this document (Tab A).

The document is one individual's interpretation of a momentous period in U.S. foreign policy, not a consensus of the Staff. But its overview of current trends is based on all the relevant official studies, documents, and analyses and on systematic discussions within the intelligence community. It indicates the emergence of an increasingly complex and pluralistic international environment and suggests some of the implications of this phenomenon for the basic pattern of U.S. policy, but it does not purport to recommend American responses.

Tab A

INTRODUCTION

In a meeting with the NSC Staff on October 2 the President suggested that, in view of basic changes in international politics over the last twenty years, it would be useful to have a reassessment of the governing assumptions underlying American foreign policy. The pages that follow may serve this purpose.

---

[1] Source: National Archives, Nixon Presidential Materials, NSC Files, Box 252, Agency Files, NSC 1969–71. Secret. Sent for information. The memorandum was stamped and initialed by Alexander Butterfield to indicate that it was seen by the President. The attached study was drafted by Robert E. Osgood of the NSC Staff.

There are three parts to this analysis. The first two parts assess the current questioning of American foreign policy in the light of basic changes—and some continuities—in the international environment and in America's position in the world. The third section spells out the most important trends in international politics over the next one to five years. In this context it suggests on pages 17–19 ways in which the dominant rationale of U.S. foreign policy during much of the cold war must be modified.

This analysis is a personal interpretation, but it is based on a thorough examination of the voluminous answers to NSSM-9[2] and all the relevant documents in the intelligence community.

I. THE REAPPRAISAL OF CONTAINMENT

Americans are questioning major features of the policy that has dominated the U.S. position in the world since the beginning of the cold war. Their questioning arises not only from disaffection with the war in Vietnam but also from a sense that familiar perceptions of the world do not fit a changing reality.

American foreign policy throughout most of the years since World War II could be summed up, with only a little exaggeration, as containment—that is, the prevention of communist expansion. Although the implementation of containment changed greatly during this period, the objective dominated American policy.

The threat of communist expansion has not disappeared, nor has the U.S. ceased being concerned about it. But the patterns of conflict and alignment, of power and political activity, among nations have changed in so many ways—and the communist world has changed so greatly—that containment no longer adequately describes the organizing concept of American foreign policy.

This change has not occurred suddenly. It is the result of a process that is in some respects at least a decade old. But its impact on American policy is sharpened now by a national mood of reappraisal—reappraisal of America's foreign interests and of how it should use its power to support them; reappraisal of familiar assumptions about international realities, of the proper extent of American involvement in the world, and of the relative weight that ought to be given to internal rather than external concerns.

---

[2] In NSSM 9, January 23, 1969, Henry Kissinger, on President Nixon's behalf, tasked the Departments of State, Defense, and the Treasury, as well as the CIA to undertake a sweeping review "to provide a current assessment of the political, economic and security situation and the major problems relevant to U.S. security interests and U.S. bilateral and multilateral relations." Kissinger structured what he referred to as an "inventory" of the international situation by appending 52 pages of questions. (Ibid., Box 365, Subject Files, National Security Study Memoranda (NSSMs), nos 1–42)

This mood of reappraisal has been precipitated by the costs and frustrations of the war in Vietnam, but it goes deeper than the reaction to the war and will outlast the war. In Congress, for example, it extends to a loss of confidence in the wisdom of the Executive Branch to define the requirements of American military security. On the campuses it is manifested in efforts to exclude military training and research. But underlying a broad spectrum of dissatisfaction with American foreign policy is an ill-defined feeling that the United States has become involved in world affairs to an extent that exceeds the imperatives of its vital interests, the efficacy of its power, and its equitable share of the burdens of international order. In short, there is a widespread feeling that the nation is "over-committed" and that the familiar rationale of American involvement—containment, falling dominoes, the Munich analogy—no longer fits the facts as it seemed to fit them in a simpler period of East-West confrontation.

At the moment this feeling reflects a mood of doubt and frustration, not a set of hardened convictions. It is "limitationist" rather than "isolationist". It does not spring from the traditional isolationist disposition to remain aloof from the world or the isolationist premise that the U.S. ought to confine the exercise of its material and economic—and especially its military—power to the protection of the United States alone. The commitments the limitationists are prepared to accept would have struck the so-called neo-isolationists of the late 1940's as the product of extravagant interventionism. On the other hand, now that the U.S. has become a global power, the impact of limitationism upon the position of the U.S. in the world could be no less significant than the impact of isolationism before World War II.

II. THE CHANGING CONTEXT OF U.S. POLICY

A brief survey of the recent history of American foreign policy indicates the extent to which both the realities and the American perception of the realities have changed. These changes are the background in terms of which the significance of current international trends for American policy should be assessed.

The Europe-Centered Bipolar Order

From the United States standpoint the cold war was at the outset dominated by a military confrontation and a political and ideological contest with the Soviet Union in Europe, although this contest had antecedents in Iran and Greece. This confrontation became the basis for the organization of most of Europe into two military alliances, each under the preponderance of a superpower. It froze the division of Germany and Europe and thereby intensified the contest between the two superpowers and their allies. At the same time, however, the management of the military balance of Europe by two extra-European superpowers also dampened intra-European power politics in both Eastern and Western Europe—politics which had repeatedly been the source of international turmoil and war—and thereby created a new kind of international order.

The bipolar order was stabilized by the consolidation of American deterrence in Europe and by the growth of nuclear inhibitions on both sides. Moreover, in the atmosphere of superpower détente following the Berlin and Cuban missile crises the danger of East-West armed conflict in Europe came to seem negligible, notwithstanding the fact that the Soviet invasion of Czechoslovakia rekindled concern about the unpredictability of Soviet military action and about the prospect of East European conflict spilling over into West Germany.

The Spread of the Cold War to the Third World

Beginning with the Korean War, the bipolar contest, having become relatively stable in Europe, spread to Asia and then, in various muted and indirect ways, to the Middle East, Africa, and the Caribbean. In spreading to the so-called Third World, this contest also became more diffuse and complicated. For the restless, mostly unstable and poor new states of the crumbling colonial world were moved by a variety of concerns having little or nothing to do with the cold war between the superpowers. Their dominant concerns, next to the achievement of full independence, were national unity, national status, modernization, and the pursuit of local state rivalries.

Nonetheless, in the mid-1950's it seemed as though the Third World might become the decisive arena of the cold war. Following the Korean War the U.S. sought to extend containment to Asia and the Middle East by means of a network of alliances and declarations intended to bolster deterrence, by economic aid and military assistance agreements intended to foster friendly stable states, and in the 1960's by more pointed appeals to nationalism and neutralism intended to identify the U.S. with the rising aspirations of the "developing" world.

Similarly, Soviet and Communist Chinese leaders switched from reviling nonaligned states to embracing them as collaborators against the remnants of imperialism. The Soviet Union launched its own selective program of economic and military assistance to gain influence and, possibly, control in areas of Western vulnerability. When the strategy of peaceful coexistence and appeals to bourgeois nationalism failed to pay satisfactory dividends, the international communist parties endorsed, in 1960, a more militant strategy of supporting "wars of national liberation".

Contrary to the popular view in Western countries, however, Soviet leaders were staunchly opposed to Peking's active pursuit of this course at the risk of involving the Soviet Union in war. They were not averse to supporting subversion where the USSR could control the subverters at a minimum cost and risk, and they could not refuse assistance to the self-proclaimed socialist state of Castro's Cuba; but they preferred to project their influence by establishing close relations with nationalist, anti-Western regimes.

The new regimes in the Third World capitalized upon the extension of the great-power contest to their domain in order to gain personal and national status and acquire material assistance. Colorful national leaders—Nehru, Sukarno, Nasser, Nkrumah—dramatized their role in world politics, exalting nonalignment as a principle of international order and touting the struggle for the moral and intellectual allegiance of the modernizing nations as the essence of international politics.

The Intractability of the Third World

The emergence of politically independent and active states in the colonial areas has exerted a tremendous impact on international politics, but the Third World has not proved to be a decisive arena of great-power conflict. Nor does it fit any of the simplifying conceptions about the climactic role of the less developed countries, such as the polarization of world politics on a North-South or rich-poor axis or on the basis of a grand ideological competition for the organization of developing societies. The area is simply too heterogeneous, disorganized, and resistant to external control and influence to fit into any such single pattern of international politics. Accentuated subnational—communal, ethnic, and tribal—and inter-state conflicts have proved to be stronger determinants of policy than any common denominator among the new states, such as the desire for economic development or even the removal of remaining colonies.

After an initial romantic period of statehood under dramatic leaders like Nkrumah, most of the LDC's have approached the developed states on more pragmatic lines as the new leadership has faced the hard problems of internal unity, national security, and economic solvency. The mystique of nonalignment has been dissipated by growing divisions among Afro-Asian states, the discovery by India and others of a national security problem that may require limited alignment with one or both superpowers, and the death or political decline of the charismatic national leaders.

Finally—as events in Greece, Burma, Malaysia, the Philippines, Guatemala, the Congo, Laos, and Indonesia show—the capacity of local communist parties to subvert or gain control of unstable states by "wars of national liberation" or any other means has proved to be quite limited. This is true even when such parties are supported by an adjacent communist power, especially if the target states receive external assistance. South Vietnam now seems to be an exception, due to a combination of unique circumstances: the sophisticated use of modern military power by North Vietnam, the organizational genius of Ho Chi Minh in developing an extensive Viet Cong infrastructure, and his ability to exploit nationalist sentiment in the war against the French. Cuba is an equally unique case of the leader of a non-communist revolution seeking Soviet assistance by appealing for membership in the communist camp.

The Loosening of Alliances

While the superpowers were growing aware of the complexity, intractability, and hazards of over-involvement in the Third World they were also becoming increasingly concerned with the cohesion of their alliances.

In NATO the growing capacity of the USSR to inflict nuclear devastation on the U.S. cast doubt on the credibility of America's nuclear protection. But the European allies were caught between the logic of a strategy of flexible response, which by 1967 prevailed on paper, and the political reality of budgetary restrictions on defense, which prevented conventional force improvements to support the strategy in practice.

President de Gaulle asserted France's independence by pulling her out of NATO's Organization and opposing American efforts to reduce allied dependence on a strategy of nuclear deterrence. Other allies were also growing restive under American preponderance, but they regarded American forces in Europe as indispensable to their security and showed few signs of being ready to supplant American preponderance with tangible efforts of their own.

At the same time, the U.S. was under steady domestic pressure to reduce its forces in Europe substantially. This prospect accentuated allied doubts about the reliability of American protection, but reinforced their own domestic pressures for reduction of defense efforts.

Now, in an atmosphere of détente, which persists despite the Czechoslovakian crisis, the appeal of East-West relations is more compelling than collective defense needs, and in the smaller countries concessions to the latter can be gained only through active deference to the former. Yet U.S. accommodations with the USSR, although welcomed in general as a contribution to détente, tend to arouse suspicion—especially in the FRG that the U.S. seeks a condominium with the USSR at the expense of allied interests. The Non-Proliferation Treaty (NPT) has been especially provocative in this respect, since it requires the FRG to sign a pledge of self-abnegation to appease special Soviet interests and fears.

Nonetheless, after twenty years the North Atlantic Alliance still serves its essential security function and still seems indispensable to its members. SEATO and CENTO (in which the U.S. is not formally a member) have increasingly shown their lack of cohesion, but the U.S. never conceived of them as being much more than means of conveying America's deterrent to the rimlands of Eurasia. America's other alliances and security commitments in Asia have served not only as deterrents against direct aggression and, indirectly, as obstacles to subversion but also (in the cases of Japan, South Korea, and Taiwan) as constraints upon the military policies and actions of allies.

The Soviet Union has encountered far more serious trouble than the U.S. from the loosening of its alliances. Since 1957 the growing split in the Sino-Soviet alliance has been a galling factor in every major Soviet policy and action throughout the world. In recent years the deterioration of this split into hostility has begun to alter fundamentally the structure of world power by establishing an incipient tripolarity at the center of international politics.

At the same time, "contradictions" in the Warsaw Pact threaten the maintenance of political and ideological control over the remaining members of the "socialist commonwealth". As long as Soviet leaders believe that the security of the Warsaw Treaty Organization depends on the political and ideological conformity of bloc members, they will have to rely heavily on armed control and threat of suppression. They will have to do this while trying to preserve an atmosphere of détente without permitting Western (and especially German) economic, political, and cultural penetration to "subvert" Eastern Europe. And at the same time they will be under steady pressure from their clients to subsidize their inefficient economics. The Soviets would face these dilemmas in their most acute form if liberal and nationalist forces were to threaten secure communist control of the GDR.

If the Soviet Union could accept liberalizing tendencies in Eastern Europe without feeling that its external security or its domestic tranquillity were threatened, it might strengthen the cohesion of its bloc by letting it evolve from an empire into a contractual alliance. But there is no assurance that Soviet leadership, foresight, or tolerance of diversity will be equal to this task. Meanwhile, Soviet burdens of empire are the more burdensome because, simultaneously, the Soviet economy (especially in the agricultural sector) is lagging in the face of rising consumer demands.

U.S.-Soviet Relations: Limited Adversaries

In some respects the U.S. and the USSR find themselves in comparable positions in the world, although for different reasons and in different ways. In military power, geographical reach, and the global scope of their interests, the discrepancy between them and the second-rank powers is greater than ever. Both have experienced a momentous expansion of powers and commitments. The United States attained its global position in pursuit of containment and a liberal conception of world order; the Soviet Union, in pursuit of an imperial status keyed to an ideological vision. In pursuit of their different aims both were sucked into the power vacuums of the world by the dynamics of their competition and the desire of others to turn it to their own advantage. Both have experienced concomitant frustrations and constraints—domestic and external—upon their ability to manage the environment within which they must exert their power and protect their commitments.

Now, having consolidated a limited core of common interests in minimizing the risks of armed conflict stemming from direct confrontation or the actions of other states, they nevertheless remain cautious adversaries on a broad spectrum of issues in an increasing portion of the world. In every important international development the relations of the superpowers are an important and often determining element. The vital interests of the U.S. can be affected far more seriously by the actions of the USSR, and vice-versa, than by the actions of any other state. The structure of military power in the world is no less dominated by the superpowers than at the outset of the cold war. The military balance between them is no less consequential for the security or insecurity of others.

Consequently, more than twenty years after World War II, despite all the diffusion of political activity, U.S.-Soviet relations continue to dominate the center stage of international politics. But their relations are the product of a substantially different mix of animosity and accommodation than in earlier periods of cold-war confrontation. Neither an unqualified adversary nor a partner in condominium, the Soviet Union seeks an international environment in which it can cope with its allies, its clients, and its internal problems—which implies a reduction of international tension and a stabilization of relations with the United States. But it also continues its efforts to overcome American strategic military superiority; to expand its air, land, and sea capacity for overseas intervention; and to eliminate American influence and enhance its own in areas like the Middle East where the stakes seem worth the costs and risks.

Having achieved a position of virtual parity with the U.S. in the capacity to inflict unacceptable nuclear retaliatory damage, the Kremlin is in a position either to consolidate détente through arms limitations with the U.S. or to try to exploit a position of strategic strength it lacked during most of the cold war. Conceivably, it could try both courses of action. But even if a bolder leadership should pursue a more aggressive foreign policy, the pattern of U.S.-Soviet relations would not return to the relatively simple confrontation that appeared to exist at the height of the cold war.

Vietnam in Perspective

Changes in the principal pattern of conflict facing the U.S. were already altering American policies and policy concerns in 1965 when the U.S. greatly expanded its direct involvement in the war in Vietnam. A more complicated mixture of containment and détente was already developing in U.S.-Soviet relations. The period of expanding American commitments had ended years before. What the agonies of Vietnam have done is to accelerate and accentuate a revision of some familiar aspects of containment which would probably have changed anyway, although more gradually and moderately.

America's assistance to South Vietnam against communist insurgency was initiated as a perfectly consistent application of the policy enunciated in the Truman Doctrine of helping independent governments resist communist incursions. The expansion of America's involvement after 1965 did not lead to any different rationale. Nevertheless, the costs and frustrations that followed, and their domestic repercussions, have called that rationale into question. In contrast, the adversities of the Korean War led only to a more intensive application of containment to Asia.

How far-reaching the current revision of America's policy and role will become depends not only upon the popular sentiment of "no more Vietnams" but on a number of other factors. Not the least of these is the government's and the nation's assessment of the nature of the international environment and especially of the nature of the communist threat to vital American interests.

III. MAJOR TRENDS

This section summarizes the most important trends in international politics that will affect America's position in the world in the next five years.

A. The Diffusion of Politics

1. Many of the salient characteristics of the present period of international politics spring from the diffusion of independent political activity among and within states following the decline of the cold war, the loosening of cold-war alliances, and the assertion of national and subnational loyalties in the wake of colonial dissolution.

2. In the Third World this diffusion of politics is marked by the consolidation of distinct national feelings, especially in opposition to for-

eign interference or dependence on foreign powers; by the assertion of national policies locally, regionally, and in international bodies; by the growing heterogeneity of interests and alignments among states; and by centrifugal tendencies toward communal, ethnic, tribal and other subnational loyalties. These tendencies toward the diffusion of politics are not accompanied by any significant consolidations of power among LDC's, although there have been some advances in economic and political cooperation among Asian states.

3. Among the developed countries diffusion of politics is marked by centrifugal tendencies within the alliances of the superpowers, and particularly by the assertion on the part of second-rank states of independence from the superpowers in policies and national will. But diffusion does not yet take the form of the emergence of significant new centers of military power, destruction of alliances (with the very large exception of the Sino-Soviet alliance), major realignments, or the consolidation of new groupings among the second rank states.

4. The diffusion of politics in the Third World provides the USSR with new opportunities to extend its influence on a government-to-government basis, as conflicting states and factions within states seek external support and as nationalist sentiments are mobilized against the manifestations of American power. But it also constrains Soviet as well as U.S. influence from going as far as interference or dominance.

5. The diffusion of power within the superpowers' European alliances confronts the U.S. with difficulties in eliciting defense contributions commensurate with stated military requirements and the concomitant accentuation of pressures to withdraw American forces. It confronts the USSR with the more severe problem of maintaining political conformity within a quasi-imperial structure against a steady tide of national self-assertion.

6. The Sino-Soviet alliance has deteriorated into deep rivalry and hostility. This is creating a tripolar relationship in which (a) the U.S., USSR, and the PRC each have an interest in preventing the other two from cooperating, (b) the Soviets have parallel interests with the U.S. in containing China, but (c) the U.S. ability to achieve closer relations with China or to exploit Moscow's fear of a U.S.-Chinese rapprochement will be quite limited unless some substantial U.S.-PRC conflicts of interest are ameliorated—which is only a distant prospect.

B. The U.S.-USSR Military Balance

1. The growth of Soviet nuclear power tends to diminish the credibility of America's nuclear protection, but it has not been incompatible with the maintenance of an adequate American deterrent against Soviet military action or with the stabilization of the U.S.-USSR military bal-

ance based on mutual deterrence between the superpowers. Indeed, it has been accompanied by a growing mutual recognition of the need to avoid war, which has become the solid basis of détente.

2. The consolidation of a situation of virtual parity in second-strike capabilities does, however, accentuate the political problems the U.S. has in retaining the confidence of its allies. And the efforts of the superpowers to stabilize the military environment, especially when directed against the spread of nuclear capabilities to other states, foster suspicion that the superpowers may pursue their common interests at the expense of friends and allies.

3. The consolidation of strategic parity also provides the USSR with the military basis for claiming general equality with the U.S. as a global power. But whether it exploits this situation to America's disadvantage depends on opportunities unrelated to the strategic military balance.

4. The USSR will be better able than in the past to capitalize on new opportunities for projecting its influence and limiting America's influence in the Third World by virtue of the increase of its (a) naval power, especially in the Mediterranean, and of its (b) overseas amphibious and air lift forces, in both of which the U.S. held a virtual monopoly.

C. East-West Relations

1. The Soviet invasion of Czechoslovakia has demonstrated the limits of the capacity of "bridge-building" to enhance the liberty or autonomy of members of the Warsaw Pact. Nonetheless, the attraction in the West of increased East-West communications is undiminished, and East European countries see such communications as a way of constraining Soviet dominance.

2. The slight prospects of a formal East-West settlement or security agreement are diminished by the added Soviet disinclination in the aftermath of the Czechoslovakian crisis to withdraw troops from the GDR. Nor are other conditions of a settlement that would be compatible with American interests—such as the emergence of Western guarantors that could supplant an American presence—any closer to realization. The prospects of a formal settlement are also diminished by the fact that every state except the FRG has come to look upon the status quo as de facto the most satisfactory settlement available and by the FRG's tendency, in practice, to subordinate unification of the Germanies to bridge-building and the normalization of relations with the GDR.

3. The most substantive East-West relations will remain in the realm of U.S.-USSR accommodation or cooperation within a framework of selective competition—a realm of political relationships that is inadequately expressed in the word "détente". In Europe the basis of détente

will continue to be the Soviet desire to stabilize and consolidate the status quo and to moderate the arms competition with the U.S.

4. The strategic arms limitation talks will be the most consequential manifestation of détente. More than any previous arms control talks, SALT will impinge upon Soviet-American political relations, the central strategic balance in the world, and the interests of the NATO allies. The talks—whether they result in a comprehensive agreement or, more likely, a limited agreement, or no agreement at all—will not end the arms race or transform Soviet-American relations, but they will tend to accentuate all the interrelated issues of U. S.-USSR and U.S.-allied relations.

D. The Third World

1. Despite some impressive achievements of economic development, as in Asia, most LDC's continue to suffer the well-known obstacles to development: population growth that exceeds food resources, lack of entrepreneurial skills, lack of the requisite political and administrative capacity, resistance of traditional elites to economic and social reform. Even among the states that are really "developing", the disparity between their standard of living and that of the developed states is increasing.

2. The frequency and intensity of political violence and disorder have been increasing. The insurgencies do not seem likely to displace existing regimes in the next five years; but in some areas (especially Latin America) they reflect economic and social developments that may create genuine although not necessarily successful revolutions. At least they will radicalize political life.

3. The high frequency and intensity of internal conflict is accompanied by an accentuation of interstate conflicts among the LDC's, but the political and military weakness of these states saves them, with a few exceptions, from organized warfare against each other.

4 The heterogeneity of interests and accentuation of conflicts among LDC's, the instability and weakness of their governments, and the growth of internal conflict and violence makes them susceptible to external political *access, penetration,* and *influence.* That is, foreign governments can readily establish lines of communication, bargaining, and inducement with not only governments but also parties, factions, and individuals within the LDC's; so that LDC's must take into account the wishes of foreign donors, and donors can marginally affect the internal and external policies of recipients. On the other hand, apart from a few exceptional cases in which actual military occupation is feasible, the capacity of foreign governments to influence the LDC's is limited far short of *control*—that is, far short of the capacity to subvert governments or to induce or compel them to follow courses of action solely in

response to a foreign government. Control is impeded by the strength of nationalist resistance to external interference, the availability of alternative sources of support, the self-restraint of foreign governments seeking official and popular approval, the strength and diversity of internal loyalties, and the disorganization and weakness of political and administrative institutions.

5. One manifestation of the susceptibility of LDC's to external influence has been the immense extension since 1950 of American involvement in the internal and external security of the LDC's in pursuit of containment. Since 1955 this development has been accompanied by growing Soviet influence and involvement, especially in the Middle East. This influence is now spreading from India to other parts of Asia. Soviet influence, however, is due to government-to-government relations (particularly through Soviet military assistance) rather than to the influence of communist parties. Indeed, the resistance of LDC's to foreign interference, the strength of subnational loyalties, and the emergence of new radical and revolutionary forces in some parts of the Third World (especially Latin America) have restricted the influence of communist parties; while the Sino-Soviet split, Soviet troubles in maintaining the cohesion of its "commonwealth" in Eastern Europe, and the effect of both of these developments in hastening the fragmentation of international communism have increased the independence of communist parties.

6. The capacity of the Soviet Union or Communist China to exploit internal conflicts so as to overthrow governments and establish political control is demonstrably limited. It is limited by the inherent obstacles to successful insurgency or revolutionary war, the limited capacity of the USSR or China to assist insurgencies except in adjacent countries, and, most important, the difficulty of controlling from the outside an insurgency or a victorious insurgent government. Although the prospects of successful insurgency may be increasing somewhat in Southeast Asia and Latin America, the Soviet or Chinese capacity to control insurgent movements or governments is, if anything, declining. This does not preclude LDC governments—revolutionary or otherwise—becoming economic and military dependents of the Soviet Union. But even then, as the cases of Egypt and Cuba illustrate, dependency is not the equivalent of subserviency.

7. As the USSR has succeeded in establishing access and influence in the Third World and as it has grown more apprehensive about Chinese competition, Soviet leaders have become more concerned with protecting their gains as opposed to simply stirring up trouble. They have also become more conscious of the limits and costs of their influence and of the hazards of becoming over-committed. Bitter experience with China and, to a lesser extent, Cuba has reinforced practical doubts

about the value of translating into reality Lenin's vision of communist governments replacing colonial or bourgeois nationalist regimes.

8. The extension of American and Soviet influence and involvement in the Third World has geographically expanded the contest and rivalry of the superpowers. Although it is not polarizing the international politics of the LDC's along the tight ideological and political lines of the cold war, the extension of Soviet and American competition to areas in which they have not worked out a modus vivendi for avoiding direct clashes and in which there are many sources of local conflict over which they have limited influence raises the risk of these powers getting into armed encounters between themselves contrary to their intentions. The risk is highest in the Middle East.

E. The Locus of International Concern

A local war or a major change in the configuration of power or alignment would probably affect American interests more seriously in Europe or the Middle East than in other parts of the world. The establishment of a communist government even in a small state would be as serious a reversal, in American eyes, in Latin America as in either of these two areas because of our special historical relationship to the Western Hemisphere. In reality, however, the area in which changes basically affecting American policy over the next ten years are most likely to take place is Asia, since international politics in Asia are in flux and since the interests of several powerful states converge in the area. If the U.S. is to have any deliberate influence on these changes, it will have to demonstrate its continuing engagement in Asian affairs—but in a selective and unobtrusive manner acceptable to an increasingly self-assertive group of Asian states, as well as to American limitationist opinion.

F. The Devolution of Power

It is logical for those who believe that America's interests continue to be affected by international developments throughout the world to look beyond the diffusion of political activity to the devolution of power; that is, to the emergence of self-reliant regional and subregional groupings that would significantly relieve the U.S. of the burden of maintaining a modicum of order and stability in the world. At present, however, there are few signs that such groupings are emerging. Indeed, powerful trends toward the fragmentation of power lead in the opposite direction.

Unless the U.S. can convince those it protects that it is going to reduce its support, they are not likely to become more self-reliant, but a precipitate U.S. withdrawal would be more likely to lead allies to seek security in neutralism, accommodation with the Soviet Union or China, or national nuclear self-reliance than to induce them to undertake creative efforts of self-defense.

In any case, if the U.S. seriously seeks to encourage the emergence of indigenous guardians of regional security, it will also have to face the prospect of new and expanded centers of nuclear power in Western Europe and Japan.

In the next five years or so, however, progress toward regional self-reliance will fall far short of "hard" military collaboration (as distinct from staff discussions, agreement on strategic guidelines, etc.) or the emergence of new centers of nuclear power capable of supplementing American nuclear power. But bilateral security exchanges between Asian countries are possible.

G. *Principal Policy Concerns*

These trends create an international environment in which America's policy concerns will arise principally from:

1. the management of détente and a stable military balance with the Soviet Union in a manner consistent with the restraint of hostile Soviet moves or adventurism and the maintenance of allied strength and cohesion;

2. the encouragement of Western European allies, Japan, and Southeast Asian countries gradually to assume in the next decade a larger share of responsibility for their own security and the stability of their regions, short of a significant devolution of power from the U.S. to regional security groupings;

3. the conduct of a geographically expanding, though diversified and limited, contest with the Soviet Union for influence in the Third World while acting on parallel interests in the moderation of local conflicts and the containment of China;

4. the gradual improvement of relations with Communist China while continuing to maintain the strength of American deterrence against direct Chinese military aggression and nuclear blackmail;

5. the problems of maintaining access and influence in the Third World, although the LDC's under radical nationalist regimes will be intractable, if not hostile, to American influence; and a number of them will be torn by subnational as well as interstate and transnational conflicts;

6. the support of vital American commitments in the Third World while minimizing the risk of involvement in local conflicts, especially when they entail the risk of an armed confrontation with the Soviet Union or China;

7. the termination of the war in Vietnam and the establishment of a postwar American position in Asia that can encourage indigenous internal and external security efforts at a reduced scale of American involvement;

8. the further development of international surveillance and management of the monetary system, exchange rates, and correction of balance-of-payments disequilibria among the developed countries;

9. the development of national and international regulations for the orderly technological development and use of man's total environment, from ocean space to outer space.

H. Beyond Containment

Clearly, the containment of communist influence and adventures is an important condition for the pursuit of these policy concerns, but it no longer serves as the dominant rationale for American policies, because:

1. the threat of the expansion of communist *control* is not sufficiently intense or clear cut;

2. the expansion of the control of one communist party or state does not necessarily increase the threat of the Soviet Union or China to American security;

3. conflicts within and among the LDC's are diversified and fragmented, not polarized into a contest between communist and non-communist ideology and power; hence, disorder in the Third World is more apt to be localized, and threats of subversion or aggression are more readily decoupled from the central balance of power;

4. in so far as the U.S. is engaged in a contest with the USSR and Communist China in the Third World, it is a limited competition for influence in which the threat of communist take-over by peaceful or violent means is considerably less than was generally supposed to be the case in the early 1960's;

5. the contest with the Soviet Union is qualified by a limited but crucial area of parallel interests arising from the concern of the superpowers to avoid armed clashes with each other and to moderate the arms race;

6. a number of problems that are only indirectly, if at all, connected with containment have become more pressing—including the problems of inter-allied relations, nuclear non-proliferation, the international monetary system, and the orderly use of man's total environment.

Although in response to these trends the tasks of American policy have become more diverse and complex, they have not become less demanding. Coping with them still implies an active global foreign policy supported by American power and resources.

Such a policy is not incompatible with a selective reduction of America's scale of effort overseas or with the avoidance of burdensome new commitments. But as the familiar rationale of containment becomes less convincing, domestic opposition to "over-commitment" will tend to constrict the resource base of policy and inhibit the exercise of American power to an extent that may jeopardize a flexible global policy and even the support of existing commitments.

The prominent role that U.S. economic, diplomatic, and military power plays in the affairs of dozens of other states—whether it is actively used or not—refutes the frequent observations by contemporary analysts about the "impotence of power". The impression of growing impotence that both of the superpowers convey, however, does have a real basis in changes that have occurred since the period in which the U.S. was establishing and extending containment: The increased fragmentation of power, the greater diffusion of political activity, and the more complicated patterns of international conflict and alignment that have emerged over the past decade have limited the capacity of the U.S. and the USSR to control the effects of their influence and have revealed the limits of their capacity to control the actions of other governments, except by direct military means. At the same time, the U.S. has discovered the great obstacles to using military power directly to achieve political ends.

It is also significant for American policy, however, that the U.S. exerts immense and growing influence in the world through a broad range of international activities conducted by nongovernmental individuals, enterprises, and organizations. While the direct influence of the U.S. Government over its international environment has been restricted in one way or another, the scope and reach of American commercial, technical, and cultural influence has continued to expand.

42.   **Letter From the Under Secretary of State (Richardson) to the President's Assistant for National Security Affairs (Kissinger)**[1]

Washington, October 27, 1969.

Dear Henry:

This is in response to your suggestion that I try to put on paper the thoughts about the President's Viet-Nam speech[2] that I touched on in our phone conversation Saturday.

In thinking about the opportunity—and the need—for a Presidential restatement of our purposes and plans for Viet-Nam, I keep coming back to the pivotal question: why are we justified in calling for additional sacrifices of American lives and the continuing diversion of American resources for something less than victory but short of defeat?

It is not enough, I believe, to point to the goal of self-determination for the people of South Viet-Nam. Only a few of the world's peoples enjoy that privilege, if by it we mean the exercise of free choice through fair and honest elections. Nor is this goal made sufficient by the circumstance that in South Viet-Nam the major danger to its fulfillment is externally supported insurgency: the President himself, in his Southeast Asian tour, made clear that assistance against insurgency, even though externally supported, will not hereafter justify the involvement of U.S. combat forces.

There is, however, an element in the South Vietnamese situation which significantly distinguishes it from other situations in which the exercise of self-determination is threatened by external force. This is that we have made a commitment—a promise—to the people of South Viet-Nam to help them preserve the opportunity to determine their own destiny. Whether or not it was wise in the first instance for us to have undertaken such a commitment is not now in issue: the important fact is that we have undertaken it.

So firmly and so frequently has the United States proclaimed this objective that upon our willingness to carry it out depends the credibility of all U.S. commitments. And upon the credibility of U.S. commit-

---

[1] Source: Library of Congress, Manuscript Division, Richardson Papers, Box CL 2, Chronological File. Secret.

[2] On November 3 President Nixon gave a nationally televised speech on Vietnam. The speech came to be known as the "silent majority speech" from Nixon's appeal for support for his policy from "the great silent majority of Americans." The full text of the speech is printed in *Public Papers of the Presidents of the United States: Richard Nixon, 1969,* pp. 901–909.

ments depends, in turn, the possibility of a relatively stable and peaceful world. Conversely, should our word be rendered doubtful by our abandonment of the people of South Viet-Nam, the risk of instability and war—even of World War III—would be measurably enhanced. Not to be willing to make such additional sacrifices as are essential to the fulfillment of our irreducible minimum objective in South Viet-Nam would thus increase the danger that we will be forced to make much greater sacrifices at some future time.

Now all this, of course, has been stated many times by the President, not only in his May 14 speech[3] but in all his talks with heads of state, who have strongly endorsed these propositions. And yet they badly need restatement, particularly for the American people. For the real point of Viet-Nam is not Viet-Nam itself but our world-wide role. By the same token, the real core of the criticism of our policies in Viet-Nam is a criticism of that role. The critics discount both the continuing causes of conflict between East and West and the continuing risks to every nation whose primary concern is the preservation of its own independence and integrity. In the case of the generation that has grown up since the events which generated the Cold War, this is understandable enough, but no less misguided on that account.

In the light of these considerations, it has occurred to me that the President in his November 3 speech, instead of restating our commitment to South Viet-Nam and then relating it to our wider responsibilities, might begin with a review of these responsibilities, explain their importance to world peace, and then show how abandonment of South Viet-Nam, by eroding confidence in our capacity to fulfill them, would prejudice the prospects of world peace. In so doing, he could also stress the point that the very opportunity for an era of negotiations depends on our adherence to our existing obligations. Unilateral concessions are the antithesis of reciprocal concessions. Negotiations, moreover, are aimed at agreement, and the validity of any agreement is dependent upon confidence between the parties that their mutual undertakings will be honored. The capacity of the United States to honor its present undertakings is thus an earnest of its capacity to honor its future undertakings, including those which contribute to a more enduring peace. Our sacrifices in Viet-Nam can thus be seen as sacrifices for a larger cause.

For a television audience, to be sure, a defect of this approach is its abstractness. This is a defect, however, which could be offset by injecting as tangible a feeling as possible for the real situation in Viet-Nam

---

[3] The text is printed ibid., pp. 369–375.

into the latter part of the address. And since the President does in fact have an extraordinarily comprehensive and integrated grasp of the U.S. role in world affairs, it would, I think, heighten the confidence of his viewers in the rightness of his Viet-Nam policies if he laid bare in a low-keyed but thoughtful way the essence of his thinking on this broader subject. In addition, his doing that would at the same time supply ammunition useful in containing other neo-isolationist pressures to roll back U.S. commitments.

Such, at any rate, for whatever they may be worth, are the thoughts I wanted to convey.

As ever,

Sincerely,

Elliot L. Richardson[4]

---

[4] Printed from a copy that bears this typed signature.

---

43.   **Notes of Telephone Conversation Between President Nixon and His Assistant for National Security Affairs (Kissinger)**[1]

Washington, November 5, 1969, 7 p.m.

The President thought of a couple of other things K might tell Sidey.[2] The President mentioned a book by Thompson, "1940" which is the story of what really happened when Churchill came in.[3] He mentioned the story about Patton and Pershing and that there were never tired decisions, only tired commanders. In terms of history, when we talk about the crusades that H.G. Wells talked about, for example the moon thing, had the effect of bringing to Western Europe not just the discovery in the East but the fact that Western Europe at that time devoted itself to a great cause beyond itself. It changed Western Europe. (The President read passages from H.G. Wells.) The President said nations must have great ideas or they cease to be great. They talked about what happened to England and France and that peoples' great-

---

[1] Source: Library of Congress, Manuscript Division, Kissinger Papers, Box 361, Telephone Conversations, Chronological File, 1–10 Nov 1969. No classification marking.

[2] Hugh Sidey of *Time* magazine.

[3] Laurence Thompson, *1940* (New York: William Morrow, 1966).

ness has to be extra-dimensional and move beyond themselves. The question is whether we do what we need to both abroad and in the ghettos. If we just go to the ghettos and let go abroad, apart from the destruction that might come from a war, we might destroy ourselves. Roosevelt talked about it as the white man's burden. Both of these people were searching for that same feeling that people need.

K said he would have a talk with Sidey and do his best.

---

44. Special Message From President Nixon to the Congress[1]

Washington, November 18, 1969.

For the past 35 years, the United States has steadfastly pursued a policy of freer world trade. As a nation, we have recognized that competition cannot stop at the ocean's edge. We have determined that American trade policies must advance the national interest—which means they must respond to the whole of our interests, and not be a device to favor the narrow interest.

This Administration has reviewed that policy and we find that its continuation is in our national interest. At the same time, however, it is clear that the trade problems of the 1970s will differ significantly from those of the past. New developments in the rapidly evolving world economy will require new responses and new initiatives.

As we look at the changing patterns of world trade, three factors stand out that require us to continue modernizing our own trade policies:

First, world economic interdependence has become a fact. Reductions in tariffs and in transportation costs have internationalized the world economy just as satellites and global television have internationalized the world communications network. The growth of multi-national corporations provides a dramatic example of this development.

Second, we must recognize that a number of foreign countries now compete fully with the United States in world markets.

We have always welcomed such competition. It promotes the economic development of the entire world to the mutual benefit of all,

---

[1] Source: *Public Papers of the Presidents of the United States: Richard Nixon, 1969*, pp. 940–946.

including our own consumers. It provides an additional stimulus to our own industry, agriculture and labor force. At the same time, however, it requires us to insist on fair competition among all countries.

Third, the traditional surplus in the U.S. balance of trade has disappeared. This is largely due to our own internal inflation and is one more reason why we must bring that inflation under control.

The disappearance of the surplus has suggested to some that we should abandon our traditional approach toward freer trade. I reject this argument not only because I believe in the principle of freer trade, but also for a very simple and pragmatic reason: any reduction in our imports produced by U.S. restrictions not accepted by our trading partners would invite foreign reaction against our own exports—all quite legally. Reduced imports would thus be offset by reduced exports, and both sides would lose. In the longer term, such a policy of trade restriction would add to domestic inflation and jeopardize our competitiveness in world markets at the very time when tougher competition throughout the world requires us to improve our competitive capabilities in every way possible.

In fact, the need to restore our trade surplus heightens the need for further movement toward freer trade. It requires us to persuade other nations to lower barriers which deny us fair access to their markets. An environment of freer trade will permit the widest possible scope for the genius of American industry and agriculture to respond to the competitive challenge of the 1970s.

Fourth, the less developed countries need improved access to the markets of the industrialized countries if their economic development is to proceed satisfactorily. Public aid will never be sufficient to meet their needs, nor should it be. I recently announced that, as one step toward improving their market access, the United States would press in world trade forums for a liberal system of tariff preferences for all developing countries. International discussions are now in progress on the matter and I will not deal with it in the trade bill I am submitting today. At the appropriate time, I will submit legislation to the Congress to seek authorization for the United States to extend preferences and to take any other steps toward improving the market access of the less developed countries which might appear desirable and which would require legislation.

[Omitted here are proposals for legislation addressing tariffs and trade.]

The trade bill I have submitted today is a necessary beginning. It corrects deficiencies in present policies; it enables us to begin the 1970s with a program geared to the start of that decade.

As we look further into the Seventies, it is clear that we must reexamine the entire range of our policies and objectives.

We must take into account the far-reaching changes which have occurred in investment abroad and in patterns of world trade. I have already outlined some of the problems which we will face in the 1970s. Many more will develop—and also new opportunities will emerge.

Intense international competition, new and growing markets, changes in cost levels, technological developments in both agriculture and industry, and large-scale exports of capital are having profound and continuing effects on international production and trade patterns. We can no longer afford to think of our trade policies in the old, simple terms of liberalism vs. protectionism. Rather, we must learn to treat investment, production, employment and trade as interrelated and interdependent.

We need a deeper understanding of the ways in which the major sectors of our economy are actually affected by international trade.

We have arrived at a point at which a careful review should also be made of our tariff structure itself—including such traditional aspects as its reliance upon specific duties, the relationships among tariff rates on various products, and adapting our system to conform more closely with that of the rest of the world.

To help prepare for these many future needs, I will appoint a Commission on World Trade to examine the entire range of our trade and related policies, to analyze the problems we are likely to face in the 1970s, and to prepare recommendations on what we should do about them. It will be empowered to call upon the Tariff Commission and the agencies of the Executive Branch for advice, support and assistance, but its recommendations will be its own.

By expanding world markets, our trade policies have speeded the pace of our own economic progress and aided the development of others. As we look to the future, we must seek a continued expansion of world trade, even as we also seek the dismantling of those other barriers—political, social and ideological—that have stood in the way of a freer exchange of people and ideas, as well as of goods and technology.

Our goal is an open world. Trade is one of the doors to that open world. Its continued expansion requires that others move with us, and that we achieve reciprocity in fact as well as in spirit.

Armed with the recommendations and analyses of the new Commission on World Trade, we will work toward broad new policies for the 1970s that will encourage that reciprocity, and that will lead us, in growing and shared prosperity, toward a world both open and just.

Richard Nixon

45. Memorandum From the President's Assistant for National Security Affairs (Kissinger) to President Nixon[1]

Washington, December 3, 1969.

SUBJECT

Pat Moynihan's Memo on the Young Demonstrators

I have several specific comments on Pat Moynihan's memo on the problem of the young demonstrators. (Tab A)

Who Are They?

They are a very mixed group—in social origin, in political outlook, in potential for help or harm. Of the young Moratorium marchers, some were certainly the offspring of the affluent, and therefore their politics are a sharp departure from their parents. Yet many probably have fathers who attended college under the GI Bill in the late '40s. Some of the marchers were likely to be the first generation to reach college. And if Tom Wicker is speaking for himself and his colleagues in claiming that "those are our children" down there in the streets, these are also the offspring of some traditionally Democratic elements.

The geographic spread of politically active young people is much broader than the East Coast. A Harvard–Princeton game might find a majority of Bostonians and New Yorkers among the alumni in the stands. But the percentage of mid-Westerners and Westerners among the students would be far, far higher than it was 10 or 15 years ago. To use Pat's comparison, the distinction between the subway to City College (or the freeway to Berkeley) as against walking across Harvard Yard has largely broken down in this age of mass higher education.

Why Do They March?

Their motives are undoubtedly varied. I think a good many of these young people simply don't know who they are—and are trying desperately to find out. In the broader sense, they are casualties of our affluence. Brooded over by too zealous, too psychologically-oriented parents, they have lost confidence in themselves as well as in their elders. Graduated into the impersonal routine of a bureaucratic-technological society, they see conformity as a lonesome life without adventure. In short, they do not find meaning or purpose in those values that guided most of their parents.

---

[1] Source: National Archives, Nixon Presidential Materials, NSC Files, Box 1050, Staff Files, Staff Memos, Moynihan 3/69–11/70. Eyes Only; Sensitive.

It is this quality of rootlessness and despair that goes to explain their quest for "instant" experience—from politics to sex. And what better refuge from loneliness than the crowd ("the happening")—from Woodstock to the Moratorium.

Confusion and outrage have taken their toll, of course, of youthful energies in every generation. The group Pat talks about is special in the sheer breadth of its political consciousness and activism. It is drawn, after all, from the largest number of educated young people in history. They have had the leisure for self-pity, *and* the learning enabling them to focus it in a fashionable critique of the "system".

To the degree that they are politically conscious, many are substantially anti-establishment simply because that is not only the natural bent of youthful alienation, but also because it is a major thrust of contemporary academic literature. Modern American sociology, psychology, political science, etc., have turned a glaring light on the faults in our society. So too is some of our modern literature social criticism. All this is bound to fall on fertile ground—and cover more of it than ever before—in a country that sends *8 million* kids to college.

The practical results are very mixed. The combination of aimlessness and skepticism of the elders has produced a sense of isolation and even of nihilism.

A small minority escapes (as it always has) in mindless radicalism. And the predictable quota of shallow minds and fanatics—the organizers rather than the thinkers—ride the crest of the wave to positions of prominence they could never claim otherwise.

There is also the danger that many of these young demonstrators—deriving passion from their personal crises—do not grasp the consequences of their actions. Some (though not all by any means) march for marching's sake with the sheepish conformity they claim to abhor. The heroes of a vocal minority among them (Che, Mao, et al) are romantic images devoid of reality. It is just unthinking emotion that links civil rights and Chinese Communism.

Yet I believe that the overwhelming majority of these young people across the country remain remarkably open in terms of their future political affiliation. Many are bright and thoughtful. They are committed to right wrongs as well as to find themselves. They are eager to participate, impatient for tangible progress. It is true that they are wary of every answer—and some are ready to suspect that arguments for gradual (realistic) progress (from peace in Vietnam to desegregation) mask some sinister conspiracy against the goal. But this skepticism can also be the bedrock of a critically intelligent and informed citizenry in the '70s and '80s.

Their Political Impact

This frame of reference will probably stay with most of these young people through their first decade as voters. Taken alone as a segment of the voting public, however, they are not significant, and you could build a broad majority however you deal with them.

They become formidable by adding to their own votes an enormous outburst of political activism, bound to have an influence on others as well as on their parents. We have ample proof of this in the McCarthy phenomenon.

In this sense, Vietnam may be only symptomatic. When that issue is gone, another will take its place. For they are fighting the established position as much as a given problem.

What Can You Do?

I think that attacking this group head-on is counterproductive. This is not to say that you should be soft on the destructive militants. There is obviously a need here for firm leadership. But when talking about the great majority of these young activists, I believe you should weigh the benefits and costs of taking them on.

My concern is that blanket condemnation, while giving no lasting benefit, will drive the young activists to focus their energies against you personally—with the fallout Pat describes in the sympathy of their elders and the influence they have in the broader arena. The best posture is that the Administration be seen to take seriously the perplexed but responsible majority of these young people. The posture would be that they may be wrong on the merits of the argument, but you do not doubt the authenticity and sincerity of their concerns.

However, we should remember that these same young people will not forgive us for letting them suffer the consequences of their own actions. To take them seriously is *not* to add one more indulgence. We need not give in to them to show our concern for their problems.

Above all, they need leadership to respect. It is the qualities they miss in their own lives—sureness of purpose, confidence in the future, the courage to stand alone—that they will recognize, whatever the differences on specific issues.

Although many do not realize it, you have something basic in common with many of them—a conviction that the machinery of New Deal liberalism has to be fundamentally overhauled. You also share a concern that America play a more balanced and restrained role in the world. You are, in fact, turning over most of the rocks at home and abroad that these kids want to see turned over. You are in addition, their best protection against the forces their impetuosity and extremism bids fair to unleash on the right.

With a concerted and sensitive effort to get across the fresh approach of your Administration, you may well gain some converts among those who now seem irretrievable.

Tab A

Memorandum From the President's Assistant for Urban Affairs (Moynihan) to President Nixon[2]

Washington, November 13, 1969.

Last night Teddy White related to me your hopes for reviving the Eisenhower–Nixon majority. This seems to me altogether a worthy goal, and a perfectly feasible one. But I fear we may be jeopardizing that outcome by certain present postures which are now in no way central to any of your other goals or policies.

The Eisenhower–Nixon majority was broadbased. (Ike got 20% of the black vote in 1952 and twice that in 1956.) But its bedrock consisted of the business and professional class of the nation. These provided the brains, the money, the elan.

Clearly your overall policies are ideal for mobilizing that group once again. Your fixed intention to get us out of that war in Asia; to put the economy back in balance; to restore the authority of public institutions; to achieve social progress with social stability—all these are precisely the goals of that group.

I think, however, you could lose much of it—needlessly—if *their children* begin to take personally your necessary, proper and essentially impersonal opposition to their own effort to make foreign policy in the streets.

It must be remembered that to an extraordinary degree the demonstrators are an elite group.[3]

—I would hazard that half their parents are Republicans.

—I would not be surprised if those parents contributed half the funds spent by either major party in the 1968 election.[4]

---

[2] No classification marking. Nixon added the following handwritten note on the memorandum and sent it to Kissinger: "K—Return to me with your comment."

[3] Nixon underlined the last five words in this sentence, and at the top of the first page of the memorandum he wrote: "Can we *win* the Harvard et al types?"

[4] Nixon added a marginal handwritten comment at this point which reads: "no—RN $ came from Midwest California & South."

—Note, for example, that much of the money behind this weekend's demonstration comes from General Motors and Singer Sewing Machine fortunes. (*The Ole Mole*, the radical journal in Cambridge, is financed by the granddaughter of Merrill, Lynch, Pierce, Fenner and Smith. There is no end to such examples.)

As with most such groups, they really are kind of arrogant. Teddy White told a (private) story. His son will be down from Harvard this weekend, demonstrating with his girl friend. She is an Auchincloss. As she put it "Uncle Mac [Bundy] and Uncle Bill [Bundy] made a terrible mistake about Vietnam, and I feel I must help rectify it."[5]

They can also be wonderful. Maureen Finch who took part in the Moratorium worked for me this summer, and was superb. I gather that Mel Laird's son who also took part is equally an attractive young man.

And in the mass they are powerful. One of the least understood phenomenon of the time is the way in which the radical children of the upper middle classes have influenced their parents. That is why *Time* Magazine, *Life, Newsweek,* NBC, CBS, the *New York Times* and the media in general will take their side against anybody whatsoever: the Democratic Party, the Pentagon, Mayor Daley. Or, if it should ever come to it . . . you.[6]

In the course of the rioting at the Chicago convention Tom Wicker of the *New York Times* uttered the famous remark "But those are our children down there on the street." It remained for Pete Hamill to comment that "You'd think no cop ever had a mother." No matter. The kids finished Humphrey.

Their parents are in a curious way proud of them. Last Saturday at half time at the Harvard–Princeton game the Harvard Band lined up and began its march with the announcement "Ladies and Gentlemen, the Effete Harvard Corps of Intellectual Snobs." There cannot have been less than $10 billion bucks of Republican money in the Stadium at the time, and as one man it roared approval, i.e., unity with the undergraduates in the face of an outsider who dared affront them.[7] After all, they *are* Harvard men, etc. (Try to remember that *I* went to the City College of New York on the subway. So I am not writing about anybody I know!)

---

[5] Brackets in the source text.

[6] Nixon underlined "against anybody whatsoever" and added the following marginal comment: "(on the left only!)."

[7] Nixon underlined portions of this paragraph, including the final four words, and added a marginal note which reads: "RN *did* so in 1947."

I sometimes like these kids. More often I detest their ignorant, chiliastic, almost insolent self confidence. But I think it extremely important for the administration not to allow itself to become an object of their incredible powers of derision,[8] destruction, and disdain.

DM

---

[8] Nixon underlined "incredible powers of derision."

---

46.   Memorandum From the Under Secretary of State (Richardson) to the President's Assistant for National Security Affairs (Kissinger)[1]

Washington, December 5, 1969.

As I have talked and thought about the emerging shape of the Nixon foreign policy, I have become increasingly struck by the extent to which its major elements form an integrated structure. Since I am scheduled to address the Boston World Affairs Council on January 12, I am contemplating trying this analysis out in that speech, but it has occurred to me that I should first bring it to your attention as a possible framework for a Presidential statement—in the State of the Union Message, in his year-end review of foreign policy, or in a major speech.

The Nixon foreign policy, as I understand it, is built first of all on a realistic awareness of changes in the world that have taken place over the past decade. For purposes of the role of the United States, the most important of these are: (a) the increasing capacity and determination of individual nations to maintain their own independence and integrity; (b) the subordination of ideologies to these over-riding national objectives; and (c) the recognition that United States economic and military resources, in light of competing domestic demands, are not as unlimited as they may once have seemed.

At the same time, however, the President affirms the indispensability of a major U.S. role in preserving a relatively stable world order and promoting a more secure peace.

---

[1] Source: Library of Congress, Manuscript Division, Richardson Papers, Box CL 2, Chronological File. Confidential.

Out of this assessment of changed circumstances and reaffirmation of U.S. responsibility, the following six propositions emerge:

(1) While scrupulously maintaining our existing commitments and being wary of assuming new ones, we should at the same time cut away any surplus fat that has accumulated around them. This, as I understand it, is the essence of the Nixon Doctrine enunciated in Guam.

(2) We should encourage national and regional efforts to achieve economic development and promote mutual security. The United States should be a helpful partner in supporting such efforts but not seek to dominate or control them. This, I take it, is implicit in the Nixon Doctrine and explicit in our Latin American policy. The same approach could well serve also for other regions, e.g., the western Mediterranean, including the Maghreb.

(3) Other advanced nations should be encouraged to contribute to the support of such regional efforts. Existing multilateral agencies should be called upon to assist and, in some instances, existing structures (e.g., CIAP) should be adapted to the purpose or new ones created.

(4) Meanwhile, as in the Middle East and Berlin, we should vigorously pursue efforts to reduce the causes of tension and conflict. Understanding that unilateral concessions do not purchase stability but stimulate the opposite, we recognize that only those settlements that are the product of hardheaded give-and-take are likely to last. Herein lies one important aspect of the significance—and the opportunity—of the "era of negotiation."

(5) We should simultaneously seek to diminish the dangers inherent in the by-products of tension, i.e., armaments and force levels since these inflict not only heavy economic burdens but tend in themselves to generate an atmosphere of tension. Here lies the other important aspect of the "era of negotiation," as evidenced by SALT and balanced force reductions.

(6) There remains the bitter residue left by past tensions, and this we are systematically seeking to dissipate through deliberate and carefully measured steps toward normalizing relations with countries with which our past relationships have, in varying degrees, been strained. Thus, Bucharest and our signals toward the Chicoms.

Not only do these propositions derive from the changed circumstances and the reaffirmed U.S. responsibility noted above, but they are mutually reinforcing. The sharper definition of our existing obligations, for example, and our wariness toward the assumption of new ones rest upon our awareness of the limitations of our resources. To the extent, however, that we succeed in encouraging national and regional self-sufficiency, the need for reliance on us correspondingly diminishes—and so on.

Articulated in this way, it seems to me these principles can be seen to be a coherent whole.

Elliot L. Richardson[2]

---

[2] Printed from a copy that bears this typed signature.

---

47. White House Background Press Briefing by the President's Assistant for National Security Affairs (Kissinger)[1]

Washington, December 18, 1969, 2:50 p.m.

[Omitted here are White House Press Secretary Ronald Ziegler's introduction of Kissinger and his explanation of the rules governing the briefing.]

Dr. Kissinger: I am ready for your questions.

Q. I thought you might have a frame, if I asked this question: Would you list briefly the accomplishments of the Administration this year and its major disappointments?

Dr. Kissinger: Let me first list the disappointments: Of course we haven't made more progress in ending the war, although we are on course. But we have always said there are two ways of ending the war. One is through essentially unilateral moves, on which we are now embarked, and the other one is through negotiations, which would be the rapid way of ending the war.

We are disappointed that there hasn't been more progress in the negotiations and we were perhaps more hopeful that there would be greater progress in the negotiations than there has in fact been, earlier this year.

In the accomplishments, let me take a few minutes on that. First, we have devised a new way of making decisions in the field of foreign policy, which I have explained to you on many occasions, and which takes a period of time to become effective; that is, we now have a reasonable opportunity to be sure that when a decision is made, we have looked at every respectable option, not only those generated within the bureau-

---

[1] Source: Library of Congress, Manuscript Division, Kissinger Papers, Box CL 425, Subject File, Background Briefings, June–Dec 1969. No classification marking.

cracy, but those that exist outside, through the NSC system, and we have engaged in a systematic review of American foreign policy with this in mind.

We have done so, moreover, because we are convinced that, while Vietnam is, of course, the most anguishing problem we face, and the one that in the short term is going to determine the success or failure of this Administration, in the long term we are in a period in which American foreign policy has to be put on a new foundation.

For about 20 years after the end of the war, American foreign policy was conducted with the maxims and the inspiration that guided the Marshall Plan, that is, the notion of a predominant United States, as the only stable country, the richest country, the country without whose leadership and physical contribution nothing was possible, and which had to make all the difference for defense and progress everywhere in the world.

Now whichever Administration had come into office would have had to face the fact, I believe, that we have run out of that particular vision. Conditions have changed enormously. We are now in a world in which other parties are playing a greater role. They have regained some of their self-confidence. New nations have come into being. Communism is no longer monolithic and we, therefore, face the problem of helping to build international relations on a basis which may be less unilaterally American.

With this in mind, we have engaged in a rather systematic review of a whole range of things. What we have done in various fields, really, ought to be seen as part of this general pattern.

You take the Nixon Doctrine for Asia, the basic philosophy of which has really guided our actions elsewhere. This is based on the proposition, not that the United States withdraws from Asia, but that the defense and progress in Asia, as elsewhere, cannot be a primarily American policy, that the United States can participate where it can make a difference, but it cannot, over an historic period, be the American role to make all the plans, to design all the programs, to execute or implement all the decisions and undertake all the defense and be in the posture where both progress and defense of other areas seem more important to the United States than it is for the countries concerned.

Therefore, what President Nixon announced in Guam is the basic policy we have followed elsewhere. We have generally approached these problems in the NSC in two bites: That is, we would make a general—the word isn't a bit philosophical—decision first, of where is it we want to go, and then we would make a number of practical decisions on how to implement it.

For example, on Latin American policy, we made the general decision of where we wanted to go in July, and then in October, after Governor Rockefeller came back from his trip, and the Department of State and other agencies had made specific recommendations, we developed the implementing decisions.

What we have done in Latin America reflects essentially the same philosophy that has guided the policy towards Asia. That is to say, we have tried to develop a pattern that to the greatest degree possible elicits Latin American initiatives and the Latin American contribution, so that the programs that emerge there are joint programs, or programs in which the Latin American countries have played an important and perhaps even predominant role in formulating.

We have seen our role in eliciting their initiative and their contribution, and within the framework of what is a fact of life—that huge sums are not available—we have tried to go as far as it is possible to go, through executive and legislative action, to elicit this set of initiatives.

The policy towards Okinawa or towards Japan was set in effect in March. We decided in March that we were going to return Okinawa to Japan and we did so because we had to weigh the benefit in terms of physical security in maintaining our base in Okinawa against the intangible benefit of being able to establish a partnership with Japan on major areas of concern in the Pacific.

We decided that the temporary continuation of a certain amount of physical security was not our primary problem, that our primary problem was to enlist Japan's cooperation in the development of Asia and in the security interests of its immediate concern; and therefore, it seemed to us important for the sake of this long-term relationship to make the decisions which we did in March.

Another major area where we have started is the relationship with the Communist world. We have taken the view that the tensions that have persisted for 25 years have not been caused by an accident and cannot be removed by primarily psychological means.

We have made it very clear that we are prepared to negotiate intensively, seriously and concretely, and unemotionally, on a whole range of issues, including SALT, which I will come back to in a minute.

We have always made it clear that we have no permanent enemies and that we will judge other countries, including Communist countries, and specifically countries like Communist China, on the basis of their actions and not on the basis of their domestic ideology.

And we hope we have started a process towards Communist China, that over a period of years, will permit a more calibrated relationship to develop, and one in which such a large part of humanity will not be excluded from the international community.

Now, let me go back to SALT because I think this is a good example of both our approach and our philosophy. There has been a lot of discussion, some discussion in the press, that the White House in contrast to previous periods is not as interested in negotiations as before, that we have not given the push to arms control that previous White Houses have given. I think it might perhaps be of some use, if I explained our general approach, because I think it is symptomatic of the Administration.

First, in the SALT talks, we are concerned not with one weapons system, but a complex inter-relationship of weapons systems, in which on both sides, the most basic elements of security are involved, and which on our side, the most fundamental issues of alliances and the conception by our allies of their security is involved.

Secondly, there are many people who like to see this as a morality play in which the good guys defeat the bad guys and in which you drive desperately or, if not desperately, in which you drive brutally, if necessary, towards one position which you impose on the bad guys with White House leverage, if necessary.

But if you look at the negotiations in this field that have taken place over the years, you will find that negotiations as relatively simple as the test ban, and as the Non-Proliferation Treaty, took five and three years respectively; that, if you look at what the classical pattern has been, that we would enter with a position.

It never happened that the other side would come in with a similar position and therefore, we were confronted with having to spend half of our time negotiating with ourselves, another quarter of our time negotiating with our allies and the rest of our time in an entirely tactical exercise with the Soviets. Therefore, what we attempted to do is to be prepared for the contingency that the other side might really be serious, and that if it was serious, it would have to address a number of fundamental questions, which would concern us as much as them, and, therefore, we did something, which has not been done, I think—I know—in the history of these arms control negotiations; that is, we made a systematic survey of every weapons system that could conceivably be the subject of negotiations, of our intelligence capabilities with respect to that weapons system, of the possibility of evasion with respect to that system, what counter measures we would have to take, if there were evasion, what risks we were running and how we could avoid these risks.

And the purpose was to avoid the sterile, theological debate where one group of the bureaucracy would say, "You are jeopardizing American security" without ever being able to define how, and the other group of the bureaucracy would be saying, "You must be able to run the risk for peace", without ever being able to tell you what the risk was.

As a result, first of all, many of the disagreements, most of the disagreements disappeared because when you define just what the evasion was that was possible, and what the risk was, it was possible to express it in a way in which most people agreed.

Secondly, we are in a position to put together almost any position, and we have in fact put together a whole variety of positions, depending on the scope of the agreement, that the other side might be prepared to undertake.

Thirdly, we were able to engage with the Soviets in the preliminary talks in Helsinki, in what I consider the most constructive talks on arms control of which I am familiar, either in or outside the government, and I had participated in almost all of the scientific exchanges outside the government that have taken place.

We were told before we went to Helsinki by many people that if we didn't go there with a position, the Soviets would lose confidence in us, or we were told if we didn't go there with a detailed position the Soviets would pre-empt the field with a spectacular of their own.

In fact, the curious thing seems to have happened that the Soviet preparations have taken about the same form as ours; that is, they have made a detailed analysis of the problems and I consider that one of the more hopeful signs, regardless of what may come out in the next phase of the talks.

We are now in a position to enter the next phase of the talks with some understanding of how the Soviets conceive the problem. And we are not flying blind and we are not just negotiating with ourselves when we put forward a position. Again, I repeat, I think we have done, in terms of preparation, more thorough, detailed, and thoughtful work than I remember having been done in the last ten years.

Another example of how this works is in the field of biological and chemical warfare, where rather than turn it into an obtuse exercise of whether one was for or against biological warfare, we went through an analysis of what could be accomplished in either of these forms.

And in short, what we have attempted to do is to be thoughtful and to look ahead and to look at matters in a comprehensive manner.

The Defense budget now is no longer looked at from a purely security point of view. We have this Defense Policy Review Committee, which has been written about, which takes into consideration political and arms controls considerations and in the consideration of our basic defense posture, we for the first time consider the relationship between the Defense spending and domestic needs.

And when it was presented to the President, he was in a position to compare what domestic priorities had to be given up, or where possible, at various levels of Defense spending.

I don't want to be misleading. No procedure and no attempt to be thoughtful guarantees that one is in fact right, or indeed that one is in fact thoughtful. And three years from now, we won't be judged by the process by which we have made the decisions, or even where we attempted to be thoughtful, but whether we were in fact thoughtful.

[Omitted here is the question-and-answer session on a variety of foreign policy issues.]

---

48.   **Memorandum From Secretary of State Rogers to President Nixon**[1]

Washington, December 24, 1969.

SUBJECT

Suggestions on a Basic Approach for your Review of American Foreign Policy

I would like to let you have my thoughts on the basic approach your Review of American Foreign Policy[2] might follow. Basically I believe the Review should serve to underscore the new direction you have given to United States involvement in world affairs in the past year.

In essence I would capsulize this new direction as follows:

At a time when we should no longer be looking back to the residue of the Second World War and of a passing colonial era but ahead to a future of international cooperation in which others will have an increasing desire and capacity to contribute fully, you have directed American foreign policy toward:

—Achieving a broader sharing of responsibility and a new equality of partnership with our friends and allies throughout the world as the foundation for a durable collaboration to achieve a world of peace with security and a higher quality of life; and toward

---

[1] Source: National Archives, Nixon Presidential Materials, NSC Files, Box 325, Subject Files, President's Annual Review of U.S. Foreign Policy. Confidential.

[2] Reference is to the report on foreign policy submitted to Congress by President Nixon on February 18, 1970; see Document 60.

—Approaching all international issues and conflicts in an atmosphere not of contention but of negotiation and with a desire to improve our relations with all countries of the world, whatever our differences may be.

I suggest that you build first upon these two broad themes and then elaborate by relating other policy developments to the relevant portions of your Inaugural Address.[3]

Broader Sharing of Responsibility

The stress should be on the importance of a broader sharing of responsibility as a basis for a sound long-term international collaboration. Five main specific elements could be developed—(1) Vietnamization, (2) Latin American policy, (3) Asian policy (including Okinawa), (4) European policy, and (5) South East Asia other than Viet-Nam.

One aspect of this basic policy thrust was at the core of your address to the Inter-American Press Association on October 31, 1969,[4] when you expressed the belief that the "future pattern of American assistance must be US support for Latin American initiatives" and when you offered them a larger role in decisions on economic aid. The efforts we have made to consult more widely with our European allies on matters of concern to them is another. The same policy was set forth in a security context in Guam on July 25,[5] when you said that the United States was going to encourage and had a right to expect that problems of internal security and national defense will be increasingly handled by the Asian nations themselves.

The Vietnamization policy is another expression of the same view, and the present success of the Government of the Republic of Viet-Nam in improving the capabilities of its armed forces and assuming a larger share of the fighting on the ground is proof that the policy is based on a realistic appraisal of the potential of South Viet-Nam.

In setting forth this policy the presentation should make it clear that we intend to continue to do our share. Our policy reflects no desire to retreat to a fortress America.[6] Indeed it is an affirmation of our intention to establish a durable basis for continued world-wide cooperation. We have reaffirmed our treaty commitments to NATO, to our Asian

---

[3] See Document 9.

[4] For text, see *Public Papers of the Presidents of the United States: Richard Nixon, 1969*, pp. 893–901.

[5] See Document 29.

[6] Nixon underlined the second half of the first sentence and all of the second sentence. He wrote in the margin: "Hit this *very hard.*"

allies, and to the attainment of a just peace in Viet-Nam. We have made clear that we will be, as you said in your Inaugural Address, "as strong as we need be for as long as we need be". We have made clear that we will judge each situation in itself and that we are prepared to assist those who are assisting themselves.

Era of Negotiation

The basis of the policy of negotiations and improved relationship was contained in the Inaugural Address in the words: "after a period of confrontation, we are entering an era of negotiation". The section should bring out that during 1969 the United States sought to bring many major problems that confront the world community to the bargaining table. It should emphasize (1) efforts to negotiate in Viet-Nam, (2) negotiations with the Soviet Union, especially on disarmament, (3) efforts to open talks with the Chinese Communists, (4) efforts to bring about negotiations on the Middle East, and (5) a negotiable stance on matters affecting us, such as in Peru and in Korea.

Your Inaugural Address keynoted other important themes which have been carried forward in the policy decisions of this Administration over the past year.

Disarmament

—You said then "let us cooperate to reduce the burden of arms". This section obviously would deal with the beginning of Strategic Arms Limitations Talks with the Soviet Union. It would also cover the seabeds, NPT, chemical warfare, balanced force reductions and arms limitations in the Middle East. It should bring out that the start of negotiations does not signal their success and that we must govern our defense policies accordingly.

Openness

—You said then that "during this Administration our lines of communication will be open" and that this "government will listen". This willingness to listen and to appreciate the position of others made a major contribution to the style and quality of our relationships with other nations. Our willingness to truly consult, to listen as well as to speak, has improved relations within the NATO Alliance. It led to a marked improvement of our relations with France. It is a major aspect of the Latin American policy. It was reflected in your trips to Europe and to Asia and in my Asian trip and UN consultations as well as in your many meetings with foreign officials in Washington. We welcome in the same vein renewal of relations with Cambodia and Mauritania.

Quality of Life

—You called then for peaceful competition "in enriching the life of man". Here there are many elements to bring out, such as the visits of Doctor DuBridge and AEC Chairman Seaborg to Romania, which could mark a new success in East-West cooperation in the scientific and technological fields; your establishment of a high priority on population matters; our leadership on the human environment; our support of the UN Decade of Developments; the Decade of Ocean Exploration and the region of the seabed; and efforts to control the narcotics trade.[7]

Open World

—You called in your Inaugural Address for a more open world, open to the free flow of people. This section might include statements of your visit to Romania as the first State visit by an American President to any country in Eastern Europe;[8] the extent of private American travel abroad; the proposed new visa regulations to encourage more people to visit the United States; our cultural exchange programs around the world; and our desire for continued and expanded exchange programs with Eastern Europe.

Trade and AID

—You also called for a world open to the free flow of goods. We have continued to encourage the growth of freer international trade. This section would develop the request for further authority to reduce trade barriers, the proposal for generalized tariff preferences for manufactured goods from developing countries; the creation of $9.5 billion of international monetary reserves—or Special Drawing Rights; our desire to negotiate reduction or removal of non-tariff barriers; the steps to liberalize economic relations with the Americas; easing of trade restrictions with Communist China; rationale and support for continued AID, and the appointment of the Peterson Commission.[9]

Lowered Voices

In addition to the Administration's many specific accomplishments, the manner in which we have conducted our foreign policy is worthy of note. We have tried, in the words of your Inaugural Address,

---

[7] Nixon highlighted this paragraph and added the marginal comment: "good theme."

[8] Nixon highlighted this paragraph to this point and added a marginal note which reads: "good to hit again."

[9] See footnote 2, Document 35.

to "lower our voices". We have curtailed American presence overseas, reducing by 8,000 the number of people employed by the United States abroad because we knew that our presence can be overbearing, and that it is not the size of the American presence that determines our influence but the soundness of our efforts. You have called for a new partnership in Latin America "in which the United States lectures less and listens more". We have taken a businesslike approach in the various negotiations we have entered. We have reduced the rhetoric and hyperbole in our speeches.

Specifics

I have not sought to set out treatments for other specific policy issues that should be covered—such as Biafra, Greece, the UN, Korea, India and Libya—as this can best be done as the outline of the entire presentation is established by the drafters.

Conclusion

Looking to the future, the conclusion might develop the theme that it is not likely that the United States will again find itself in the position it held after World War II of being the single country in the Free World with the national will and resources to make a major impact on world events. National capacity and strength will continue to grow among the nations of the world. We have not sought to impede or deflect this trend. Instead we have made clear by word and deed that we will continue to cooperate with and to encourage the increasingly self-reliant members of the world community in the cause of progress, peace and security.

WPR

49. **Memorandum From Marshall Wright of the National Security Council Staff to the President's Assistant for National Security Affairs (Kissinger)**[1]

Washington, January 10, 1970.

SUBJECT

Revised Drafts of African and UN papers for Annual Report[2]

Here are the latest versions of these two papers, revised to reflect your comments as relayed by Dick Kennedy.

In connection with these drafts I want to remind you that both in Africa and in the UN our policy is essentially defensive. Neither is central in any way to US foreign policy operations or interests. We deal with them because they are there, not because we hope to get great things out of our participation. We aim at minimizing the attention and resources which must be addressed to them. What we really want from both is no trouble. Our policy is therefore directed at damage limiting, rather than at accomplishing anything in particular.

That being true, there is (or at least, I can find) no broad and positive conceptual base which can credibly be put forward to explain why we do what we do in Africa and the UN. The real base we cannot mention. The task then is to put the best possible face upon essentially negative roles, and to try to make them sound more positive and more integrated than they actually are.

I call this to your attention so that you will be under no illusions that I consider the attached drafts to be what you asked for.

---

[1] Source: National Archives, Nixon Presidential Materials, NSC Secretariat Files, Box 1303, Richard M. Nixon Annual Review 1970–1974, Annual Review 1970. Secret.

[2] Attached are an 8-page paper outlining the Nixon administration's policy toward Africa and a 7-page paper which addressed the administration's view of the United Nations. Neither draft is dated nor is drafting information provided. Regarding the annual report to Congress, see Document 60.

---

50. **Editorial Note**

Henry Kissinger telephoned President Nixon on January 14, 1970, to report on negotiations with the North Vietnamese in Paris. Kissinger called the President in Camp David, Maryland, from his office in the

White House. (National Archives, Nixon Presidential Materials, White House Central Files, Staff Members and Office Files, Office of Presidential Papers and Archives, Daily Diary) During the course of the conversation, Nixon and Kissinger concluded that the experience of history highlighted the serious risks involved in negotiating with the Soviet Union. Nixon apparently applied the lesson to negotiations with North Vietnam. His opening and concluding comments relate to negotiations with North Vietnam:

"P: I suppose they will want to take the line they will say what have you got to say. I was reading a couple of nights ago the whole record of Churchill's account on Teheran, Malta and his negotiations with Harriman and what happened in terms of Yugoslavia, Czechoslovakia, Poland, etc. And really it is a shameful record. It is an outrage. I thought Eisenhower was taking the orders from the top but the whole emphasis was on getting along with the Russians whereas Churchill was concerned with re-drawing the map of Europe.

"K: He was thinking of what would happen after the war.

"P: Right. And the whole thing was the absolute hardness of Stalin during the whole thing. The Russians did not give anything on anything.

"K: The Russians got us so focused on victory they never talked about peace.

"P: You know that in the days of McCarthy and Jenner they really overstated it but basically they happened to be right. We did screw up the peace.

"K: For example, the invasion of Southern France. If those units had been put into the Balkans the whole thing would have been different.

"P: I think you should scan through it and see just what happened. He would send a message over and obviously the American President was responding and was responding in an almost unbelievably naive way.

"K: And these Kremlinologists were saying just what Thompson told you. 'You have to be in good faith.'

"P: Right and Truman turned down a meeting with Churchill first and then came back with the proposition that Truman ought to meet with Stalin first. Well that would have been the most terrible thing. It is well to read this stuff in order to know what we are dealing with now.

"K: Hopkins wanted Truman and Roosevelt to be the intermediary between England and Russia, grossly overestimating the British strength and grossly underestimating the Russian intentions.

"P: What I am getting at is that I don't know what these clowns want to talk about but the line we take is either they talk or we are going to sit it out. I don't feel this is any time for concession. And mainly because I feel that the only way we are going to get anywhere is by talking this way."

Later in the conversation, Nixon outlined those elements of his administration's foreign policy he wanted to emphasize in his forthcoming State of the Union address:

"P: We have to say a little about Vietnam—maybe pick up what we said Nov 3rd and say it a little differently. We are for a just peace. We have seen progress in Asia, in Japan. We have seen progress here. There are other areas in the world where there are still problems. The Mid-East is still difficult. I will cover it all. We are not going to retreat from our world commitments. We are going to keep them. I would use it to make another whack at the Nixon Doctrine. The Nixon Doctrine is not a retreat from our world responsibilities. It is a method—a new way. Whether it is Latin America or any other area in the world. If you don't mention everybody they will feel hurt. My point is that we feel that it is time for the industrial nations of the world—all the nations of the world. You might give it a historical slant. As we enter the '70's more than 25 years have passed since WW II—we made a new policy to deal with the new situation. For 25 years the US had to assume the major responsibility. We are for negotiation rather than for confrontation." (Memorandum of telephone conversation; Library of Congress, Manuscript Division, Kissinger Papers, Box 361, Telephone Conversations, Chronological File, 3–14 Jan 1970)

For the reference to Thompson, see footnote 3, Document 43.

51.　　Address by Secretary of State Rogers[1]

Washington, January 15, 1970.

In this first year the Nixon administration has put its own stamp on United States foreign policy. It is a mix of continuity and change.

There is a necessity for continuity in our foreign policy which derives from the fact that we are the world's greatest power. Nothing

---

[1] Source: Department of State *Bulletin*, February 2, 1970, pp. 118–120. Secretary Rogers addressed the National Foreign Policy Conference for Editors and Broadcasters in the Department of State.

can relieve us of the inescapable responsibilities that go with that status. Certainly one of the most stabilizing influences in world affairs today is that other nations, friendly and not so friendly, take it for granted that the United States will live up to its obligations. Without the element of continuity in basic United States foreign policy, world affairs would be much more unstable and dangerous.

Yet there must be change, too, because world events require a dynamic foreign policy. When this administration took office, our participation in the war in Viet-Nam had come to pervade and color the whole of our foreign policy. In fact, it consumed much of the time and energy of our top leaders. The alternatives seemed to be either to negotiate a settlement or to go on fighting indefinitely.

It was clear that we needed another approach. President Nixon decided that our policy should be to negotiate a settlement or, if that were not possible, to transfer the responsibility for combat activities to the South Vietnamese in a way which would assist them to achieve self-determination. As you know, that has come to be known as Vietnamization, and we are cautiously optimistic about its success. It will be carried out until all combat forces and ultimately other forces have been withdrawn or until Hanoi decides to work out a peace through negotiation which will give the people of South Viet-Nam the right of free choice.

President Nixon's program to end American participation in combat in Viet-Nam is irreversible. We are training and equipping the forces of the Republic of Viet-Nam to take care of themselves as we transfer to them the whole of the combat role. There is a growing confidence in South Viet-Nam that this can be done. Assuming its success—and our policy makes this assumption—the result will be valuable for the future security of the area: a feeling of independence and self-reliance not just in South Viet-Nam but in Southeast Asia as a whole.

We believe we are on the right track toward national release from total preoccupation with this one area of foreign affairs.

If United States foreign policy a year ago was overly concentrated on Viet-Nam, the foreign policy of the Soviet Union was equally preoccupied with the quarrel with Communist China. As far as we can see this is still the case, and there is no reason to believe that it is likely to change dramatically in the near future.

It therefore seemed wise to us to make known what our position was with respect to the Sino-Soviet border dispute and the general tensions between those governments. This we have done.

We have made it clear that we have no intention of attempting to exploit their differences.

We intend to negotiate with the Soviet Union, hopefully in a meaningful way, in pursuit of common ground and mutual advantage.

We also intend to seek ways to have better relations with Communist China. Consequently, we are pleased that we now have an agreement to meet in Warsaw on January 20.

To have better relations with the Soviet Union and with Communist China, we believe, would be in our national interest, and our policy is to seek sensible ways to accomplish this. The fact that a Sino-Soviet conflict exists is strictly their affair, but it should not be a restraint on our efforts to improve relations with both.

I think I should mention two other powerful nations in the world which are making new contributions to the dynamics of world affairs.

The first is Japan. Japan has become the third industrial power of the world. She is ready to play a part in the affairs of the Asian and Pacific community of nations more commensurate with that status. In recognition of this fact our administration decided to return Okinawa to Japan in 1972. This historic decision should be looked upon as the closing act of the postwar period of United States-Japanese relations. Our relations with Japan now enter a new stage of close and friendly cooperation at the beginning of a new decade.

The Pacific community provides a bright picture. The highest rates of sustained economic growth in the world are found today in Japan, Korea, Taiwan, and Thailand. The picture in Indonesia is most encouraging. Cooperative regional organizations in the Pacific area have come into being; and as I have indicated, the new strength and energy of Japan is an outstanding factor in that regional picture.

The fourth most productive economy in the world is the Federal Republic of Germany. There is a new government in Bonn with which we have excellent relations, both bilaterally and within NATO.

The German Government is seeking in every practical way to reduce tensions that made the German question the most dangerous of the cold-war issues. The North Atlantic Council serves as a good forum for close consultation on policies and methods of improving relationships with the countries of Eastern Europe. But if East-West relations are to return to a more normal state, Germany obviously must play a major role in that process. The present German Government is engaged in an effort to do this in consultation with, and with the support of, its allies, including, of course, the United States.

These brief remarks serve to highlight the fact that in this next decade glacial changes will undoubtedly occur. The Nixon administration's general approach to foreign policy as we enter the decade of the seventies is:

First, to try to move from stalemated confrontations to active negotiations on outstanding issues with the Soviet Union and others;

Second, to encourage other more developed nations, and especially in the framework of regional organizations, to assume greater responsibility for leadership and initiative in the affairs of the major regions of the world;

Third, to lower our voice and our visibility on the world stage to accord with what we intend to be a more moderate dialogue and a greater degree of partnership with our friends and allies; and

Fourth, to make it clear that the United States has no intention of renouncing its treaty obligations, of withdrawing from the international scene, or of failing to play a proper and active role in the constant search for security and for a better life for all of mankind.

On the negotiating front, we have successfully launched the strategic arms limitations talks; we have agreed with the Soviet Union on a draft treaty banning the emplacement of weapons of mass destruction on the ocean floor; we are seeking to discuss arrangements to normalize access to Berlin; we have negotiated intensively, but with disappointing results so far, to find a framework on which the parties may negotiate a lasting settlement in the Middle East; and we have indicated a willingness to negotiate with the Warsaw Pact nations on mutual and balanced reduction of forces in Europe.

We shall make some proposals next week to the Communist Chinese in Warsaw in the hope that we can improve relations with them.

On the second point—encouraging greater responsibility for regional leadership by the nations of the area—we have moved forward in Europe, Asia, and Latin America.

To our NATO allies, President Nixon has offered to consult more on subjects of mutual concern. This has eliminated the fear of unilateral action, and our Western allies are appreciative.

In Asia our friends and allies have agreed that henceforth, if it should be required, they will provide the necessary military forces to cope with subversion, both internally and externally promoted, with the United States providing appropriate support by way of equipment and training, et cetera. We have agreed, too, that the proper role of the United States is that of partner and participant in regional activities, for which Pacific and Asian countries will undertake initiatives and provide leadership. This is the way we want it and the way the Asians want it.

In Latin America a comparable development has taken place. In accord with our neighbors to the south, we are proceeding on the basis of a more mature and a more equal partnership. Our hemisphere friends have accepted responsibility for providing a leading voice in inter-American affairs and in setting their own course in the struggle for economic development and social reform.

I have not mentioned Africa, but next month I shall visit Africa. I will in particular discuss with African leaders their views of how best to find a steady, long-term basis for relating our interest in helping them raise standards of living to their own efforts.

Overall, I believe that the United States, under the leadership of President Nixon, has had a successful year in the conduct of its foreign affairs.

Finally, I want to underscore that the foreign policy of this administration cannot be characterized as tending toward isolationism—as a curtailment of interests or a shedding of responsibility in world affairs. We cannot retreat from a world in which we will increasingly be involved, however longingly some might glance in that direction.

What we *can* do and what we propose to do is to alter the character of our involvement, to make that involvement more consistent with present-day realities, to give it a sound footing for the long term. We can be less intrusive and less domineering. We can have a lower profile. We can speak with a less strident voice. By working more effectively with other nations, by conducting our international affairs with a bit more modesty, we hope that we may become more successful and effective partners in the search for peace and security in the world during this last third of the 20th century.

---

52. Address by President Nixon on the State of the Union[1]

Washington, January 22, 1970.

Mr. Speaker, Mr. President, my colleagues in the Congress, our distinguished guests and my fellow Americans:

[Omitted here are general introductory remarks.]

When we speak of America's priorities the first priority must always be peace for America and the world.

---

[1] Source: *Public Papers of the Presidents of the United States: Richard Nixon, 1970*, pp. 8–16. The President delivered the address at 12:30 p.m. in the House of Representatives before a joint session of Congress.

The major immediate goal of our foreign policy is to bring an end to the war in Vietnam in a way that our generation will be remembered—not so much as the generation that suffered in war, but more for the fact that we had the courage and character to win the kind of a just peace that the next generation was able to keep.

We are making progress toward that goal.

The prospects for peace are far greater today than they were a year ago.

A major part of the credit for this development goes to the Members of this Congress who, despite their differences on the conduct of the war, have overwhelmingly indicated their support of a just peace. By this action, you have completely demolished the enemy's hopes that they can gain in Washington the victory our fighting men have denied them in Vietnam.

No goal could be greater than to make the next generation the first in this century in which America was at peace with every nation in the world.

I shall discuss in detail the new concepts and programs designed to achieve this goal in a separate report on foreign policy, which I shall submit to the Congress at a later date.[2]

Today, let me describe the directions of our new policies.

We have based our policies on an evaluation of the world as it is, not as it was 25 years ago at the conclusion of World War II. Many of the policies which were necessary and right then are obsolete today.

Then, because of America's overwhelming military and economic strength, because of the weakness of other major free world powers and the inability of scores of newly independent nations to defend, or even govern, themselves, America had to assume the major burden for the defense of freedom in the world.

In two wars, first in Korea and now in Vietnam, we furnished most of the money, most of the arms, most of the men to help other nations defend their freedom.

Today the great industrial nations of Europe, as well as Japan, have regained their economic strength; and the nations of Latin America—and many of the nations who acquired their freedom from colonialism after World War II in Asia and Africa—have a new sense of pride and dignity and a determination to assume the responsibility for their own defense.

That is the basis of the doctrine I announced at Guam.[3]

---

[2] See Document 60.

[3] See Document 29.

Neither the defense nor the development of other nations can be exclusively or primarily an American undertaking.

The nations of each part of the world should assume the primary responsibility for their own well-being; and they themselves should determine the terms of that well-being.

We shall be faithful to our treaty commitments, but we shall reduce our involvement and our presence in other nations' affairs.

To insist that other nations play a role is not a retreat from responsibility; it is a sharing of responsibility.

The result of this new policy has been not to weaken our alliances, but to give them new life, new strength, a new sense of common purpose.

Relations with our European allies are once again strong and healthy, based on mutual consultation and mutual responsibility.

We have initiated a new approach to Latin America in which we deal with those nations as partners rather than patrons.

The new partnership concept has been welcomed in Asia. We have developed an historic new basis for Japanese-American friendship and cooperation, which is the linchpin for peace in the Pacific.

If we are to have peace in the last third of the century, a major factor will be the development of a new relationship between the United States and the Soviet Union.

I would not underestimate our differences, but we are moving with precision and purpose from an era of confrontation to an era of negotiation.

Our negotiations on strategic arms limitations and in other areas will have far greater chance for success if both sides enter them motivated by mutual self-interest rather than naive sentimentality.

It is with this same spirit that we have resumed discussions with Communist China in our talks at Warsaw.

Our concern in our relations with both these nations is to avoid a catastrophic collision and to build a solid basis for peaceful settlement of our differences.

I would be the last to suggest that the road to peace is not difficult and dangerous, but I believe our new policies have contributed to the prospect that America may have the best chance since World War II to enjoy a generation of uninterrupted peace. And that chance will be enormously increased if we continue to have a relationship between Congress and the Executive in which, despite differences in detail, where the security of America and the peace of mankind are concerned, we act not as Republicans, not as Democrats, but as Americans.

[Omitted here is the remainder of the address devoted largely to domestic issues.]

---

53. Memorandum From the Under Secretary of State (Richardson) to the President's Assistant for National Security Affairs (Kissinger)[1]

Washington, January 22, 1970.

"A Cause Bigger than Ourselves . . ."

Two thoughts which I have been meaning to suggest for Presidential utterance at some future date now—in the light of his State of the Union Message[2]—seem to me appropriate for his foreign policy message. They are:

1. Having outlined the importance of emerging nationalism in terms of its significance for self-reliance, regionalism, etc., and having emphasized the essentiality of our role in maintaining the relative stability of a world structure composed of sovereign states, the President could go on to say that for the long future such a structure is not enough. We must look, rather, toward ways in which the peacekeeping role of the UN as a supra-national structure can be strengthened, ways in which the rule of law can be expanded.

This can be said in a way, I think, which need not undercut the realism and the practicality with which he approaches today's and tomorrow's problems. To say it, however, could help to express the larger vision called for by his State of the Union address. It would, moreover, supply what has heretofore seemed to me a missing ingredient in the articulation of our policy.

The theme would, of course, be an appropriate one for further development in an address to the UN on the celebration of its 25th anniversary.

---

[1] Source: National Archives, Nixon Presidential Materials, NSC Files, Box 325, Subject Files, President's Annual Review of U.S. Foreign Policy. No classification marking.

[2] See Document 52.

2. The youthful idealism and impatience that have fastened on the squalor and misery of our domestic ghettos is bound, I believe, eventually to be extended to the vastly greater squalor and misery in which most of the world lives. I just don't believe that young people who are so much concerned with the poverty, hunger and disease within our own borders will long continue to be indifferent to the much worse conditions beyond our borders.[3]

As the President said months ago in our NSC meeting on foreign assistance, its most important justification is, after all, moral. To sound this note and to affirm the goal of a more adequate world order are the only ways I can think of for the President to sustain in the foreign policy message the inspirational tone so impressively achieved in his State of the Union message.

Again, the theme could be further developed in a later message—in this case, in a message based on the Peterson Task Force recommendations[4] and in compliance with the Javits Amendment.[5]

ELR

---

[3] Kissinger highlighted this paragraph and the next one and put a checkmark in the margin.

[4] Regarding the establishment of the President's Task Force on International Development, see footnote 2, Document 35. The task force submitted its report and recommendations to President Nixon on March 8, 1970. (*Report to the President of the United States From the Task Force on International Development: U.S. Foreign Assistance in the 1970's,* Washington, D.C., U.S. Government Printing Office, 1970) The White House released the report on March 8 along with a statement by President Nixon indicating his intention to reform the foreign assistance programs in light of the task force recommendations. (*Public Papers of the Presidents of the United States: Richard Nixon, 1970,* pp. 253–254)

[5] Reference is to an amendment offered by Senator Jacob Javits on December 12, 1969, during debate in the Senate on foreign assistance legislation. The amendment to H.R. 14580, which was adopted by the Senate, restored authorization for the Overseas Private Investment Corporation. (*Congressional Quarterly Almanac,* Vol. XXV, 1969, p. 445)

54.   Paper Prepared in the National Security Council Staff[1]

Washington, undated.

THE NIXON DOCTRINE FOR ASIA: SOME HARD ISSUES

It is useful at the outset to recognize that there is no such thing as a grand strategy for Asia. If we can restrain the natural impulse to package a grand strategy, future discussions of American policy in Asia will be more illuminating than past ones. Most treatment of possible U.S. post-Vietnam Asian policies has tended to compartmentalize them neatly under strategic labels that describe U.S. base postures and imply U.S. political postures, e.g., "mainland", "offshore", "Pacific outposts". Such treatment is misleading. The strategic headings are oversimplified and just won't hold up under the glare of Asian complexities. It is fruitless to try and draw abstract defense lines which represent "vital interest" boundaries on which we would "fight". And even if we could construct a master plan, we would not adhere rigidly to it for the sake of consistency if events dictated tactical aberrations.

The Nixon Doctrine Is Already Being Implemented

In current discussion of U.S. policy for post-Vietnam Asia, the conventional wisdom is that:

—The President, Vice-President and Secretary of State during their Asian trips have sketched the outlines of a significant new policy for the region in the 1970s.

—However, this outline has as yet little operational significance, and we must await specific actions in order to assess the real implications of any new policy.

This is not really true:

—Our various statements are very significant, demonstrating a new tone and suggesting a new direction. However, if read literally, the proposed policy is not all that different from the rhetoric of past policy.

---

[1] Source: National Archives, RG 59, Policy Planning Staff Files: Lot 77 D 112, Director's Files, Selected Lord Memos. Confidential. The paper was sent to Kissinger on January 23 under a covering memorandum from Winston Lord of the NSC Staff. (Ibid.) No drafting information is provided but Lord's covering memorandum suggests that it was drafted by Lord or by Lindsey Grant, another Asian specialist on the NSC Staff. Kissinger subsequently returned the memorandum to Lord with the following handwritten comment: "Winston—I've read belatedly—1st class. How do you suggest we get policy resolutions of unresolved issues?"

—What is even more significant is the many concrete actions that we have already taken or plan to take which have us moving down a clear policy path. These actions, although often not taken with a strategic concept in mind, are already putting flesh on our pronouncements and demonstrating that there is indeed a significant new policy thrust.

We are beginning to implement what in the past we attempted only in part, paid lip service to, or postponed to a vague longer term. There are already many examples and they are beginning to form a consistent pattern, even if this has not been consciously constructed. In some cases our actions have been proposed to us by others—but we have not resisted as we might have previously. In other cases we are taking actions for reasons not primarily keyed to an Asian strategy—but they are consistent with our approach nevertheless. In many cases we are making moves with an awareness of the general direction they are taking us. We do not yet appear to be following any policies which are strikingly discordant with our overall approach. However, Laos—where we have yet to make a clear choice—holds the potential for a very serious diversion.

Major examples of concrete actions that are already reflecting and implementing the Nixon doctrine include:

—*Vietnam.* Turning the war over to the South Vietnamese and reducing American presence to a supporting role illustrate the precept that the target country bear the brunt of battle.

—*General Purpose Forces.* Our projected cut in post-Vietnam ready forces underlines the policy that our friends must provide the bulk of the manpower for their defense against non-nuclear aggression.

—*Japan.* The Nixon–Sato Communiqué[2] points up U.S.-Japanese partnership and the need for greater regional contributions by our ally.

—*Thailand, Philippines, Japan.* U.S. troop withdrawals and/or consolidation of bases lowers the American profile.

—*China.* Trade and travel moves, the Warsaw talks, neutrality in Sino-Soviet dispute punctuate our approach of diminishing confrontation, dealing with countries on the basis of their actions, not their ideology; we recognize Peking's impact on the region while we maintain our treaty commitments for Taiwan.

—*Cambodia.* Reestablishment of diplomatic relations was pragmatic step designed to improve communications and prevent misunderstandings.

---

[2] Reference is to the joint communiqué issued in Washington on November 21, 1969, at the conclusion of a 3-day State visit by Prime Minister Eisaku Sato. For text, see *Public Papers of the Presidents of the United States: Richard Nixon, 1969*, pp. 953–957.

—*Australia–New Zealand.* Our encouragement of their forward deployment in Malaysia–Singapore reflects our emphasis on allied contributions and regional cooperation.

—*Safeguard.* Protection against Chinese-scale attack is a component of our nuclear shield for Asia.

—*Overseas Reduction of U.S. Personnel.* The 10 percent cutback worldwide slims the American presence in Asia.

Therefore it is now moot to debate, as the forthcoming NSSM 38[3] on this subject does, whether we should continue to follow our past approach to Asia ("high strategy") or whether we should move to a lower profile and a more supporting role ("low strategy"). *This Administration is already set on the latter course, through actions as well as words.* What remains to be determined—and this of course is crucial—is how we manage the trend and cumulative impact of our policy and how we apply our new approach to the really tough questions that we will face in the 1970s.

Some Hard Issues for the 1970s

It is useful to run through the major components of our Asian approach and suggest some of the difficult questions that they could involve during the next decade. The following is by no means exhaustive and includes some relatively unlikely contingencies as well as predictable issues. There is no attempt to explore the questions in depth or recommend U.S. actions. In some cases the policy implications of our new approach seem clear. In many instances—unsurprisingly—the general guidelines don't give us the answer now. We cannot paint in all the factors in advance; a degree of ad hocism is necessary. This section is designed to locate some of the issues imbedded in our Asian policy components and to begin exploring their ramifications. These issues are not treated in any particular order of importance.

Commitments—The U.S. will keep all of its treaty commitments.

Issue: How do we interpret them when their fuzzy edges are involved?

"Commitment" is a slippery concept. Our actions on specific cases will be guided not by legal phrases but by an assessment of the significance of our interests involved and the nature of the threat. We have said we will "honor" our formal treaty obligations and these are imprecise in the areas where the definition of our interests is especially impre-

---

[3] Reference is to anticipated agency responses to NSSM 38, which on April 10, 1969, tasked the Departments of State and Defense and the CIA to assess post-Vietnam Asian policy. (National Archives, Nixon Presidential Materials, NSC Files, Box 365, Subject Files, National Security Study Memoranda (NSSMs) Nos 1–42)

cise. Some specific examples come to mind. Our defense obligations for the offshore islands have been purposely ambiguous to maintain our flexibility and keep Peking guessing. Our explicit commitment is to help defend Taiwan and the Penghus only. Presidential discretion is formally reserved for the offshore islands, which the U.S. would defend only if the President deems such action necessary to secure Taiwan/Penghus. There are no indications that Peking intends to move against the islands, but such a contingency is plausible in the 1970s, if, for example, the communists misread the reduction in our Taiwan Straits patrol. Our new Asian approach does not predict our reaction, especially if we are confronted with pressures like a blockade rather than a naked assault.

We have encouraged Australia and New Zealand to maintain ground and air forces in Malaysia and Singapore after 1971 when the British will have withdrawn. To date our allies have agreed to do so and have not pressed us very hard on the applicability of our ANZUS commitments to their forces in the Malaysia–Singapore area. However, Australian and New Zealand intentions are not firm and they continue to seek general reassurance of American help if their forces get into trouble. As 1971 draws near they could press us for more specific understandings under ANZUS (which obligates us only in the "Pacific area" as well as homelands) as the price for maintaining a forward presence. We would then have to weigh our objectives of regional cooperation and a greater allied defense role against the principle of no new "commitments." The threat to Malaysia–Singapore seems sufficiently remote and our aversion to new obligations sufficiently strong to suggest that we might forego the forward allied presence.

We are committed to defense of the Philippines, and the enemy need not be "communist". Presumably we would choose to stay out of Philippine hostilities with Malaysia over Sabah, but this could involve some bending of our mutual treaty.

Our obligation to defend South Korea is unambiguous. How would we interpret this obligation if our *allies* initiated hostilities or if it were at least clear that Seoul provoked Pyongyang? Such a contingency might look more likely if there were a substantial reduction in U.S. troops, and with it U.S. operational control, in South Korea.

Nuclear Policy—We will maintain a nuclear shield for our allies or for nations whose survival we consider vital to our security.

Issue: Which is the lesser of two evils—nuclear proliferation or the extension of more concrete American nuclear assurances?

India is likely to pose this issue. It has a nuclear capability, fears the Chinese and is very reluctant to sign the NPT. The obligations of the nuclear powers toward non-nuclear signatories of the NPT are imprecise. While suggesting their importance to countries like India we stressed their unimportance to Senators like Fulbright. Indian nationalism and the Chinese threat could induce New Delhi to demand from us (and the Soviets) much more explicit nuclear assurances as the price of nuclear abstention. We would have to choose between our objectives of non-proliferation of nuclear weapons and non-proliferation of U.S. "commitments".

Japan is the other prime nuclear candidate in Asia—it too is on the nuclear threshold and has been slow to sign the NPT. Unlike the Indian case, we cannot be much more explicit in our nuclear assurances for Japan. If it inclines towards the nuclear club it will mean that it is shedding its unique nuclear aversion and it prefers to assume its own defense against China. Such a development would be a function of growing Japanese nationalism/militarism and declining confidence in the American umbrella. Would this necessarily be against our long range interests? If so, what steps, if any, would we take—could we take—to keep Japan from going nuclear?

Conventional Aggression—We will assist our allies but expect them to provide the bulk of the manpower.

Issue: How do we square reaffirmation of treaty obligations with the reductions in our standing forces in Asia?

The NSSM 3[4] projected cutback in our ready divisions after Vietnam is a fundamental manifestation of the Nixon doctrine for Asia. It was based on a realistic downgrading of likely threats, the feeling that five or six divisions couldn't stop Chinese hordes anyway, the aversion to another Asian ground war, and the need for defense budget savings. We have recognized in effect that for Asia we have been spending a great deal of money for forces that we suspect are insufficient against a threat which we do not believe will materialize.

Closely related to the numbers of our Asian divisions is their deployment. Our main decision will be in South Korea where the return of capable ROK forces from Vietnam (if not before) will provide a logical opportunity to implement our new approach of greater allied self-reliance and a lower American profile by slicing our two divisions.

The fact remains that we are taking a gamble, albeit sensible and conscious. We judge conventional aggression in Asia to be both unlikely and containable by our allies, including in Korea where the threat is

---

[4] NSSM 3, issued on January 21, 1969, instructed the Departments of State and Defense and the CIA to analyze the U.S. military posture and the balance of power. (Ibid.)

most plausible. Reduction of our capabilities, however, at best will not decrease the threat of conventional aggression (although some would argue that a less "provocative" American posture could ease tensions). It might tempt potential adversaries. Our new Asian approach does not—cannot—instruct us in advance on how we would meet our treaty obligations and assist an overwhelmed ally when we have substantially less power than we do now. We would have to explore our options of military assistance, air and naval support, mobilization, tactical and strategic nuclear response.

Insurgency—U.S. supporting role only.

Issue: Would we ever provide American manpower—even where there is massive external intervention—so long as there were an indigenous movement?

Our public and background statements have all but ruled out the use of U.S. troops in any future insurgency. This is an unchallengeable policy where the conflict is wholly domestic, such as Malay-Chinese communal strife in Malaysia. Or where external support for the insurgency is clearly limited, such as Burma (where in addition we have little interest). Or where outside help, though significant, does not tip the scales against the target government, such as Thailand today.

Our new Asian approach is, however, obscure on those cases where massive external intervention shades the nature of the conflict from insurgency towards conventional aggression, such as happened at some point (whether before or after American intervention is debatable to say the least) in South Vietnam. Laos, with 50,000 North Vietnamese troops, and perhaps 5,000 Chinese, is the obvious present case. Our equivocation there reflects not only what we inherited in the past and the linkage with Vietnam but also our uncertainty about how to apply our Asian doctrine in the future. One doubts, for example, that a couple of years ago we would have displayed our current restraint on the Chinese road-building exercise. No one advocates committing American ground forces to Laos, but American manpower is there, however we may choose to label pilots and Meo advisers as non-combat personnel. We do not know what we will do if the enemy, who can overrun Laos if they wish, decide to do so. Our diplomatic and military maneuvers are designed to forestall this contingency, but if we fail we presumably will let Laos go rather than risking another Vietnam-type quagmire.

This would bring us of course to Thailand. A communist takeover of Laos could lead to greatly increased external support for the Thai insurgents. There might be the prospect of semi-conventional aggression, with thousands of North Vietnamese forces, Chinese advisers. In this situation Bangkok could present us with two choices: massive U.S.

reassurances or Thai accommodation with their adversaries. The former would have to consist of actions, such as increased military assistance and probably American deployments, as well as words, which would sound hollow to our ally after Vietnam and Laos. Our other option would be acquiescence in Thai overtures to Hanoi and Peking which would no doubt have to include Thai neutrality, renunciation of SEATO, and removal of all American bases and troops. Would this be more palatable than direct American intervention and would it be consistent with our new Asian approach?

Foreign Assistance and Trade—No clear policy yet.

Issue: Are increased aid levels and greater access to the American market necessary components of our new approach and are we willing to push a reluctant Congress on these matters?

Although we have not been precise on the point, increased assistance to our friends might seem to be a logical corollary to our moving toward a supportive, less conspicuous role. Reduction in the American presence, both in Vietnam and generally, will have both military and economic impact on various countries. We expect them to become more self-reliant, but at least for certain countries for a certain transitional period compensatory American assistance might be in order. This need runs up against a Congress that has steadily whittled down Presidential requests for foreign assistance. A coherent Administration approach and strong Presidential leadership will be required. Perhaps the political and budgetary appeal of a leaner American deployment abroad will produce Congressional support for the aid levels needed to ease the way. However, if Congress remains balky, we might face choices on slowing down our Asian slimming process or running some security, political or economic risks in the area. This general problem will translate into specific issues such as which countries should receive priority; the tradeoffs between military and economic assistance; the proper use of Vietnam surpluses, etc.

Our future emphasis on Asian prescriptions has relevance for our aid programs. This emphasis suggests that we will encourage Asian nations (and regional groupings) to fashion their own security and development needs and then come to us with their proposals. Aside from aid levels and priority recipients, we might face some sticky questions concerning the nature of the proposed hardware or projects. As donor—but less as seller—of the goods and services, we obviously have a strong say on what transactions make sense. Nevertheless our new themes of Asian initiative and Asian definition may make it more awkward for us than now to turn down a request for a jet plane (which *we* don't think fits the country's security needs) or a steel mill (which *we* think deserves a lower priority) that the recipient country deems important. It would be more awkward still if a regional grouping presented the request. For economic assistance, we can often use multilateral groups—such as the IBRD or ADB—as a buffer; we cannot do so on military requests.

Our aid and trade policies are closely related, and we face some tough Asian trade issues in the 1970s. The goal of our aid program is to help developing countries stand on their own: Taiwan is a recent graduate, Korea a prospective one. Both are prospering, bolstered by healthy exports in fields our aid programs have encouraged. Their economic performances rely heavily on the American market as our textile manufacturers well know. They will in any event need to find new markets for their expanding exports, but restricting their access to our own greatly exacerbates their difficulties. So will the fading of economic stimuli from the Vietnam War. There may be good domestic reasons for limiting our imports from our friends, but such a policy clashes with our aid policy and our objectives of greater Asian development and self-reliance.

Alliances—No changes.

Issue: What do we do about SEATO?

Our approach to our non-SEATO formal Asian alliances seems relatively clear. We will continue to maintain them—and negotiate their terms if necessary—on the basis of mutual perceptions of national interest. Thus the joint reaffirmation of U.S.-Japanese ties and the upcoming adjustments in our Philippine arrangements. Our formal ties with Korea present no immediate issue. As already noted, possible problems with Taiwan concern the offshore islands, with ANZUS the Malaysia–Singapore area.

Our handling of SEATO is less clear. It is essentially an anachronism, designed against unlikely threats, filled with unenthusiastic members. Its main purpose is to cover our defense obligations to Thailand. French and Pakistani membership are meaningless, the British almost so. What would be our reaction if any or all of these countries decide to leave SEATO? Presumably we would acquiesce in their definition of their national interest, but the exodus would prompt a debate about the future of the organization. Our Philippine and ANZUS treaties cover the SEATO Asian members except Thailand, where our formal commitment remains multilateral, although the 1962 Rusk–Thanat communiqué[5] stipulated that we would be prepared to

---

[5] Secretary of State Rusk and Thai Foreign Minister Thanat Khoman issued a joint communiqué in Washington on March 6, 1962, at the conclusion of a visit by Thanat to the United States. The communiqué addressed the related issues of the SEATO treaty and the security of Thailand. For text, see *American Foreign Policy: Current Documents, 1962*, pp. 1091–1093.

act on our own if necessary. The Thai recently professed unhappiness with the organization, but they have done this before to reflect uneasiness over U.S. intentions; when pressed by Vice President Agnew they backed off from their threat to opt out of SEATO.

There is little inclination from any quarter to attempt to revitalize SEATO, find new tasks for it or draw other Asian nations into the organization. Any fresh regional security efforts will flow from Asian initiatives, perhaps evolving from existing economic and technical groupings like ASEAN. Thus our options on SEATO boil down to either maintaining its facade of a multilateral commitment to Thailand or dismantling the alliance and making our Thai commitment strictly bilateral. Secretary Rogers' attendance and statements at the SEATO Ministerial last spring were essentially a holding action. The Vice-President was more positive about the organization in Thailand. As our Asian doctrine continues to be fleshed out we will have to decide on our SEATO policy in the context of our overall approach to Asian regional security and our relationship with Bangkok.

Regionalism—We welcome and support.

Issue: To what extent do we attempt actively to promote regional cooperation?

Being against regionalism is like being against motherhood. We have always endorsed the principle of regional cooperation, with the major policy questions centering on the extent to which we led and shaped regional efforts. We are now set on a more reactive and supportive course where we will encourage Asian leadership. However, our encouragement can take many forms. For example, we recently tried to relate prospective arms sales to Singapore to its cooperation with Malaysia and to regional Commonwealth defense efforts with Australia, New Zealand and the UK. This proved somewhat premature and we have backed off from anything more than suggesting that Singapore keep its partners informed.

This minor issue shadows significant future decisions wherein we will have to weigh other countries' national prerogatives and U.S. restraint against our desire to encourage regionalism. Will we balk at an Asian country's prescription when it appears to undercut regional cooperation? Will we try to induce regionalism through our assistance policies even though this suggests a more aggressive American role in shaping Asian ventures? Does our emphasis on Asian initiative mean that we merely sit back and wait for regional groupings to get together, no matter how faltering the pace, or will we be prepared to make suggestions to promote their cooperation?

Japan is at the center of any discussion on Asian regionalism. Our policy, culminating in the Nixon–Sato communiqué, has been to prod our ally towards a leadership role in the region that reflects its dominant power, in part to relieve us of some of our responsibilities. We know that we want Japan to increase its economic assistance, its political clout, even its self-defense capacity. We do not know the degree to which we want Japan to participate or take the lead in regional security efforts. Are we—and the rest of Asia—not too close to World War II to contemplate easily a remilitarized Japan? Even a strong Japanese economic and military presence could disturb other Asians. For example, Indonesian Foreign Minister Malik has just told our Ambassador of his apprehension over Japan's growing influence in the region. Certain aspects of Sato's speech to the National Press Club might be interpreted as an impulse toward a U.S.-Japanese blueprint for Asia. We will need to avoid suggestions that our two countries might play the type of dominant regional role that could disturb other Asian countries and would clash with our new doctrine of Asian self-expression.

The Quadrilateral Relationship of Major Asian Powers—No clear policy yet.

Issue: How do we reconcile our policies toward China, Japan, and the Soviet Union?

The interaction of the four great powers in Asia will clearly be crucial, and our policies toward any one of them will have to take into account the impact on the others. Several factors converge to highlight the quadrilateral relationship. These include:

—The general shift in the Asian scene from bipolar confrontation between united blocs toward multipolarity and regionalism.

—Movement in our China policy which will bring into play both the Soviets and the Japanese.

—The Sino-Soviet dispute which makes both communist nations especially sensitive to Japanese and American designs.

—The growing Soviet interest in Asia, including its vague collective security scheme.

—The growing power of Japan and the new U.S.-Japanese partnership whose future health depends greatly on how the two allies manage China policy.

—Japan's conflicting historical, political, and commercial interests in both mainland China and Taiwan.

—Japan's ambivalent relations with the Soviet Union which include the northern territories question and possible Siberian interests.

In the past we have generally focused on our bilateral relationships, although lately we have been sensitive to the U.S.-USSR-China triangle. Japan must clearly be brought into the equations from here on out.

New Neutralism—No clear policy yet.

Issue: What kind of Asia are we prepared to see?

This is a fundamental question that lurks behind all the other issues. It is not the same as asking what kind of Asia we want. While we can influence events, we cannot control, nor do we wish to prescribe, the region's future.

The cumulative impact of the Nixon doctrine—implemented against the backdrop of a world-weary American public, Congressional assertiveness and domestic problems—could move certain of our Asian allies toward neutralism. The doctrine has some suggestive ingredients —our reluctance to commit manpower, fewer U.S. forces and bases, gestures toward Peking, lower American profile.

Are we willing to witness an evolution toward neutralism in Asia? What would this concept mean? Is it a pattern we can or should be trying to encourage? If not, why not? If so, how?

---

55.   Editorial Note

During a conversation in the Oval Office of the White House on January 27, 1970, President Nixon and British Prime Minister Harold Wilson discussed arms control negotiations in the context of the rift between China and the Soviet Union. The President said: "We are taking the line that we cannot have one billion Chinese sitting outside the international community. Dobrynin says this is a dirty trick, but we will move at our pace and in our direction. Some of the Kremlinologists believe we should stonewall the Chinese lest we irritate the Russians, but the SALT talks prove we can talk to the Russians and to the Chinese simultaneously.

"The President then turned to a discussion of ABM and MIRV. He said we won't pay any advance price to get a SALT settlement, but we were very flexible in the SALT discussions. 'You know and I know', he said, 'that it is essential that we don't have a nuclear blowup. You recognize that better than any other world leader.' The Prime Minister said that the Soviet military leaders have more power than the military in our own countries. The President said our line at the talks is this: First, we want agreement; we want to be forthcoming. Second, we won't give up any cards in advance. On Vietnam, he said, our best position is to accept Russian help, but not to ask for it. They won't help us because we ask them; they will help us because they will face the necessity.

"Returning to SALT, the President said that before talks began he had had very little optimism. Now he thinks there's a chance they may need a control on arms because of their problem with the Chinese. A situation may be arising where self-interest requires give and take.

"He then asked Wilson to comment on the possibilities for a détente. Wilson said he agreed with everything the President had said, and added that anything that makes the Soviet Union swallow their words on Germany is harder than either on ABM or Vietnam. We have told Kosygin, Wilson continued, that the Common Market may be a good way to contain Germany.

"Wilson said he had the impression that the President, through his very subtle China policy, was trying to use China to ruffle the back hair of the Soviets. The President said we just don't want them to take us for granted." (Memorandum of conversation; National Archives, Nixon Presidential Materials, NSC Files, Box 1024, Presidential/HAK Memcons, Memcon: Nixon–Prime Minister Wilson Jan 27, 1970)

---

56.   Editorial Note

At a National Security Council meeting on January 28, 1970, with British Prime Minister Wilson attending, President Nixon emphasized the importance of coordinating with Western European allies in formulating an approach to the Soviet Union:

"Often we read that the columnists say that Europe does not really matter. What is needed is for the United States and the Soviet Union to sit down and cool the whole process. If this means cooling relations with our Western European friends they say, then so be it. If it means antagonizing China—again, so be it.

"As I said in February and again in August, I reject this approach categorically. First, there is no reduction of our NATO commitment. Certainly this can be a matter for negotiation, but we cannot reduce our level of commitment except on a mutual basis. Second, on Soviet-US relations, there is not a lack of interest in finding an arrangement, but it is vitally important to establish a relationship within the Alliance. We must know what we are going to talk about before getting into summitry."

Later in the discussion, Nixon outlined his support for the development of a strong, independent European community which could provide "friendly competition" for the United States:

"I have never been one who believes the US should have control of the actions of Europe. It is in the interests of the United States to have a strong economic, political and military European community, with the United Kingdom in that community. I have preferred that Europe move independently, going parallel with the United States. A strong, healthy and independent Europe is good for the balance of the world. For the US to play a heavy-handed role would be counter-productive. What we want is friendly competition with the United States." (Minutes of NSC meeting; National Security Council, Secretariat Files, NSC Meeting Minutes, Originals, 1970)

---

57.   Memorandum From President Nixon to His Assistant for National Security Affairs (Kissinger)[1]

Washington, February 10, 1970.

A general reaction to the State of the World message[2] is that it might be strengthened to knock down the assumption that is gaining disturbing currency abroad and in the United States—that this Administration is on an irreversible course of not only getting out of Vietnam but of reducing our commitments around the world. I realize that this thesis is answered in several places with phrases like "This is not a retreat from our obligations but a sharing of obligations," but this is not enough. I think high up in the lead of the introductory statement should be some strong assertions to the effect that the United States recognizes that because of our economic and military position the fate of freedom and peace in the last third of this century will depend upon how we meet our responsibilities in the world. We did not ask for this role but now because the force of circumstances has imposed it upon us we shall meet our responsibilities. However, we believe that our goal of nations

---

[1] Source: National Archives, Nixon Presidential Materials, NSC Files, Box 325, President's Annual Review of U.S. Foreign Policy, 2/8/70, Vol. I. No classification marking.

[2] Reference is to the foreign policy report submitted to Congress on February 18; see Document 60.

living in independence and freedom in a peaceful world will be better achieved if other nations assume responsibilities to the extent of their capabilities just as we do.

In other words, get back to my theme that the Nixon doctrine rather than being a device to get rid of America's world role is one which is devised to make it possible for us to play a role—and play it better, more effectively than if we continued the policy of the past in which we assume such a dominant position. I would suggest that you take a look at the Colorado Springs speech[3]—some of the tone and strength of that speech on this issue is very much needed in the introductory portion.

I realize that your staff may well object to this because the peacenik types who will be primarily the reading audience for this report will want to find any evidences possible which will give comfort to their feeling that "the United States should reduce its world role and start taking care of the ghettoes instead of worrying about Afghanistan."

For over twenty years, however, I have been saying "that we can have the best social programs in the world—ones that will end poverty, clean up our air, water and land, provide minimum income, etc., and it isn't going to make any difference if we are not around to enjoy it." I am not suggesting that this be put into the report in such specific, blunt terms but the *thought* must be put in just as strongly because I feel that the people of the country and even more so our troubled allies in Asia and Europe, as well as our potential enemies, need to hear this.

·

---

[3] See Document 27.

58. White House Background Press Briefing by the President's Assistant for National Security Affairs (Kissinger)[1]

Washington, February 16, 1970.

[Omitted here are White House Press Secretary Ron Ziegler's introduction of Kissinger, Richardson, and Packard, and Kissinger's comments on specific references in the President's report.]

Q. Dr. Kissinger, the President used the word "watershed" in introducing this briefing this afternoon.[2] If I understand watershed correctly, it means a separation, division, going in a new direction. I have not had a chance to read this. What are the watershed points in this foreign policy statement?

Dr. Kissinger: What the President meant is the fact that there now exists a comprehensive, philosophical statement of American foreign policy. It makes it clear that for better or worse our policies are not simply tactical responses to immediate situations, but that there exists a coherent picture of the world; that we are taking our action in relation to this picture; and that this document outlines his experience in foreign policy, national security policy and his expectations for the future.

So whatever debate is generated by this would have to be in terms of a general concept of foreign policy and not simply in terms of tactical responses to immediate situations.

Secondly, it is his belief and it is the Administration's belief that we are reaching the end of the post-war era, the end of the post-war era in the sense that in the immediate period after World War II the United States, among the non-Communist countries, was the only one that had emerged from the war with its society and its economy relatively intact. Therefore, it was natural that the United States would assume a predominant role anyplace where it felt that security of the non-Communist world was threatened.

---

[1] Source: Library of Congress, Manuscript Division, Kissinger Papers, Box CL 425, Subject File, Background Briefings, Feb–June 1970. Kissinger, Under Secretary of State Elliot Richardson, and Deputy Secretary of Defense David Packard were responding to questions concerning an advance text of the President's report to Congress on foreign policy, which had been distributed to reporters. The report was sent to Congress on February 18; see Document 60. Kissinger opened the briefing.

[2] In his remarks to the reporters, President Nixon characterized the report to Congress, which ran to some 40,000 words, as "the most comprehensive statement on foreign and defense policy ever made in this country." As such, he styled it "a watershed in American foreign policy." (*Public Papers of the Presidents of the United States: Richard Nixon, 1970*, p. 114)

This, in turn, imposed on us the requirement that we were trying to remedy immediate crisis situations rather than deal with the overall structure of peace, or, rather, we identified the overall structure of peace with the solution of immediate crisis.

This is ending now for a number of reasons. It is ending, according to this document and our convictions, because many other parts of the world have now regained a degree of cohesion, have grown into independence, which was, of course, not the case at the end of World War II, and are capable of assuming a greater responsibility, both for their security and for their problems.

In these conditions, the United States should not be the fireman running from one conflagration to the other, but can address itself to the longer-term problems of a peaceful international structure and leave to local responsibilities the immediate task of construction.

In other words, the United States will participate where it can make a difference. It will attempt to contribute to the creation of regional organization where that is appropriate, but the United States in this new era will have to change its position from one of predominance to one of partnership.

Now, we recognize—and to pick up a point that the President made in introducing this report—that there is a danger that in moving from predominance to partnership some people may believe that we are moving towards disengagement or returning to isolation. This is not the philosophy of this Administration.

The philosophy of this Administration is to find a basis for a long-term engagement in the world, one that is consistent with the realities of the contemporary world, one that we can sustain over an indefinite period of time, and one that will give an impetus to our foreign policy of the same order that the Marshall Plan conception did to the conditions of 1947. Those conceptions were appropriate to the realities of the '40s and '50s and early '60s and we are attempting to find conceptions that are appropriate to the realities of the '70s.

[Omitted here are exchanges with reporters about questions arising from the report.]

Q. Dr. Kissinger, I am not sure from all of this whether you think the Cold War is increasing or lessening. Do you think it is increasing or lessening from this broad philosophical statement?

Dr. Kissinger: The Cold War, as it came to be known in the immediate post-war period, we would say has in that forum lessened. At that time, there was a belief in a monolithic communism, and that no longer exists in this forum.

At that time, there was a belief in the notion of irreconcilable hostility. On the other hand, we believe that there are objective causes for the tension that has existed over this period. We believe that we are doing no one a service by pretending that these tensions do not exist or that they can be removed by mere atmospherics.

We are prepared to negotiate seriously, either individually or comprehensively, on these issues with either of the great Communist countries. And, therefore, the foreign policy that was appropriate to the period that was called the Cold War is not appropriate to the period into which we believe we are now entering.

But we make this statement without under-estimating that there are still serious causes of tension, that ideology is not dead, even though it has changed some of its character, and that large areas of potential discord and of hostility remain. But we are prepared to work seriously, and as energetically as we can.

[Omitted here is the remainder of the briefing, which ranged over questions relating to SALT negotiations and developments in the Middle East, Latin America, and Vietnam.]

---

59.   Memorandum From the President's Special Assistant
       (Buchanan) to President Nixon[1]

Washington, February 18, 1970.

Notes from Legislative Leadership Meeting[2]
Tuesday, February 17, 1970

The bulk of the leadership meeting was devoted to discussion of the State of the World message[3] which Dr. Kissinger outlined in extensive and brilliant detail.

---

[1] Source: National Archives, Nixon Presidential Materials, White House Special Files, President's Office Files, Box 80, Memoranda for the President, Jan 4–May 31, 1970. No classification marking.

[2] The meeting with Republican Congressional leaders was held in the Cabinet Room of the White House from 8:34 to 10:51 a.m. Six Senators and nine Representatives attended. In addition to the President, Vice President Agnew, Secretary of Health, Education and Welfare Robert Finch, and nine members of the White House staff, including Haldeman and Kissinger, were also present. (Ibid., White House Central Files, Staff Members and Office Files, Office of Presidential Papers and Archives, Daily Diary)

[3] Reference is to the report submitted to Congress on February 18; see Document 60.

The President opened the discussion by saying his message would cover foreign and defense policy of the entire world. It was in effect 40,000 words of policy. He described it as the most important statement made by this Administration; that all our foreign and defense policies had been gathered together in one place, that there would be a summary of 3,000 words, and a briefing had been held on the total message and one would be held this afternoon for the bipartisan leadership. The message had been put together over many weeks. It had been put into its final form over the weekend in Key Biscayne. The President described it as interesting reading, and not hard reading.

Henry outlined the extensive message and his discussion took about three quarters of an hour. At the end of it, the President interjected a number of comments in response to some points that had been raised. On Japan for example, the President said it was absolutely indispensable for political reasons that we train troops in Japan, and that we have some U.S. forces there. In the event that China should try to take on Japan, we would not, of course, try to fight it out with conventional forces. The purpose of the troops was to maintain the U.S. presence and involvement in the security of Japan.

Moving on to another point, the President said unless the United States does play a role in the world, if, for example, the United States should return home, the rest of the world in his opinion would come under Communist domination.

One of the questions we answered, he said, is how we can meet our responsibilities without draining ourselves economically and psychologically. The purpose of this foreign policy is to find a way to stay in the world, not a way to get out of the world. The message puts great responsibility indirectly in its language on the other nations of the free world to do more in their own behalf. They must assume an increasing share of the burden of their own defense, said the President. Returning to Japan, he said that while admittedly some time ago there was a good deal of reluctance on the part of the Japanese to involve themselves in world affairs, he wouldn't be surprised if "in five years we didn't have to restrain them." They have gone through a traumatic period since the bomb dropped, he said. Now they are going to do something.

The President indicated that he felt that in Asia the major counterforce to China should not be the U.S. but Japan. He indicated that both the Chinese and the Soviets recognized this; there had been far more interest in the cables on the part of the Chinese and Russians in the reversion of Okinawa to Japan than any other facet of US policy in the area.

Discussion of the difference between soft line and hard line began, and the President said he would consider this policy neither. It is more a pragmatic and realistic line, a peace line. He said in the past it has been his experience that the soft line has led to war more often than the hard line. He can recall some two or three occasions in the post-war era when a soft line resulted in a war where he could not recall a single incident where a hard line had.

The President eschewed gushy optimism of any kind. He said that some Americans think that we can rely on peace by sending a few Fulbright scholars abroad or even Fulbright himself, but that doesn't bring peace. We can avoid war if we are realistic and not soft-headed, he indicated.

As for Laird's report on Vietnam after his return,[4] the President described it in a single word: encouraging.

Moving on to the Middle East, he said that many American politicians took it that it should be the basis of American foreign policy the simple question of whether or not Israel is to survive. That cannot be the basis of American foreign policy, he said. The interest of the US policy in the Middle East is designed to advance the United States interests primarily. Those interests involve vital stakes in the Mediterranean and Iran; they involve oil interests in the Arab world; they also are coincidental with the survival of Israel as a state. For one hard reason the Israelis are currently the strongest buffer against Soviet expansion in the entire region.

The President asked what the Soviet objectives in the Middle East were, and answered his own question. They want control of the Middle East; they want the oil it contains; they want a land bridge to Africa. Looking over the Middle East, the President said Tunis is too weak to matter. Morocco is distant, out on the Atlantic Coast, and you know what happened in Libya. Algeria, the UAR, Syria, Iraq, the Sudan are all either under great Soviet pressure or Soviet influence at this time. As for Spain, it has been relegated to outer darkness until Franco's death. Italy is paying now for the opening to the left of a few years back, which the President had opposed. We intend to see to it that Israel is not overrun for the reason that Israel is the current most effective stopper to the Mideast power of the Soviet Union. Our policy, said the President, will not be pleasing to some of our political friends. But it is not in Israel's interest for American policy to be one sided. Israel ought to make a deal when it is strong enough to whip anyone in the Middle East and will be strong enough for the next five years. The President said he indicated to

---

[4] Secretary of Defense Laird visited South Vietnam February 10–17. He submitted a report on his trip to the President on February 17. The report is in the National Archives, Nixon Presidential Materials, NSC Files, Box 224, Agency Files, DOD, Vol. IV, 1 Feb 70–20 April 70; it is scheduled for publication in *Foreign Relations*, 1969–1976, Vietnam, 1969–1970.

Golda Meir when she was in the country that he had only gotten 8% of the Jewish vote and he was supporting the Israelis not for political reasons for the first time in recent history. He was supporting Israel because it was in the interest of the United States to do so.

[Omitted here is discussion of a visit to the United States by French President Pompidou.]

Discussion was now brought up of the withdrawal of all American forces. The President said he thought the withdrawal of all American forces from Europe, for example, would be very detrimental policy. At the very least we ought to retain a "trip-wire." He said there is a significant shift indicated in this statement. We are telling all Asia and Europe they must do more on their part and we are going to do less on our part. Griffin[5] indicated the President should emphasize how he has reorganized and taken control of policy development. Taft[6] asked what effect it has on the National Commitments Resolution.[7] I have no precise response on that.

Another point made by Dr. Kissinger was that we are being "absolutely candid" with the American people on this. With regard to someone recommending the proposal for mutual cooperation in Latin America, Kissinger indicated it should not be the US proposition for "if it is a US proposal, it tends to be counter-productive." In other words, the countries of Latin America tend to reject out of hand something that bears the American stamp of American initiative. The President indicated that he would hope Congressmen would pick out eight or ten points to be drawn from the message by Safire and Kissinger and others and repeat these points in speeches around the country.

Allott[8] now returned to the Mansfield resolutions.[9] He said that the NATO countries had not, were not, and are not doing their share and there was a general feeling in the Senate that the only way they could be forced to do so is for the reduction of American contribution to the

---

[5] Senator Robert Griffin of Michigan.

[6] Representative Robert Taft of Ohio.

[7] The National Commitments Resolution was a non-binding resolution adopted by the Senate on June 25, 1969, which defined a national commitment and expressed the sense of the Senate that a commitment could only result from a treaty, statute, or concurrent resolution of both Houses of Congress providing for such a commitment. As defined by the resolution, a national commitment involved the promise or use of U.S. financial resources or armed forces to assist a foreign country. S. Res. 85 is summarized in the *Congressional Quarterly Almanac*, Vol. XXV, pp. 178–181.

[8] Senator Gordon Allott of Colorado.

[9] Reference is apparently to the resolution introduced in the Senate on December 1, 1969, by Senate Majority Leader Mike Mansfield which called for a "substantial reduction" of U.S. troops in Europe. Mansfield had initially introduced this resolution in 1966. S. Res. 292 is summarized in *Congressional Quarterly Almanac*, Vol. XXV, p. 999.

effort. Allott said this is the feeling that has to be considered when you take into account the vast American investment in places like France and the pipeline arrangement we put into France and our difficulty in getting satisfaction. The President said this is a difficult problem, but if the US were to withdraw now under the pressure of this resolution, the whole thing (NATO) would unravel. On the other hand, we do have a new attitude. And we must remember we are there in Europe not to defend Germany or Italy or France or England, we are in Europe to save our own hides.

Returning again to the Middle East, he said as for Israel, it's a pretty weak argument when we say we are supporting Israel for simply political reasons. The strongest foundation for our support is that it is in our national interest.

Again to the Mansfield Resolution to bring home troops from Europe, if they pass the resolution to bring home two divisions, said the President, it would have a detrimental impact. We may do it ourselves, but we have to do it our way.

The President then summarized a number of points that he had taken since his Administration had begun that should be emphasized in speeches. First, his new control and coordination of planning and foreign policy. Second, there has been no major crisis with the Soviet Union. Third, there is normalization of relations with Japan after the reversion of Okinawa. Fourth, steps have been taken in CBW warfare. Five, the Middle East's problems were inherited. Six, we have reopened lines of communication with Communist China. For a number of reasons we have done this "which have nothing to do whatever with what we think of them." The President had made successful visits to Asia and Europe which could not have been done under the previous administration. We have put relations in Western Europe on a new perspective. We have re-established contact with General DeGaulle, and from that contact come our current discussions with Georges Pompidou.

[Omitted here is discussion of domestic issues.]

60.   Report by President Nixon to the Congress[1]

Washington, February 18, 1970.

U.S. FOREIGN POLICY FOR THE 1970s:
A NEW STRATEGY FOR PEACE

Introduction

"A nation needs many qualities, but it needs faith and confidence above all. Skeptics do not build societies; the idealists are the builders. Only societies that believe in themselves can rise to their challenges. Let us not, then, pose a false choice between meeting our responsibilities abroad and meeting the needs of our people at home. We shall meet both or we shall meet neither."

—The President's Remarks at the Air Force Academy Commencement, June 4, 1969.[2]

When I took office, the most immediate problem facing our nation was the war in Vietnam. No question has more occupied our thoughts and energies during this past year.

Yet the fundamental task confronting us was more profound. We could see that the whole pattern of international politics was changing. Our challenge was to understand that change, to define America's goals

---

[1] Source: *Public Papers of the Presidents of the United States: Richard Nixon, 1970*, pp. 116–190. The report, the first annual report on foreign policy, was transmitted to Congress under a covering letter signed by Nixon. (Ibid., p. 115)

According to Henry Kissinger's memoirs, the idea of preparing a comprehensive report on foreign policy originated with a memorandum Kissinger sent to the President-elect shortly before the new administration took office. Kissinger envisioned a document that would "serve as a conceptual outline of the President's foreign policy, as a status report, and as an agenda for action." He anticipated that it would "simultaneously guide our bureaucracy and inform foreign governments about our thinking." (*White House Years,* p. 158) President Nixon approved the concept on January 30, 1969. (Chronology attached to a memorandum from Haig to Kissinger, February 12, 1970; National Archives, Nixon Presidential Materials, NSC Files, Box 148, Kissinger Office Files, State-WH Relationship) On October 27 Kissinger sent NSSM 80 to the Secretaries of State, Defense, and the Treasury, and the Director of Central Intelligence directing on the President's behalf the preparation of an unclassifed annual report on foreign policy. Kissinger indicated that the report to be submitted to Congress should be analogous to the Defense Posture Statement previously submitted to Congress by Secretary of Defense McNamara. (Ibid., Box 365, Subject Files, National Security Study Memoranda, NSSMs 43–103) Additional documentation on the preparation of the annual report is ibid., Boxes 325–326, Subject Files, The President's Annual Review of U.S. Foreign Policy, and ibid., NSC Secretariat Files, Boxes 1303–1309, Richard M. Nixon Annual Review 1970–1974.

[2] See Document 27.

for the next period, and to set in motion policies to achieve them. For all Americans must understand that because of its strength, its history and its concern for human dignity, this nation occupies a special place in the world. Peace and progress are impossible without a major American role.

This first annual report on U.S. foreign policy is more than a record of one year. It is this Administration's statement of a new approach to foreign policy to match a new era of international relations.

A New Era

The postwar period in international relations has ended.

Then, we were the only great power whose society and economy had escaped World War II's massive destruction. Today, the ravages of that war have been overcome. Western Europe and Japan have recovered their economic strength, their political vitality, and their national self-confidence. Once the recipients of American aid, they have now begun to share their growing resources with the developing world. Once almost totally dependent on American military power, our European allies now play a greater role in our common policies, commensurate with their growing strength.

Then, new nations were being born, often in turmoil and uncertainty. Today, these nations have a new spirit and a growing strength of independence. Once, many feared that they would become simply a battleground of cold-war rivalry and fertile ground for Communist penetration. But this fear misjudged their pride in their national identities and their determination to preserve their newly won sovereignty.

Then, we were confronted by a monolithic Communist world. Today, the nature of that world has changed—the power of individual Communist nations has grown, but international Communist unity has been shattered. Once a unified bloc, its solidarity has been broken by the powerful forces of nationalism. The Soviet Union and Communist China, once bound by an alliance of friendship, had become bitter adversaries by the mid-1960's. The only times the Soviet Union has used the Red Army since World War II have been against its own allies—in East Germany in 1953, in Hungary in 1956, and in Czechoslovakia in 1968. The Marxist dream of international Communist unity has disintegrated.

Then, the United States had a monopoly or overwhelming superiority of nuclear weapons. Today, a revolution in the technology of war has altered the nature of the military balance of power. New types of weapons present new dangers. Communist China has acquired thermonuclear weapons. Both the Soviet Union and the United States have acquired the ability to inflict unacceptable damage on the other, no matter which strikes first. There can be no gain and certainly no victory for the power that provokes a thermonuclear exchange. Thus, both sides have recognized a vital mutual interest in halting the dangerous momentum of the nuclear arms race.

Then, the slogans formed in the past century were the ideological accessories of the intellectual debate. Today the "isms" have lost their vitality—indeed the restlessness of youth on both sides of the dividing line testifies to the need for a new idealism and deeper purposes.

This is the challenge and the opportunity before America as it enters the 1970's.

The Framework for a Durable Peace

In the first postwar decades, American energies were absorbed in coping with a cycle of recurrent crises, whose fundamental origins lay in the destruction of World War II and the tensions attending the emergence of scores of new nations. Our opportunity today—and challenge—is to get at the causes of crises, to take a longer view, and to help build the international relationships that will provide the framework of a durable peace.

I have often reflected on the meaning of "peace," and have reached one certain conclusion: Peace must be far more than the absence of war. Peace must provide a durable structure of international relationships which inhibits or removes the causes of war. Building a lasting peace requires a foreign policy guided by three basic principles:

—Peace requires *partnership*. Its obligations, like its benefits, must be shared. This concept of partnership guides our relations with all friendly nations.

—Peace requires *strength*. So long as there are those who would threaten our vital interests and those of our allies with military force, we must be strong. American weakness could tempt would-be aggressors to make dangerous miscalculations. At the same time, our own strength is important only in relation to the strength of others. We—like others—must place high priority on enhancing our security through cooperative arms control.

—Peace requires a *willingness to negotiate*. All nations—and we are no exception—have important national interests to protect. But the most fundamental interest of all nations lies in building the structure of peace. In partnership with our allies, secure in our own strength, we will seek those areas in which we can agree among ourselves and with others to accommodate conflicts and overcome rivalries. We are working toward the day when *all* nations will have a stake in peace, and will therefore be partners in its maintenance.

Within such a structure, international disputes can be settled and clashes contained. The insecurity of nations, out of which so much conflict arises, will be eased, and the habits of moderation and compromise will be nurtured. Most important, a durable peace will give full opportunity to the powerful forces driving toward economic change and social justice.

This vision of a peace built on partnership, strength and willingness to negotiate is the unifying theme of this report. In the sections that follow, the first steps we have taken during this past year—the policies we have devised and the programs we have initiated to realize this vision—are placed in the context of these three principles.

I. Peace Through Partnership—The Nixon Doctrine

As I said in my address of November 3,[3] "We Americans are a do-it-yourself people—an impatient people. Instead of teaching someone else to do a job, we like to do it ourselves. This trait has been carried over into our foreign policy."

The postwar era of American foreign policy began in this vein in 1947 with the proclamation of the Truman Doctrine and the Marshall Plan, offering American economic and military assistance to countries threatened by aggression. Our policy held that democracy and prosperity, buttressed by American military strength and organized in a worldwide network of American-led alliances, would insure stability and peace. In the formative years of the postwar period, this great effort of international political and economic reconstruction was a triumph of American leadership and imagination, especially in Europe.

For two decades after the end of the Second World War, our foreign policy was guided by such a vision and inspired by its success. The vision was based on the fact that the United States was the richest and most stable country, without whose initiative and resources little security or progress was possible.

This impulse carried us through into the 1960's. The United States conceived programs and ran them. We devised strategies, and proposed them to our allies. We discerned dangers, and acted directly to combat them.

The world has dramatically changed since the days of the Marshall Plan. We deal now with a world of stronger allies, a community of independent developing nations, and a Communist world still hostile but now divided.

Others now have the ability and responsibility to deal with local disputes which once might have required our intervention. Our contri-

---

[3] Reference is to a televised address on the war in Vietnam. For text, see *Public Papers of the Presidents of the United States: Richard Nixon, 1969*, pp. 901–909.

bution and success will depend not on the frequency of our involvement in the affairs of others, but on the stamina of our policies. This is the approach which will best encourage other nations to do their part, and will most genuinely enlist the support of the American people.

This is the message of the doctrine I announced at Guam—the "Nixon Doctrine." Its central thesis is that the United States will participate in the defense and development of allies and friends, but that America cannot—and will not—conceive *all* the plans, design *all* the programs, execute *all* the decisions and undertake *all* the defense of the free nations of the world. We will help where it makes a real difference and is considered in our interest.

America cannot live in isolation if it expects to live in peace. We have no intention of withdrawing from the world. The only issue before us is how we can be most effective in meeting our responsibilities, protecting our interests, and thereby building peace.

A more responsible participation by our foreign friends in their own defense and progress means a more effective common effort toward the goals we all seek. Peace in the world will continue to require us to maintain our commitments—and we will. As I said at the United Nations,[4] "It is not my belief that the way to peace is by giving up our friends or letting down our allies." But a more balanced and realistic American role in the world is essential if American commitments are to be sustained over the long pull. In my State of the Union Address,[5] I affirmed that "to insist that other nations play a role is not a retreat from responsibility; it is a sharing of responsibility." This is not a way for America to withdraw from its indispensable role in the world. It is a way—the only way—we can carry out our responsibilities.

It is misleading, moreover, to pose the fundamental question so largely in terms of commitments. Our objective, in the first instance, is to support our *interests* over the long run with a sound foreign policy. The more that policy is based on a realistic assessment of our and others' interests, the more effective our role in the world can be. We are not involved in the world because we have commitments; we have commitments because we are involved. Our interests must shape our commitments, rather than the other way around.

We will view new commitments in the light of a careful assessment of our own national interests and those of other countries, of the specific threats to those interests, and of our capacity to counter those threats at an acceptable risk and cost.

---

[4] See Document 37.
[5] See Document 52.

We have been guided by these concepts during the past year in our dealings with free nations throughout the world.

—In Europe, our policies embody precisely the three principles of a durable peace: partnership, continued strength to defend our common interests when challenged, and willingness to negotiate differences with adversaries.

—Here in the Western Hemisphere we seek to strengthen our special relationship with our sister republics through a new program of action for progress in which all voices are heard and none predominates.

—In Asia, where the Nixon Doctrine was enunciated, partnership will have special meaning for our policies—as evidenced by our strengthened ties with Japan. Our cooperation with Asian nations will be enhanced as they cooperate with one another and develop regional institutions.

—In Vietnam, we seek a just settlement which all parties to the conflict, and all Americans, can support. We are working closely with the South Vietnamese to strengthen their ability to defend themselves. As South Vietnam grows stronger, the other side will, we hope, soon realize that it becomes ever more in their interest to negotiate a just peace.

—In the Middle East, we shall continue to work with others to establish a possible framework within which the parties to the Arab-Israeli conflict can negotiate the complicated and difficult questions at issue. Others must join us in recognizing that a settlement will require sacrifices and restraints by all concerned.

—Africa, with its historic ties to so many of our own citizens, must always retain a significant place in our partnership with the new nations. Africans will play the major role in fulfilling their just aspirations—an end to racialism, the building of new nations, freedom from outside interference, and cooperative economic development. But we will add our efforts to theirs to help realize Africa's great potential.

—In an ever more interdependent world economy, American foreign policy will emphasize the freer flow of capital and goods between nations. We are proud to have participated in the successful cooperative effort which created Special Drawing Rights, a form of international money which will help insure the stability of the monetary structure on which the continued expansion of trade depends.

—The great effort of economic development must engage the cooperation of all nations. We are carefully studying the specific goals of our economic assistance programs and how most effectively to reach them.

—Unprecedented scientific and technological advances as well as explosions in population, communications, and knowledge require new forms of international cooperation. The United Nations, the symbol of international partnership, will receive our continued strong support as it marks its 25th Anniversary.

2. America's Strength

The second element of a durable peace must be America's strength. Peace, we have learned, cannot be gained by good will alone.

In determining the strength of our defenses, we must make precise and crucial judgments. We should spend no more than is necessary. But there is an irreducible minimum of essential military security: for if we are less strong than necessary, and if the worst happens, there will be no domestic society to look after. The magnitude of such a catastrophe, and the reality of the opposing military power that could threaten it, present a risk which requires of any President the most searching and careful attention to the state of our defenses.

The changes in the world since 1945 have altered the context and requirements of our defense policy. In this area, perhaps more than in any other, the need to re-examine our approaches is urgent and constant.

The last 25 years have seen a revolution in the nature of military power. In fact, there has been a series of transformations—from the atomic to the thermonuclear weapon, from the strategic bomber to the intercontinental ballistic missile, from the surface missile to the hardened silo and the missile-carrying submarine, from the single to the multiple warhead, and from air defense to missile defense. We are now entering an era in which the sophistication and destructiveness of weapons present more formidable and complex issues affecting our strategic posture.

The last 25 years have also seen an important change in the relative balance of strategic power. From 1945 to 1949, we were the only nation in the world possessing an arsenal of atomic weapons. From 1950 to 1966, we possessed an overwhelming superiority in strategic weapons. From 1967 to 1969, we retained a significant superiority. Today, the Soviet Union possesses a powerful and sophisticated strategic force approaching our own. We must consider, too, that Communist China will deploy its own intercontinental missiles during the coming decade, introducing new and complicating factors for our strategic planning and diplomacy.

In the light of these fateful changes, the Administration undertook a comprehensive and far-reaching reconsideration of the premises and procedures for designing our forces. We sought—and I believe we have achieved—a rational and coherent formulation of our defense strategy and requirements for the 1970's.

The importance of comprehensive planning of policy and objective scrutiny of programs is clear:

—Because of the lead-time in building new strategic systems, the decisions we make today substantially determine our military posture—and thus our security—five years from now. This places a premium on foresight and planning.

—Because the allocation of national resources between defense programs and other national programs is itself an issue of policy, it must be considered on a systematic basis at the early stages of the national security planning process.

—Because we are a leader of the Atlantic Alliance, our doctrine and forces are crucial to the policy and planning of NATO. The mutual confidence that holds the allies together depends on understanding, agreement, and coordination among the 15 sovereign nations of the Treaty.

—Because our security depends not only on our own strategic strength, but also on cooperative efforts to provide greater security for everyone through arms control, planning weapons systems and planning for arms control negotiations must be closely integrated.

For these reasons, this Administration has established procedures for the intensive scrutiny of defense issues in the light of overall national priorities. We have re-examined our strategic forces; we have reassessed our general purpose forces; and we have engaged in the most painstaking preparation ever undertaken by the United States Government for arms control negotiations.

3. Willingness to Negotiate—An Era of Negotiation

Partnership and strength are two of the pillars of the structure of a durable peace. Negotiation is the third. For our commitment to peace is most convincingly demonstrated in our willingness to negotiate our points of difference in a fair and businesslike manner with the Communist countries.

We are under no illusions. We know that there are enduring ideological differences. We are aware of the difficulty in moderating tensions that arise from the clash of national interests. These differences will not be dissipated by changes of atmosphere or dissolved in cordial personal relations between statesmen. They involve strong convictions and contrary philosophies, necessities of national security, and the deep-seated differences of perspectives formed by geography and history.

The United States, like any other nation, has interests of its own, and will defend those interests. But any nation today must define its interests with special concern for the interests of others. If some nations define their security in a manner that means insecurity for other nations, then peace is threatened and the security of all is diminished. This obligation is particularly great for the nuclear superpowers on whose decisions the survival of mankind may well depend.

The United States is confident that tensions can be eased and the danger of war reduced by patient and precise efforts to reconcile conflicting interests on concrete issues. Coexistence demands more than a spirit of good will. It requires the definition of positive goals which can be sought and achieved cooperatively. It requires real progress toward resolution of specific differences. This is our objective.

As the Secretary of State said on December 6:[6]

"We will continue to probe every available opening that offers a prospect for better East-West relations, for the resolution of problems large or small, for greater security for all.

"In this the United States will continue to play an active role in concert with our allies."

This is the spirit in which the United States ratified the Non-Proliferation Treaty and entered into negotiation with the Soviet Union on control of the military use of the seabeds, on the framework of a settlement in the Middle East, and on limitation of strategic arms. This is the basis on which we and our Atlantic allies have offered to negotiate on concrete issues affecting the security and future of Europe, and on which the United States took steps last year to improve our relations with nations of Eastern Europe. This is also the spirit in which we have resumed formal talks in Warsaw with Communist China. No nation need be our permanent enemy.

America's Purpose

These policies were conceived as a result of change, and we know they will be tested by the change that lies ahead. The world of 1970 was not predicted a decade ago, and we can be certain that the world of 1980 will render many current views obsolete.

The source of America's historic greatness has been our ability to see what had to be done, and then to do it. I believe America now has the chance to move the world closer to a durable peace. And I know that Americans working with each other and with other nations can make our vision real.

[Omitted here is the 68-page body of the report.]

---

[6] Reference is to an address by Secretary Rogers to the Belgo-American Association in Brussels, Belgium. For text, see Department of State *Bulletin*, December 29, 1969, pp. 622–625.

61. **Memorandum From President Nixon to His Assistant (Haldeman), His Assistant for Domestic Affairs (Ehrlichman), and His Assistant for National Security Affairs (Kissinger)**[1]

Washington, March 2, 1970.

For discussion with the group and implementation.

After a great deal of consideration of our performance during the first year, I have decided that our greatest weakness was in spreading my time too thin—not emphasizing priorities enough. This may sound strange in view of the fact that I did arrange my time to do the November 3rd speech and the State of the Union adequately; but the balance of this memorandum will demonstrate what I want implemented for the future. Also, while this applies primarily to my time, I want Ehrlichman and Kissinger to apply the same rules to allocating their time to the extent that they find it possible.

What really matters in campaigns, wars or in government is to concentrate on the big battles and win them. I know the point of view which says that unless you fight all the little battles too that you do not lay the ground work for winning the big ones. I do not agree with this point of view to the extent that it means that I will have to devote any significant part of my time to the lower priority items, or to the extent that Ehrlichman and Kissinger have to do so.

This means that there must be delegation to the Departments and within the White House staff of complete responsibility for those matters which are not going to have any major effect on our success as an Administration.

Applying this general rule to specifics, in the field of Foreign Policy, in the future all that I want brought to my attention are the following items.

1. East-West relations.

2. Policy toward the Soviet Union.

3. Policy toward Communist China.

4. Policy toward Eastern Europe, provided it really affects East-West relations at the highest level.

5. Policy toward Western Europe, but only where NATO is affected and where major countries (Britain, Germany and France) are affected.

---

[1] Source: National Archives, Nixon Presidential Materials, NSC Files, Box 341, Subject Files, HAK/President Memos 1969–1970. Eyes Only.

The only minor countries in Europe which I want to pay attention to in the foreseeable future will be Spain, Italy, and Greece. I do not want to see any papers on any of the other countries, unless their problems are directly related to NATO. At the next level out where I am indicating policy toward the Mid-East and then finally in the last is policy with regard to Vietnam and anything that relates to Vietnam, Laos, Cambodia, etc. As far as the balance of Asia is concerned, that part of Africa which is not directly related to the Mid-East crisis, and all of Latin America and all countries in the Western Hemisphere with the exception of Cuba and anything else that may be concerned with the East-West conflict, I do not want matters submitted to me unless they require Presidential decision and can only be handled at the Presidential level.

This is going to require a subtle handling on Kissinger's part. He must not let members of his staff or members of the establishment and the various Departments think that I do "not care" about the under-developed world. I do care, but what happens in those parts of the world is not, in the final analysis, going to have any significant effect on the success of our foreign policy in the foreseeable future. The thing to do here is to farm out as much of the decision-making in those areas to the Departments, and where Kissinger does not have confidence that State will follow up directives that I have previously laid down with regard to Latin America, Africa and the under-developed countries of Asia, he should farm that subject out to a member of his staff but he, himself, should not bother with it. I want him to concentrate just as hard as I will be concentrating on these major countries and these major problem areas.

In the future, all that I want to see with regard to what I consider the lower priority items would be a semiannual report indicating what has happened; and where a news conference is scheduled, of course, just enough information so that I can respond to a question, although it is interesting to note that we have received very few questions on the low priority items in news conferences to date.

Haldeman, in the arranging of my schedule, have in mind these priorities. Great pressures will build up to see this and that minor or major official from the low priority countries. All of this is to be farmed out to Agnew. For example, the Minister of Mines from Venezuela is a case in point; he should not have been included on the schedule, and I do not want this to happen again.

With regard to domestic affairs, our priorities for the most part will be expected but a couple will be surprising for reasons I will indicate.

I want to take personal responsibility in the following areas:

1. Economic matters, but only where the decisions affect either recession or inflation. I do not want to be bothered with international monetary matters. This, incidentally, Kissinger should note also, and I

will not need to see the reports on international monetary matters in the future. Problems should be farmed out, I would hope to Arthur Burns if he is willing to assume it on a confidential basis, and if not Burns to Houthakker[2] who is very capable in this field. I have confidence in the Treasury people since they will be acting in a routine way. International monetary matters, incidentally, are a case in point in making the difficult decision as to priorities. I feel that we need a new international monetary system and I have so indicated in several meetings. Very little progress has been made in that direction because of the opposition of Treasury. I shall expect somebody from the White House staff who will be designated who will keep the pressure on in this area. The man, however, who could really be the lead man is Arthur Burns because he feels exactly as I do and it might be that he could exert some influence on the others. Ehrlichman, of course, could be helpful on the staff side but he is not familiar enough with the intricacies of the problem to assume the lead responsibility.

[Omitted here is a rank ordering of the President's priorities on domestic issues.]

In writing this memorandum I failed to include under the Kissinger section the national defense positions. Here I am interested only in those positions where they really affect our national security and East-West relations. That means that in the case of ABM I, of course, will consider that a high-priority item as long as it is before us. Where an item like foreign aid is concerned I do not want to be bothered with it unless it directly affects East-West relations. I have already indicated in my meeting with Pedersen[3] (?) that I want some reform here and I shall expect that reform to be accomplished in some degree or the other.

A lot of miscellaneous items are not covered in this memorandum but I think you will be able to apply rules based on what I have already dictated.

For example, trade policy is a case in point. This is something where it just isn't going to make a lot of difference whether we move one way or another on the glass tariff. Oil import is also a case in point. While it has some political consequences it is not something I should become deeply involved in. A recommendation should be made and responsibility given at other levels and I will then act without getting involved at lower levels of the discussion.

[Omitted here is a concluding paragraph on government reorganization.]

---

[2] Hendrik S. Houthakker, member of the Council of Economic Advisers.

[3] Reference is to Rudolph Peterson; see Document 35.

62. Editorial Note

On March 26, 1970, Secretary of State Rogers sent to President Nixon a policy overview prepared in the State Department on the "U.S. and Africa in the 70's." The 25-page paper ranged over the full spectrum of relations with the nations of Africa. The essence of the approach to Africa, as defined in the paper, derived in considerable measure from a statement made by then Vice President Nixon in 1957:

"We seek a relationship of constructive cooperation with the nations of Africa—a cooperative and equal relationship with all who wish it. We are prepared to have diplomatic relations under conditions of mutual respect with all the nations of the continent. We want no military allies, no spheres of influence, no big power competition in Africa. Our policy is a policy related to African countries and not a policy based upon our relations with non-African countries.

"As early as 1957, when he returned from a mission to Africa on behalf of President Eisenhower, the then Vice President Nixon recommended that the U.S. assign a higher priority to our relations with Africa, which he recognized to be of growing importance to the United States. Specifically he said:

"'The United States must come to know these leaders better, to understand their hopes and aspirations, and to support them in their plans and programs for strengthening their own nations and contributing to world peace and stability. To this end, we must encourage the greatest possible interchange of persons and ideas with the leaders and peoples of these countries. We must assure the strongest possible diplomatic and consular representation to those countries and stand ready to consult these countries on all matters affecting their interests and ours.'" (Letter with attached enclosure from Secretary Rogers to President Nixon, March 26, 1970; National Archives, Nixon Presidential Materials, NSC Files, Box 281, Agency Files, State, Vol. VI)

The full text of the policy statement is scheduled for publication in *Foreign Relations, 1969–1976, Africa, 1969–1972.*

In a letter to Rogers on the same day, Nixon approved the policy statement on Africa. In doing so, he wrote: "You know of my keen personal interest in relations with the African countries. We have both felt the spirit and dynamism of this continent and its people. I believe we now have a special opportunity to maintain and to expand our present relationships and am pleased that you and your staff have made so positive an examination of the paths that are available to us." (National Archives, Nixon Presidential Materials, NSC Files, Box 281, Agency Files, State, Vol. VI)

63. Letter From President Nixon to President Chiang[1]

Washington, March 27, 1970.

Dear Mr. President:

Your letter of March 1 was most welcome.[2] I greatly appreciated your frankness and your sincere concern for the success of my efforts to bring a lasting peace to East Asia.

From the conversations which we had together before I became President and from the previous correspondence which we have exchanged, I know of your deep distrust of Communist China's motives. In my own evaluation of Communist China, I do not ignore the legacy of the past, nor do I ignore the threat which the Chinese Communist regime may pose in the future. In my report to the Congress of February 18, 1970 on United States Foreign Policy,[3] I stated that in dealing with the Communist countries we would not underestimate the depth of ideological disagreement or the disparity between their interests and ours. You may recall, too, that in my press conference of January 30 I cited the potential danger to the United States posed by the growth of Communist China's nuclear weapons capability.

At the same time, Mr. President, I believe that I would be remiss in my duty to the American people if I did not attempt to discover whether a basis may not exist for reducing the risk of a conflict between the United States and Communist China, and whether certain of the issues which lie between us may not be settled by negotiation. The alternative of maintaining a hostile relationship indefinitely while weapons of mass destruction increase in numbers and power is a terrible one, and demands that every reasonable effort be made to promote understandings which will contribute to peace and stability in Asia.

In undertaking this effort, I of course have in mind not only the essential interests of the American people, but of our allies as well. In your letter you have expressed concern for certain aspects of our talks

---

[1] Source: National Archives, RG 59, S/S Files: Lot 72 D 230, Presidential and Secretary of State Correspondence with Heads of State, 1961–1971, Box 18, China (Nationalist). Nodis. Also printed in Foreign Relations, 1969–1976, China, 1969–1972.

[2] In his March 1 letter to Nixon, Chiang Kai-shek wrote that he did not object to talks between the United States and Communist China, but he warned that accepting Peking's five principles of peaceful coexistence or discussing the "so-called Taiwan problem" would be "infringing on the sovereign rights of the Republic of China." (Ibid., Nixon Presidential Materials, NSC Files, Box 520, Country Files, Far East, China, Vol. IV)

[3] Document 60.

with the Chinese Communists at Warsaw. Secretary Rogers has received from your Ambassador in Washington a detailed statement of your Government's views on these matters and is replying to them.

I wish, however, to assure you personally and in the strongest terms of my determination that there shall be no change in the firmness of our commitment to the defense of Taiwan and the Pescadores and of my earnest desire that these talks will not affect the friendship and close cooperation which has existed between our Governments for so many years. I deeply value our long personal relationship as candid friends and am confident that this will serve us well in the future.

Mrs. Nixon joins me in extending our best wishes and warmest regards to you and Madame Chiang. We trust that Madame Chiang's health has improved.

Sincerely,

Richard Nixon

64. Memorandum From President Nixon to His Assistant for National Security Affairs (Kissinger)[1]

Washington, April 22, 1970.

I think we need a bold move in Cambodia, assuming that I feel the way today (it is five AM, April 22) at our meeting as I feel this morning to show that we stand with Lon Nol. I do not believe he is going to survive. There is, however, some chance that he might and in any event we must do something symbolic to help him survive. We have really dropped the ball on this one due to the fact that we were taken in with the line that by helping him we would destroy his "neutrality" and give the North Vietnamese an excuse to come in. Over and over again we fail to learn that the Communists never need an excuse to come in. They didn't need one in Hungary in 1956 when the same argument was made by the career State people and when Dulles bought it because he was tired and it was during the campaign. They didn't need one in

---

[1] Source: National Archives, Nixon Presidential Materials, NSC Files, Box 341, Subject Files, HAK/President Memos 1969–1970. Confidential. Also scheduled for publication in *Foreign Relations*, 1969–1976, Southeast Asia, 1969–1972.

Czechoslovakia when the same argument was made by the State people, and they didn't need one in Laos where we lost a precious day by failing to make the strike that might have blunted the whole offensive before it got started, and in Cambodia where we have taken a completely hands-off attitude by protesting to the Senate that we have only a "delegation of seven State Department jerks" in the Embassy and would not provide any aid of any kind because we were fearful that if we did so it would give them a "provocation" to come in. They are romping in there and the only government in Cambodia in the last 25 years that had the guts to take a pro-Western and pro-American stand is ready to fall. I am thinking of someone like Bob Murphy who would be sent there on a trip to report back to me and who would go in and reassure Lon Nol. This, of course, would be parallel to your activities which will be undertaken immediately after the NSC meeting,[2] in the event that I decide to go on this course,[3] with some of the lily-livered Ambassadors from our so-called friends in the world. We are going to find out who our friends are now, because if we decide to stand up here some of the rest of them had better come along fast.

I will talk to you about this after the NSC meeting.

---

[2] An NSC meeting on Cambodia took place on April 22 but at the President's instruction no notes were taken. Additional information on the meeting is scheduled for publication ibid.

[3] On May 1 U.S. forces crossed the border of South Vietnam into Cambodia. They followed South Vietnamese forces which had invaded North Vietnamese sanctuaries in Cambodia 2 days earlier.

65.   Memorandum of Conversation[1]

Washington, May 6, 1970, 3–4:15 p.m.

SUBJECT

Mr. Kissinger's Meeting with Eleven Students and Five Faculty Members of Stanford University[2]

Mr. Kissinger opened by stating the ground rules for the meeting; namely, that he did not mind how they characterized or described the meeting, but that in the interest of promoting a frank discussion he did not want to be quoted. They agreed.

Q: Patrick Shea, Student Body President from Stanford, read part of a resolution adopted by the Stanford Academic Senate which, in effect, stated that they believed that the machinery which was used for making decisions in the country did not seem legitimate and that they were therefore sending a delegation to express their concern to the President and to deliver to him a petition signed by 3,800 students from Stanford. Mr. Shea stated that the violence, which seemed to be increasing, was outrageous and that the situation was becoming impossible; but that the students could not condemn the violence here when what the U.S. government was doing in Southeast Asia was so violent. He continued that there was what he called a "generational solidarity" developing which was more than a gap and that the student generation was seeking to mobilize itself to solve the problems which the older generation did not seem to be able to solve.

A: Mr. Kissinger was asked if he had any comments. He replied that he thought Mr. Shea's remarks were too sweeping for direct comment but that he would like to start by stating a few of his observations on the current situation. He stated that we must assume that both sides realize that no one has a monopoly on righteousness and that, as a former pro-

---

[1] Source: National Archives, Nixon Presidential Materials, NSC Files, Box 340, Subject Files, Stanford University, May 1970. No classification marking. Drafted by David Young of Kissinger's office and initialed by Kissinger. The meeting was held in the Situation Room of the White House.

[2] The reaction on the campuses of American colleges and universities to what was generally perceived as the "invasion" of Cambodia was widespread, largely peaceful, but occasionally violent. It turned tragic on May 4 at Kent State University in Ohio when anti-war demonstrators were killed by Ohio National Guardsmen. The effects of anti-war demonstrations are not often cited in official documents but as Haldeman makes clear in *The Haldeman Diaries*, pp. 158–164, they had a profound effect on the state of mind of the President and his advisers. Kissinger recalls in *White House Years*, p. 510, that he met with 10 student groups on Cambodia during May 1970 alone. Memoranda of these conversations are in the Library of Congress, Manuscript Division, Kissinger Papers, CL 268, Memoranda of Conversation, 1968–1977, Dec 1968–Nov 1970.

fessor, what students thought and felt was of great significance to him. Mr. Kissinger then expressed his own personal view, drawing upon his practice while at Harvard to meet with the SDS members there in order to find out what they represented. He concluded that they were characterized by two things: one, extraordinary intensity and two, an extraordinarily superficial knowledge of the facts.

Mr. Kissinger continued that we agree on ending the war in Vietnam; there is no doubt about that. We also agree that it should be ended as quickly as possible. Our only difference is in what is meant by "as quickly as possible." This in his view was not worth tearing the country apart. He then commented on the problem of the generation gap which he felt was inevitable. In the present circumstances, however, the younger generation had very good reason to attack the older generation because, in Mr. Kissinger's opinion, his generation had failed—it had become cynical and skeptical. It had "taken the clock apart" without being able to put it together and it collapses and turns into mush when it is pushed.

Q: Mr. Shea commented that in the past a war would destroy lives and property, but that today it might destroy humanity.

A: Mr. Kissinger agreed and went on to point out that even if we did away with all the nuclear weapons in the world we would not have solved the problem of being able to destroy humanity since you cannot destroy the technology—men would still know how to produce nuclear weapons. The problem is how to relate knowledge to the preservation of humanity.

Q: Professor Lewis asked what had occurred within the Administration since March 18, the date of the Cambodian coup. It had been his understanding that the Administration's policy was to contain the war but that it now appeared that it was being expanded. China was even being brought into it in view of its expressed solidarity with the Indochinese people. The resulting situation therefore is not what he had understood the Administration's objective to be. In short, what puzzled him was that it seemed that certain political ramifications were not anticipated. Do the professors know more than the policy-makers?

A: Mr. Kissinger replied that he would first like to make some general comments before answering the specific question. In the process by which decisions are made it is possible for a judgment to be wrong, but that does not justify attacking the fabric of the society. The press has characterized this as an "invasion" of Cambodia. But this territory was not controlled by the Cambodians. The primary objective of the operation was simply to remove supplies, and it is limited in time. (Shea interjected, "Even if Phnom Penh falls?", and Mr. Kissinger replied, "We intend to stick by what we have said.")

On the disaffection of political science professors, Mr. Kissinger stated that he had seen the impact of the war on academicians and that he understood their misgivings. He pointed out that the thrust of their point of view had always been against the war and that it was difficult for them to believe that anything we did could be an improvement. Vietnamization was not a brilliant choice, but it was the best we had in January of 1969. We had to respond not in light of what people would think tomorrow but in light of what people would think five years from now.

In regard to the events since March 18, Mr. Kissinger stated that it may be difficult for the persons present to believe but we had nothing to do with the overthrow of Sihanouk. There were no CIA personnel there and, in fact, we did not even have an Ambassador, but only a chargé d'affaires there. Indeed, it would have been better for us to have Sihanouk in Cambodia with a rough equilibrium than to have the conflict expand. We were, are, and remain committed to extricating ourselves from Vietnam and ending the war. We have made very strenuous efforts to bring about serious negotiations, some of which cannot be made public at this time, and we continue to keep these channels open.

In response to the question of whether or not the Administration had reversed its policy and was now expanding the war, Mr. Kissinger replied, "No, we were not altering our policy." In fact, the Administration believed that what it had done would shorten the war.

Q: Mr. Shea mentioned that earlier today they had talked with Congressman McCloskey who stated that Mr. Kissinger had recently told him that one of the two alternatives of the Nixon plan for ending the war had failed.

A: Mr. Kissinger replied that this was untrue. What Mr. McCloskey may have been thinking of was that our policy is based on two tracks— one negotiation, and two, Vietnamization—and that Mr. Kissinger had told him that the negotiations were not proceeding as rapidly as everyone had hoped.

Q: Professor Lewis then asked how much political input there had been in the decision to attack the sanctuaries in Cambodia, whether it was based on soft or hard intelligence, and why we had not let the dust settle before making our decision.

A: Mr. Kissinger replied that he seems to always be conducting both tactical and theoretical conversations simultaneously. On the tactical side, there is no doubt that we ought to talk to concerned people as to whether or not the tactical decision was wise, but it does not seem to be worth tearing our campuses apart. On the theoretical side, Mr. Kissinger stated that his own conclusions, for what they were worth, were as follows: The North Vietnamese people were a very heroic and tenacious people and they were very good at making war, as their history proves. But the question remains as to whether or not they can also make peace. Mr. Kissinger noted that we also see this problem in the Middle East.

The North Vietnamese tactic has been to sell us the beginning of negotiations over and over again. Some people think that negotiating with them is like a detective story in which they throw out vague clues and it is up to us to discover them. There are a number of channels through which they can communicate with us directly, and we believe that when they are serious about negotiating they will not let us know through vague clues. The more fundamental problem, however, is that they cannot conceive of sharing political power. They want it foreordained that they will have control.

Q: Professor Lewis then asked whether we had given sufficient attention to Sihanouk's position or whether we had gotten him into the situation which brought about the coup.

A: Mr. Kissinger replied that, for what it was worth, his analysis of what caused Sihanouk's downfall was as follows: First of all, Mr. Kissinger stated that he considered Sihanouk a political genius in that he managed to keep himself in power between the right and the left. This depended on his maintaining Cambodia's international neutrality and his manipulating the internal political structure so that he appeared to the Communists to be as far left as he could be without provoking a reaction from the right. Sihanouk therefore needed a strong right, and it was he who put Lon Nol and Matak into power. Sihanouk, when he left the country, was trying through political means to squeeze the Viet Cong and North Vietnamese there. He had gone to Paris and was on his way to Moscow and Peking to pursue this course on the diplomatic front. Consequently, he approved of Lon Nol's activities since they gave him evidence of the troubles he was having on his right. The result, however, was that the assumption by Lon Nol got out of hand and the right wing took over. The problem now is that if Sihanouk came back he would not be the same because the balance has changed. For this reason, we cannot seek to bring him back. Our position has been the same as the French, the U.K., and most every other nation (even the Chinese until yesterday) in that we have continued to deal with the existing government.

As a result of the Lon Nol takeover, the Viet Cong and North Vietnamese started to expand their sanctuaries. We warned them, publicly and privately, and we even approached the Russians to try to discourage such expansion. Finally we did not act against the sanctuaries until they moved out.

Q: A professor of anthropology stated that he wanted to impress upon Mr. Kissinger the gravity of the situation on the campuses, that the middle ground had disappeared, and that there had been a drastic change. After Cambodia it was not just a strike but a complete stoppage in order to determine a political consensus as to what was to be done. This dissent was not going to fade away and there was a growing feeling that one could not work through the existing political structure.

Q: Another professor stated that in view of the report of the Cambodian tribesmen being trained by the Green Berets, does this mean that we are now going to go to "Cambodianization" and "Laosization." He felt (1) that unless we stopped the war our credibility would be zero, (2) that there was growing feeling among academics that they could no longer be believed since their universities were so closely related to defense operations, and (3) that many of the students consider the war a racist war and that it was time for us to get back to the problems of the United States. In this connection, he mentioned that the attitude of the Vice President was not very helpful since it seemed to represent a repressive atmosphere.

Q: A Mexican-American student spoke next and explained how tired the minority groups were with handouts. He said that he also spoke for the Indian-American and Chinese-American students present in expressing the frustration and alienation they felt with the system. He stated that they did not feel that minority problems should be dealt with by programs. He also felt that it was inconsistent to fight Communism in Europe with Radio Free Europe but in Southeast Asia with bullets. He mentioned that minorities die in the war at a disproportionately higher rate than do whites. Finally, he stated that he was not concerned about saving the university since it was so closely associated and involved with the war-death machine.

Another professor stated that Cambodia really was the straw that broke the camel's back, that there had been great division and distrust on the campuses already. He went on to state that if Cambodia is only a tactical question and Vietnam is the moral question, what are the Administration's long-range plans; or what kind of peace are we planning for in Asia?

A: Mr. Kissinger replied that he thought the students had given a correct and factual description of the campuses of the country. The real question here is, faced with this situation, what can be done? Cambodia made it easy for some to do what they wanted to do anyway, but they confused a tactical question with a fundamental question. The real issue is that any society to survive must have a modicum of trust. The bureaucracy is the curse of the modern state, and there is profound dissatisfaction with it. Mr. Kissinger stated that on the other hand he did not know what student riots contributed to the solution of the problem.

In order to have world order we must maintain a modicum of confidence in authority. Anything worth doing takes time and order.

It is a very simple rule but whenever the scope for action is the greatest, the knowledge of the facts is the least. Whether an assessment is right or wrong can never be proved until afterwards. Our view is that we must get out of Vietnam in a way that the peace does not divide the country more than the war. Historically, a student revolution has never succeeded. If there is a revolution, it will not be by a bunch of upper-middle class college students on the left, but by some other more uncivilized group on the right. We are not playing with lives to prove our manhood. It may be one of the curses of our age that to be thoughtful requires one to be tough.

Mr. Kissinger stated that the Administration had made an effort to look many years ahead and to make decisions which would produce the kind of world and peace vehicle we all sought. Politics, however, is a grubby business and the easy decision is usually the immediate tactical one. One does not always have the time or room to make the decision that is in the long-term best interests of world peace. There have been institutions, however, in which we have had room to make long-range decisions such as in the SALT talks, the Nuclear Non-Proliferation Treaty, and the Chemical and Biological Warfare decision.

In Southeast Asia we do not believe that the situation is going to be improved simply by giving economic aid. Nor do we subscribe to the more conservative view that guerrilla warfare can solve all these problems. We are trying to ask the right questions, to stop the pedantic Americanization approach, and to get more regional cooperation. Our specific answers are not going to be very profound but they will be even less promising if we have to take a good part of our energy to deal with the present problems on our own campuses.

Q: Dean Gibbs interrupted here to ask why there was so much reverse rhetoric, for instance, from the Vice President, which in no way seemed conducive to a forward look.

A: Mr. Kissinger replied that the Administration had a spectrum of opinion and that each person there knew how difficult it would have been for Mr. Kissinger to have the dialogue he had had with them today if they had met on the campus at Stanford. He concluded by saying that he recognized the inadequacies of his own side, but that he also thought the universities should recognize the inadequacies on their part and on the part of their faculties. It seemed that too many professors were more interested in being popular than in being right, and that a resolution voted on in a large academic senate would tend to be the result of the emotions of the moment.

Mr. Patrick Shea, the incoming Student Body President, summed up the attitude of the students in a prepared statement saying that they hoped the Administration would re-evaluate its position in Southeast Asia.

David R. Young

66.   Memorandum for the President's File[1]

Washington, May 7, 1970, 11:12 a.m.–12:32 p.m.

SUBJECT

Mid-day meeting in the President's office with eight university presidents, members of the Association of American Universities

Present at this meeting with the President were eight members of the Association of American Universities and three members of the White House staff. The names of those attending are attached at Tab A.[2]

After some opening small talk regarding the redecorating of the Oval Office, the President began by stating that in view of the conversation he had had with this group a couple of weeks ago,[3] and given the recent developments on college campuses, there were certain questions he would like to consider with them. Namely, what ought to be the Federal role, even the Presidential role, regarding student problems? Should the Federal government step into university administration in some way? And the more sensitive question, What is, or should be, the relationship of state and local governments and the national guard to the university?

---

[1] Source: National Archives, Nixon Presidential Materials, White House Special Files, President's Office Files, Box 81, Memoranda for the President, May 3, 1970. No classification marking. Drafted and sent to the President by Edward L. Morgan, Deputy Assistant to the President for Domestic Affairs.

[2] Not printed. The university presidents were William C. Friday of the University of North Carolina, Fred H. Harrington of the University of Wisconsin, G. Alexander Heard, Chancellor of Vanderbilt University, Charles C. Hitch of the University of California (Berkeley), Edward Levi of the University of Chicago, Malcolm Moos of the University of Minnesota, Nathan M. Pusey of Harvard University, and W. Allen Wallis of the University of Rochester. Ziegler, Kissinger, and Morgan also attended.

[3] The President met with the same group of university presidents on April 22 from 10:35 to 11:23 a.m. (National Archives, Nixon Presidential Materials, White House Central Files, Staff Memos and Office Files, Presidential Papers and Archives, Daily Diary)

The President noted that the National Guard tends to be thought of as Federal, even though it is not, which probably grew in part out of the federalizing of national guard troops by President Eisenhower in Little Rock.

He stated that there is probably no question that the Cambodian action sparked a considerable amount of the current turmoil. Kent State certainly dramatized it all.[4] He further noted that he was not asking the support of the college presidents for his action in Cambodia, an action that he had to take, ironically, for the very reason that the demonstrations are about. He stated that when the Cambodian action is completed in early June, he will have bought at least ten months more time. Our actions in Cambodia avoid either complete capitulation on the one hand or leaving our forces indefensible on the other.

The President then went on to note that he met yesterday with six Kent State students, all of whom were basically against the war in Viet Nam.[5] The students had stated to him that their purpose in coming to Washington was not just to protest the war but to try and explain what was happening. The students noted that the origin of the Ohio State disturbances had not been a protest against the war but against the curriculum. The students said that the issue of Black Power had actually started the demonstration at Kent State, although Cambodia and Viet Nam were soon added as issues.

The President then noted that while he has made a difficult decision in Cambodia, he is the one who must take the responsibility and see it through. Nonetheless, he absolutely respects everyone's right to disagree.

---

[4] In a telephone conversation on May 4 at approximately 4:45 p.m., Nixon told Kissinger that: "At Kent State there were 4 or 5 killed today. But that place has been bad for quite some time—it has been rather violent." Kissinger suggested that they would be blamed for the killings and he noted that 33 university presidents were appealing to the President to leave Vietnam. The President asked about the student strike, observing: "If it is peaceful it doesn't bother me." He worried, however, that if the students were "out of classes they'll be able to raise hell." Kissinger thought they would hold teach-ins and possibly march on Washington. Nixon hoped "we can get some people of our own to speak out." (Memorandum of telephone conversation; Library of Congress, Manuscript Division, Kissinger Papers, Box 363, Telephone Conversations, Chronological File, 1–5 May 1970)

[5] Nixon met with the students on May 6 from 10:41 to 11:36 a.m. In addition, Congressman William Stanton from Ohio and Thomas Bell of the Kent State University Alumni Association of Washington, D.C. attended. (National Archives, Nixon Presidential Materials, White House Central Files, Staff Memos and Office Files, Presidential Papers and Archives, Daily Diary) Nixon was still reflecting on the student demonstrations on June 8 when he told Kissinger "we ought to think what we are going to do with our young people. We don't want to set up opposition." He would continue to meet with them, he said. (Memorandum of telephone conversation, June 8, 1970, 10:15 p.m.; Library of Congress, Manuscript Division, Kissinger Papers, Box 363, Telephone Conversations, Chronological File, 6–10 June 1970)

The President went on to ask the broader question: Once we are out of Cambodia, what happens? He stated that it would be a mistake to consider that solving the war problem would solve the campus problem, and that we must get to the more fundamental roots of the issue of campus turmoil.

The President passed on some more of the observations of the Kent State students: the student body at Kent State is basically apathetic; a well organized group of about 200 has been developing destructive activities; at least 18,000 had not been involved in the disturbance but were *spectators*. The students further pointed out that the student body generally hates the City of Kent police, who they feel are ill trained; and finally they noted that if the President of the school, or someone with like authority, had stepped up and tried to negotiate the situation, the resulting tragedy might not have occurred. The President indicated that the students might have been naive in this conclusion; however, he indicated that the students said that when the national guard comes on campus, the university administration abdicates. Thus, the President raised the question of "communication" and "control" between the national guard and the university administration.

The President indicated that at Yale we sent troops at the governor's request, but we had also been working with the situation quietly. He noted that the October and November moratoriums had been handled by regular army troops, who were better trained, and that even though there was $100,000 damage done in the city, no one was killed or injured. At this point the President said that he had personally gotten the Court to waive the thirty (fifteen?) day notice requirement for demonstrations for whatever demonstrations are planned this Saturday.

The President asked what the Federal government can do, if anything, noting that when state and local governments cannot handle situations the question immediately becomes, "What is Washington going to do?" He said that the usual answer is that we will study the problem and it is clear that students would reject just another commission. The question today is, "What can we do *now*?"

Dr. Nathan Pusey: Stated the group was grateful to be asked to come to see the President and they all wanted to be candid, even though most of them were sleepy as the result of the week's activities on their respective campuses. He stated that the situation on campus this week seems new, different, and terribly serious. The question has become whether or not we can get through the week. He indicated that no longer are we dealing with a small group of radicals, but rather a broad base of students and faculty who are upset. Even the conservatives are filled with anxiety and he feels that this new unrest springs from three things:

(1) Cambodia. He indicated that none of the men present were there to pass judgment on Cambodia, but it does seem on campus to have been the last straw. The students just don't see it the same way the President must see it, but rather feel it is an expansion of the war, or sort of a "here we go again."

(2) Kent State, which needs no elaboration.

(3) Speeches from the administration about campus events. The students feel that the Vice President does not understand the campus community. He apparently doesn't understand or believe in the freedom of speech and right of dissent.

Pusey feels the next three days may see a "terrible thing." He noted that students and faculty are now convening numerous meetings, turning away from their academic duties, and a feeling that they want to declare war is increasing.

Pusey stated that he feels we (the college presidents) must speak to the academic community. He indicated the group feels that if the President could find a man (for instance, a university president or even a Senator) who would represent a rallying point for the President it would be very helpful. Such a man should know and appreciate college institutions and be presented as a channel of communication to the President. Perhaps he could be placed temporarily on the White House staff for a month and even have a student assistant.

Allen Wallis: Noted that he was very surprised to learn that the President had been surprised regarding what the Kent State students had said. He further noted that he continues to be surprised that the White House staff is always surprised to learn what is going on. Finally, he was even more surprised that the President would raise the long range question of campus disturbance, which seemed to him analogous to discussing future insurance policies while your building was ablaze. He wonders whether these institutions will even hold together 'til Monday without more people getting killed. Up until now we were gaining a coalescence of people against violence who were willing to work in such things as Congressional elections and were opposing student occupation of buildings, but that may be lost.

Fred Harrington: Stated that Wisconsin does not share the same concern about the national guard that Kent State does, but at Wisconsin the university is in control over the national guard when they move onto campus. He expressed great concern that the moderates are going over to join the radicals.

William Friday: Noted that students and faculty are now beginning to hire busses to come to Washington next week to talk to Congressmen, not the President, about Cambodia and Viet Nam. He stated that there is a real need to stabilize this situation and felt the President is the only person who can do this.

The President: Inquired whether appointing a man to be a listener isn't somewhat like appointing a commission. Wouldn't it indicate that we are just trying to push the students off? He further asked if this wouldn't look like a scholar in residence?

(The group generally felt that such an appointment would be very helpful and would not be analogous to appointing a commission.)

Malcolm Moos: Felt that any repressive moves would be bad. He categorically stated that the Vice President must be muzzled. When the Vice President attacked the president of the University of Michigan, things exploded beyond control. Stated that the President must let the country know that this is not what *he* (the President) believes. Asked whether the Vice President was going to make the speech at Stone Mountain.

The President: Replied that he was, and indicated that these men should not worry about the speech, since he (the President) wrote the Vice President's speech himself. The President indicated that it would be a good speech and that it would say the right things.

Mr. Moos further indicated that the students are now going to the Congressmen and not to the President.

Malcolm Levi: Stated that the President must give the impression that he cares and is willing to talk to people. He noted that those who want violence may now have the ability to take over. Stated that he feels the President has been isolating himself and should come out now and say that he welcomes student views. Naturally, one cannot open up this solicitation of student views to questions of whether or not students should be running the universities, making the decisions in Cambodia, or anything like that.

The President: Noted that he was having a press conference on Friday and pointed out to the group that it was he who had arranged for the administration to communicate with people such as Sam Brown during the moratoriums. Naturally, decisions such as Cambodia cannot be made based upon how many people come in and out of the White House.

Levi: Stated that he felt it was unfortunate that the President had gone to the Pentagon after the Cambodia speech, which made the whole thing seem quite military.

The President: Stated that we're not going to fight in Cambodia or Laos, and that this summer should well bring the best news out of the Viet Nam war.

Alexander Heard: Said that the message he brought was one of attitude being communicated. Feels the students believe that it's their lives that are at issue and we are facing a fundamental crisis in our political system. The moderate students are saying, "Here we are, working away, wanting to change the system in an orderly fashion (such as by protest or demonstration) and yet we are derided and condemned and our motives impugned by the Vice President and the Attorney General, who lump us together with those who would burn buildings.

He further stated that somehow the President should convey a feeling of sympathy and understanding to those willing to work in outspoken ways short of violence. The students are asking, "Where do I go now, if I'm condemned when I work within the framework of the system?" Feels that the students must sense a warmth and receptivity from the administration or they will join the other side.

Moos then stated that the universities are being separated from the nation and that perhaps this group could meet with the President from time to time to keep some visibility.

Dr. Pusey indicated that they would like to hold a press conference this afternoon and indicate that they had been here, stated their views, and found the President concerned and receptive.

The President said that they should naturally meet with the press and he certainly wouldn't tell them what to say. The President went on to say that no one believes more strongly in the right to dissent than he does, short, of course, of the right to violence.

Dr. Kissinger: Stated that we are listening and certainly have compassion with their anguish.

The President said the issue is the *means*.

Kissinger indicated that we get only one guess when we take such actions as Cambodia, and we must often act on things we cannot always prove.

A short discussion followed regarding who such a man might be, if the President appointed one as a "listening post." Those mentioned were Roben W. Fleming, President of the University of Michigan, and Charles Young of the University of California at Los Angeles.

Pusey noted that the black issue is still smoldering and should not go unnoticed.

Wallis came down rather hard on the Vice President, noting that the Vice President had attacked Cornell when he didn't even have the facts straight and really meant Connecticut. He stated he feels the Vice President is somewhat like McCarthy, who goes around hitting individuals who can't defend themselves or possibly recover. He noted that in many cases he agreed with the Vice President regarding the merits of what he is saying, but he nonetheless feels somewhat outraged that the Vice President would attack persons individually and name them. Even if what he's saying makes sense, does he consider what effect it's having?

The President stated that of course one must assume the responsibility for any remarks he's made, even if they are taken out of context.

There was some final discussion regarding the selection of a man to work at the White House for the President. Some suggested possibly Secretary Shultz or Secretary Finch. Mr. Levi felt that it should not be someone from within the administration.

The President noted all this, but did not commit to appointing someone.

---

67.   Interview With President Nixon[1]

Los Angeles, California, July 1, 1970.

[Omitted here is the opening portion of the interview which dealt with Southeast Asia.]

Mr. Smith. Mr. President, one of the things that happened in the Senate last week was the rescinding of the Gulf of Tonkin resolution[2] by the Senate. Mr. Katzenbach,[3] in the previous administration, told the Foreign Relations Committee that resolution was tantamount to a congressional declaration of war. If it is rescinded, what legal justification do you have for continuing to fight a war that is undeclared in Vietnam?

The President. First, Mr. Smith, as you know, this war, while it was undeclared, was here when I became President of the United States. I do

---

[1] Source: *Public Papers of the Presidents of the United States: Richard Nixon, 1970*, pp. 546–549. The interview, conducted by Howard K. Smith of ABC, John Chancellor of NBC, and Eric Sevareid of CBS, was broadcast live at 7 p.m. on television and radio from an ABC studio in Los Angeles. The interview focused primarily on the fighting in Southeast Asia and, to a lesser extent, on U.S. policy in the Middle East.

[2] On August 7, 1964, Congress responded to a North Vietnamese attack on U.S. destroyers in the Gulf of Tonkin by passing a joint resolution expressing Congressional approval and support of the "determination of the President, as Commander in Chief, to take all necessary measures to repel any armed attack against the forces of the United States and to prevent further aggression." On August 10 President Johnson signed the joint resolution into law as Public Law 88–408. (78 Stat. 384)

[3] Nicholas deB. Katzenbach, Under Secretary of State from 1966 to 1968. [Footnote in the source text.]

not say that critically. I am simply stating the fact that there were 549,000 Americans in Vietnam under attack when I became President.

The President of the United States has the constitutional right—not only the right, but the responsibility—to use his powers to protect American forces when they are engaged in military actions, and under these circumstances, starting at the time that I became President, I have that power and I am exercising that power.

Mr. Smith. Sir, I am not recommending this, but if you don't have a legal authority to wage a war, then presumably you could move troops out. It would be possible to agree with the North Vietnamese. They would be delighted to have us surrender. So that you could—

What justification do you have for keeping troops there other than protecting the troops that are there fighting?

The President. A very significant justification. It isn't just a case of seeing that the Americans are moved out in an orderly way. If that were the case, we could move them out more quickly, but it is a case of moving American forces out in a way that we can at the same time win a just peace.

Now, by winning a just peace, what I mean is not victory over North Vietnam—we are not asking for that—but it is simply the right of the people of South Vietnam to determine their own future without having us impose our will upon them, or the North Vietnamese, or anybody else outside impose their will upon them.

When we look at that limited objective, I am sure some would say, "Well, is that really worth it? Is that worth the efforts of all these Americans fighting in Vietnam, the lives that have been lost?"

I suppose it could be said that simply saving 17 million people in South Vietnam from a Communist takeover isn't worth the efforts of the United States. But let's go further. If the United States, after all of this effort, if we were to withdraw immediately, as many Americans would want us to do—and it would be very easy for me to do it and simply blame it on the previous administration—but if we were to do that, I would probably survive through my term, but it would have, in my view, a catastrophic effect on this country and the cause of peace in the years ahead.

Now I know there are those who say the domino theory is obsolete. They haven't talked to the dominoes. They should talk to the Thais, to the Malaysians, to the Singaporans, to the Indonesians, to the Filipinos, to the Japanese, and the rest. And if the United States leaves Vietnam in a way that we are humiliated or defeated, not simply speaking in what is called jingoistic terms, but in very practical terms, this will be immensely discouraging to the 300 million people from Japan clear around to Thailand in free Asia; and even more important it will be ominously encouraging to the leaders of Communist China and the Soviet Union who are supporting the North Vietnamese. It will encourage them in their expansionist policies in other areas.

The world will be much safer in which to live.

Mr. Smith. I happen to be one of those who agrees with what you are saying, but do you have a legal justification to follow that policy once the Tonkin Gulf Resolution is dead?

The President. Yes, sir, Mr. Smith, the legal justification is the one that I have given, and that is the right of the President of the United States under the Constitution to protect the lives of American men. That is the legal justification. You may recall, of course, that we went through this same debate at the time of Korea. Korea was also an undeclared war, and then, of course, we justified it on the basis of a U.N. action. I believe we have a legal justification and I intend to use it.

Mr. Sevareid. Mr. President, you have said that self-determination in South Vietnam is really our aim and all we can ask for. The Vice President says a non-Communist future for Indochina, or Southeast Asia. His statement seems to enlarge the ultimate American aim considerably. Have we misunderstood you or has he or what is the aim?

Mr. President. Mr. Sevareid, when the Vice President refers to a non-Communist Southeast Asia that would mean of course, a non-Communist South Vietnam, Laos, Cambodia, Thailand, Malaysia, Singapore, and Indonesia. That is the area we usually think of as Southeast Asia.

This is certainly something that I think most Americans and most of those in free Asia and most of those in the free world would think would be a desirable goal.

Let me put it another way: I do not think it would be in the interest of the United States and those who want peace in the Pacific if that part of the world should become Communist, because then the peace of the world, the peace in the Pacific, would be in my opinion very greatly jeopardized if the Communists were to go through that area.

However, referring now specifically to what we are doing in Vietnam, our aim there is a very limited one, and it is to provide for the South Vietnamese the right of self-determination. I believe that when they exercise that right they will choose a non-Communist government. But we are indicating—and incidentally, despite what everybody says about the present government in South Vietnam, its inadequacies and the rest, we have to give them credit for the fact that they also have indicated that they will accept the result of an election, what the people choose.

Let us note the fact that the North Vietnamese are in power not as a result of an election, and have refused to indicate that they will accept the result of an election in South Vietnam, which would seem to me to be a pretty good bargaining point on our side.

Mr. Chancellor. Mr. President, I am a little confused at this point because you seem in vivid terms to be describing South Vietnam as the first of the string of dominoes that could topple in that part of the world and turn it into a Communist part of the world, in simple terms.

Are you saying that we cannot survive, we cannot allow a regime or a government in South Vietnam to be constructed that would, say, lean toward the Communist bloc? What about a sort of Yugoslavia? Is there any possibility of that kind of settlement?

The President. Mr. Chancellor, it depends upon the people of South Vietnam. If the people of South Vietnam after they see what the Vietcong, the Communist Vietcong, have done to the villages they have occupied, the 40,000 people that they have murdered, village chiefs and others, the atrocities of Hue—if the people of South Vietnam, of which 850,000 of them are Catholic refugees from North Vietnam, after a blood bath there when the North Vietnamese took over in North Vietnam—if the people of South Vietnam under those circumstances should choose to move in the direction of a Communist government, that, of course, is their right. I do not think it will happen. But I do emphasize that the American position and the position also of the present Government of South Vietnam, it seems to me, are especially strong, because we are confident enough that we say to the enemy, "All right, we'll put our case to the people and we'll accept the result." If it happens to be what you describe, a Yugoslav type of government or a mixed government, we will accept it.

Mr. Chancellor. What I am getting at, sir, is, if you say on the one hand that Vietnam—South Vietnam—is the first of the row of dominoes which we cannot allow to topple, then can you say equally, at the same time, that we will accept the judgment of the people of South Vietnam if they choose a Communist government?

The President. The point that you make, Mr. Chancellor, is one that we in the free world face every place in the world, and it is really what distinguishes us from the Communist world.

Again, I know that what is called cold war rhetoric isn't fashionable these days, and I am not engaging in it because I am quite practical, and we must be quite practical, about the world in which we live with all the dangers that we have in the Mideast and other areas that I am sure we will be discussing later in this program.

But let us understand that we in the free world have to live or die by the proposition that the people have a right to choose.

Let it also be noted that in no country in the world today in which the Communists are in power have they come to power as a result of the people choosing them—not in North Vietnam, not in North Korea, not in China, not in Russia, and not in any one of the countries of Eastern Europe, and not in Cuba. In every case, communism has come to power by other than a free election, so I think we are in a pretty safe position on this particular point.

I think you are therefore putting, and I don't say this critically, what is really a hypothetical question. It could happen. But if it does happen that way we must assume the consequences, and if the people of South Vietnam should choose a Communist government, then we will have to accept the consequences of what would happen as far as the domino theory in the other areas.

Mr. Chancellor. In other words, live with it?

The President. We would have to live with it, and I would also suggest this: When we talk about the dominoes, I am not saying that automatically if South Vietnam should go the others topple one by one. I am only saying that in talking to every one of the Asian leaders, and I have talked to all of them. I have talked to Lee Kuan Yew—all of you know him from Singapore of course—and to the Tunku[4] from Malaysia, the little countries, and to Suharto from Indonesia, and of course to Thanom and Thanat Khoman, the two major leaders in Thailand—I have talked to all of these leaders and every one of them to a man recognizes, and Sato of Japan recognizes, and of course the Koreans recognize that if the Communists succeed, not as a result of a free election—they are not thinking of that—but if they succeed as a result of exporting aggression and supporting it in toppling the government, then the message to them is, "Watch out, we might be next."

That's what is real. So, if they come in as a result of a free election, and I don't think that is going to happen, the domino effect would not be as great.

[Omitted here are the concluding questions relating to Southeast Asia and the Middle East.]

---

[4] A Malaysian title meaning Prince or My Lord; Tunku Rahman Al-Haj was Prime Minister. [Footnote in the source text.]

68. Press Conference by President Nixon[1]

Los Angeles, California, July 30, 1970.

[Omitted here are the President's introductory remarks and his responses to questions dealing with the Middle East, Vietnam and the Paris peace talks, arms control negotiations, price trends, and school desegregation.]

Q. To pursue the question of our military preparedness a bit further, twice within the past week statements have been made by high ranking naval officers, Admiral Rickover and Admiral U.S. Grant Sharp, to the effect that our military preparedness is suspect. And they went further. Each gentleman said that in his opinion it is doubtful that we could win a war with the Soviet Union. Given the eminence of these gentlemen, as Commander in Chief, how do you regard the validity of those statements?

The President. Well, I would first react by saying that if there is a war between the Soviet Union and the United States, there will be no winners, there will be only losers. The Soviet Union knows this and we know that.

That is the reason why it is vitally important that in areas like the Mideast that we attempt to avoid to the greatest extent possible being dragged into a confrontation by smaller powers, even though our interests in the area are very, very great. That is why it is very much in our interests in the SALT talks to work out an arrangement if we can, one which will provide for the interests of both and yet not be in derogation of the necessity of our having sufficiency and their having sufficiency.

One other point I would make briefly is this: What the Soviet Union needs in terms of military preparedness is different from what we need. They are a land power primarily, with a great potential enemy on the east. We are primarily, of course, a sea power and our needs, therefore, are different. But what is important now is to find a way to stop this escalation of arms on both sides, and that is why we have hopes in the SALT talks which, I emphasize again, do not involve disarmament for the United States or the Soviet Union, but do involve a limitation and then eventually a mutual reduction.

[Omitted here are questions and answers on domestic issues and Vietnam.]

---

[1] Source: *Public Papers of the Presidents of the United States: Richard Nixon, 1970*, pp. 626–635. The press conference was held at 8 p.m. in the Century Plaza Hotel and was broadcast on television and radio.

69.   Background Press Briefing by the President's Assistant for National Security Affairs (Kissinger)[1]

New Orleans, Louisiana, August 14, 1970.

[Omitted here are Klein's introductions and Kissinger's opening remarks.]

I will talk to you for a bit about our general approach to foreign policy, and specifically also about the disarmament talks, relations with the Soviets and Vietnam, maybe a word about the Middle East. Then Secretary Sisco can talk to you in somewhat greater detail about the specifics of recent events in the Middle East.

Let me begin with a general statement first. I believe that when the history of American post-war foreign policy is written, it will turn out that the big turning point occurred not in 1961 when it was very eloquently announced, but in 1969, when no claims were made.

At the end of April of this year when the President spoke about Cambodia, many of my colleagues complained bitterly—many of my ex-colleagues complained bitterly—about the polarizing effect that his speech was supposed to have had with its emphasis on commitments to friends abroad and the desire to see to it that the self-determination of South Vietnam be preserved.

But if you read, for example, the Inaugural Address of President Kennedy, you will find such phrases—I don't have the exact text here but I think this is reasonably accurate—as: "We will pay any price, we will bear any burden, we will meet any hardship, we will fight any enemy, we will support any friend, to assure the survival of liberty."

I am not saying this as a criticism. It moved me, too, very much. I am citing it as an example of the enormous transformation that has taken place in the situation in the world and in the situation in America since the early 60's.

The period of the 60's, in retrospect, will probably appear as the last flowering of that era of American foreign policy which we initiated in 1948, when we threw ourselves into international affairs with the same enthusiasm, impetuosity, and dedication with which we had built our country.

---

[1] Source: Library of Congress, Manuscript Division, Kissinger Papers, Box CL 426, Subject File, Background Briefings, July–August 1970. No classification marking. Herbert Klein, White House Director of Communications, introduced Kissinger and Assistant Secretary of State Joseph Sisco and explained the rules governing a background briefing. Kissinger and Sisco conducted the briefing.

The belief was after our long history of isolation that any problem in the world that was not solved by America would probably not be solved at all. All over the world the United States found itself in the position of designing all the programs, selling them, executing them, running them. Part of this reflected the realities of the postwar situation.

Every major country in Europe, except Great Britain, had been defeated at one stage or another during the war.

Every country in Europe, with the exception of Great Britain, had been occupied at one stage or another during the war.

Every country in the world that had ever played a major role in foreign policy had been significantly smashed or reduced in influence, power and capacity to conduct foreign affairs, by the war. Economies were shattered. Civil government was very often threatened by domestic discord.

In these conditions, it was, in fact, true that if the United States did not play the major role, no one else possibly could.

Many of the transformations that I am talking about, therefore, are not criticisms of previous Administrations. They were made possible or, indeed, necessary, by the successes of previous policy and not always by the failures—although some of them also reflect certain failure.

A number of big changes have occurred. First, since 1948 over sixty new states have come into being. Since 1948 many of the traditional countries of Europe and Asia regained a great deal of their strength and vigor. Since 1948, the Communist world, which appeared monolithic, has appeared to have many profound divisions. And since 1948, and especially through the 1960's, we have had to learn that the United States cannot be in the position where other countries can pretend that their development is more important to us than it is to them, and that if their security is threatened, it is worse for us than it is for them. The United States cannot be in this position because to conduct foreign policy on this basis may be beyond our physical resources. It surely is beyond our psychological resources. No one can ask the U.S. Government to take the principal responsibility for every decision at every point in the world at every moment in time. It is not healthy for us and it is not healthy for other countries. It enables them to shift the burden of difficult decisions to the United States. It demoralizes their domestic situation. It exacerbates our domestic decisions when all the burdens have to be borne by the United States at every point throughout the world.

It was in this situation, in the fifth year of a war that seemed inconclusive, that this administration has come into office. It is in these conditions that we have tried to adjust the American foreign policy to realities of both our domestic and our foreign situation.

I read in the newspapers always very exciting accounts of the tremendous disputes that go on within the Administration, and who is up and who is down at any particular point, and who did or did not know about this or that decision. The basic charge that the President has given me and to his senior advisors is, first of all, to ask ourselves where we are going. The President, on the whole, is not interested in tactical questions. I remember four weeks after we came into office, if I can mention a personal vignette, the Viet Cong and the North Vietnamese started an offensive. The government was then still geared to the pace of the previous administration. A number of senior officials wanted to come over and assemble in the Situation Room so that the President could conduct that battle. I told them to wait a minute and let me find out what the President wanted to do. I asked the President whether he wanted to conduct these tactical operations from the White House. He said, "Is there any decision that I need to make?" I said no. He said, "Is there any decision that I can make now that would make any difference?" I said no. Then he said, "I don't want to see them. When there is a decision that I need to make, let me know. Let me know what my choices are."

He was absolutely right. There was nothing he could do at that point when the attack started that would not drive everybody crazy. The important concern that the President has put before us is to know where we are going, to put before him the fullest range of choices that he can develop; and then, of course, the final decision, which of the options he would choose, is up to him. He has steadfastly refused to leap on the basis of what seems temporarily fashionable.

This has been terribly important because, as a result of the frustration of some of the previous events, and partly as a result of the fact that we had, or maybe have, outrun our intellectual capacity in some areas, there has been a tendency to have a rote answer to every question. The President mentioned the issue of disarmament. When we came into office, we were confronted with the prospect of talks on strategic arms limitations with the Soviets. We received a great deal of vociferous pressure from many well-meaning groups that we should immediately plunge into these negotiations. We hesitated. Indeed, we did not do it. We did not [sic] hesitate, but we did not do it because we did not want to engage in negotiations on a subject of this magnitude until we knew what we were talking about.

The danger of going into these negotiations precipitately was that we would spend two-thirds of the time negotiating with ourselves and one-third of the time negotiating with the Soviets. If you look at the history of the nuclear ban, for example, we spent five years on that subject. On the Non-Proliferation Treaty, which didn't even concern us, primarily, but other countries, we spent four years.

It would have been an easy matter to slap together a position and meet the Russians and put our position on the table. Then the Soviets would put their position on the table. There would have been a deadlock. We would have had to renegotiate our position within our bureaucracy. We would go back to the Russians.

This process could have been repeated indefinitely for five or six years. Instead, the President ordered the fullest study that has been made in or outside the government of just exactly what one would do if one wanted to limit any conceivable weapon system that has any conceivable application for strategic warfare.

We went through this weapon system by weapon system. We analyzed what our means of inspection were, what the dangers of violation were, what we would do if we spotted a violation, what the strategic significance would be if there was an agreement or if there were not an agreement.

In that process, incidentally, most of the usual bureaucratic disputes were avoided because we looked at it as an analytical problem and not as a bureaucratic problem.

Having made this survey, we were then in a position to put together four positions of various degrees of comprehensives, of which the President chose the two most comprehensive ones, which we put to the Soviets. The Soviets, as was predictable—and this I am not saying critically, the issue is so complex—had a slightly different view of the problem. But the work we had done enabled us to shift within a matter of three weeks from one position to another where previously this would have taken a year of internal fighting within our Administration.

Therefore, we are extremely optimistic about the progress in strategic arms talks. The Soviets have been constructive and without their cooperation it wouldn't have been possible. But I think it is fair to say that without the particular approach that the President insisted we introduce into the decision-making process, we could not have gotten to where we are today.

I will come back to that in a moment. I wanted to use it only as an illustration of the general approach.

Let me go back, then, and say that in the light of the philosophy I have described, and say what the guiding principle of the Administration is with respect to foreign policy.

This was expressed by the President at Guam, and has been popularly described as the Nixon Doctrine. It states the following: One, of course, we will maintain any commitments that the United States has. Two, that in the case of a threat by a nuclear country against a non-nuclear country, we feel that we have a special obligation since we are the only major nuclear country in the free world. Three, with respect to other threats, or with respect to other programs, the initial and principal responsibility has to be borne first by the country concerned and secondly by the region concerned.

We will assist where our interests are involved and where what we can do can make a difference. But we will not be in a position where the principal programs or the principal defense are borne in the first instance by the United States if the countries concerned do not make the effort themselves.

This we view not as a way of withdrawing from the world, but as a way of remaining related to the world in a way that is historically, psychologically and domestically bearable for us. It is a way of shifting to the other countries what has to be the normal position of the primary burden of their responsibilities, intellectually, physically, politically and militarily.

Enunciating a doctrine is a lot easier than implementing it. Obviously, as one goes into a new phase, it is only at universities that one has sharp dividing lines. In reality, there are always vestiges of the old together with the beginning of the new. Obviously, for example, when you have 550,000 Americans engaged in combat, you cannot shift to the Nixon Doctrine the day after you have announced it. That will have to be obviously, in those areas, a gradual progress.

So, I am describing a direction and not a cookbook, a recipe, that can be applied literally to every situation from one day to the next.

The reason why we believe that this doctrine can, should and will characterize American foreign policy in the next decade is not only because of the developing strength and self-confidence of other countries, but also because of the different conditions that exist in the world compared to the late 1940's.

In the late 1940's and the 50's, and, indeed, the early 60's, one thought of Communism as a monolith, inherently and eternally aggressive and run from a central core. No one who has seen the Communist world operate would underrate the aggressiveness of many of their leaders and many of their countries. But there has been an important historical change in a number of respects.

One is that the Communist system simply isn't working very well domestically, and that the Communist Party really does not have a very meaningful domestic function any more.

This has good and bad consequences. It leads on the one hand to a certain bureaucratization of life. On the other hand, it may give the Communist Parties a vested interest in foreign dangers. You don't need an ideological party to run a country. You don't need them to run an economy. So, they may have a vested interest always in being in a position of some tension in at least some part of the world.

The second important and perhaps decisive feature is the split between the Soviet Union and Communist China. According to Communist doctrine, the spread of Communism is to insure eternal peace. The fact of the matter is that the Red Army has been used four times since World War II, always against allies, only against allies.

The fact of the matter is that the deepest rivalries that exist in the world today are between Communist countries. First, the split that existed between the Soviet Union and Yugoslavia, and now the enormous tension that exists between the Soviet Union and Communist China, which may be the deepest factor in Soviet foreign policy and for which they really have no mechanism of handling it. It would be bad enough as a problem among states, that is, if states of the size of Communist China and the Soviet Union were in conflict that would be serious enough, but when you add to it a quasi-religious struggle of who is going to define the true orthodoxy so that it has profound ideological, semi-religious overtones, it has many insoluble aspects. And if the Soviet Union is more conciliatory towards the West at the moment, the consciousness of what seems to them the impending danger from the East is one of the most crucial factors.

There are, therefore, openings in negotiations with the Soviet Union that simply did not exist even ten years ago, much less 20 years ago, produced by this new aspect of international relations. These are the basic realities with which we deal.

Let me now make a few remarks about some specifics in the conduct of foreign policy.

We have a difficult problem in the sense that when the President came into office he announced that it would be an era of negotiations, that he was aiming for an era of negotiation and not confrontation. Many Americans tend to believe that you fuel negotiations primarily by endless demonstrations of unilateral good will.

On the other hand, history tends to indicate that negotiations depend to an important extent, especially with Communist countries, on the balance of risks and opportunities that they perceive.

Last year, when the President announced the ABM program, there were many who argued with us and said that if we developed the ABM, this would spark a new round of the arms race and it would forever doom the SALT negotiations.

The fact of the matter is, as the President pointed out, and as we can easily demonstrate, that without the ABM there probably wouldn't be any meaningful SALT negotiations. What possible incentive would the Soviets have? We have stopped developing offensive weapons. We have stopped building offensive weapons. Why should they make an agreement with us to stop doing something that we have already stopped doing and that they are continuing to do.

We didn't say that last year. At that time, we did it mostly on strategic claims, so I don't want to claim a foresight that we didn't insist on last year. Last year we did it because we were getting worried about the tremendous build up of the Soviet land based missile force.

As it turned out in the evolution of the negotiations, it is the ABM which is one of the main reasons why we can be so optimistic about the fact that we will get a fairly comprehensive agreement that we expect will include both offensive and defensive weapons within a reasonable time period, certainly a much shorter time period than was spent on any other set of negotiations.

The second area which I will not cover in detail, but which Joe Sisco will talk about is, of course, the Middle East.

I will confine myself to this general set of remarks. In many respects, the Middle East is a more difficult and in some of its aspects a more dangerous problem than, say, Southeast Asia. It is more difficult and more dangerous because we and the other side are not so completely in control of our actions. The characteristic of the Middle East that has caused the President and others to describe it as similar to the Balkans before World War I is that you have two groups of countries with very intense emotions who are very conscious of their local rivalries, but not primarily responsible for the peace of the world, two groups of countries that are, however, tied to the two opposing major camps, so that if these countries can get into conflict without the desire of the major countries, that is, specifically if there is an Arab-Israeli war that is not caused either by a decision in Washington or a decision in Moscow, it can nevertheless happen that Washington and Moscow, or the United States and the Soviet Union may get involved despite the fact that they were not involved in the initial decision.

This is why the Administration has been so interested in bringing about a settlement in the Middle East, and why Joe Sisco has been so invaluable in coming up with a formula. I will not say anything more about it except to underline our concern about the Middle East, the fact that the Administration has had a united policy on that issue, and that we consider it one of our high priority items.

Now let me make a few remarks about Southeast Asia. If the Middle East is our most dangerous area, there is no doubt that Southeast Asia is our most anguishing problem. We came into office while the level of troops was, in fact, still increasing in Vietnam, in the fifth year of a war that had been inconclusive, in negotiations which had never yet reached substance, and we faced the problem of bringing the war to a conclusion as the President promised, and in conformity with the principles that he has himself outlined to you.

There is a liturgical quality about the Vietnam debate that causes the participants to take fixed positions, that causes people to take fixed positions, and makes it very difficult to have a meaningful debate. I recognize that the concerns that have been expressed by many of our critics are based on very thoughtful analysis. Let me therefore state briefly where we think we are going, and why we do what we are doing.

First of all, the other day I met with a group of Princeton students whose emotions exceeded their knowledge, and who said, Why are you simply continuing old policies? Why don't you have the courage to change the policy? I reminded them that in August 1968, Senator Edward Kennedy made a speech in which he said he was picking up the fallen banner of his brother as a declaration of conscience of what should be done in Vietnam. I asked them to read that speech because it turns out there is nothing in that speech that we have not already done and exceeded. So what the professors of 1968 considered a daring program, we have gone far beyond. In 1968 [sic] when we came in, the number of troops was still increasing.

We have announced withdrawals of over 260,000. In 1968 the issue of whether one would even talk to the National Liberation Front was not settled. There is no question now that they can participate in the political process of Vietnam.

I don't want to repeat all the details which we can furnish you in writing. The major point I want to make is that this Administration is committed to ending the war, and it will end the war. But in order to end the war, it must carry out a number of steps which lend themselves to relatively easy attack. Obviously, at this stage of the war, there are no brilliant solutions available. The easy things have all been done. Therefore, anyone who takes the negative of any proposition can point out many weaknesses in any course that may be pursued.

Let me give you an example. One of our basic policies is the policy of Vietnamization, which is really an application of the Nixon Doctrine to South Vietnam, in which we want to put more and more responsibility on the South Vietnamese for their defense and for their political development.

There are many people who specialize in pointing out that this cannot possibly work, and others who say, "You mustn't have Vietnamization; you should have negotiation."

Let me say two things about it. First, if Vietnamization doesn't work, negotiation will not work either. Let me say flatly the whole thrust of our policy is to promote negotiation. We are convinced that the only quick way to end the war is through negotiation. The only reliable way of ending the war is through negotiation. No one familiar with the history of Vietnam can have any doubt that any program that depends entirely on local conditions has major problems connected with it.

But what we are saying is this: To the extent that the North Vietnamese look at the situation in South Vietnam and see that there develops there a structure that at least will give them a major problem after we withdraw, to that extent they will have an incentive to negotiate.

To the extent that the North Vietnamese looking at South Vietnam see a structure that is certain to collapse, to that same extent negotiations cannot work.

Therefore, there is no opposition between negotiation and Vietnamization. If Vietnamization works, negotiation may work—will work. If Vietnamization doesn't work, then both policies do not work.

Secondly, on the issue, there are many proposals, some of which have found their way into editorial pages, to the effect that we should put a deadline on our withdrawals. First of all, no one really knows whether we have an internal deadline or not. Secondly, whether we should announce a deadline raises a whole series of questions.

One reason we don't announce a deadline is because we want to beat any of the deadlines that I have seen written about. The reason we think we want to beat it is because we still have not given up on negotiations.

Once you have committed yourself irrevocably to getting out on a certain date, regardless of consequences, the other side has no conceivable interest left in negotiation. At that time, their only task is to hold on until that deadline is reached.

We are reasonably optimistic, insofar as one can be that in Vietnam, that Vietnamization is progressing satisfactorily enough, in order to support negotiations.

We will have setbacks and there won't be an uninterrupted progress. But the major trend we believe will either lead to a situation in which the other side may negotiate or to a situation in which we can withdraw and leave the country in a position where it has at least a chance to take care of itself.

Let me mention a few questions that are always put to us. A friend of mine wrote a letter a few months ago in which he said he wanted to put a few questions that concerned thoughtful people. One of his questions was: To what extent is your policy dictated by the Saigon Government? Or, are you independent of the Saigon Government?

I know the fashionable thing, at least in my former stamping grounds, would be to say we are completely independent of the Saigon Government and we do exactly what we believe. That would be a demagogic thing to say.

Obviously, when you fight in another country, you are allied with that other country, and you are affected by the actions of that country. Of course, we are influenced by some of their views.

What we are trying to do, however, through the process of Vietnamization, is to put them into a position, and ourselves in a position, where we are less and less dependent on their actions and they are less and less dependent on our views. That is the purpose of Vietnamization. We are not there yet, but we are trying to be there.

Secondly, are we independent of Hanoi's action?

Of course we are not completely independent of Hanoi's action. They, to some extent, influence us.

The third question is in negotiations, why don't you propose—and then you can have any list that human ingenuity can devise.

Let me make one observation about negotiations. First, there is a myth that negotiation with the North Vietnamese is like a detective story, in which they throw out their clues and we have to guess at the answer. Then if we don't get the answer correctly we are at fault for the failure of the negotiations.

I have been visited by more self-appointed peace emissaries who have picked out a phrase from some delegate in Paris that they thought was terribly significant, that we had been told about already, 50 times before.

The chief problem in negotiations is not lack of ingenuity on our part in coming up with a formula. The chief problem in negotiations is that we are confronting a country that has fought for 25 years with great courage, but whose very quality of courage may not make it capable of visualizing a compromise.

We have paid for the beginning of negotiations five different times. First we were told that if there were a bombing halt there would be substantive negotiations. Then we were told if we talked to the NLF there would be substantive negotiations; if we made a symbolic withdrawal of troops, if we announced the withdrawal of 100,000 troops, if we made the withdrawal of 100,000 troops, if we announced a new senior negotiator in Paris.

We have done every one of these things. There have not yet been substantive negotiations, and that for one simple reason. The last convinced Leninists in the world may be the North Vietnamese, and the sharing of political power is not the most obvious conclusion to which you are driven by the study of Leninism. Indeed, the opposite is true.

Secondly, Vietnamese, North or South, find it very difficult to visualize anything else but total victory. As soon as North Vietnam indicates that it is ready for serious negotiations, it will not be lack of ingenuity on our part that will start the negotiating process. Of this I can assure you flatly.

So, the missing ingredient at this moment is the beginning of a serious negotiation. But we haven't given up hope. You read in the paper yesterday that their senior negotiator is coming back to Paris. Whenever there has been a break in these Vietnam negotiations, it has come suddenly. I am not saying it is coming now, but whenever it will come, if it ever comes, it will be relatively sudden.

Let me make one final point to sum up all these observations. We had some difficult months after the President's decision to go into Cambodia. We have been told on a number of occasions how desirable it would be if we yielded to the pressures of so many dedicated and concerned groups, and if we only stopped what is often called the polarization of our society.

We have not done it, as the President said, because history tends to prove that the people do not forgive leaders who produce disasters, even if these disasters are following the recommendations made by the public. We believe that our obligation is to make a peace that will last; that a peace cannot last if in the process confidence in the United States is shaken.

Nor do we believe that the answer to our domestic difficulties is to yield to any group that smashes the china and then says, "Look what you have made me do."

We believe it is important that the way we end the war and the way we build the peace reflects the best judgment of the best thought that can be brought to bear on the problem.

In doing this, we believe, even though this wouldn't be recognized, that we may be the best protection of the very people who have been most vociferously protesting against us. If this country is taken over by a radical group, it will not be by upper middle class college kids. There will be a much more elemental group taking it over.

We cannot permit the political contests to be fought out by rival groups of demonstrators. We think this is terribly important, to conclude, because we are at a point where except for the war in Vietnam, there are possibilities of bringing about a more reliable peace in the world than we have known in the whole post-war period.

We are at a point where we can re-define the American position with respect to the world, where, for whatever reasons, it may be that even the Soviet Union has come to a realization of the limitations of both its physical strength and of the limits of its ideological fervor.

But none of these possibilities can be realized except by an American Government that is confident that it knows what it is doing, that can respond to its best judgment, and by an American public that has enough confidence in its leaders so that they are permitted the modicum of ambiguity that is sometimes inseparable from a situation in which you cannot, at the beginning of a process, know completely what all the consequences are.

The tragic aspect of policy-making is that when your scope for action is greatest, the knowledge on which you can base this action is always at a minimum. When your knowledge is greatest, the scope for action has often disappeared. This is the problem that we face. This is why no society can operate without confidence. But the reason despite this turmoil is because in any new creation one is very conscious of the symptoms of the turmoil. One is very aware of the things that are being changed. It is always a painful process to see it come about. But we think there is a very good chance that by the end of this term we will have laid the foundations for a period to which many of those who were most worried a few months ago can not only reconcile themselves, but can support and in which the whole American public will feel that this was the beginning of an era of constructive peace.

[Omitted here are Sisco's comments and his and Kissinger's answers to questions.]

---

70.   Message From President Nixon to the Congress[1]

Washington, September 15, 1970.

FOREIGN ASSISTANCE FOR THE SEVENTIES

Today, I am proposing a major transformation in our foreign assistance programs.

For more than two decades these programs have been guided by a vision of international responsibilities conditioned by the aftermath of World War II and the emergence of new nations. But the world has been changing dramatically; by the end of the 'Sixties, there was widespread agreement that our programs for foreign assistance had not kept up with these changes and were losing their effectiveness. This sentiment has been reflected in declining foreign aid levels.

The cause of this downward drift is not that the need for aid has diminished; nor is it that our capacity to help other nations has dimin-

---

[1] Source: *Public Papers of the Presidents of the United States: Richard Nixon, 1970,* pp. 745–756. President Nixon signed the message for transmittal to Congress in a ceremony in his office attended by the members of the Presidential Task Force on International Development.

ished; nor has America lost her humanitarian zeal; nor have we turned inward and abandoned our pursuit of peace and freedom in the world.

The answer is not to stop foreign aid or to slash it further. The answer is to reform our foreign assistance programs and do our share to meet the needs of the 'Seventies.

A searching reexamination has clearly been in order and, as part of the new Administration's review of policy, I was determined to undertake a fresh appraisal. I have now completed that appraisal and in this message I am proposing a set of fundamental and sweeping reforms to overhaul completely our entire foreign assistance operation to make it fit a new foreign policy.

Such a major transformation cannot be accomplished overnight. The scope and complexity of such an undertaking requires a deliberate and thoughtful approach over many months. I look forward to active discussion of these proposals with the Congress before I transmit my new assistance legislation next year.

Reform No. 1: I propose to create separate organizational arrangements for each component of our assistance effort: security assistance, humanitarian assistance, and development assistance. This is necessary to enable us to fix responsibility more clearly, and to assess the success of each program in achieving its specific objectives. My proposal will overcome the confusion inherent in our present approach which lumps together these separate objectives in composite programs.

Reform No. 2: To provide effective support for the Nixon Doctrine, I shall propose a freshly conceived International Security Assistance Program. The prime objective of this program will be to help other countries assume the responsibility of their own defense and thus help us reduce our presence abroad.

Reform No. 3: I propose that the foundation for our development assistance programs be a new partnership among nations in pursuit of a truly international development effort based upon a strengthened leadership role for multilateral development institutions. To further this objective,

—The U.S. should channel an increasing share of its development assistance through the multilateral institutions as rapidly as practicable.

—Our remaining bilateral assistance should be provided largely within a framework established by the international institutions.

—Depending upon the success of this approach, I expect that we shall eventually be able to channel most of our development assistance through these institutions.

Reform No. 4: To enable us to provide effective bilateral development assistance in the changed conditions of the 'Seventies, I shall transmit legislation to create two new and independent institutions:

—A U.S. International Development Corporation, to bring vitality and innovation to our bilateral lending activities and enable us to deal with lower income nations on a businesslike basis.

—A U.S. International Development Institute to bring the genius of U.S science and technology to bear on the problems of development, to help build research and training competence in the lower income countries themselves, and to offer cooperation in international efforts dealing with such problems as population and employment.

Their creation will enable us to phase out the Agency for International Development and to reduce significantly the number of overseas U.S. Government personnel working on development programs.

Reform No. 5: To add a new dimension to the international aid effort insuring a more permanent and enduring source of funds for the low income countries, I have recently proposed that all nations enter into a treaty which would permit the utilization of the vast resources of the seabeds to promote economic development.

Reform No. 6: I propose that we redirect our other policies which bear on development to assure that they reinforce the new approach outlined in this message. Our goal will be to expand and enhance the contribution to development of trade and private investment, and to increase the effectiveness of government programs in promoting the development process. A number of changes are necessary:

—I propose that we move promptly toward initiation of a system of tariff preferences for the exports of manufactured products of the lower income countries in the markets of all of the industrialized countries.

—I am ordering the elimination of those tying restrictions on procurement which hinder our investment guarantee program in its support of U.S. private investment in the lower income countries.

—I propose that all donor countries take steps to end the requirement that foreign aid be used to purchase goods and services produced in the nation providing the aid. Complete untying of aid is a step that must be taken in concert with other nations; we have already begun discussions with them toward that end. As an initial step, I have directed that our own aid be immediately untied for procurement in the lower income countries themselves.

The Foundations of Reform

These are the most fundamental of the many far-reaching reforms I propose today. To understand the need for them now, and to place them in perspective, it is important to review here the way in which we have reexamined our policies in light of today's requirements.

Two steps were necessary to develop a coherent and constructive U.S. assistance program for the 'Seventies:

—As a foundation, we needed a foreign policy tailored to the 1970's to provide direction for our various programs. For that, we developed and reported to the Congress in February the New Strategy for Peace.[2]

—Second, to assist me in responding to the Congress and to get the widest possible range of advice on how foreign assistance could be geared to that strategy, I appointed a distinguished group of private U.S. citizens to make a completely independent assessment of what we should be trying to achieve with our foreign aid programs and how we should go about it.

The Task Force on International Development, chaired by Rudolph Peterson, former President of the Bank of America, drew upon the considerable experience of its own members and sought views from Members of the Congress and from every quarter of U.S. society. In early March the Task Force presented its report to me, and shortly thereafter I released it to the public.[3] The Task Force undertook a comprehensive assessment of the conditions affecting our foreign assistance program and proposed new and creative approaches for the years ahead. Its report provides the basis for the proposals which I am making today.

I also have taken into account the valuable insights and suggestions concerning development problems which were contained in the Rockefeller Report on our Western Hemisphere policy.[4] Many of the ideas and measures I am proposing in this message in fact were foreshadowed by a number of policy changes and program innovations which I instituted in our assistance programs in Latin America.

The Purposes of Foreign Assistance

There are three interrelated purposes that the U.S. should pursue through our foreign assistance program: promoting our national security by supporting the security of other nations; providing humanitarian relief; and furthering the long-run economic and social development of the lower income countries.

The national security objectives of the U.S. cannot be pursued solely through defense of our territory. They require a successful effort by other countries around the world, including a number of lower income countries, to mobilize manpower and resources to defend themselves.

---

[2] See Document 60.

[3] See footnote 4, Document 53.

[4] See footnote 5, Document 35.

244 Foreign Relations, 1969–1976, Volume I

They require in some cases, military bases abroad, to give us the necessary mobility to defend ourselves and to deter aggression. They sometimes require our financial support of friendly countries in exceptional situations.

Moreover, our security assistance programs must be formulated to achieve the objectives of the Nixon Doctrine, which I set forth at Guam last year. That approach calls for any country whose security is threatened to assume the primary responsibility for providing the manpower needed for its own defense. Such reliance on local initiative encourages local assumption of responsibility and thereby serves both the needs of other countries and our own national interest. In addition, the Nixon Doctrine calls for our providing assistance to such countries to help them assume these responsibilities more quickly and more effectively. The new International Security Assistance Program will be devoted largely to these objectives. I shall set forth the details of the proposed program when I transmit the necessary implementing legislation to the Congress next year.

The humanitarian concerns of the American people have traditionally led us to provide assistance to foreign countries for relief from natural disasters, to help with child care and maternal welfare, and to respond to the needs of international refugees and migrants. Our humanitarian assistance programs, limited in size but substantial in human benefits, give meaningful expression to these concerns.

Both security and humanitarian assistance serve our basic national goal: the creation of a peaceful world. This interest is also served, in a fundamental and lasting sense, by the third purpose of our foreign assistance: the building of self-reliant and productive societies in the lower income countries. Because these countries contain two-thirds of the world's population, the direction which the development of their societies takes will profoundly affect the world in which we live.

We must respond to the needs of these countries if our own country and its values are to remain secure. We are, of course, wholly responsible for solutions to our problems at home, and we can contribute only partially to solutions abroad. But foreign aid must be seen for what it is—not a burden, but an opportunity to help others to fulfill their aspirations for justice, dignity, and a better life. No more abroad than at home can peace be achieved and maintained without vigorous efforts to meet the needs of the less fortunate.

The approaches I am outlining today provide a coherent structure for foreign assistance—with a logical framework for separate but interdependent programs. With the cooperation of Congress, we must seek to identify as clearly as possible which of our purposes—security, humanitarianism, or long-term development of the lower income countries—to pursue through particular U.S. programs. This is necessary to enable us to determine how much of our resources we wish to put into each, and to assess the progress of each program toward achieving its objectives.

There is one point, however, that I cannot over-emphasize. Each program is a part of the whole, and each must be sustained in order to pursue our national purpose in the world of the 'Seventies. It is incumbent upon us to support all component elements—or the total structure will be unworkable.

Effective Development Assistance—The Changed Conditions

The conditions that surround and influence development assistance to lower income countries have dramatically changed since the present programs were established. At that time the United States directly provided the major portion of the world's development assistance. This situation led to a large and ambitious U.S. involvement in the policies and activities of the developing countries and required extensive overseas missions to advise governments and monitor programs. Since then the international assistance environment has changed:

First, the lower income countries have made impressive progress, as highlighted by the Commission on International Development chaired by Lester Pearson, the former Prime Minister of Canada. They have been helped by us and by others, but their achievements have come largely through their own efforts. Many have scored agricultural breakthroughs which have dramatically turned the fear of famine into the hope of harvest. They have made vast gains in educating their children and improving their standards of health. The magnitude of their achievement is indicated by the fact that the lower income countries taken together exceeded the economic growth targets of the First United Nations Development Decade. These achievements have brought a new confidence and self-reliance to people in communities throughout the world.

With the experience that the lower income countries have gained in mobilizing their resources and setting their own development priorities, they now can stand at the center of the international development process—as they should, since the security and development which is sought is theirs. They clearly want to do so. Any assistance effort that fails to recognize these realities cannot succeed.

Second, other industrialized nations can now afford to provide major assistance to the lower income countries, and most are already doing so in steadily rising amounts.

While the United States remains the largest single contributor to international development, the other industrialized nations combined now more than match our efforts. Cooperation among the industrialized nations is essential to successful support for the aspirations of the lower income countries. New initiatives in such areas as trade liberalization and untying of aid must be carried out together by all such countries.

Third, international development institutions—the World Bank group, the Inter-American Development Bank and other regional development organizations, the United Nations Development Program, and other international agencies—now possess a capability to blend the initiatives of the lower income countries and the responses of the industrialized nations. They have made effective use of the resources which we and others have provided. A truly international donor community is emerging, with accepted rules and procedures for responding to the initiatives of the lower income countries. The international institutions are now in a position to accelerate further a truly international development effort.

Fourth, the progress made by lower income countries has brought them a new capability to sell abroad, to borrow from private sources, and to utilize private investment efficiently. As a result, a fully effective development effort should encompass much more than government assistance programs if it is to make its full potential contribution to the well-being of the people of the developing nations. We have come to value the constructive role that the private sector can play in channeling productive investments that will stimulate growth. We now understand the critical importance of enlightened trade policies that take account of the special needs of the developing countries in providing access for their exports to the industrialized nations.

Effective Development Assistance—The Program for Reform

To meet these changed international conditions, I propose a program for reform in three key areas: to support an expanded role for the international assistance institutions; to reshape our bilateral programs; and to harness all assistance-related policies to improve the effectiveness of our total development effort.

My program for reform is a reaffirmation of the commitment of the United States to support the international development process, and I urge the Congress to join me in fulfilling that commitment. We want to help other countries raise their standards of living. We want to use our aid where it can make a difference. To achieve these goals we will respond positively to sound proposals which effectively support the programs of the lower income countries to develop their material and human resources and institutions to enable their citizens to share more fully in the benefits of worldwide technology and economic advance.

[Omitted here is a detailed exposition of the proposed program for reform.]

---

71.   Off-the-Record Remarks by President Nixon[1]

Chicago, Illinois, September 16, 1970.

[Omitted here are Herbert Klein's introduction of President Nixon and his admonition that the President's remarks were on "deep background" and should be used without direct attribution. Nixon began by explaining that an off-the-record approach gave him the latitude to discuss matters he might not otherwise feel free to discuss. He then praised Henry Kissinger and Joseph Sisco, who had provided the group with a prior briefing on the administration's foreign policy.]

If I could come to some other points, the greatest need that I felt we had in the field of foreign policy when we came into office was for perspective, for a long historical perspective.

What I say now is not intended to be critical of previous administrations, any of them. It is basically an observation about American foreign policy generally.

Throughout the years, American foreign policy has been basically one that reacts to events. That is why, as a matter of fact, when you see young people outside carrying signs, "Peace now, Peace now," it should not be surprising. We are that kind of people. "Bring the boys home immediately after World War II" regardless of what was going to happen. "End the war," do this and that and the other thing.

The United States people are people who are impatient people. We are a people who find it difficult to take the long view. There is a fundamental reason for that, which is very much to our credit, in my opinion.

We are the only world power that got to that position without intending to do so. We didn't have a policy to become a world power. It

---

[1] Source: Library of Congress, Manuscript Division, Kissinger Papers, Box CL 426, Subject File, Background Briefings, September–October 1970. No classification marking. The President spoke from 4:47 to 5:25 p.m. in the Embassy Room of the Blackstone Hotel in Chicago. He addressed 60 editors and broadcasters from Illinois, Indiana, Iowa, Kentucky, Michigan, Minnesota, Nebraska, North Dakota, Ohio, and Wisconsin. (National Archives, Nixon Presidential Materials, White House Central Files, Staff Members and Office Files, Office of Presidential Papers and Archives, Daily Diary)

happened that by the acts of World War II, the fact that all the other major powers in the free world, except the United States, were decimated by the war, all of the powers of Europe, the Japanese in Asia, and all the other industrial powers. Of course, none of them had the ability.

Here sat the United States. The action was all in our court. We had to act. Here we were. We didn't plan it that way. We did not have a policy to reach that point.

Then, we suddenly found ourselves in the position where what happened in Asia, what happened in the Middle East, what happened in Latin America, what happened in Africa, what happened in Europe, all over the world, we in the United States some way—not because we wanted it, for most Americans didn't want it as a matter of fact, and don't want it, but because no one else was there to fill the vacuum of leadership—we in the United States had to have policies.

And that is why we, of course, developed a policy with regard to the defense of Europe. That is why we developed our policy in the field of economic assistance to Latin America and to all the other countries of the world.

That is why we had a policy in the Middle East. That is one of the major reasons why we developed a capability in our Armed Forces far beyond the necessity simply to defend the fortress of America. Because we had to have and we did have the responsibility, at least we felt we did, to look to other nations including even our defeated enemies—perhaps them more than others, Japan and Germany, because they, as a result of the war, were forced to complete disarmament and were denied the right to obtain the only armament that means anything for world power, nuclear power.

Here sits the United States with the responsibility on our hands.

With this kind of background, I have found and I would say this about all of our Administrations, I sat in the Eisenhower Administration for eight years. I know the discussions that were made there.

General Eisenhower had a longer view than most Americans. He had been through part of World War I at a very early age and he had seen, of course, much of World War II and had dealt with the great problems of the world. But even then there had not yet developed a long-term perspective. Then came the situation in the years after that.

I was not in government. But I think, as I look at the papers that were written at that time, a long-term perspective was not there.

So our first instruction to all of the people in our Administration when we came in—Joe Sisco knows this is what we said, not only with regard to the Middle East, but with regard to India, Pakistan, areas also under his control, and Henry Kissinger who had general charge of it all recognizes that, and I won't go into all the areas we have tried to cover.

It is a mountain of work—we are re-examining every policy and trying to look ahead, not one year, two years, not even five years, not even to the end of this Administration, whether it is two years or six years or what have you, but ahead to the end of a century. That is about as far as we probably can look.

As we look ahead at the end of the century, that brings me, if I can for just a moment, come, to the subjects that Dr. Kissinger probably has covered in some perspective already, because his presentations are always in this vein.

But I would like for you to hear directly from me, to hear first very briefly about the war in Asia and what our plans are, and then if we could look at the Mediterranean and the trip we are planning there, and why it is really being taken. It really isn't a junket, it is for very important reasons which I will not discuss publicly for reasons you will soon see.

Then, look at the relations between the two super powers and perhaps one brief look at what the world will be like 10 or 15 years from now if we do play a role.

Many years ago, at the time of the Korean War, when it was a great debate as to whether Truman should or should not have gone into Korea, I was talking to a man who is a great expert on the World Communist Movement. He said something that stuck in my mind ever since that time. He said, "Truman had to go into Korea. We had to go into Korea, because what we must remember is that the war in Korea for the Communists is not about Korea. It is about Japan." Of course, it was.

If you look back at it now and see the weak Japan at that time, if Korea had been overrun, and Japan with its very, very strong Socialist party leaning toward the Communists might have—even with the enormous dependence it had at that time upon the United States economically and with certainly even the power that we guaranteed in terms of their defense—Japan would have been pulled inevitably into orbit and toward that orbit. So Korea was about that.

I think we could say and we don't need to talk about any common theory. We all argue whether or not that is right. But the point is that as far as the war in Vietnam is concerned, history will record that it was about Vietnam, yes, and the Vietnamese people and whether they survive and have the right to choose their form of government and so forth.

But in terms of its impact of how it is ended, that war is not just about Vietnam. It is about Southeast Asia, the Pacific, about Japan, and about, we think, peace in the world generally. Because, if it is ended in a way that encourages those who might embark on any kind of aggression in that part of the world, if it is ended in a way that is interpreted by the Japanese, for example, the Indonesians, even by our friends in India and Pakistan—that far away not to mention our friends in Europe—if it is interpreted as the failure of the United States in this part of the world in its very difficult but relatively small action, as our failure to achieve a minimum goal, not victory over North Vietnam, but simply the right of the South Vietnamese to choose their own way without having it imposed, the impact would be enormous and I think devastating.

That is why despite the great political temptation—and how great it really is—to get it over right now, pull them out, blame whoever started it, et cetera, despite all of that we, I think, have to take the position that we will end the war. We are ending it. It is winding down. It will continue to. But we are going to end it in a way which will discourage those who might engage in aggression, that will not in terms of our enemies and those who might be our enemies encourage those who are, shall we say, the hawks as against the doves, and also in a way that particularly will not dismay our friends in Asia and that part of the world.

That is why the long view requires not only ending the war, but then a plan after that, and that is why right at the present time, Mr. Shultz, Mr. Ehrlichman, two of our top domestic advisers, are in Japan and will shortly be going to South Vietnam for the purpose of taking the long view—what happens afterwards; the development of Southeast Asia, our relations with Japan, and so on.

Let me come to the Mediterranean and put it in the same context for a moment. This is a trip to the Sixth Fleet.[2] It could be looked upon as what Presidents do in political campaigns. You go and inspect the fleet or inspect a base. It has been done before. I didn't bring it up for the first time, as you are all aware.

The Sixth Fleet, however, has implications far beyond simply a routine Presidential inspection. I have gone to carriers before and I have looked at them. I have no reason to want to see how a carrier operates and how the Navy with its marvelous flyers are able to land in a small space and so forth and so on.

But when we look at the Mediterranean and the Sixth Fleet—let me try to put that in the context of history as I see it.

If there is one thing that can be said, over the past ten years the American position in the Mediterranean has been rapidly deteriorating and has deteriorated there more than any place in the world.

---

[2] Reference is to the President's impending trip to the Mediterranean, which included a visit to the Sixth Fleet. The trip began on September 27, concluded on October 5, and included stops in Italy, Yugoslavia, Spain, England, and Ireland.

Look at the southern rim of the Mediterranean. Look at the eastern rim of the Mediterranean and the northern rim of the Mediterranean and see what has happened, and you will see why this is the case.

When you look at the southern rim of the Mediterranean, ever since the June war in 1967, while the United States still has a strong friend in Morocco, and also a strong friend in Tunisia, both of these countries are relatively weak, both economically and certainly militarily.

Next door is Algeria. Algeria is more hopeful at the moment, even though we don't have diplomatic relations established on a formal basis. They have been making certainly rather generous comments, or at least more generous than you would normally expect. I think Mr. Sisco would agree.

Libya is a country which is enormously affected by the fact that about half of its population is Palestinian refugees. Libya with all of that oil, and with the kind of government it has—who knows what will happen there; the influence, whether the influence will be within Libya, whether it will be by Nasser hanging over them, or for that matter from the Soviet Union. I don't need to talk about Nasser and his problems in Egypt. You are aware of that. It has been discussed earlier.

But looking further around, Lebanon always was shaky, and still is, of course.

Jordan, a country where you wonder why anybody would ever insure the king. I am sure nobody does. And there are reasons there that have already been discussed.

Iraq and Syria, countries that at the present time are, as far as we are concerned, ones we have very little information about, except that they are basically irrational and usually antagonistic towards our views.

Then we have to go clear over to Iran, which is not in the Middle East, to find a strong, effective support of the United States, or to Saudi Arabians. That is about it.

You look at all of that area, sitting in the heart of it is Israel. There is a tendency to look at the Mideast and say, "This conflict is about Israel and its neighbors." Of course it is. It is about the survival of Israel. But we couldn't make a greater mistake than to think of it in those terms even primarily. Certainly the United States stands for the survival of Israel and the survival of other countries in that area and for their independence and for their ability to defend themselves.

But on the other hand, if we look at the Arab-Israeli conflict, we have to remember they have hated each other for thousands of years and they are going to continue for another thousand years and nothing we do or they do is going to solve that—no cease fires, no agreements, no border guarantees, no U.N. guarantees, no U.S.-Soviet guarantees, nothing.

What is it all about then? What it is about in terms of historical perspective is this: A policy which will keep, if we can, this relationship of an uneasy ceasefire, fragile, as has already described, attempting to look down the road when Israel will be able to live with its neighbors in a relative period of live and let-live.

That is about all that they can hope for and all that we can hope for. It is putting it in the perspective of history for them and it is very difficult for them to think in this perspective, just as it is for us. They look down the road five years and they realize that they are going to be able to handle any of their neighbors without any question, even though their neighbors have many more planes, many more tanks, and everything else.

But looking down the road, 10, 15, 20 years, Egyptians supported enough by the Soviet Union or some other power, can learn to fight and Iraqis and Syrians and all the rest. They never have, but it can be done. We used to not think that Asians could fight. They have proved they could fight pretty well in Korea, and then in Vietnam. So it will be here.

So far as Israel is concerned, it has an interest, in my belief at least, it has an interest in making, at least attempting, attempting to bargain when its bargaining position is strong rather than waiting for the time when its bargaining position becomes much more equal with that of its neighbors. So be it.

I only indicate that as one of the factors that may eventually bring these nations to some kind of a live-and-let-live attitude.

But let us look further. Looking at the northern Mediterranean and some of the policies we have there, I know many in this room—I have seen a few editorials—that are concerned about our policy toward Greece; critical of the fact that we continue to provide military aid to the Greek government for its NATO forces, due to the fact that the Greeks have a government that we disapprove of. We do disapprove of their government. They are aware of that.

But Greece has 11 divisions in NATO. It is on the southern hinge of NATO. It is right next to Turkey, which also has a number of divisions. And as far Greece is concerned, while we of course try to use our influence as effectively as we can, but not in a way that will put them on the spot publicly and create exactly the opposite effect that we want, it is essential that the United States continue to support NATO forces in Greece and we will do so.

You move on over. Italy has had problems ever since World War II; a divided government, too many parties and not one strong enough— not a really strong man since De Gasperi, except for Saragat, the

President, who of course has never been head of the government. His party is too small; he has just been head of state.

We go on to Spain. Here again we have one of those tough ones. From an ideological standpoint, people in this country don't like the idea of America supporting a man, Franco, who 35 years ago left the taste in the mouth of dictatorship. And we would, I think, in this room subscribe to our antipathy to the kind of rule that he imposed then and that he has now.

Yet here is Spain, the western hinge. And if Spain, is what we are involved in there, where our bases are involved, if we look at the whole Mediterranean policy and speak of it completely, shall we say, in the idealistic terms that I would like to always speak of, and that you would like to write about and speak of, we shouldn't have any bases in Spain.

We should let the Greeks go.

The Turks, we don't like their government too well either because it isn't too democratic. As far as the southern hinge is concerned, the southern part of the Mediterranean is concerned, we just let that slip and slide.

That is what the short-range attitude would be. But we have to look at the whole Mediterranean. We are looking at the whole Mediterranean. And there are times we are going to have to make decisions that will have to put first things first. We are going to use our influence always to bring other people toward those kinds of principles that we believe people throughout the world, regardless of their background, have a right to have in their governments.

But we, on the other hand, feel that where American interests are involved, the interests of free nations generally, it is vitally important that the Mediterranean not be allowed to create the vacuum, to continue to deteriorate as it has been deteriorating.

Now comes the Sixth Fleet. What good do a few carriers and cruisers and the rest do down there? It has an enormous effect, an enormous effect because it is a presence. If we have any doubt about what good it does, we can look to see what our potential opponents in the world— when I say "potential opponents", I don't use the word "enemy" because we live in a world that is too dangerous for super powers to be enemies. We hope to work out with the Soviet Union a live-and-let-live attitude, even though their interests are very different.

The way to work out that attitude, live-and-let-live policy, is to recognize once and for all that we aren't going to agree on everything, we aren't going to like each other too well as far as our systems are concerned, they are going to be different, our interests are going to conflict. They have a different attitude about Europe, about Asia, about Africa, about Latin America, and they are still expansionists.

We are, on the other hand, thinking in terms of defense all around the world. But when we look at the situation—what are they doing about the Mediterranean? If you have any doubts about sea power, you will see. It grows. It is still far short of ours. It will not catch ours, not in the foreseeable future.

I am speaking not of its nuclear submarine power where they will catch us in 1974 nuclear missile-carrying submarines, but I am speaking in terms of sea power generally.

And if that sea power is allowed to grow to the point which it could, with our doing nothing—where it is superior to ours in the Mediterranean, you can see the effect that is going to have on the American presence in the Mediterranean.

When we speak of the Mediterranean, the Mideast and the rest, you have got to put it in the larger context. We all know the Mideast is the gateway to Africa. We all know that the Mideast is the source of 80 percent of Europe's oil and 90 percent of Japan's oil. We all know too that it is the southern hinge of NATO.

That is why we try to think not in terms simply of the hijackers on four planes: Arabs versus Israeli, of what we do about the Italian Government today, and Spanish bases, we have to look at the whole picture and see what kind of a situation we are going to be faced with five or ten years from now.

How can we improve the American and free-world position in the Mediterranean? We don't do it alone. That is why we are helping the British, the Italians, to the extent they can, the Spanish, the French and everybody else to play their role.

So much for that bit of analysis, a case history.

Now, I would go on to a couple of other points, and I will be through, to illustrate. In the perspective of history, let me talk briefly about ABM.

ABM can be looked upon as a new defensive weapons system, of very doubtful efficiency, doubtful until it is tried, and nobody knows. I hope we never find out, or have to find out, whether or not it will be useful.

We think it might. Certainly the Soviet Union thinks it might.

But as we look today at the power balance and Henry Kissinger has covered this already with you I am sure, we find that the enormous advantage that the United States had in 1961 has gone down. This is not said critically of the Administrations of the past. It was inevitable to go down, because the United States maintained its level, the Soviet Union came up.

Whereas, there was at least a ten to one advantage of the United States over the Soviet Union at the time of the Cuban missile crisis in terms of Intercontinental Ballistic Missiles. Today it is even, with the throw weight, three to one in their favor.

That doesn't mean that at this point the United States is behind, because we have been doing some things, too, that are effective. The development of our MIRV program, moving on certain areas, and we still have enormous advantages in air power. We have enormous advantages on the sea still at this point.

But looking to the future, what the United States must remember is this: Take, for example, the field of nuclear submarines. If we decided now that we had to do something to maintain an adequate number of nuclear submarines vis-à-vis the Soviet Union, we couldn't have the first one until eight years from now. That is why decisions have to be made in the long term, rather than the short term. That is why again we look at the Sixth Fleet, not just in terms of its mission in the Mediterranean today, but where is it going to be six, eight years from now and what should we do in this country having that in mind.

Again, getting back to ABM, so we decide at this point that we will go for a defensive system in order to maintain what we describe as sufficiency for the United States, and not to allow the balance to get out.

Let me talk very candidly about why I think that is important. An argument can be made, I have heard it made quite eloquently often around our Cabinet tables from time to time, particularly by outside experts, to the effect that enough is enough. It doesn't make any difference if the Soviet Union has ten times as much as we have, or Communist China 25 years from now might have that much.

The answer is maybe. But on the other hand, try to tell that to your European allies. Tell it to a Germany, or a Japan, with no nuclear power.

The point that I make is this: I do not suggest that the United States for some jingoistic reason, because of cold war rhetoric, as it is described, has to be number one in the world in every respect, but I do say that as far as that when the time comes, when those who depend upon the umbrella of U.S. power, when they reach the conclusion that the United States has settled for an inferior position on the sea, or in terms overall roughly of the balance between missiles, offensive and defensive, then the United States no longer can play the role which unfortunately—I say unfortunately because it would be so much easier to concentrate on all of these domestic problems that start crying out for a solution—we could not play the role that history has cast upon us to play of being the nation that makes it possible for other nations to grow up in freedom and independence, without having a Soviet or Chinese and Communist system imposed upon them.

That finally brings me to the last point I would like to make. I often get the question, "As you look way ahead, what is the most difficult problem the United States has?" And I could say, of course, "Well, it is ending the war in Vietnam, the policy in the Mid East, a new policy in Europe, maintaining the weapons balance," and the rest. All of those things are important, not the most difficult, because they are soluble in the long run either by diplomacy or money or some other method.

But the real problem basically goes much deeper than that. And it basically is something that I particularly convey to you. I know that in this room there are very honest men who disagree with some of our policies, our Cambodian decision, our decision to continue the war in Vietnam to what we believe is a just peace, rather than ending it more precipitately, people who disagree with our decision to go on ABM, who may disagree with some of the things I have said in other areas.

That I understand, I appreciate, I respect. I hope we always have it in this country.

But one thing I would say very strongly at this point is as I look down the road, the next 25 years, I am convinced that there isn't any question about the ability of the United States to continue to play a helpful and constructive role in the world. I say thank God the United States is the nation that has the responsibility of leadership. The United States isn't going to attack anybody else. The United States isn't trying to get anything from anybody else. We are not trying to extend or impose our system on anybody else.

All we want is peace for ourselves, freedom for ourselves, and we hope peace and freedom, if we can, for other nations in the world.

That is the kind of a leader that the free world, I think, desperately needs and would want and would trust.

The question is, whether we in this country—our young people, for that matter, older people with all of our tremendous domestic problems—whether we have the stamina and the character and basically I come back to the fundamental point, whether we have the wisdom to take the long view, to see what the world would be like if the United States did draw into itself and say, "Who else, who is left?" Not the Germans, not the Japanese, not the British, not the French, no one else in the world can assume this responsibility of leadership.

So, as we look at that world and what it is going to be like, I am convinced that this Administration will do the best it can for the balance of the time we are there.

But I am convinced that you gentlemen have in your hands, through your editorials, through your television commentary, over the period of time, that you have an even greater responsibility and one that can have an ever greater impact to develop within this country the sense of perspective and sense of judgment.

I could even say a sense of destiny which a nation like ours needs—which we need, not because we want to be number one or Mr. Big or anything like that, but because at this time we happen to live in a world where unless we do, the situation as far as the rest of the world is concerned would be that most of the nations of the world, except for the other two great super powers, the Soviet Union and China, would simply be living in terror of what would happen.

So, we appreciated a chance to come here and share some thoughts with you at this media briefing. We have now had three of them, we are going to have another one in the Northeast shortly, and I am sorry that I have gone over the time that I expected to talk.

But I did want to share with you, not simply the decisions that we make and why we make them—that has been done better than I can by the experts who work on it day to day—but I did want you to know some of the things that sometimes you wonder, "What does he think about when he goes in the Lincoln sitting room and sits up late at night? What does he think about when he goes to Camp David and the rest?"

I don't think always simply about subjects as heavy as this. But I can assure you that at this time, above everything else, I try not to become enmeshed in the details that someone else can handle, not to become bogged down in making decisions like what is going to be the bombing run tomorrow, here, there and everyplace.

But I try constantly to bring to these discussions the sense of perspective that America has never had because we didn't need it, but now that we have got to have because not only we need it, but the world needs it.

Thank you.

72.   **Background Press Briefing by the President's Assistant for National Security Affairs (Kissinger)**[1]

Naples, Italy, September 29, 1970.

[Omitted here are Press Secretary Ronald Ziegler's introduction of Kissinger, his explanation of the rules governing a background briefing, and the initial questions fielded by Kissinger in the briefing, relating largely to the Yugoslav portion of the trip.]

Let me say a word about the general objective of the President in the last two days and then fit the *Springfield* into it.[2]

Many of you have heard me talk about the Nixon Doctrine at perhaps exorbitant length. But one of the problems that we have faced in connection with our foreign policy and with the transition from a period in which the United States carried the almost exclusive responsibility to one in which we are trying to share increasingly our responsibility with others, is the fear of many countries, particularly of many allies, that the United States might withdraw from its responsibilities altogether.

Whenever we have met Europeans over recent months, European leaders over recent months, this has been one of their principal concerns. It turned out to be one of the important concerns of Italian leaders when we saw them yesterday, one of whom pointed out to us that the first visit of the President here in February was very important but the one this week was really quite crucial in reassuring the Europeans, and particularly the countries of the Mediterranean, that the United States was not withdrawing into isolationism, but, rather, remained committed to its alliances.

I mention this because the President has reiterated wherever he has been that the United States did not intend to make any unilateral reductions of its forces; that we considered the problems of the Western Alliance a concern for all the countries.

What we attempted to do this afternoon was to review with our commanders in the Mediterranean two problems. One, the problems

---

[1] Source: Library of Congress, Manuscript Division, Kissinger Papers, Box CL 426, Subject File, Background Briefings, September–October 1970. No classification marking. The briefing took place from 7:10 to 7:45 p.m. local time.

[2] The question Kissinger was responding to at this point was: "What did the President discuss in his conference today with the military commanders on the *Springfield*?" Nixon had met with the commanders of the Sixth Fleet aboard the U.S.S. *Springfield* earlier in the day. (National Archives, Nixon Presidential Materials, White House Special Files, Staff Members and Office Files, Office of Presidential Papers and Archives, Daily Diary)

posed for the southern flank of NATO by the developments in the Mediterranean over recent years and partly by the growth of the Soviet naval presence in the Mediterranean, and, secondly, to draw some lessons from the experiences of recent weeks, to review the experiences of recent weeks, and to see about the relationship between our strength in this area and the prospect for stability in this area.

We thought that this was particularly important, because, as I pointed out in the backgrounder I gave before we left, we are not only interested, obviously, in the aspect of how to protect the security of these countries, or help to protect the security, but how we can contribute to a more stable and more permanent peace, a problem which we want particularly to explore in our next stop when we visit Yugoslavia.

So, what we had this afternoon was a full review of the various capabilities in the Mediterranean, both as they affected NATO and as they affected other areas.

[Omitted here is discussion of official U.S. attendance at the funeral of United Arab Republic President Nasser.]

Q. Doctor, it seems at times that the relationship between the Nixon Doctrine as enunciated at Guam was not entirely clear in relationship to the President's statements concerning our role and our future role and our intentions in the Mediterranean.

Specifically, in his opening remarks with President Saragat,[3] I believe he was talking along the lines that we intend to see to it that this will not become the place where future wars will begin. Can you talk about this statement in connection with the Nixon Doctrine?

Dr. Kissinger: This is great for my ego, but it is very dangerous. The question is that the relationship between the Nixon Doctrine and some of the pronouncements on this trip did not seem self-evident to the questioner, particularly the opening remarks to President Saragat where the President said, "We will see to it", or some words to that effect, "that peace in this area will be maintained."

Let me say two things about it. First, we have always brought out the fact that there can never be a neat breakoff point between American foreign policy in one place and another.

Secondly, it is clear that the Nixon Doctrine had always envisaged a continuation of some significant American presence in crucial areas of the world where that American presence was necessary and was considered to be in the American interest.

---

[3] Reference is to Nixon's arrival statement in Rome on September 27. For text, see *Public Papers of the Presidents of the United States: Richard Nixon, 1970*, p. 772.

Both of these conditions obtain in the Mediterranean. The objective of the Nixon Doctrine continues to be one of the guidelines, or the guideline, of our foreign policy. We intend to shift an increasing amount of responsibility to our allies. We intend to cooperate with them more fully than has been the case in the past, and we do look to them to make their contribution.

But we also recognize that the threat in the Mediterranean may have grown larger than anyone assumed over, say, 10 years ago, and, therefore, we recognize that some of the measures that are possible in other parts of the world do not apply with equal force here. But the basic objectives remain.

[Omitted here is the remainder of the briefing, devoted largely to questions relating to the Middle East.]

73.   Statement by President Nixon to the Press[1]

Newmarket-on-Fergus, Ireland, October 4, 1970.

[Omitted here are introductory remarks.]

The purpose of this trip, just as has been the purpose of my other trips abroad, is to strengthen the structure of peace throughout the world, and particularly is to strengthen the structure of peace in the Mediterranean area which, because of recent events, has been an area of very great concern for all those interested in peace.

Now, in analyzing what the threat to peace in the Mediterranean is, we must realize that it is not the conventional threat of one nation possibly engaging in overt action against another. It is more difficult than that, more difficult because it is the threat which arises from irresponsible radical elements which might take action which, in turn, would set in the course of events, the train of events, set in motion—I meant to say—a train of events, that would escalate into a possible confrontation between major powers in the area. That is what we saw in the Jordanian crisis and that is the kind of threat to the peace that we will have to be

---

[1] Source: *Public Papers of the Presidents of the United States: Richard Nixon, 1970*, pp. 804–809. The President spoke at 6:35 p.m. at a reception given for the press in Dromoland Castle. His purpose, indicated in his opening remarks, was to summarize the European trip he was concluding.

guarding against in the months and possibly the years ahead in the Near East and the Mediterranean generally.

Now, when you have that kind of a threat, in order to meet it the primary need is for elements of stability in the area, economic and political stability, yes, but primarily, where the threat is irresponsible and where it resorts to violence, unexpected and unpredictable violence, without reason, without cause—sometimes—there must be military stability and military strength. That is why I first visited the 6th Fleet.

The 6th Fleet is one element of military stability in the Mediterranean. After visiting the 6th Fleet and being briefed by its commanders and our commanders there, I became convinced that the 6th Fleet is able to meet its mission of deterring irresponsible elements in the Mediterranean area.

After meeting with the 6th Fleet commanders and, also, after having discussed this matter with our NATO allies and with our ambassadors from the Mediterranean countries, I am convinced that it is essential that the 6th Fleet continue to have this capability in the event that other powers, with other designs on the area, other than ours and our friends who have no designs except the peace in the area, and the right of each individual nation to maintain its own integrity—in the event that other forces, naval forces, should threaten the position of strength which the 6th Fleet now enjoys, then the United States must be prepared to take the action necessary to maintain that overall strength of the 6th Fleet.

So what I am saying here is the 6th Fleet presently can meet its mission and, second, we shall be prepared to increase its strength in the event that its position of overall strength is threatened by the actions of other powers who take another position in the area than we do.

Another element of strength in the Mediterranean area is, of course, NATO, and particularly its Southern Command. Without going into the specific conversations that we had with the NATO Southern Commanders, I would emphasize here that this provided an opportunity for me to state very strongly and unequivocally these principles with regard to the United States association with NATO.

Considerable concern, I find, has arisen among many of the NATO nations, the major nations and the smaller NATO nations, as a result of some comments by political figures in the United States as well as some of those commenting upon the American role in the world, that the United States might not meet its NATO responsibilities and was on the verge of reducing its contribution to NATO. I stated categorically to the NATO Commanders, and I do it here publicly again, that the United States will, under no circumstances, reduce, unilaterally, its commitment to NATO. Any reduction in NATO forces, if it occurs, will only take place on a multilateral basis and on the basis of what those who are lined up against the NATO forces—what they might do. In other words, it would have to be on a mutual basis.

I know that the Nixon Doctrine has sometimes been inaccurately described as one that would allow the United States to reduce its responsibilities in the world. That is not the case. The purpose of the Nixon Doctrine is to provide a policy under which the United States can meet its responsibilities more effectively in the world by sharing those responsibilities with others. And in NATO that is our policy.

To summarize, with regard to NATO, we will maintain our present strength. We will not reduce it unilaterally. We will continue to talk with our NATO allies with regard to how, overall, we can meet our responsibilities together.

Moving from NATO now to the Mideast, I found in the conversations that I had with all of the leaders that I met—and, as you know, they covered not only our allies and friends but also they covered President Tito of Yugoslavia, a nonaligned state—I found general agreement on these propositions: strong support for the American cease-fire initiative; and, second, I found that, as far as that cease-fire initiative is concerned, that there is not the pessimism that we sense in some quarters, as a result of what happened in Jordan and as a result of the new instability that inevitably will follow the death of President Nasser, that the cease-fire initiative's days were numbered.

I do not suggest that the road ahead is not difficult. But I think we have to separate our peace initiative into two parts: one, the cease-fire part of the initiative; and, second, that part of the initiative that has to do with negotiation.

With regard to negotiation, the prospect for immediate negotiation between the two or three or other parties involved on either side—as far as those prospects are concerned—they are, at this time, not bright because of the introduction of missiles into the 50-kilometer zone.

The reaction of the Israelis, of course, has been not to participate in negotiation.

However, we are going to continue to attempt to get the negotiating process started and, of course, in the process, to do what we can diplomatically to see that there are no further violations of the standstill, and dealing, of course, diplomatically, with the violations that have occurred. So much for the negotiation side of it.

On the cease-fire side of it, however, I think I can say quite unequivocally that neither party—and by neither party I say neither the Israelis on the one side or the other nations, the U.A.R. and others involved in the cease-fire initiative—will gain by breaking the cease-fire. That is why we believe that our acting and talking strongly in behalf of an extension of the cease-fire for another 90 days is the proper course and that it has considerable chance to succeed. Because any party at this time that would break the cease-fire initiative would have very, very little support in the world. It would be acting alone against the whole weight of the world public opinion and also against the weight of public opinion, I should say, in the United States.

Another comment with regard to the Mideast that I think should be made: We tend in the United States to see our role as being predominant and, of course, it is because of our strength. On the other hand, we must recognize, and this trip brought this home to me and underlined it again, that there are other powers in the Mediterranean area that can play, that are playing, and that must play, a significant role in the peace-keeping area.

The Italians, for example, have a very significant interest in the Mediterranean and have contacts that we do not have that are better than ours. The Spanish also have very significant interests in the Mediterranean and have been very helpful. And the British, in addition, of course, have had a traditional, longtime interest in the Mediterranean area. My talks with the leaders of these three countries were very helpful in that respect because it is not a healthy situation in the world for the United States to be alone, whether it is in the Far East, where we welcome the fact that the British are maintaining a presence there, or whether it is in the Mideast, or in the Mediterranean.

That is why the Secretary of State and I have worked, both before we arrived on this trip and during this trip, on developing not only consultation but participation on the part of other Mediterranean powers who share our views about the area, and participation and responsibility for keeping the peace in that area.

[Omitted here are the President's concluding remarks devoted primarily to his impressions of the trip and the leaders with whom he met.]

74.   **Memorandum for the President's File by the President's Special Assistant (Keogh)**[1]

Washington, October 7, 1970.

Cabinet Meeting, October 7, 1970

[Omitted here are a preview and discussion by President Nixon of a new proposal for a settlement in Southeast Asia he intended to deliver in a televised speech later that day, related discussion of problems within the South Vietnamese economy that complicated prospects for a settlement, and limited discussion of the President's European trip. For the text of the President's speech, see *Public Papers of the Presidents of the United States: Richard Nixon, 1970*, pages 825–828.]

Turning to a more general theme, the President remarked to the Cabinet that "We have been through some difficult times since we came here." But he added that he was not pessimistic about the international situation. He said he found on his European trip that "other countries want the U.S. to play a role in the world." While there is often shouting against the U.S., he said, the attitude becomes quite different when a suggestion is made seriously that the U.S. should "go home." Then, he said, the attitude becomes "Oh, no, don't go." He remarked that President Marcos of the Philippines had told him earlier that while it was politically popular to say that the United States must go, it was also quite necessary to say privately, "I hope that you don't."

"We are the most powerful nation in the world," the President said. "But no nation in the world *fears* the United States. This is the greatest asset we have in diplomacy." The U.S., the President went on, is "the only nation in history that hasn't used its power to acquire more power. This country can be proud of its role in the world and we should stand up and say so."

As the President reached this point in his remarks, Secretary of Housing and Urban Development, George Romney, said he felt that everyone in the room "thanks God that you, Mr. President, are at the head of this country's government at this time and are handling our role in the world with such great skill."

The President said he believed that "it may take 40 years for it to be written but it is the truth that America never worked for a better cause

---

[1] Source: National Archives, Nixon Presidential Materials, White House Special Files, Box 82, President's Office Files, Memoranda for the President, August 16–October 25, 1970. No classification marking.

than it has in Vietnam. If we can bring the war to a close, if we can give South Vietnam a chance, this will be an achievement of which we can be extremely proud. I am sorry that a Republican Mayor said that our best young men went to Canada to avoid serving in the Armed Forces. I say our best young men went to Vietnam."

As the President left the room, the Cabinet gave him a standing ovation.

---

75.   **Editorial Note**

During the course of a general discussion of foreign policy issues and domestic considerations on October 12, 1970, President Nixon and Henry Kissinger weighed the responsibilities of leadership:

"P: The US—what it will be like for the next 25 years depends on whether we have the guts, the stamina, the wisdom to exert leadership, will determine whether the future of the country . . . that is really what the facts are. People may want to put their heads in the sand; they may want to clean up the ghettos. All right, we will get out of the world. Who is left? The two activists, Russia and Communist China.

"K: If you will look at countries like Austria. When they had great political power they also did great things domestically. Now they are just shrunk into weak petty countries.

"P: All these people are concerned about peace in the world. We go to the sidelines and there are a couple of big boys out there ready to play—China and Russia. All we are doing is fighting for the right of countries to be free.

"K: Their conflicts are going to be infinitely more bitter than anything we participate in." (Memorandum of telephone conversation, October 12, 1970, 6:10 p.m.; Library of Congress, Manuscript Division, Kissinger Papers, Box 365, Telephone Conversations, Chronological File, 12–16 Oct 1970)

76.   Statement by Secretary of State Rogers Before the Senate
       Finance Committee[1]

Washington, October 12, 1970.

Mr. Chairman[2] and members of the committee, I welcome the
opportunity to discuss with your committee the pending Trade Act. My
comments will be made against the background of our relations with
friendly countries and in the light of our position in world affairs.

Last year the President sent to the Congress a proposed Trade Act[3]
which followed in the tradition of American trade legislation designed
to increase trade and prosperity by reducing barriers and obstacles to
peaceful commerce in the world. In major part because of vigorous
American leadership, international trade since World War II has been
substantially relieved of the restrictions and distortions that we had
inherited from the 1930's.

I would remind the committee that in the 25 years since the end of
the Second World War the world has had the longest period of sustained and rapid income growth in history, thanks in very important
part to the unblocking of the channels of trade. The American people,
along with peoples everywhere, have been the beneficiaries of this
unprecedented period of prosperity.

The legislation before you incorporates many of the provisions that
the President requested in his initial proposal to the Congress, including limited tariff cutting authority, liberalization of adjustment assistant
provisions of the present Trade Expansion Act, and authority to eliminate the "American Selling Price" system of valuation.

It includes also a provision for the establishment of domestic international sales corporations, intended to assist our exports, which the
administration subsequently had requested. The President has also
indicated his willingness to accept a provision for restrictions on certain
textile imports because our efforts to find other solutions to problems in
our textile trade have thus far been unsuccessful.

The administration recognizes that the world environment is
changing, that new economic, trade, and investment problems are

---

[1] Source: *Trade Act of 1970: Amendments 925 and 1009 to H.R. 17550, Social Security
Amendments of 1970: Hearings and Informal Proceedings Before the Committee on Finance,
United States Senate, Ninety-First Congress, Second Session* (Washington, 1971), pp. 266–269.

[2] Senator Clinton P. Anderson of New Mexico was Acting Chairman in the absence
of Senator Russell B. Long of Louisiana.

[3] See Document 44.

appearing and that new approaches may be necessary. The President, therefore, has commissioned a group of distinguished Americans under the leadership of Albert Williams to study the emerging situation and to recommend a comprehensive set of foreign trade and investment policies for the 1970's.

In the meantime, a bill limited to the provisions I have just enumerated would be a positive factor in our relations with the rest of the world. It would be accepted by our trading partners as evidence of American intention to continue along the broad lines of the postwar commercial policy that has served us all so well. It would be taken as a signal that the United States will maintain its place of leadership in the development of the world economy.

It would put us in a favorable position to achieve further reductions in barriers to our exports. It would permit us, I believe, to deal with the difficult problems in our textile trade in a manner calculated to minimize difficulties with supplying nations.

Unfortunately, the bill before you includes a number of additional provisions which the President did not request and which the administration considers to be contrary to the national interest. Primary among these are, first, provisions for quotas on individual items apart from textiles and, second, the potential extension of restrictions, including quotas, to many other products through an excessive loosening of the escape clause.

Additionally, the proposed bill would depart from past escape-clause procedure by setting an arbitrary arithmetic formula to be used in assessing injury. I must tell you that if other countries were to apply this approach to our own exports, there would be grave damage to the sales of hundreds of American firms and to the jobs of hundreds of thousands of American firms and to the jobs of hundreds of thousands of American workers.

I urge this committee, therefore, to recommend to the Senate the elimination of these undesired and potentially damaging features of the legislation.

We have made a careful assessment of the impact of this bill, not only upon our economic interests, but also upon our international interests. We are convinced that it would cause serious harm to the United States.

Naturally, we have heard from other countries about their views of the legislation as it now stands. The President and I heard some of these views at firsthand during our recent journey to Europe. The reactions abroad to the pending bill are those of deep concern and even alarm at the apparent direction of American policy.

Our trading partners fear that the United States is about to make an historic turn in its foreign trade policy. Just as we have led the trading world on the way to a steady reduction of trade barriers, it is now feared that our example could drive the trading world back to the kind of bilateralism and restrictionism that crippled international commerce, including our own, in the 1930's, and contributed to the disastrous consequences that we all know.

It may be said that these fears are unjustified, that the proposed legislation merely seeks to deal with certain special and urgent problems of the United States, and that other nations too have restrictions on imports. The fact is, however, that the legislation before you could lead to restrictions on a very large volume of U.S. trade, as much as $3 billion or more, and other nations are acutely aware of this.

It is also a fact that the very size of the United States in the world economy lends special weight and emphasis to everything we do and that our actions do set an example, for good, or bad, for everyone else. Obviously, other nations have trade restrictions, as of course we do. But we and the rest of the world recognize that the way to a reduction of the remaining obstacles to trade in the world is through hard, reciprocal bargaining, not by adding new and unnecessary obstacles.

Considering the potential damage to trade and the amount of public attention that has been and will be given to this matter, it must be expected that other governments would not be able to accept passively increased trade restrictions by the United States.

There is widespread fear of an impending trade war that no one wishes, neither we nor our trading partners. But we must realize that the political pressures on other governments could be so great as to lead to retaliatory actions against our trade. We are a very large exporter and in some fields the volume of our more dynamic export items already gives rise to foreign concern.

I hope that the Congress will give us a trade bill which will preclude any possibility of serious retaliation. I think it is my duty, nevertheless, to tell you what easily might happen, and it would be wrong for us to minimize the travesty of the situation that we might come to face.

Let me add that a liberal trade policy is essential if the developing countries are to achieve the self-reliance that the Nixon doctrine seeks to encourage. If we are going to foster self-reliance by the developing countries of the world, we must not deny to them the possibility of earning their own way. If we do that, we shall undermine the very processes that generate self-confidence and growth. The consequence will be that we will hurt them and ourselves as well.

The legislation before you appears in some respects to give the President a wide degree of flexibility in the application of the provisions of the legislation. Some may argue that this will enable the President to avoid the application of the worst features of the bill. But in many instances, this flexibility could not be used.

Specifically, it would be extremely costly to discriminate among countries in order to moderate the impact of the legislation. We are solemnly committed, in the General Agreement on Tariffs and Trade and in many bilateral treaties, to treat other countries on a nondiscriminatory, most-favored-nation basis. To do otherwise would be to dishonor our obligations.

We have economic and trading interests everywhere. We do not want to become a victim of a world fragmented into trading blocs and bilateral arrangements. It would ill serve our Nation to take the lead in restricting trade and damaging or destroying the principle of most-favored-nation treatment that is now written in our own basic trade law.

Mr. Chairman, I have spoken out of deep concern for the potential damage to our industry and agriculture of certain features of the legislation that you are considering. It is possible for this committee to propose to the Senate a bill that will advance our economic interests, not retard them, that will uphold our status and position in world affairs and that will still enable the administration to deal effectively and constructively with the pressing problems of specific firms and industries in our domestic economy.

A statute that is limited to the provisions recommended or supported by the administration will do that. A statute with additional and restrictive features, such as are contained in H.R. 18970, on the other hand, would threaten our economic interests and would undermine our position in the world, without meeting the true nature of our particular problems at home.

I earnestly invite you to look upon our trade legislation as part and parcel if our total national interests and in the framework of a coherent political and economic policy that takes into account our domestic needs and our world responsibilities.

I urge this committee, therefore, and the Senate to remove from the bill these unneeded and dangerous features and to send to the President trade legislation consistent with our tradition of leadership and with our national interests.

Thank you, Mr. Chairman.

77.   Memorandum of Conversation[1]

Washington, October 22, 1970, 11 a.m.–1:30 p.m.

PARTICIPANTS

The President
Soviet Foreign Minister A. A. Gromyko
Soviet Ambassador A. F. Dobrynin
Secretary Rogers
Mr. Kissinger
Viktor Sukhodrev, Interpreter, Soviet Ministry of Foreign Affairs
William D. Krimer, Interpreter, State Department

[Omitted here is the opening portion of the conversation, in which Nixon welcomed Gromyko, suggested topics for discussion, and invited Gromyko's response. Gromyko began by expressing his government's concern about the tenor of U.S.-Soviet relations, which he said seemed to be at variance with the President's stated intent to convert an era of confrontation into an era of negotiation. Speaking for his government, he said the Soviet Union would like to see a lessening of tensions and an improvement and expansion of relations with the United States.]

The President replied that with respect to the bilateral relations between our two countries, Mr. Gromyko had indeed described his policy correctly, the policy on moving from an era of confrontation into a era of negotiation. The President also agreed with Mr. Gromyko's comments to the effect that the internal situation of a country should not be allowed to influence its foreign relations. However, since both countries are great powers, he was enough of a realist to know that when great powers are involved there were inevitably bound to be some misunderstandings. He thought Mr. Gromyko would agree that the President had been extremely careful to try to limit differences between them to private discussions rather than discussions in public. Mr. Gromyko, being a realist, would know that in our country whenever elections approached political leaders were tempted to take a belligerent anti-Communist line. As for the President personally, he did not consider such an approach to be in the interests of world peace or of Soviet-American relations. For this reason, he had personally tried to avoid any statement that might make the situation worse.

The President continued that he felt very strongly that both sides, allies during World War II, who were instrumental in bringing into

---

[1]   Source: National Archives, Nixon Presidential Materials, NSC Files, Box 71, Kissinger Office Files, Country Files, Europe, USSR, Gromyko 1970. Top Secret; Sensitive. The conversation was held in the Oval Office of the White House.

being the United Nations, must realize on this 25th anniversary of the UN that the relations and the interests of the two great powers could hardly be submitted to the United Nations where their differences would be publicly resolved [*exposed*?]. Mr. Gromyko had spoken before the General Assembly yesterday and the President intended to do so tomorrow. However, in the next 25 years, world peace in general and, more precisely even, avoidance of smaller wars would depend to a much greater extent on the relations between the United States and the Soviet Union than on anything else. For this reason, he felt unhappy that the relations between our countries were now the coolest since the cold war began. He had been very careful not to contribute to the difficult situation by rhetoric. He thought it was of greatest importance now to give a signal to the world that the United States and the Soviet Union were not looking for areas in which to confront each other. To be honest, we had to realize that our interests in many parts of the world differed and that on some questions it would be most difficult to reach agreed positions. However, it was clearly in the common interests of both great powers to limit the burden of armaments, to increase trade and communications between them. It was in this spirit that he was resolved to view our bilateral relations.

Mr. Gromyko replied that he found the President's appraisal of the situation to be a reasonable one. He asked the President's permission to summarize what had been said to the effect that the policy of the United States would be directed at reducing the tensions which were bound to arise from time to time and that the President's formula of negotiation rather than confrontation remained in effect; also that the President personally intended to work for an improvement and deepening of the relations between the two countries and the international situation in general.

The President agreed that this was correct and added the further point that in the past we had been reasonably successful and it was his hope that we would be even more successful in the future whenever difficulties arose to keep them in private channels rather than expose them in public. In the past we may have been at fault to some extent, and so was the Soviet Union, in publicizing our differences. This was in the past, however, and it would be important to avoid that in the future.

Mr. Gromyko said this was correct. Articles in the Soviet press in the past reporting what was being said in the United States in regard to the Soviet Union had been but a small fraction of unfavorable American statements about the Soviet Union. After all, when hostile statements appeared in the U.S., what was there left for the Soviet Union to do but to react accordingly? The Soviet side would not remain indebted when it came to hostile statements. This was not the right path, however. He noted that the President had mentioned the development of trade relations between the two countries. In this respect, we were faced by almost a vacuum. Was this indeed the policy of the United States Government? He simply would like to know the President's attitude to this question.

The President said that there were possibilities in this field. He thought one would have to be realistic and say that some of the other problems come into play when it comes to considering the possibility of increasing trade between the two countries. For example, the Vietnam war, which involved our primary and basic interests, was bound to have an inhibiting influence upon the possibilities of trade. Due to the fact that under our legislative arrangements some items which could be used to aid North Vietnam could not be exported to the Soviet Union. We were indeed prepared to explore ways in which trade between our two countries could be increased. He did not like to use the word "linkage", but it was true nevertheless that a settlement of these other matters would lead to increasing economic exchanges between us. He therefore felt that if our political relations improved, increased trade would follow naturally. This was in our interest as well as in the interest of the Soviet Union.

[Omitted here is discussion of the Middle East, Berlin, Vietnam, the SALT negotiations, and the possibility of convening a European security conference.]

Conclusion

The President said he believed we have covered most of the subjects that required discussion. Referring to earlier discussions, he said that as realists we knew and Mr. Gromyko knew that the question of the future of Europe, as well as the question of arms control would depend upon whether the United States and the Soviet Union could work out solutions aimed at strengthening peace. We recognized that there are also a number of other factors threatening peace, but if the great powers worked together, the peace could be kept. As practical men, we knew that US-Soviet understanding was essential for the future of the world. He wanted to be sure that Mr. Gromyko would not leave with the impression that the internal political situation in the United States would lead the President to take a course opposite to the one he had followed until now. He noted that Mr. Gromyko had made a temperate speech before the UN yesterday, and said that he would make a temperate speech there tomorrow. Both Mr. Gromyko and Mr. Dobrynin were well acquainted with U.S. politics. Both had been in this room before with President Johnson and President Kennedy. The President said that he was in an unusual position. When he was elected to office it was said that President Nixon would not be able to work with the Soviet leaders because of his past background of anti-Communism. He did not believe this to be so. More than any other President since World War II, he felt that he could be flexible. He was prepared to be flexible in all negotiations with the Soviet Union and wanted Mr. Gromyko to realize that his approach would not be doctrinaire on any subject, but, rather, pragmatic in all cases.

Mr. Gromyko thanked the President for his views and said that the President had correctly emphasized the role of the Soviet Union and the United States as the two great powers responsible for keeping peace in the world. The Soviet leadership was in full agreement with the premise that the future of the world depended to an enormous extent upon the relations between the Soviet Union and the United States. If the U.S. Government worked in the direction of peace, if it respected the interests of the Soviet Union, it would find a vigorous, energetic and determined partner in its search for ways to improve relations. This policy of the Soviet Union was not new. It had been inviolable since the very inception of the Soviet State. It was important, however, to stress the concept of reciprocity. Mr. Gromyko repeated this statement for emphasis. As for what the President had said about the internal political situation influencing American foreign policy, it was not for him to offer any evaluation of this influence. He repeated however that his government sometimes had the impression that the U.S. Government paid some tribute to the internal political situation in the U.S. in the conduct of foreign affairs. If this was indeed so, it could only be harmful to the relations between our two countries. Mr. Gromyko said that he was gratified to learn that President Nixon's speech before the UN would be temperate. One should be able to rise above transitory phenomena and guide our two countries to work for the interests of peace.

78.   Address by President Nixon to the United Nations General Assembly[1]

New York, October 23, 1970.

Mr. President, Mr. Secretary General,[2] distinguished Chiefs of State and Heads of Government, Your Excellencies the Foreign Ministers, and Delegates here assembled:

I am honored to greet the members of the United Nations on behalf of the United States as we celebrate this organization's 25th anniversary. On this historic occasion I wish to pay a special tribute to the founders of the United Nations—to Secretary General U Thant and to all others who have played indispensable roles in its success.

In considering an anniversary and in celebrating one, there is a temptation to recount the accomplishments of the past, to gloss over the difficulties of the present, and to speak in optimistic or even extravagant terms about our hopes for the future.

This is too important a time and too important an occasion for such an approach. The fate of more than 3-1/2 billion people today rests on the realism and candor with which we approach the great issues of war and peace, of security and progress, in this world that together we call home.

So I would like to speak with you today not ritualistically but realistically; not of impossible dreams but of possible deeds.

The United Nations was born amid a great upwelling of hope that at last the better nature of man would triumph. There was hope that Woodrow Wilson's dream of half a century ago—that the world's governments would join "in a permanent league in which they are pledged to use their united power to maintain peace by maintaining right and justice"—would at last be realized.

Some of those early hopes have been realized. Some have not.

The U.N. has achieved many successes in settling or averting conflicts.

The U.N. has achieved many successes in promoting economic development and in fostering other areas of international cooperation, thanks to the work of dedicated men and women all over the world.

---

[1] Source: *Public Papers of the Presidents of the United States: Richard Nixon, 1970*, pp. 926–932. The President spoke at 3:55 p.m. at the UN Headquarters. His address was broadcast live on television and radio.

[2] The President of the General Assembly was Dr. Edvard Hambro of Norway; the Secretary-General was U Thant.

These are matters that all the members of the United Nations can point to with very great pride.

But we also know that the world today is not what the founders of the U.N. hoped it would be 25 years ago. Cooperation among nations leaves much to be desired. The goal of the peaceful settlement of disputes is too often breached. The great central issue of our time—the question of whether the world as a whole is to live at peace—has not been resolved.

This central issue turns in large part on the relations among the great nuclear powers. Their strength imposes on them special responsibilities of restraint and wisdom. The issue of war and peace cannot be solved unless we in the United States and the Soviet Union demonstrate both the will and the capacity to put our relationship on a basis consistent with the aspirations of mankind.

Commenting here today on U.S.-Soviet relationships, I see no point in responding in kind to traditional cold war rhetoric. The facts of the recent past speak for themselves. An effort to score debating points is not the way to advance the cause of peace.

In fact, one of the paramount problems of our time is that we must transcend the old patterns of power politics in which nations sought to exploit every volatile situation for their own advantage, or to squeeze the maximum advantage for themselves out of every negotiation.

In today's world, and especially where the nuclear powers are involved, such policies invite the risk of confrontations and could spell disaster for all. The changes in the world since World War II have made more compelling than ever the central idea behind the United Nations: that individual nations must be ready at last to take a farsighted and a generous view. The profoundest national interest of our time—for every nation—is not immediate gain but the preservation of peace.

One of the reasons the world had such high hopes for the United Nations at the time of its founding was that the United States and the Soviet Union had fought together as allies in World War II. We cooperated in bringing the U.N. into being. There were hopes that this cooperation would continue.

It did not continue, and much of the world's—and the U.N.'s—most grievous troubles since have stemmed from that fact of history.

It is not my intention to point fingers of blame, but simply to discuss the facts of international life as they are.

We all must recognize that the United States and the Soviet Union have very profound and fundamental differences.

It would not be realistic, therefore, to suggest that our differences can be eliminated merely by better personal relationships between the heads of our governments. Such a view would slight the seriousness of our disagreements.

Genuine progress in our relations calls for specifics, not merely atmospherics. A true détente is built by a series of actions, not by a superficial shift in the apparent mood.

It would not be realistic to suggest that all we need to improve our relations is "better mutual understanding."

Understanding is necessary. But we do understand one another well enough to know that our differences are real, and that in many respects we will continue to be competitors. Our task is to keep that competition peaceful, to make it creative.

Neither would it be realistic to deny that power has a role in our relations. Power is a fact of international life. Our mutual obligation is to discipline that power, to seek together with other nations to ensure that it is used to maintain peace, not to threaten the peace.

I state these obstacles to peace because they are the challenge that must be overcome.

Despite the deep differences between ourselves and the Soviet Union, there are four great factors that provide a basis for a common interest in working together to contain and to reduce those differences.

The first of these factors is at once the most important and the most obvious. Neither of us wants a nuclear exchange that would cost the lives of tens of millions of people. Thus, we have a powerful common interest in avoiding a nuclear confrontation.

The second of these factors is the enormous cost of arms. Certainly we both should welcome the opportunity to reduce the burden, to use our resources for building rather than destroying.

The third factor is that we both are major industrial powers, which at present have very little trade or commercial contact with one another. It would clearly be in the economic self-interest of each of us if world conditions would permit us to increase trade and contact between us.

The fourth factor is the global challenge of economic and social development. The pressing economic and social needs around the world can give our competition a creative direction.

Thus, in these four matters, we have substantial mutual incentives to find ways of working together despite our continuing difference of views on other matters.

It was in this spirit that I announced, on taking office, that the policy of the United States would be to move from an era of confrontation to one of negotiation.

This is a spirit that we hope will dominate the talks between our two countries on the limitation of strategic arms.

There is no greater contribution which the United States and the Soviet Union together could make than to limit the world's capacity for self-destruction.

This would reduce the danger of war. And it would enable us to devote more of our resources—abroad as well as at home—to assisting in the constructive works of economic development and in peaceful progress: in Africa, for example, where so many nations have gained independence and dignity during the life of the United Nations; in Asia, with its rich diversity of cultures and peoples; and in Latin America, where the United States has special bonds of friendship and cooperation.

Despite our many differences, the United States and the Soviet Union have managed ever since World War II to avoid direct conflicts. But history shows—as the tragic experience of World War I indicates—that great powers can be drawn into conflict without their intending it by wars between smaller nations.

The Middle East is a place today where local rivalries are intense, where the vital interests of the United States and the Soviet Union are both involved. Quite obviously, the primary responsibility for achieving a peaceful settlement in the Middle East rests on the nations there themselves. But in this region in particular, it is imperative that the two major powers conduct themselves so as to strengthen the forces of peace rather than to strengthen the forces of war.

It is essential that we and the Soviet Union join in efforts toward avoiding war in the Middle East, and also toward developing a climate in which the nations of the Middle East will learn to live and let live. It is essential not only in the interest of the people of the Middle East themselves, but also because the alternative could be a confrontation with disastrous consequences for the Middle East, for our nations, and for the whole world.

Therefore, we urge the continuation of the cease-fire and the creation of confidence in which peace efforts can go forward.

In the world today we are at a crossroads. We can follow the old way, playing the traditional game of international relations, but at ever-increasing risk. Everyone will lose. No one will gain. Or we can take a new road.

I invite the leaders of the Soviet Union to join us in taking that new road—to join in a peaceful competition, not in the accumulation of arms but in the dissemination of progress; not in the building of missiles but in waging a winning war against hunger and disease and human misery in our own countries and around the globe.

Let us compete in elevating the human spirit, in fostering respect for law among nations, in promoting the works of peace. In this kind of competition, no one loses and everyone gains.

Here at the United Nations, there are many matters of major and immediate global concern on which nations even when they are competitors have a mutual interest in working together as part of the community of nations.

In approaching these matters each of us represented here, in our national interest as leaders and in our self-interest as human beings, must take into consideration a broader element: "The World Interest."

It is in the world interest to avoid drifting into a widening division between have and have-not nations.

Last month I proposed a major transformation of the American foreign aid program.[3] A major thrust of my proposals is to place larger shares of American assistance under international agencies, in particular the World Bank, the U.N. Development Program, the Regional Development Banks. We seek to promote greater multilateral cooperation and the pooling of contributions through impartial international bodies. We are also encouraging developing countries to participate more fully in the determination of their needs. Within the inter-American system, for example, new mechanisms have been established for a continuing and frank dialogue.

In the spirit of the U.N.'s second development decade, we shall strive to do our full and fair share in helping others to help themselves—through government assistance, through encouraging efforts by private industry, through fostering a spirit of international volunteer service.

It is in the world interest for the United States and the United Nations, all nations, not to be paralyzed in its most important function, that of keeping the peace.

Disagreements between the major powers in the past have contributed to this paralysis. The United States will do everything it can to help develop and strengthen the practical means that will enable the United Nations to move decisively to keep the peace. This means strengthening both its capacity for peacemaking, settling disputes before they lead to armed conflict, and its capacity for peacekeeping, containing and ending conflicts that have broken out.

It is in the world interest that we cooperate, all of us, in preserving and restoring our natural environment.

Pollution knows no national or ideological boundaries. For example, it has made Lake Erie barely able to support life, it is despoiling Lake Baikal, and it puts Lake Tanganyika in future jeopardy. The U.N.

---

[3] See Document 70.

is uniquely equipped to play a central role in an international effort to curtail its ravages.

It is in the world interest for the resources of the sea to be used for the benefit of all—and not to become a source of international conflict, pollution, and unbridled commercial rivalry.

Technology is ready to tap the vast, largely virgin resources of the oceans. At this moment, we have the opportunity to set up rules and institutions to ensure that these resources are developed for the benefit of all mankind and that the resources derived from them are shared equitably. But this moment is fleeting. If we fail to seize it, storm and strife could become the future of the oceans.

This summer the United States submitted a draft United Nations convention on this matter which I hope will receive early and favorable attention.

It is in the world interest to ensure that the quantity of life does not impair the quality of life.

As the U.N. enters its second development decade, it has both the responsibility and the means to help nations control the population explosion which so impedes meaningful economic growth. The United States will continue to support the rapid development of U.N. services to assist the population and family planning programs of member nations.

It is in the world interest that the narcotics traffic be curbed.

Drugs pollute the minds and bodies of our young people, bringing misery, violence, and human and economic waste. This scourge of drugs can be eliminated through international cooperation. I urge all governments to support the recent recommendations of the U.N. Commission on Narcotic Drugs, to take the first step toward giving them substance by establishing a United Nations Fund for Drug Control. And I urge all governments to support a strengthened narcotics treaty that would govern all production by restricting it solely to medical and scientific purposes. The United States has already circulated such a proposal for consideration at the next session of the U.N. Narcotics Commission.

It is in the world interest to put a decisive end to sky piracy and the kidnapping and murder of diplomats.

In this assembly last year, I called for international action to put an end to air piracy. This problem has grown even more acute. Recent events have dramatically underscored its gravity and also underscored the fact that no nation is immune from it. The United States has taken a number of steps on its own initiative. But this issue requires effective international actions, including measures to permit the suspension of airline services to countries where such piracy is condoned.

The increase of kidnappings of accredited diplomats is a closely related matter that should urgently concern every member of this Assembly.

Finally, it is in the world interest to ensure that the human rights of prisoners of war are not violated.

In an address earlier this month proposing a cease-fire in Indochina, I called for the immediate and unconditional release by both sides of prisoners of war and innocent victims of the conflict. This is not a political or a military issue. It is a humanitarian issue. The United Nations should register its concern about the treatment of prisoners of war and press all adversaries in this conflict, indeed in every conflict, to honor the Geneva Convention.

I have mentioned some of the problems on which the United Nations can—if its members have the will—make substantial progress. There are many others. I urge this body, and the U.N. system, to move ahead rapidly with effective action. And as we move ahead, the United States will do its full share.

The United States came to its present position of world power without either seeking the power or wanting the responsibility. We shall meet that responsibility as well as we can.

We shall not be so pious or so hypocritical as to pretend that we have not made mistakes, or that we have no national interests of our own which we intend to protect.

But we can with complete honesty say that we maintain our strength to keep the peace, not to threaten the peace. The power of the United States will be used to defend freedom, never to destroy freedom.

What we seek is not a Pax Americana, not an American Century, but rather a structure of stability and progress that will enable each nation, large and small, to chart its own course, to make its own way without outside interference, without intimidation, without domination by ourselves or any other nation. The United States fully understands and respects the policy of nonalignment, and we welcome joint efforts, such as the recent meeting in Lusaka, to further international cooperation.

We seek good relations with all the people of the world. We respect the right of each people to choose its own way.

We do hold certain principles to be universal:

—that each nation has a sovereign right to its own independence and to recognition of its own dignity.

—that each individual has a human right to that same recognition of his dignity.

—that we all share a common obligation to demonstrate the mutual respect for the rights and feelings of one another that is the mark of a civil society and also of a true community of nations.

As the United Nations begins its next quarter century, it does so richer in experience, sobered in its understanding of what it can do and what it cannot, what should be expected and what should not.

In the spirit of this 25th anniversary, the United States will go the extra mile in doing our part toward making the U.N. succeed. We look forward to working together—working together with all nations represented here in going beyond the mere containment of crises to building a structure of peace that promotes justice as well as assuring stability that will last because all have a stake in its lasting.

I remember very vividly today my visit to India in 1953 when I met for the first time one of the world's greatest statesmen, Prime Minister Nehru. I asked him, as he considered that great country, with its enormous problems, what was its greatest need? He replied: The greatest need for India, and for any newly independent country, is for 25 years of peace—a generation of peace.

In Africa, in Asia, in Latin America, in Western Europe, in Eastern Europe—in all the 74 nations I have now visited, one thing I have found is that whatever their differences in race or religion or political systems, whatever their customs, whatever their condition, the people of the world want peace.

So let the guns fall silent and stay silent.

In Southeast Asia, let us agree to a cease-fire and negotiate a peace.

In the Middle East, let us hold to the cease-fire and build a peace.

Through arms control agreements, let us invest our resources in the development that nourishes peace.

Across this planet let us attack the ills that threaten peace.

In the untapped oceans of water and space, let us harvest in peace.

In our personal relations and in our international relations, let us display the mutual respect that fosters peace.

Above all, let us, as leaders of the world, reflect in our actions what our own people feel. Let us do what our own people need. Let us consider the world interest—the people's interest—in all that we do.

Since the birth of the United Nations, for the first time in this century the world's people have lived through 25 years without a world war.

Let us resolve together that the second quarter century of the United Nations shall offer the world what its people yearn for, and what they deserve: a world without any war, a full generation of peace.

79.   Editorial Note

Romanian President Nicolae Ceausescu came to Washington on October 26, 1970, for a 2-day official visit following his participation in the 25th anniversary session of the UN General Assembly. During the course of a conversation between President Nixon and President Ceausescu in the Oval Office of the White House on October 26, Ceausescu expressed the hope that improved relations between the United States and Romania would serve as a model for relations between large and small countries as well as between those with differing social systems:

"The President responded by saying that this is what the United States has in mind with countries like Romania and Yugoslavia—that this kind of cooperation can be the basis for cooperation between countries with different systems, especially having in mind that this is a cooperation without strings, with no intention to influence the internal affairs of the other country."

President Nixon also addressed concerns that U.S. efforts to develop a modus vivendi with the Soviet Union would be undertaken at the expense of countries such as Romania:

"The President then said there was one point he would like to emphasize. After his talk to the UN, some observers in the press had speculated that he was committed to develop with the USSR a condominium to the detriment of other countries. The President continued by saying that he wished to state American policy quite directly. He had had a long talk with Gromyko. There would be other discussions in the future. The purpose of these discussions with the Soviets would be to explore areas where the United States and the Soviet Union could reduce the level of world conflict and the burden of arms. Under no circumstances will the direction of any discussions be toward a result where the independence of any country, especially any country in Eastern or Western Europe will be compromised. The future of each country in Europe must be determined by itself not by the USSR nor by the United States.

"That is why we will continue, the President added, in the future to attempt to explore ways we can talk with the People's Republic of China again because it is necessary to have avenues of communication with all nations in the world if we are going to have a world safe from the danger of a nuclear war."

Nixon reiterated this assurance later in the conversation:

"The President assured Ceausescu, however, that under no circumstances would the United States cooperate with any country, including the USSR, at the expense of another country or American relations with that country. This would be contrary to American tradition. He could also assure Ceausescu that the American position was clear, namely that the United States wants good relations with all countries of Eastern Europe. It rejects the idea that two great powers should sit down at a summit meeting and determine the future of smaller countries. That is wrong and the United States will not proceed on such a course."

Near the end of the conversation, discussion turned to the desire of the United States to improve relations with China, and Nixon expressed his appreciation for Romania's efforts to facilitate expanded contacts between the United States and China:

"Ceausescu remarked that Romania has especially cordial relations with China. Since his last meeting with the President, there have been several fairly high level delegations which have visited China and discussed many subjects including relations between China and the United States and China's presence in the UN. It is important to note from these discussions the point that China desires to have improved relations with the United States and is ready at any moment to occupy its place in the UN, including this year. This morning, Ceausescu added, he had just received a message from Chou En-lai on behalf of the Chinese leadership, thanking him for the clear Romanian pronouncement at the UN in favor of China's taking its place there. He believes that the United States should take the first steps in that direction, especially after the Cambodian events. Such steps could open the way to increased contacts with the Chinese. Ceausescu then said he must tell the President frankly that the Chinese have some of the same feelings of concern, some of the same doubts as those he had mentioned earlier regarding problems being solved by only two large countries.

"The President commented that the other side of the coin was that the Soviets do not look with much sympathy on American moves to normalize relations with China.

"Ceausescu replied why should they not. Otherwise things would be impossible. The Romanians have told the Soviets more than once that there should be good relations between China and the U.S. A lack of understanding of this problem will not help solve it. Ceausescu said he did not believe that an improvement in U.S.-Chinese relations would be directed against the USSR or others. He noted that he had had lots of discussions with Chinese leaders and knew how they thought. He was convinced that they are not pursuing such a goal.

"The President stated that American policy is one of wanting friendly relations with both the USSR and eventually with Communist China. We do not intend to play one against another. Our desire is to have independent relations with each, not directed against the other.

The President added that this seems to be President Ceausescu's viewpoint as well. He then remarked that President Ceausescu's continued role as a peacemaker is very useful in regard to U.S.-Chinese relations. He can talk to both parties which is very helpful and in the end, in the President's opinion, this will produce results." (Memorandum of conversation, October 26, 1970, 10:55 a.m.–12:55 p.m.; National Archives, Nixon Presidential Materials, NSC Files, Box 936, VIP Visits)

---

80.   Memorandum of Conversation[1]

Washington, December 9, 1970, 1–2:45 p.m.

PARTICIPANTS

Hedley Donovan
Hugh Sidey
William Mader
Herman Nichol
John Steele
Henry A. Kissinger
David R. Young (note taker)

The luncheon opened with a general discussion about the student movement. Mr. Kissinger explained that when he met with the students around the time of the Cambodian operation he did so on the condition that they return after the summer or in six months to discuss it and other matters of foreign policy again. By and large the result has been that the students' interest has petered out. In fact it has now become necessary for us to take the initiative to encourage students to come down. The groups that we now have are no longer protest groups and they are asking more serious questions. The earlier groups were characterized by incredible ignorance. A good example is the question that Safire asked them, that if the Administration did certain things would they be satisfied. When they said yes, he revealed that these steps had already been taken, but they were not satisfied. The same ploy was used by the Vice President on TV a short time later.

---

[1] Source: Library of Congress, Manuscript Division, Kissinger Papers, Box CL 269, Memoranda of Conversation, 1968–1977, Chronological File. No classification marking. Prepared by David Young of Kissinger's office. The interview was conducted by *Time* magazine correspondents at the Washington offices of the magazine.

The students seem to only know the standard questions and after they had said, "What about Cambodia?" and one has replied, "yes, what about Cambodia?", they did not know what to say. They seem quite bored with probing into the reasons behind decisions, etc.

Mr. Donovan mentioned Bator's[2] complaint about the coverage of the visit of the Harvard professors and Sidey explained that this involved their disagreement with the article he had written stating that one of the implied messages of their visit was that in view of the recent Cambodian actions and Mr. Kissinger's part in it, he would no longer be welcome back at Harvard. The group claimed that they had never said this and Sidey agreed but said it was implicit in their coming down and he was not questioning their integrity but their judgment.

Mr. Kissinger explained how the meeting took place and that he was completely unaware of their purpose in coming. They opened the meeting by stating that everything he said would be completely on the record. As a result he could not really give any explanations. Many have since felt somewhat guilty of their role because they acted at a time of considerable emotion. Mr. Kissinger also explained that he had since been in touch with just about all of the members of the group and he thought their communications were relatively open in spite of the confrontation.

[The discussion then turned to a general question and answer format.][3]

[Omitted here is an exchange concerning problems coloring the Nixon administration's dealings with Congress on foreign policy issues.]

Q. Mr. Donovan: In the last ten years do you think there had been any constructive public opinion intervention in the formulation of foreign policy?

A. Dr. Kissinger: The whole debate on commitments has indirectly been somewhat helpful. The problem is that the debate has concentrated on our commitments and not our interests. It is really our interests that should get us involved, not our commitments. The real debate therefore should be on *what* and *where* are our interests, and only then should we look at our commitments. The whole public debate on commitments, however, has at least focused our attention in the right direction. In Vietnam there never was an adequate analysis of what our strategic interests were. The theory was that Vietnam was a test case for

---

[2] Francis M. Bator, professor of political economy at the John F. Kennedy School of Government, Harvard, and former Deputy Special Assistant to President Johnson.

[3] Brackets in the source text.

what appeared to be centrally directed guerrilla wars; if we could stop the war there, we could stop it worldwide. There was no real examination of our interests vis-à-vis the Soviets or the Chinese. If LBJ had known that the one division he committed would grow to 550,000 men he would never have done what he did.

Q. Mr. Steele: It seems that in the past many commitments were made simply by the military in the field. How do you look at the making of our commitments now?

A. Dr. Kissinger: Our procedure now is much more formal. One of the jobs of the Washington Special Action Group is to develop contingency plans which have an integrated political/diplomatic/military scenario even down to the point of preparing draft cables on what we should say to particular countries. And more importantly, we examine where we will be two years after a certain plan is followed. This procedure was first followed after the shoot-down of the EC-121.

One of the discoveries made since assuming this position has been the realization that it is not simply enough to be able to identify a problem. This is what I thought was the objective when I was a consultant on the outside. The problem I now realize is to get time to address a particular issue. Our commitment to Ethiopia is an example of a situation where we have not yet had time to give it the attention we should.

One additional practice which we have instituted is to formally review our major programs and reassess our covert operations on a periodic basis. If this is not done from time to time, programs have a habit of just going on even though the initial reason for their implementation may have disappeared.

Q. Mr. Donovan: Who do you think really carries the responsibility for understanding and implementing a new direction in our foreign policy?

A. Dr. Kissinger: The answer would seem to be the "establishment", whatever that means. Specifically, it would seem to be those who are concerned about our foreign policy, who have an influence on the media and who have the means to form a consensus of opinion in the country. These seem to be the ones who carry the responsibility for understanding and giving us a new direction, but one of the more disturbing aspects of the Cambodian operation was the total collapse of the establishment at a time when it should have stood up. One can understand the students' reaction, but it is not as easy to excuse the establishment and its leaders for attacking the President and the system on such an issue. They should have known better and have realized that, regardless of what they said, the only one that could bring the war in Vietnam to an end was the President and that it was not in the best interests of the country to seek to destroy it [him?].

It is surprising how preoccupied outsiders are in operational matters. On such matters the government official can invariably outpoint his outside opponent, not because he is brighter but simply because he has more information at his disposal. What the outsider should concentrate on doing is asking the right questions, then the government official can try to get the answers. If they are wrong that is his fault, not the fault of the questioner. One of the great dangers with trying to deal with such a high number of issues and problems is that the urgent ones seem to displace the more important ones. It is a constant fight to find time to address those questions which have long range implications. The bureaucracies also do not help one in this connection since they almost always give us three options in which the first and third are the extremes and the second is what they are doing or what they propose to do.

To answer your questions directly, yes, the formulation of informed and reasoned public opinion is needed very badly.

Q. Mr. Donovan: How many people would you say in a country are reasonably well informed, 100,000, 200,000, 10,000?

A. Dr. Kissinger: The number of people who cause senior people in the government to think would be more restricted. We do care about the League of Women Voters in Iowa, but the groups that I think would be the opinion molders would be various foreign relations committees around the country such as the Council on Foreign Relations. The problem with such a group as the CFR is that the membership must really be changed since they are all thinking on the basis of post World War II 1940's assumptions. McCloy[4] was in the other day bemoaning the lack of leadership in Europe. What he wants is something like the Marshall Plan. But the situation has changed. The Marshall Plan was okay in the 1940's but not now.

Q. Mr. Steele: What is your present analysis of the "cold war?"

A. Dr. Kissinger: In June, despite Cambodia, it was fairly optimistic. We had the likelihood of progress in SALT, a visit to the US by Kosygin in connection with the UN anniversary and an apparent willingness to keep the Middle East quiet. We never even anticipated a problem in Cuba. In the middle of June, however, there seemed to be a sudden shift and the flexibility that we had earlier experienced disappeared. This was at about the same time as the Soviet decision to delay their Party Congress.

---

[4] John J. McCloy, member of the law firm of Milbank, Tweed, Hadley, and McCloy, and Chairman of the President's Advisory Committee on Arms Control and Disarmament.

There are three possible explanations for this change:

—First, that it was part of a master plan that each one of these decisions which seemed to be gratuitously aggressive was made as part of an integrated scheme.

—A second explanation would be that the leaders are so grossly incompetent that they made these decisions on an ad hoc basis simply without studying the relation of one to the other.

—Thirdly, it can be explained as the outgrowth of a collective leadership in which there is no dominant personality and which has become divided into divisive factions.

Each faction is seeking to outdo the other, no one has the power of a veto but neither does anyone have the power to make a generous deal with the US which might produce some long-term advantages. It is entirely possible that the Middle East actions were decided by one group, the Cuban ones by another and the SALT ones by still another.

Dobrynin, notwithstanding the element of flattery, has told me that the problem is that the Kremlin does not have an office such as an advisor for national security affairs which can pull together all the various points of view. It is equivalent to each of our Cabinet members having access to all cables and papers. The result is obviously that there is more likely to be discordant decisions. And this, incidentally, is also what Tito believes to be the case.

Q. Do you think the cold war is over?

A. By all reason it should be over but it obviously is not. It would seem that the Soviet [Union] would realize that it is to its advantage to deal with Nixon since he has far more flexibility in reaching agreement with them than either Kennedy or Johnson had. For example, in SALT or in the Middle East if they would pull themselves together and forget about gigging us and trying to take advantage of every tactical situation, we could have progress. But it must be admitted that so far in this Administration there has been no conversation resulting in a fundamental agreement.

Q. Mr. Mader: Are not these divisive factions also at the Politburo level?

A. Dr. Kissinger: Yes; that is exactly where they are and where they are most apparent. In fact, it would not seem to be unusual for one faction to make a deal with another faction in order to get reciprocal support from their divisions.

Q. Mr. Nichol: How would you apply this analysis of the Soviet regime to its actions on Berlin?

A. Dr. Kissinger: It would seem that what West Germany is doing—their Ostpolitik—is in the best interests of the Soviet Union. The Soviet reaction is therefore puzzling. With regard to the question of access to Berlin, there is no doubt that the East German regime is gaining increased sovereignty over the routes. And even if an access agreement is worked out, there is no end to the harassments an imaginative bureaucracy can think up. And they can even be legal. Therefore, if the Soviets wanted to put West Germany in a fairly tough spot, it would seem that they would give some concessions in order to facilitate an agreement on Berlin thereby removing the West German precondition to ratification of their treaty with the Soviets. But it may be that the Soviets think that they can get their ratification without any Berlin concessions. It may also be that the Soviets believe that no West German government can take responsibility for not ratifying the treaty.

Q. Mr. Nichol: Will we make it easier or tougher for West Germany to ratify the treaty with the Russians?

A. Dr. Kissinger: As long as the agreement on Berlin is confined to the question of access, we will go as far as the Germans want us to. But we cannot be more German than the Germans. We have not been tough on Berlin, the comments of Ehmke[5] notwithstanding. We will not hold up the Berlin agreement unless it is a patent turnover to the other side. We will not push Germany into a soft position. It should be remembered that it was the Germans who started the negotiations. They said that they had a deal with the Soviets to get improvements on Berlin in exchange for their Ostpolitik. But as yet, we have not seen any sign of such a deal.

Q. Mr. Mader: How would you describe your present concern about Cuba?

A. Dr. Kissinger: It is a fact that the Soviets constructed a submarine facility in Cienfuegos such as we have at Holy Loch. It was done with a maximum of deception and speed in a little over three weeks.

We challenged them along the line that we knew what they were doing but without saying it precisely. We said if this facility turns into a military base, we would not be pleased. The Soviets then came back and said specifically they were not building a military base. The 1962 Understandings[6] therefore were extended on the public record to include this type of military facility. The Soviets at the same time pulled

---

[5] Horst Ehmke, Head of the Federal Chancellery and Minister for Special Tasks, Federal Republic of Germany.

[6] An apparent reference to the exchange of letters between President Kennedy and Soviet Chairman Khrushchev on October 27 and October 28, 1962, which ended the initial phase of the Cuban missile crisis. As outlined in Kennedy's letter of October 27, the "understandings" involved the dismantling and removal from Cuba of "all weapon systems capable of offensive use" combined with an assurance that the Soviet Union would not introduce such systems into Cuba in the future. In return, the United States agreed to lift the naval quarantine in effect and offer assurances against an invasion of Cuba. Khrushchev accepted Kennedy's proposal on October 28, but further negotiations to establish formal understandings based on the exchange of letters foundered on the issues of verification of the removal of weapons from Cuba and on the unwillingness of the Kennedy administration to provide a formal non-invasion pledge. See *Foreign Relations, 1961–1963*, vol. XI, Documents 95 and 102.

out their tender so that, while they would not admit that they were building a nuclear submarine facility, their actions betrayed them.

Q. Mr. Donovan: Isn't this sort of action insulting?

A. Dr. Kissinger: Yes, it is. It may be indicative of the petty type of leadership that the Soviets now have, but the positive result is that the 1962 Understandings have been extended to cover the submarine facility. If the tender services nuclear subs, it is breaking the agreement. If it does not tend the subs, then it is no good to them. The question here is why do they continue to horse around. The way that they are putting the tender in here, pulling out something else there, putting the tender back over here does not give one confidence that he is dealing with big people. If they do set up a facility and it operates sufficiently, it can increase their patrolling by 35 per cent. The thing they do not seem to realize, though, is if they do get away with a partial establishment of a base, they are hurting our confidence in them in relation to other more significant areas of agreement

Q. Mr. Mader: Do we have any confidence in them now at all?

A. Dr. Kissinger: In the SALT talks, we can still see areas for progress. The reason here is that the SALT preparations were so thorough that if any agreement is reached it will be so precise that there will probably be about a two-year period in which to react to any violation. We can therefore go ahead regardless of how they behave elsewhere in the world.

We would have liked to have been known as the Administration that developed a new international system not based on rivalry but which took into account the abyss before which we stand as nations.

It may be that after the Party Congress next year there will be a crystallization of leadership and more likelihood of agreement. But, we must realize that the Soviet leadership is a bunch of thugs. Krushchev's memoirs[7] and specifically his account of Beria's downfall are good examples of this brutal system.

The Soviets also have the China problem which is both geopolitical and ideological. They want to free their Western rear so that they can focus more on China, but when they do so, it complicates their ideological problem since the Chinese will say that they are not the "true church" because they have become soft on the West. In this sense, a détente in Europe is a God-send for the Soviets. Europe will protect their rear (e.g., Pompidou's visit, Brandt's Ostpolitik, disintegration on the Italian political scene) while they continue to maintain a stiff attitude toward us and thereby lay claim as "the true church."

---

[7] Reference is to an advance copy of Nikita Khrushchev, *Khrushchev Remembers*, translated and edited by Strobe Talbott (Boston: Little, Brown, 1971).

This, however, in my opinion is an illusion. For the same reason that a détente is important, it does not bring about anything permanent. It only defers decisions for three to four years. Hence, Ostpolitik may indirectly contribute to increased tensions with the US.

Q. Mr. Donovan: Is there any likelihood that there will be a warm-up of US/Chinese relations?

A. Dr. Kissinger: It seems that the quickest way for us to get the Soviets' attention is to put out the word that we are restudying the China question. It is indeed worrisome to Moscow whether we will develop a dialogue with the Chinese. We have floated all sorts of signals to the Chinese, but as yet, we really don't know how to get in touch with them. In Warsaw, the Chinese have enjoyed trying to drive the Soviets crazy by various approaches to us. But the Chinese are really trying to play the same game as the Soviets; namely, to first isolate us and then deal with the other. Our China strategy has been both to develop a dialogue with them for its own sake and then to have a counterweight with the Soviets.

[Omitted here is discussion of developments in Vietnam.]

81.   Editorial Note

President Nixon used the occasion of a visit to White House by Israeli Defense Minister Moshe Dayan on December 11, 1970, to define one of his administration's fundamental objectives in the Middle East. During a conversation in the Oval Office that began at 3:30 p.m.:

"President Nixon stated that his policy had been, from the outset, to counterbalance Soviet power in the Middle East. He was confident that the Arabs alone would be no match for Israel's military. For this reason, it was his concern that the Soviets recognize that the U.S. would guarantee Israel's survival. He had followed this policy since the first days of his Administration, both in public and in private contacts with the Soviets.

"The President added that U.S. actions during the Jordan crisis were designed to demonstrate this point. The movement of the Sixth Fleet was ordered to convey to the Soviet Union that the U.S. would not stand idly by in this situation. The President also complimented the Israeli Government for the readiness measures which they took and which were also an operative factor in de-escalating the situation."

Nixon made it clear later in the conversation that he expected that U.S. economic and military support for Israel would provide the security to enable Israel to participate in good faith in the effort to find a peaceful solution to the Arab-Israeli dispute:

"President Nixon stated that he would never mislead the Prime Minister or the people of Israel. He intended to be forthright and honest and make no promises that he would not deliver or provide any assurances that he would not keep. He stated that from time to time friends would disagree on particulars but that the essence of international friendship was mutual trust. He trusted Prime Minister Meir and anticipated that she shared this trust in him.

"The President added that it was quite evident to him that the American people anticipated that Israel would move to the conference table under the auspices of Jarring. He pointed out that this was expected in light of the $500 million assistance being provided by this government which he hoped would soon be approved by the Congress. He stated that it was important that the youth of Israel be permitted to apply their great talents, ingenuity and industry to peaceful pursuits and that for this reason the time was right to enter into the talks. He pointed out further that Israel at this time could move with an air of confidence since the military balance would be re-established through the current aid package and since the overall international environment dictated such a move. He emphasized that all responsible U.S. officials were of one mind on this." (National Archives, Nixon Presidential Materials, White House Special Files, President's Office Files, Memoranda for the President, November 1–January 17, 1971)

---

82.   **Editorial Note**

At a meeting with his senior staff in the Pentagon on December 14, 1970, Secretary of Defense Laird discussed President Nixon's desire for a new strategic concept:

"Mr. Laird said we still face tremendous problems in having everyone fully understand our national strategy. This is of major concern to him. We will have tremendous problems in preserving our present force capabilities and to gain or create options to add to our capabilities. We have cut the Defense budget as far as we can. The President has expressed a desire for a new strategic concept that is tied to his foreign policy objectives and that is not necessarily tied to detailed specifics on forces and weapons. Mr. Laird said his basic desire in responding to the President's desire is to develop a strategy comprehended by a majority of the country and one which both House and Senate can support. We must recognize realities, protect the FY 1972 forces as a minimum, provide the basis for increased flexibility in the short-term, and lay the foundation now for strengthening forces of all major categories during the next 5 years. He has put together a new concept paper linked closely to the Nixon Doctrine, with its emphasis on increased strength for air and sea forces as well as the emphasis in NSDM-95 on maintaining our ground commitment in NATO. He will issue this paper this week as tentative strategic guidance for FY 1973. He will also submit it to the NSC and DPRC meetings this week for consideration.

"It is important to bear in mind as we finalize the strategic guidance that what we are trying to do is have a strategy that can be understood by the American people and the Congress and which at the same time will give us the necessary flexibility in operating under the kind of budget situation that we have now and will have in the future. Naturally, there won't be complete agreement by everyone on the strategy. It has not had the major staffing many of the papers in the building have had. It is important to have a strategy that can be understood if we are to have the options and capabilities we need during the upcoming period." (Minutes of Secretary of Defense staff meeting; Washington National Records Center, Department of Defense, OSD Files: FRC 330 76–0028, Box 11, Secretary of Defense Staff Minutes, July–December 1970)

Thirty-four people attended the meeting, including Deputy Secretary of Defense David Packard, Secretary of the Army Stanley Resor, Secretary of the Navy John Chafee, Secretary of the Air Force Robert Seamans, Chairman of the Joint Chiefs of Staff Admiral Thomas Moorer, Army Chief of Staff General William Westmoreland, and Chief of Naval Operations Admiral Elmo Zumwalt. The concept paper cited by Laird has not been found. National Security Decision Memorandum 95, dated November 25 and entitled "U.S. Strategy and Forces for NATO," is in the National Archives, Nixon Presidential Materials, NSC Files, Box 363, Subject Files, National Security Decision Memoranda (NSDMs), Nos 51–96.

83.   Editorial Note

On December 17, 1970, Henry Kissinger met a number of reporters from the *Washington Post* in the offices of the newspaper. In the course of responding to a variety of questions relating to foreign policy, Kissinger addressed the complex problems posed by tensions in the Middle East, and the likelihood that a stalemate in the Arab-Israeli dispute was "inevitable":

"There are three basic issues when one looks at the Middle East. First, one can look at it solely as an Arab-Israeli problem; secondly, one can focus on the significance of the Soviet presence there; or thirdly, one can also focus on the nature of the Arab states, their autonomy. Our objective has been to try to get each of these issues in phase with each other. Some however think that only the first issue is of any consequence and it is therefore the key. They believe that if it can be solved, the rest will fall in place.

"We believe however that each of these issues is related; that there are a number of problems which have to be resolved or at least addressed. A good example is the likelihood of a stalemate once negotiations are started.

"In fact, stalemate is really inevitable. It seems to be an obsession in Washington to focus only on the next step. One of the things that surprised me most when I came here was the singlemindedness with which the immediate step was addressed and the lack of attention paid to what was going to happen next. Starting negotiations is of second order priority; breaking the stalemate is really the critical issue. Examples of the questions we should address are: With whom are we going to deal when there is a stalemate? Is it going to be in a four-power forum, two-power forum, the Security Council at the UN? Are we going to move alone? There are numerous other crucial questions which have to be answered, but they will not be addressed until the problem is on top of us." (Memorandum for the Record, December 17, 1970; Library of Congress, Manuscript Division, Kissinger Papers, Box CL 269, Memoranda of Conversation, 1968–1977, Chronological File)

The reporters who questioned Kissinger included Donald Oberdorfer, Marylin Berger, Chalmers Roberts, Murrey Marder, Meg Greenfield, and Henry Hubbard.

84.   Memorandum From the President's Assistant for National
        Security Affairs (Kissinger) to President Nixon[1]

Washington, February 10, 1971.

SUBJECT

NSC Meeting on Annual Report

[Omitted here are general comments on the status of the report and anticipated agency views in advance of an NSC meeting scheduled for the following morning.]

Like last year, this year's report emphasizes the purposes and objectives of our foreign policy rather than a mere recital of events. It is designed to stress not so much *what* we have done, but *why* we have done it. The major thrust of this report is that conditions which have changed since World War II call for a new type of American leadership, rather than an abdication of leadership. It pictures our basic task to be the enlisting of the resources and concepts of other nations to help build a stable peace.

Outline of Report

We have been following a tentative outline which looks as follows:

—*Introduction*

This briefly recalls the historical changes that have taken place which call for a new foreign policy: stronger friends and allies; a shift in military relationships from U.S. predominance to relative equality; the fragmentation of the Communist world; and new technological problems and challenges which call for world cooperation. The implications for our policy are sketched: a partnership that enlists greater contributions from others; a new doctrine for our strategic and general forces purposes; dealing in different ways with various Communist countries; and cooperating with friends and adversaries alike to meet global issues such as pollution, space and the seabeds.

—*Nixon Doctrine*

This chapter spells out the core of the new foreign policy: the philosophy of the Nixon Doctrine and its theme of partnership: It discuss-

---

[1] Source: National Security Council, NSC Meetings File, February 11, 1971, Annual Review. Confidential. Sent for information. The first page of the memorandum is stamped: "The President Has Seen . . .". In the section of the memorandum not printed here, Kissinger noted: "We have stressed throughout your wish that the report be a substantial and thoughtful presentation of the main strands of this Administration's foreign policy." Reference is to the administration's second annual report on foreign policy; see Document 85.

es its application to security and development and its invocation of the ideas as well as the resources of other nations. A basic theme is that the greater the involvement of other nations in helping to build peace, the greater their stake in preserving the peace. There is emphasis on the need for careful application of our changed approach so as to instill confidence abroad and evoke domestic support for a continuing positive American role.

—Partnership With Other Nations

This principal section of the report explains the application of the new foreign policy to the various regions of the world. In these chapters we generally (1) state our basic approach, (2) illustrate how this approach has been applied with major events and achievements, and (3) list the basic agenda for the future. Among the major chapters in this section are Europe, the Middle East and Indochina.

—National Security

This section will focus on the two ways of enhancing national security, through a strong defense and through arms control. There are individual chapters on *strategic forces* (including a discussion on sufficiency and the growing Soviet strength); *general purpose forces* (the need to tailor our conventional forces to those of our allies); *security assistance* (the need to help our friends make the transition to greater self-sufficiency) and *arms control* (with emphasis on SALT).

—Soviet Union and the People's Republic of China

Our overall approach to the Soviet Union is treated in this section although, of course, our specific dealings are sprinkled throughout the report. The emphasis is on the need for mutual respect for legitimate interests, concrete negotiations, and focusing on broader interests rather than maneuvering for tactical advantages. It reflects many of the themes in your United Nations speech. A brief chapter on China states our readiness to deal constructively with Peking while firmly maintaining our commitment to Taiwan.

—Global Issues

This section treats a new dimension in foreign affairs in a technological age, discussing issues that are common to all countries regardless of ideology, such as pollution, the exploration of space and the oceans, narcotics and hijacking.

[Omitted here is a brief comment on the upcoming NSC meeting to discuss the report.]

85.   Radio Address by President Nixon[1]

Washington, February 25, 1971.

[Omitted here are comments on Vietnam.]

To understand the nature of the new American role we must consider the great historical changes that have taken place.

For 25 years after World War II, the United States was not only the leader of the non-Communist world, it was the primary supporter and defender of this free world as well.

—But today our allies and friends have gained new strength and self-confidence. They are now able to participate much more fully not only in their own defense but in adding their moral and spiritual strength to the creation of a stable world order.

—Today our adversaries no longer present a solidly united front; we can now differentiate in our dealings with them.

—Today neither the United States nor the Soviet Union has a clear-cut nuclear advantage; the time is therefore ripe to come to an agreement on the control of arms.

The world has changed. Our foreign policy must change with it.

We have learned in recent years the dangers of over-involvement. The other danger—a grave risk we are equally determined to avoid—is under-involvement. After a long and unpopular war, there is temptation to turn inward—to withdraw from the world, to back away from our commitments. That deceptively smooth road of the new isolationism is surely the road to war.

Our foreign policy today steers a steady course between the past danger of over-involvement and the new temptation of under-involvement.

That policy, which I first enunciated in Guam 19 months ago,[2] represents our basic approach to the world:

We will maintain our commitments, but we will make sure our own troop levels or any financial support to other nations is appropriate to current threats and needs.

We shall provide a shield if a nuclear power threatens the freedom of a nation allied with us or of a nation whose survival we consider vital to our security.

---

[1] Source: *Public Papers of the Presidents of the United States: Richard Nixon, 1971*, pp. 213–214. The address coincided with the submission to Congress of the Nixon administration's second annual comprehensive report on the conduct of U.S. foreign policy. The President spoke at 11 a.m. from the White House. The text of the report is ibid., pp. 219–345.

[2] See 1969 volume, Item 279. [Footnote in the source text. See Document 29.]

But we will look to threatened countries and their neighbors to assume primary responsibility for their own defense, and we will provide support where our interests our call for that support and where it can make a difference.

These principles are not limited to security matters.

We shall pursue economic policies at home and abroad that encourage trade wherever possible and that strengthen political ties between nations. As we actively seek to help other nations expand their economies, we can legitimately expect them to work with us in averting economic problems of our own.

As we continue to send economic aid to developing nations, we will expect countries on the receiving end to mobilize their resources; we will look to other developed nations to do more in furnishing assistance; and we will channel our aid increasingly through groups of nations banded together for mutual support.

This new sharing of responsibility requires not less American leadership than in the past, but rather a new, more subtle, form of leadership. No single nation can build a peace alone; peace can only be built by the willing hands—and minds—of all. In the modern world, leadership cannot be "do-it-yourself"—the path of leadership is in providing the help, the motive, the inspiration to do it together.

In carrying out what is referred to as the Nixon Doctrine, we recognize that we cannot transfer burdens too swiftly. We must strike a balance between doing too much and preventing self-reliance, and suddenly doing too little and undermining self-confidence. We intend to give our friends the time and the means to adjust, materially and psychologically, to a new form of American participation in the world.

How have we applied our new foreign policy during the past year? And what is our future agenda as we work with others to build a stable world order?

In Western Europe, we have shifted from predominance to partnership with our allies. Our ties with Western Europe are central to the structure of peace because its nations are rich in tradition and experience, strong economically, vigorous in diplomacy and culture; they are in a position to take a major part in building a world of peace.

Our ties were strengthened on my second trip to Europe this summer and reflected in our close consultation on arms control negotiations. At our suggestion, the NATO alliance made a thorough review of its military strategy and posture. As a result, we have reached new agreement on a strong defense and the need to share the burden more fairly.

In Eastern Europe, our exchange of state visits with Romania and my meeting last fall with Marshal Tito in Yugoslavia are examples of our search for wider reconciliation with the nations that used to be considered behind an Iron Curtain.

Looking ahead in Europe:

—We shall cooperate in our political and economic relations across the Atlantic as the Common Market grows.

—We and our allies will make the improvements necessary to carry out our common defense strategy.

—Together we stand ready to reduce forces in Western Europe in exchange for mutual reductions in Eastern Europe.

The problems of Africa are great, but so is her potential. The United States will support her peoples' efforts to build a continent that provides social justice and economic expansion.

Turning to our own hemisphere: In Latin America, there was too much tendency in the past to take our closest friends and neighbors for granted. Recently, we have paid new respect to their proud traditions. Our trade, credit, and economic policies have been reexamined and reformed to respond to their concerns and their ideas, as well as to our own interests.

Our new Latin American policy is designed to help them help themselves; our new attitude will not only aid their progress but add to their dignity.

Great changes are brewing throughout the American hemisphere. We can have no greater goal than to help provide the means for necessary change to be accomplished in peace and for all change to be in the direction of greater self-reliance.

Turning to the Far East: a new Asia is emerging. The old enmities of World War II are dead or dying. Asian states are stronger and are joining together in vigorous regional groupings.

Here the doctrine that took shape last year is taking hold today, helping to spur self-reliance and cooperation between states. In Japan, South Korea, Thailand, and the Philippines, we have consolidated bases and reduced American forces. We have relaxed trade and travel restrictions to underline our readiness for greater contact with Communist China.

Looking ahead in that area:

—While continuing to help our friends help themselves, we must begin to consider how regional associations can work together with the major powers in the area for a durable peace.

—We will work to build a strong partnership with Japan that will accommodate our mutual interests.

—We will search for consecutive discussions with Communist China while maintaining our defense commitment to Taiwan. When the

Government of the People's Republic of China is ready to engage in talks, it will find us receptive to agreements that further the legitimate national interests of China and its neighbors.

In Asia, we can see tomorrow's world in microcosm. An economically powerful democratic free nation, Japan, is seeking new markets; a potentially powerful Communist nation, China, will one day seek new outlets and new relations; a Communist competitor, the Soviet Union, has interests there as well; and the independent non-Communist nations of Southeast Asia are already working together in regional association. These great forces are bound to interact in the not too distant future. In the way they work together and in the way we cooperate with their relationship is the key to permanent peace in that area—the Far East, the scene of such a painful legacy of the recent past, can become an example of peace and stability in the future.

In the Middle East, the United States took the initiative to stop the fighting and start the process of peace.

Along the Suez Canal a year ago, there was daily combat on the ground and in the air. Diplomacy was at an impasse. The danger of local conflict was magnified by growing Soviet involvement and the possibility of great powers being drawn into confrontation.

America took the lead in arranging a cease-fire and getting negotiations started. We are seeing to it that the balance of power, so necessary to discourage a new outbreak of fighting, is not upset. Working behind the scenes, when a crisis arose in Jordan, the United States played a key role in seeing that order was restored and an invasion was abandoned.

We recognize that centuries of suspicion and decades of hostility cannot be ended overnight. There are great obstacles in the way of a permanent, peaceful settlement, and painful compromise is required by all concerned.

We are encouraged by the willingness of each of the parties to begin to look to the larger interest of peace and stability throughout the Middle East. There is still the risk of war, but now—for the first time in years—the parties are actively calculating the risks of peace.

The policy of the United States will continue to be to promote peace talks—not to try to impose a peace from the outside, but to support the peace efforts of the parties in the region themselves.

One way to support these efforts is for the United States to discourage any outside power from trying to exploit the situation for its own advantage.

Another way for us to help turn a tenuous truce into a permanent settlement is this: The United States is fully prepared to play a responsible and cooperative role in keeping the peace arrived at through negotiation between the parties.

We know what our vital interests are in the Middle East. Those interests include friendly and constructive relations with all nations in the area. Other nations know that we are ready to protect those vital interests. And one good reason why other nations take us at our word in the Middle East is because the United States has kept its word in Southeast Asia.

We now come to a matter that affects every nation: the relations between the world's two great super powers.

Over the past 2 years, in some fields the Soviet Union and the United States have moved ahead together. We have taken the first step toward cooperation in outer space. We have both ratified the treaty limiting the spread of nuclear weapons. Just 2 weeks ago, we signed a treaty to prohibit nuclear weapons from the seabeds.

These are hopeful signs, but certain other Soviet actions are reason for concern. There is need for much more cooperation in reducing tensions in the Middle East and in ending harassment of Berlin. We must also discourage the temptation to raise new challenges in sensitive areas such as the Caribbean.

In the long run, the most significant result of negotiations between the super powers in the past year could be in the field of arms control.

The strategic arms limitation talks with the Soviet Union have produced the most searching examination of the nature of strategic competition ever conducted between our two nations. Each side has had the chance to explain at length the concerns caused by the posture of the other side. The talks have been conducted in a serious way without the old lapses into propaganda.

If both sides continue in this way, there is reason to hope that specific agreements will be reached to curb the arms race.

Taking a first step in limiting the capacity of mankind to destroy itself would mark a turning point in the history of the postwar world; it would add to the security of both the Soviet Union and the United States, and it would add to the world's peace of mind.

In all our relations with the Soviets, we shall make the most progress by recognizing that in many cases our national interests are not the same. It serves no purpose to pretend they are; our differences are not matters of mood, they are matters of substance. But in many other cases, our separate national interests can best be pursued by a sober consideration of the world interest.

The United States will deal, as it must, from strength: We will not reduce our defenses below the level I consider essential to our national security.

A strong America is essential to the cause of peace today. Until we have the kind of agreements we can rely on, we shall remain strong.

But America's power will always be used for building a peace, never for breaking it—only for defending freedom, never for destroying it.

America's strength will be, as it must be, second to none; but the strength that this Nation is proudest of is the strength of our determination to create a peaceful world.

We all know how every town or city develops a sense of community when its citizens come together to meet a common need.

The common needs of the world today, about which there can be no disagreement or conflict of national interest, are plain to see.

We know that we must act as one world in restoring the world's environment, before pollution of the seas and skies overwhelms every nation. We know we must stop the flow of narcotics; we must counter the outbreaks of hijacking and kidnapping; we must share the great discoveries about the oceans and outer space.

The United States is justly proud of the lead it has taken in working within the United Nations, and within the NATO alliance, to come to grips with these problems and with these opportunities.

Our work here is a beginning, not only in coping with the new challenges of technology and modern life but of developing a worldwide "sense of community" that will ease tension, reduce suspicion, and thereby promote the process of peace.

That process can only flourish in a climate of mutual respect.

We can have that mutual respect with our friends, without dominating them or without letting them down.

We can have that mutual respect with our adversaries, without compromising our principles or weakening our resolve.

And we can have that mutual respect among ourselves, without stifling dissent or losing our capacity for action.

Our goal is something Americans have not enjoyed this century: a full generation of peace. A full generation of peace depends not only on the policy of one party or of one nation or one alliance or one bloc of nations.

Peace for the next generation depends on our ability to make certain that each nation has a share in its shaping, and that every nation has a stake in its lasting.

This is the hard way, requiring patience, restraint, understanding, and—when necessary—bold, decisive action. But history has taught us that the old diplomacy of imposing a peace by the fiat of great powers simply does not work.

I believe that the new diplomacy of partnership, of mutual respect, of dealing with strength and determination will work.

I believe that the right degree of American involvement—not too much and not too little—will evoke the right response from our other partners on this globe in building for our children the kind of world they deserve: a world of opportunity in a world without war.

---

86. Interview With the President's Assistant for National Security Affairs (Kissinger)[1]

February 26, 1971.

[Omitted here is general discussion about the second annual report on foreign policy, released February 25, 1971.]

M. Kalb: Dr. Kissinger, in going through the report, and in discussing the basic philosophy of the foreign policy, time and again the word isolationism comes up. Now, one could easily get the impression that the President fears just over his shoulders this terrible specter of a nation turning in on itself. One, is that really a paramount fear in his mind and two, do you think it will happen?

Dr. Kissinger: This country has gone through a very searing experience in the last 25 years and particularly in the last decade. We went from isolationism in the pre-war period to total involvement overseas, in a way in which problems in almost every part in the world became a direct American responsibility which [and?] we designed the programs around them with optimism, enthusiasm and dedication. Now in the '60s and particularly the latter half of the '60s, we came up against a number of situations that didn't prove very attractive and many profound disappointments; the war in Viet Nam and many other things of that nature. So that is a danger that we will swing in the opposite direction, that having decided that too much involvement is wrong, we will go to little involvement. But we are too powerful and too important to withdraw and what the President attempts to do is to establish a balance to do the things that only we can do but not to do the things for others that they can and should do for themselves. There is some dan-

---

[1] Source: Library of Congress, Manuscript Division, Kissinger Papers, Box CL 426, Subject File, Background Briefings, December 1970–December 1971. No classification marking. The interview took place on CBS Morning News. Interviewers included John Hart, Marvin Kalb, and Bernard Kalb.

ger that disappointed idealism may turn into withdrawal and some of the most disillusioned people at the moment are precisely those groups who deserve the greatest credit for having shaped the previous period of foreign policy. We are concerned with the danger of withdrawal.

M. Kalb: Is it a fear of the right more than the left? Is this what he's talking about here?

Dr. Kissinger: I don't think you can characterize the American discussion on foreign policy primarily in terms of right and left. But for much of the post-war period we've had a bi-partisan foreign policy. And even today it doesn't lend itself to such easy characterization but what we are trying to do is to steer a course that avoids extremes on either side of an unthinking, chauvinistic, self-righteous, American fortuitous mentality and on the other hand of a sort of undifferentiated involvement in international affairs in which we just multiply our commitment, so there is a fear of both of these extremes and an attempt to hold together the widest possible group that we can.

[Omitted here is discussion of the war in Vietnam.]

87.   Address by President Nixon[1]

Newport, Rhode Island, March 12, 1971.

[Omitted here are the President's opening personal comments.]

The pursuit of peace is the opportunity which lies before you, and the preservation of peace will be the special obligation of your generation. There is no greater opportunity, and there is no greater responsibility.

It may be difficult now to appreciate this fully. Our involvement in the war in Southeast Asia is drawing to an end. The next 3 years stretch before you, with the prospect of danger or boredom or both. And I know some of you will wonder about the significance of serving, about the need for it. I know that many of you resent the time taken away from the pursuit of other careers. You see these years as lost years.

---

[1] Source: *Public Papers of the Presidents of the United States: Richard Nixon, 1971,* pp. 428–430. The President spoke at the graduation exercises of the Naval Officer Candidate School.

I tell you, they will not be lost. Rather, I believe that nothing you do in your life will be more important than the service you give in the next 3 years. Out of the sacrifice and the bitterness and the testing of the last 10 years has come the opportunity to achieve at last what Americans all want and what we have not had in this whole century: a full generation of peace. It is for us now to seize that opportunity, to win the peace. It will be for you to keep it.

You serve in the peace forces of the world. There are those in America who question this, but the record is clear. Our power has always been used for building the peace, never for breaking it—for defending freedom, never for destroying it.

America has fought in four wars in this century. Yet, we did not seek war; we did not plan war; we did not begin war. But when it came, young Americans fought courageously.

Today, despite the terrible evidence of this century, there are those who have refused to learn the hard lessons of the history of tyranny. They would tell us, as their predecessors in other times have told us, that the appetite for aggression can be satisfied only if we are patient and that the ambitions of the aggressor are justified if only we understand them properly.

I am never surprised to see these positions held. But I am always astonished to see them held in the name of morality. We know too well what follows when nations try to buy peace at the expense of other nations. I do not believe we are prepared to take that course. What is more important: No other nation believes it either. That is why the United States of America is represented and why it is respected among the nations of the free world—not because we are rich and not because we are powerful, but, above all, because we can be trusted. We have been, we continue to be, willing to pay the price for peace. And we pay in the hard currency of deeds—not with hollow threats and empty promises.

There can be no advantage to concealing hard facts in soft words. We know that when force is rewarded, the cost of peace and the only alternative to war will be tyranny. This fact dominated the first half of this century. We are determined that it will not dominate the last half. For this reason we have accepted the necessity of war. But our purpose is peace.

Peace with freedom—so that peace may be worth having.

Peace with justice—so that peace may be worth keeping.

And peace with strength—so that peace may be preserved.

We must have strength. If all the world were free, we might have no need of arms. If all the world were just, we would have no need of valor.

But as we see that the values we cherish are not cherished universally, and that there are those who feel threatened by the prospects of freedom and justice, then we must keep the strength we need to keep the values we cherish.

I know the arguments of the new isolationists. Though we cut defense spending, we can't cut it enough. Though we greatly increase domestic spending in proportion to defense spending, we can never increase it enough.

I understand those arguments, and I understand the sentiments behind them. But I understand the cost of weakness, too.

The question of what is enough is not academic. It is crucial to the survival of this Nation.

If we have the most extensive urban renewal programs, the most far-reaching medical care programs, the finest highways, the most comprehensive educational assistance efforts, the most effective anti-poverty programs—if we have all this and more, and if we have it all at the expense of our ability to defend ourselves, then we would soon enjoy none of the fruits of our efforts, and the only peace we would know would be that terrible peace imposed upon those who are the victims of their own lack of vigilance.

And so today we will look to the possibilities of the future with a careful regard for the realities of the present and the lessons of the past.

As you serve in our peace forces, you can be proud of this great fact: We Americans firmly believe in what we are and in what we have. But we do not choose to go the way of those ancient crusaders who sought to civilize the world one grave at a time. We do not seek power as an end in itself. We seek power adequate to our purpose, and our purpose is peace.

I have no illusions about the difficulty of achieving that purpose. I do not believe that peace will suddenly descend upon us like the answer to a prayer. I do not believe we should confuse the things we can expect from God with the things God may expect from us. Rather, we have to build peace, you and I together. We have to do it with our own hands because there is no other way. And we have to do it with our own brains and our own courage and our own faith.

I do not believe it will be done otherwise. But neither do I despair of its being done, because I believe you will do the job, and not only you here in uniform but your generation.

I remember very clearly an address President Eisenhower made in March of 1960 to a White House Conference on Children and Youth. He said, "our children understand, as we did not in our own youthful days, the need—now approaching the absolute—for peace with justice . . . .

among the things we teach to the young are such truths as the transcendent value of the individual and the dignity of all people, the futility and stupidity of war, its destructiveness of life and its degradation of human values."

In a decade of war since that time, the children he was talking about have grown up. Some of you are here today. As the years have passed and I have watched your generation, I have understood the wisdom of his words. The man the French called the peace general had a vision of "the peace generation," and it has come to pass. You will be that generation.

As you take up your responsibilities today, as you begin the great work before you, I want to remind you that you are not alone, that people of other nations have served bravely and do so today in behalf of a lasting peace. We are not the only nation that desires the end of war. We are the most powerful nation, but gallant people around the globe share our faith that the world is moving in the way of peace with freedom and with justice for all. Some of them are here today. I want to salute those members of the naval forces of the Republic of Vietnam who are here today.

I have known their country. I have known their struggle for almost 20 years. I have visited Vietnam seven times. I have seen firsthand the courage of the Vietnamese people, their endurance, their sacrifice, their will to be free.

The rights we have learned to take for granted, they are still fighting for.

War has been the condition of man from the dawn of history. Some have said that wars are made by something ignorant in the human heart. If this is so, then perhaps peace will come through something splendid in the human soul. Perhaps man will learn not to answer what is primeval in his blood, but rather to heed what is divine in his humanity.

However it may come, it is certain that peace and the greedy ambitions of governments cannot survive in the same world. But I believe it is the ambition of governments that is going to fail, because from having seen the world, almost all the world, I know the people of the world want peace.

Through time they have watched the harvest of the plowshare rot in the fields and on the vines while they have reaped the harvest of the sword. It would be difficult to suppose that God created man for this end, and difficult to doubt the wisdom of the Prophet, that "the work of righteousness shall be peace . . . ."

So we have dreamed no small dream. We have set ourselves no easy task. We seek to do the work of righteousness. In that work the years you give will not be lost. They will be redeemed along with the hopes of humanity.

[Omitted here are brief closing personal comments.]

---

88.   **Editorial Note**

President Nixon met on April 20, 1971, with members of the Republican Congressional leadership in the Cabinet Room of the White House between 8:06 and 9:44 a.m. The group included Vice President Agnew as well as more than a dozen members of the White House staff. (National Archives, Nixon Presidential Materials, White House Central Files, Staff Members and Office Files, Office of Presidential Papers and Archives, Daily Diary) According to the notes prepared that day by the President's Special Assistant, Patrick J. Buchanan, the discussion opened mainly on economic matters.

"Following this the President went into a dissertation on American foreign policy. It was one many of the members had probably heard before. The President spoke against the new isolationism, saying that if we abandon the world, pull back our aid, pull back our troops, it's not just economically what is going to happen to the United States, but what kind of world is it going to be. If we leave a vacuum in the world, then the other powers are going to fill that vacuum. The President noted that these individuals you see now up on Capitol Hill who are shouting the loudest about peace or calling for cutbacks in aid and bringing home the troops, these individuals are the ones who represent the greatest danger to peace; they are the ones whose policies would generally invite a large war. With that kind of reasoning, it will bring on war as sure as we're sitting here."

After a brief discussion of extension of the draft, Nixon continued his comments on foreign policy:

"Here and on several occasions during the meeting, the President indicated that a lot of things are looking good for the doves right now, those who vote against American armaments or who vote to bring the troops home, that aren't going to be looking good in the near future. One came away with the impression that the President was aware of something taking place or something occurring which would make the policy of isolationism, the policy of weakening America defensively, a disastrous one politically and a dangerous one for the country.

"The President told the Congressmen that the Republicans there should not run with these people, they are on the wrong course, and history will show they were.

"The President then gave a brief talk about the ablest, most dynamic, most energetic people in Europe were the Germans, in Asia they were the Japanese; that these two peoples were with us now, not simply because of economics, although there were strong economic ties, but because the United States was the first power in the world and presented for them an umbrella for their national security. When the United States ceases to be the first power in the world, then these great powers are going to be looking elsewhere for their deals, for their arrangements, and when that happens, the President said, the United States is in serious trouble. That is why we've got to remain number one.

"He used the steel figures of America and Japan to indicate the tremendous growth of the Japanese empire. He said in 1950 the United States produced about 47–48% of all the steel in the world; today we produce about 20% of the steel. In 1950 Japan produced 5 million tons of steel; today she produces over 100 million tons, and by 1974 she will exceed the United States in production unless we do something with our productivity. One hundred million Japanese, he said, produce twice as much as 800 million Chinese. This is an indication of the capability of these people; we need them on our side.

"Whittaker Chambers told me one time, he said, that the war in Korea was not about Korea but was about Japan. In that sense, in that strategic sense, the war in Vietnam is also about Japan.

"The President told an interesting anecdote. He said when he was down in Williamsburg yesterday a little teenager came up to him and said, Mr. President, how does it feel to be a war criminal. He said, well, what we are doing in Vietnam today may make it possible that that young fellow won't have to go off and fight and die in a war. If we remain strong, the President said, we can establish a modus vivendi with the Soviet Union, a modus vivendi with Red China. But we cannot if we weaken ourselves. In the long run, the President said again, the others may look good for a while, but down the road they are going to look very bad for the country, and bad for themselves." (National Archives, Nixon Presidential Materials, White House Special Files, President's Office Files, Memoranda for the President, Box 84, January 24–April 25, 1971)

Later in the day, in a meeting with Republican Senators and members of the President's staff, Nixon expounded further on the dangers of a U.S. retreat from world affairs. According to notes prepared by Kenneth Belieu, the President's Deputy Assistant for Senate Relations:

"The President said, 'I know that you gentlemen are concerned about the Vietnam War. The whole country is and many would like me to announce a specific date of withdrawal. Actually it would be improper for me to tell you, at this time, much more than I can tell anyone else. We must not publicly indicate how, when and where we will do certain things, but you will see from my announcements from time to time where we are going.'

"'The real issue, however, is where the United States will be after Vietnam. Currently the popular thought is for us to cut back and to cease all actions now. But, we are engaged in difficult negotiations around the world, especially in the SALT talks. Some think the simplest thing we could do would be to negotiate only on ABM, but we must look at the whole picture. Let's analyze just where we are now in national strength. We are ahead in conventional power. We are roughly equal in air power. With regard to nuclear punch they have approximately 1,500 ICBMs—we have 1,000. They have bigger warheads or throw-weight. By 1974 they will catch up to us in nuclear subs. We must negotiate on the broad picture. We have to consider where we will be after Vietnam. We need to end the war in Vietnam so the South Vietnamese will have a chance to survive. We can't guarantee their perpetual survival, but we certainly owe it to them and to the Free World to give them a chance for survival. Not only for their sake, but for our sake because the other nations on the perimeter of Asia: the Philippines, Korea, Japan itself, etc., cannot be allowed to lose confidence in us, and they will if we leave precipitously.'

"'If the world begins to think that the United States is content to be a second rate power (and even if that seems to fit well within the United States) it will not be conducive to peace in the world.'

"The President went on to explain, as he had in the Leadership meeting earlier in the day, that there were two great and key nations or peoples on the periphery of the Communist bloc that looked to us for a guarantee of their own security. They are Japan and Germany—neither of them have nuclear power. Germany, in Europe, will watch us. If she is convinced that America is satisfied to become a second rate power—if she once loses confidence in the American nuclear umbrella, she will accommodate herself with the East. Then all the peoples inhabiting the rim lands around the Communist bloc nations, who produce three times as much as the Communist countries, will have second thoughts. The same situation could happen with respect to Japan. Japan has 110 million people, and produces 2-1/2 times as much as China. It sits on the western borders of the Pacific in geographical position relative to Germany on the western borders of Russia and if Japan thinks the U.S. protection is not enough, then despite all else, despite its ties with us, economic links, its preference to deal with the West, it will look elsewhere. Then, where would we stand? And, what change in U.S. stature would occur over the long run? What this would do to our Nation's soul is frightening to contemplate.

"The President pointed out that any President, especially the one occupying the White House at this time, with the delicate balance existing in the world, needed strength and evidence of such strength—not only military but cohesive political backing to enable him to play the proper cards to have the 'blue chips' essential in the international poker game.

"'We could well be the last Administration that cares about America's future in the international field. That is why ABM cannot be the only issue in negotiations at the SALT talks. The SALT talks have to look to the entire field of armament in an attempt to reduce the offensive power of weapons or to limit their future construction and deployment.'"

After commentary by Kissinger relating to Soviet and U.S. missile strength (some of which was not recorded because of its highly classified nature), Nixon returned to his theme: "the President said there is a brighter side we can look at. We should not always look at the negative side. Both China and Russia want to increase their consumer goods. Russia especially. The consumer pressure is building up. The world wants peace and we must take this opportunity to get it. He said, 'One thing I want to point out. If SALT is to have a chance—the negotiations in SALT—we cannot give away in the Senate things we might want to discuss in SALT. Now is a critical time. If the USSR sees the United States ignoring its responsibilities in the draft for instance, in maintaining an adequate Armed Force, or on the Foreign Aid program, she could obviously take this as a sign of weakness and say; Why should we continue to negotiate SALT when the United States is going to take these actions itself unilaterally?'

"'The USSR has strong reasons to have an agreement, but we know for a fact that they will only deal from strength and that they respect those who have strength, otherwise they have historically moved into the power vacuums.' The President said, 'I know it is difficult for you gentlemen to always stand firm on these hard issues; but this is the better part of valor and the greater part of statesmanship. Even though it is hard, it is terribly important to the United States and that in itself is good politics.'

"He pointed out that those who are for unilateral disarmament are the ones who will really put the world into jeopardy as far as the future is concerned. Past history shows that aggression moves into areas of weakness."

The meeting concluded with general discussion of the President's war-making powers and U.S. missile strength. (Ibid.) The meeting was held in the Cabinet Room of the White House between 5:17 and 6:21 p.m. (Ibid., White House Central Files, Staff Members and Office Files, Office of Presidential Papers and Archives, Daily Diary)

---

89.   Special Message by President Nixon to the Congress[1]

Washington, April 21, 1971.

On September 15, 1970 I proposed a major transformation in the foreign assistance program of the United States.[2] My purpose was to renew and revitalize the commitment of this Nation to support the security and development objectives of the lower income countries, and thereby to promote some of the most fundamental objectives of U.S. foreign policy.

Today, I report to you on the progress of the last seven months in effecting that transformation and ask the Congress to join me in taking the next creative step in our new approach—the reform of the United States bilateral assistance program.

To achieve such reform, I am transmitting two bills—the proposed International Security Assistance Act and International Development and Humanitarian Assistance Act—and announcing a number of actions which I intend to take administratively. Taken together, they would:

—Distinguish clearly between our security, development and humanitarian assistance programs and create separate organizational structures for each. This would enable us to define our own objectives more clearly, fix responsibility for each program, and assess the progress of each in meeting its particular objectives.

—Combine our various security assistance efforts (except for those in Southeast Asia which are now funded in the Defense budget) into one coherent program, under the policy direction of the Department of

---

[1] Source: *Public Papers of the Presidents of the United States: Richard Nixon, 1971*, pp. 564–567.

[2] See Document 70.

State. This would enable security assistance to play more effectively its critical role in supporting the Nixon Doctrine and overall U.S. national security and foreign policy in the 1970s.

—Create a U.S. International Development Corporation and a U.S. International Development Institute to replace the Agency for International Development. They would enable us to reform our bilateral development assistance program to meet the changed conditions of the 1970s.

—Provide adequate funding for these new programs to support essential U.S. foreign policy objectives in the years ahead.

The Importance of Foreign Assistance

U.S. foreign assistance is central to U.S. foreign policy in the 1970s in three ways:

First, we must help to strengthen the defense capabilities and economies of our friends and allies. This is necessary so that they can increasingly shoulder their own responsibilities, so that we can reduce our direct involvement abroad, and so that together we can create a workable structure for world peace. This is an essential feature of the Nixon Doctrine.

Second, we must assist the lower income countries in their efforts to achieve economic and social development. Such development is the overriding objective of these countries themselves and essential to the peaceful world order which we seek. The prospects for a peaceful world will be greatly enhanced if the two-thirds of humanity who live in these countries see hope for adequate food, shelter, education and employment in peaceful progress rather than in revolution.

Third, we must be able to provide prompt and effective assistance to countries struck by natural disaster or the human consequences of political upheaval. Our humanitarian concerns for mankind require that we be prepared to help in times of acute human distress.

The Need for Reform

We cannot effectively pursue these objectives in the 1970s with programs devised for an earlier period. The world has changed dramatically. Our foreign assistance programs—like our overall foreign policy—must change to meet these new conditions.

In my September special message to the Congress I spelled out the major changes in the world which require new responses. Let me summarize them here:

—Today the lower income countries are increasingly able to shoulder the major responsibility for their own security and development and they clearly wish to do so. We share their belief that they must take the lead in charting their own security and development. Our new foreign assistance programs must therefore encourage the lower income countries to set their own priorities and develop their own programs, and enable us to respond as our talents and resources permit.

—Today the United States is but one of many industrialized nations which contribute to the security and development of the lower income countries. We used to furnish the bulk of international development assistance; we now provide less than half. The aid programs of other countries have grown because they recognize that they too have a major stake in the orderly progress which foreign assistance promotes, and because their capabilities to provide such assistance have grown enormously since the earlier postwar period.

—Today the international institutions can effectively mesh the initiatives and efforts of the lower income countries and the aid efforts of all of the industrialized countries. We can thus place greater reliance on such institutions and encourage them to play an increasing leadership role in the world development process.

Our ideas on the reforms needed in the world of the 1970s have evolved significantly since I received the Report of my Task Force on International Development, chaired by Mr. Rudolph Peterson, and since my special message of last September, as the result of our own deliberations and our further consultations with the Congress, the business community and many other sectors of the American public, and our friends abroad. Before spelling out a new blueprint for our bilateral assistance program, however, I wish to report to you on the gratifying progress achieved since last September in reorienting our assistance policies.

Progress Toward Reform

First, the Congress in December passed supplemental assistance legislation for FY 1971 which represented a major step in implementing the security assistance component of the Nixon Doctrine. This legislation authorized additional funds for military assistance and supporting economic assistance for countries in which the U.S. has major interests and which have convincingly demonstrated the will and ability to help themselves—including Israel and Jordan in the Middle East and Cambodia, Vietnam and Korea in East Asia.

Such support is necessary to carry out one of the central thrusts of the Nixon Doctrine—moving us from bearing the major responsibility for the defense of our friends and allies to helping them achieve an increasing capability to maintain their own defense. This increase in security assistance enables us to continue to reduce our direct presence abroad, and helps to reduce the likelihood of direct U.S. military involvement in the future.

Second, the international development institutions have continued their progress toward leadership in the international development process. For example:

—*The World Bank* continues to increase the size and improve the effectiveness of its operations. It also has decided to broaden the scope of its lending beyond the traditional financing of projects to the provision of funds to support overall development programs in appropriate circumstances, and it is developing an improved internal evaluation and audit system.

—*The United Nations Development Program* has initiated a reorganization to improve its administration. In time this will enable it to assume a leading role in coordinating the international technical assistance effort.

—*The World Health Organization* has effectively guided and coordinated the worldwide effort to cope with the present cholera epidemic in Africa.

Third, the industrialized countries have now agreed on comparable systems of tariff preferences for imports from the lower income countries. The preferences plan is a major step in the crucial international effort to expand the export earnings of these countries, and hence to reduce their reliance on external aid. The European Community has indicated that it plans to put its tariff preferences into effect on July 1, and Japan has announced that it will do so before October 1.

Fourth, there has been satisfying progress toward achieving the untying of bilateral development loans on a fully reciprocal basis. This action will enhance the value of economic assistance to recipient countries, and eliminate the political frictions which tied aid now causes. Virtually all of the industrialized countries have agreed to the principle of untying. Details of a system offering suppliers of all participating countries a fair and equitable basis for competition are now being worked out in the Organization for Economic Cooperation and Development.

Fifth, I have established a Council on International Economic Policy, which I chair, to coordinate all aspects of U.S. foreign economic policy, including development assistance. It will provide top-level focus for our policies in this area, and accord them the high priority which they require in our foreign policy for the 1970s.

I am heartened by this progress, but much more remains to be done:

—I again urge the Congress to vote the additional funds which I have requested for the Inter-American Development Bank and the Asian Development Bank.

—We will shortly transmit legislation to authorize the U.S. contribution to the doubling of the resources of the International Development Association, the soft-loan affiliate of the World Bank, which stands at the center of the network of international financial institutions, and I urge the Congress to approve it.

—We are working with others to help establish a soft-loan window for the African Development Bank.

—We will shortly transmit legislation to authorize U.S. participation in the system of generalized tariff preferences for developing countries, and I urge Congress to approve it.

The New U.S. Bilateral Assistance Program

The next major step is the reform of the U.S. bilateral assistance program, incorporated in the proposed International Security Assistance Act and International Development and Humanitarian Assistance Act.

Our new bilateral assistance program must achieve several objectives. It must:

—Clearly identify our distinct aid objectives: security assistance, development assistance and humanitarian assistance.

—Be truly responsive to the initiatives of the lower income countries themselves and encourage them to play the central role in solving their own security and development problems. In the area of development assistance, this means working within a framework set by the international institutions to the maximum extent possible.

—Be concentrated in countries of special interest to the United States, and in projects and programs in which the United States has a special ability to be of help.

—Recognize the improved economic capacity of many of the lower income countries in establishing the terms of our assistance.

—Assure improved management.

—Reduce substantially the number of U.S. Government officials operating our assistance program overseas.

[Omitted here are details of the new foreign assistance program.]

90.   Editorial Note

On April 21, 1971, the same day the President sent to Congress his message on foreign assistance reform (see Document 89), Peter G. Peterson, Executive Director of the Council on International Economic Policy, conducted a press briefing on the subject of the President's message. He was accompanied by C. Fred Bergsten, Assistant for International Economic Affairs, National Security Council; James R. Schlesinger, Assistant Director, Office of Management and Budget; and Ernest Stern, senior staff member, Council on International Economic Policy. The press conference began with a briefing by Peterson, in which he provided the context for the President's proposals:

"The changes in our foreign policy are very familiar to you already. The new foreign policy concepts that are implied in the Nixon Doctrine call for a new partnership, the primary purpose of which is to achieve a generation of peace in a durable world order. More specifically, it means a greater sharing with others in the definition of policy and in the bearing of costs.

"It means the encouragement of others to participate fully in the creation of plans and designing programs. And while it means continuing U.S. leadership, it means a leadership within an active partnership rather than a leadership of unilateral decision.

"The reorganization reflects these basic policy objectives. It brings under one authority the economic and military assistance programs which are necessary to shoulder the responsibility for defense without endangering the freedom and independence of our allies and friends.

"The resources that are being requested are approximately at the same [level] as the funding of these programs last year. They are small, we believe, compared to the savings and reductions of American troops overseas.

"On the other hand, the International Development Assistance Act will provide us with a vital instrument to support our long-term foreign policy interests in developing countries.

"As I will show you in a moment with some charts, about two-thirds of the world lives in these countries. And I thought you might be interested in my telling you about some data that might help orient you a little better to the Message as a whole.

"When we talk about the less-developed countries, let's remember we are talking about roughly two-thirds of the free world and while there has been growth over the last ten years at a slightly higher rate than developed countries in their Gross National Product, one of the particular problems is that the per capita growth in population during this period has been at significantly higher levels in less-developed countries than in the industrialized countries, with the result that, if you will look at the per capita income, you will see that the growth continues to be significantly higher for the developed countries than for the less-developed countries.

"If I may show you this chart, in general, there was a watershed date here in this period, but for the first time, the rest of the world contributed more official aid to less-developed countries than the United States, until at the present time, we account for about 45 percent of the total aid, official aid, that is.

"You will also notice, however, that the rest of the free world is putting in a great deal of private investment into these less-developed countries.

"As one looks at numbers of these kinds, he often sees them expressed in terms of per capita income in these particular countries. If you take them as a whole, you will find that the per capita income is approximately $200 for these countries that constitute two-thirds of the world.

"Numbers have a way sometimes of not conveying the human meaning of $200 versus $3,000 to $4,000 in the industrialized countries of the world.

"Let's think of it perhaps in human terms, whether these people want—I am sure they want a job. The numbers there are sobering. About 20 percent to 50 percent of the people in these less-developed countries are unemployed. They undoubtedly want good health. About one out of four children in this two-thirds section of the free world die before the age of one. About half of the children die before the age of four. Obviously these people want food. I have been impressed with the number that three-fourths of the children in this two-thirds of the world suffer from serious malnutrition to the point where, as you all well know, their human development is retarded in one way or another.

"Finally, there is a world where education is important. In this two-thirds of the world, only about five percent of the children ever reach high school. So that is a part of the world in which many of America's and the world's most important political issues will certainly be tried and many of these political issues have a very basic economic origin to them.

"Another question that is raised, aside from the political and humanitarian aspects of this, is how is this related to the economic interests of America?

"I might point out that there is a high correlation between the rate at which these countries grow in their exports and the rate in turn in which their Gross National Product grows.

"If we want them to get stronger and more industrialized, we must also think about their exports. One might say, 'Well, these exports are certainly in their interests. Are they in the interest of the United States?'

"Well, aside from assuring a more stable and peaceful structure, I would want to remind you that in many of these rapidly growing markets our exports to these countries from America have doubled in the last four years.

"So, aside from the political and humanitarian issues, I think there are some very important issues in terms of our own economic development."

Peterson then discussed the essentials of the new proposals:

"Under this new structure, you will see an International Security Assistance Act where, for the first time, all of the security assistance is looked at together and hopefully in a more integrated way and includes all of these categories of international security assistance.

"Then all of the development and humanitarian assistance is grouped together in this set of categories here. I hope most of you can read those. I am sure you read at least as well as I do.

"The Overseas Private Investment Corporation, which is set up to guarantee U.S. overseas private investment has already been passed. But I did want you to recall that. Here is the Inter-American Foundation, which was authorized by Congress last year and is now operating and it finances the social development programs in Latin America.

"The Peterson Task Force and the subsequent Presidential decision on this new development assistance part of the program—and we have experts here who will be happy to answer your questions on any specific aspects you want—but on the development side, there are distinct objectives now for each of these agencies. Each of them has a mission. The President has been quite emphatic in being sure that this program be very responsive to initiatives by the less developed countries; that they have come up with, to the maximum extent possible to function in a frame work set by international institutions.

"We want to have as cooperative an effort in this important field as we can, concentrating on countries of special interest to the United States and on projects where the United States has special competence—that is, really having something to contribute; match the terms of our assistance to the economic capacity of the recipient, which is, I think, an important way of increasing the productivity; extremely important, improving the management to carry out these basic reforms; and an important byproduct of this program will be to reduce substantially the number of U.S. Government officials overseas that have previously been involved in these programs.

"The first structure is in the development side, the U.S. International Development Corporation. Its basic activities are development loans to developing countries, very often on a project or program basis and important technical services that are related to either preparing the loan request or implementing the program. Here are the operating principles that are implied here. They will be run in response to specific proposals where the United States has a long-term interest. They will function in the framework set by the international institutions and very often in coordination and cooperation with other bilateral donors.

"The loan terms will be tailor-made to the repayment capacity of the recipient: the valuation of the loans on sound business and development criteria; and operations will be centralized in Washington, thereby reducing field staff and relying more on the recipients for relevant information.

"In the management sense, there will be a Board of Directors. You will notice here that this will include not only the Secretaries of State and Treasury, but three private individuals. This group will have its own charter. The President will be the operating head and the request is for a three-year, $2.5 billion authorization, both appropriated funds and borrowing authority.

"The U.S. International Development Institute, we think, also fills an important need. One is to finance research that is relevant to development, strengthen research capacity which is very much lacking, as all of you know, in less-developed countries; provide training. Know-how is a very important part of this process; and to help build institutions with emphasis on agriculture and education that can continue this development process within the country; and finance advisers on development problems.

"The operating principles, again, will be to be very responsive to proposals that come from them; to concentrate on development problems in which we believe the United States has special competence; to try to build and emphasize research capacity within the less-developed countries; to provide grant financing but insisting on LDC contributions; more from the more advanced countries and less from the poorest; and implement projects through the private sector reducing official U.S. overseas personnel.

"Management and finance, the two will have a Board of Trustees. You will notice that the majority will be private citizens. Again, the Executive Director will be the operating head and again we are asking for a three-year authorization of $1.3 billion. I would emphasize here the concept of continuity and forward planning.

"The very nature of the development process is a long-term process and all of the people who know this field best believe that the long-range planning requirements should be reflected in the way the funds are authorized for it to operate.

"I should want you to know that there has been careful consultation with the legislature in this program and that one of the questions that has come up from the beginning of the Task Force and certainly recently is the whole question of coordination of this development assistance operation.

"Under this bill, there will be a U.S. coordinator of bilateral development assistance. He or she will be appointed by the President with the advice and consent of the Senate, responsible to the President, accountable to the Congress as the Administration spokesman on bilateral development assistance. He will exercise his authority by being Chairman of each of these boards that I have mentioned. He will chair an Executive Committee, the operating heads of the three agencies. He will operate under the foreign policy guidance of the Secretary of State, coordinate with the National Security Council, and of course security issues are involved and under the coordination of the new Council on International Economic Policy and Economic Development Issues.

"In terms of the funds that are involved here, we have them broken down as between nearly $2 billion, $1.993 billion for the international security assistance portion and $1.245 billion for the development assistance portion.

"I might say that in hearing the President discuss this program, he has said that this is not the kind of world where we dare leave a vacuum and it is not the kind of world where we can withdraw our physical presence as we are in key areas of the world and, at the same time, withdraw our economic presence.

"If we are going to have a generation of peace, it is not going to be simply by ending a war, but by building a structure for peace. And he believes that one of the key foundations of that structure for peace has to do with the vital and viable group of less-developed countries, which, as I have indicated, account for two-thirds of the world's population where many of the political issues of the '70's will arise and where in turn many of the political issues are at their core economic issues." (The Richard Nixon Library, Nixon Papers)

A period of questions and answers followed Peterson's briefing, which began at 10:25 and ended at 11:05 a.m.

91. Memorandum for the President's File by the President's Special Assistant (Safire)[1]

Washington, June 29, 1971.

"The most significant areas of the world in the immediate future are like five fingers of the hand. Other areas like Africa and Latin America are 50 years away. But here are the five fingers: (The President held up his hand and ticked them off.) First the thumb, the US, still the strongest; next Western Europe and, boy, that Common Market is coming along fast; third, the Soviet Union; fourth, China; fifth, Japan.

"With that kind of world, the United States of America is now entering a very interesting period.

"Our vision is obscured by our obsession with the war in Vietnam. God knows, that war will be over quite soon. If we had such control over our other problems, it would all be easy.

"We will have a live-and-let-live situation with the Soviet Union; we will have a strong ally in Western Europe, but not doing much for its own defense; we will have a competing China, no longer isolated; and we will have a growing Japan.

"Now, the US looks at low labor rates around the world and its immediate reaction is, 'Boy, we better put up some quotas.' Congressional pressure along these lines is enormous. But the US cannot build a fence around itself and expect to survive as a great nation. If we did, the rest of the world, still having to make it, would out-produce us. Soon, the US would not be #1, and there are areas in which I am for the US being #1.

"Here's the irony: the success of US diplomacy will lead to greater dangers and opportunities economically.

"This morning, in the Cabinet meeting, Secretary Rogers saw a period of five to ten years from now when 75% of our foreign policy would be economics. We either have to come to the mark, or we will be #2 economically. If that should happen, something will go out of the American spirit. That's why I don't like to give up on the SST, and that's why we are ending the war the way we are. Difficult as it is, that's the easiest thing we have to do.

---

[1] Source: National Archives, Nixon Presidential Materials, White House Special Files, President's Office Files, Memoranda for the President, Box 85, May 2–August 15, 1971. No classification marking. The memorandum is Safire's record of the President's comments before a meeting of the President's Commission on Productivity, which met between 10:07 and 10:47 a.m. in the Cabinet Room of the White House. (Ibid., White House Central Files, Staff Members and Office Files, Office of Presidential Papers and Archives, Daily Diary)

"It's terribly important we be #1 economically because otherwise we can't be #1 diplomatically or militarily. You hear a lot of stuff around that the US is not to be trusted with power. You hear that our Presidents lie us into wars—though I think, when all the facts come out, we will have a better view. You hear that the US is imperialistic and aggressive. But we build up our enemies after wars, and we ask for not one acre. What will we get for ourselves out of Vietnam? Nothing.

"As distinguished from other great powers throughout civilization, we did not ask for our position of power, nor did we even have a policy for acquiring the power. It fell into our lap.

"For the next quarter century, let us see to it that we do play this role. We care when there is an earthquake in Peru or a famine in India. Never has a nation given more and gotten less.

"I have been more melodramatic than I meant to be, but if the moment comes when we are not competitive, our standard of living will go down, inflation will go up, and something will go out of the American spirit.

"This would diminish the chances for a generation of peace. The future of the economy is in our hands—and also the future of peace."

---

92.   **Remarks by President Nixon to the Nation**[1]

July 15, 1971.

Good evening:

I have requested this television time tonight to announce a major development in our efforts to build a lasting peace in the world.

As I have pointed out on a number of occasions over the past 3 years, there can be no stable and enduring peace without the participation of the People's Republic of China and its 750 million people. That is why I have undertaken initiatives in several areas to open the door for more normal relations between our two countries.

---

[1] Source: *Public Papers of the Presidents of the United States: Richard Nixon, 1971,* pp. 819–820. Nixon's remarks were broadcast live on radio and television at 7:31 p.m. from the NBC studios in Burbank, California.

In pursuance of that goal, I sent Dr. Kissinger, my Assistant for National Security Affairs, to Peking during his recent world tour for the purpose of having talks with Premier Chou En-lai.[2]

The announcement I shall now read is being issued simultaneously in Peking, and in the United States:

Premier Chou En-lai and Dr. Henry Kissinger, President Nixon's Assistant for National Security Affairs, held talks in Peking from July 9 to 11, 1971. Knowing of President Nixon's expressed desire to visit the People's Republic of China, Premier Chou En-lai, on behalf of the Government of the People's Republic of China, has extended an invitation to President Nixon to visit China at an appropriate date before May 1972. President Nixon has accepted the invitation with pleasure.

The meeting between the leaders of China and the United States is to seek the normalization of relations between the two countries and also to exchange views on questions of concern to the two sides.

In anticipation of the inevitable speculation which will follow this announcement, I want to put our policy in the clearest possible context.

Our action in seeking a new relationship with the People's Republic of China will not be at the expense of our old friends. It is not directed against any other nation. We seek friendly relations with all nations. Any nation can be our friend without being any other nation's enemy.

I have taken this action because of my profound conviction that all nations will gain from a reduction of tensions and a better relationship between the United States and the People's Republic of China.

It is in this spirit that I will undertake what I deeply hope will become a journey for peace, peace not just for our generation but for future generations on this earth we share together.

Thank you and good night.

---

[2] For a first-hand account of Kissinger's visit to Peking, see Kissinger, *White House Years*, pp. 714–755.

---

93.   Editorial Note

On July 16, 1971, Henry Kissinger provided a briefing on a background basis to members of the press on his visit to Peking and the upcoming Presidential visit to China publicly announced the previous evening. In response to a question about recent public statements by the administration cautioning against exaggerated expectations of improved relations with China, Kissinger explained:

"Well, we have had a difficult problem with maintaining a public posture on this issue. The relationships with the People's Republic have gone in essentially two phases: (1) In the first year and a half of the Administration, there was a general attempt on our part to communicate to Peking that we were prepared to have a serious dialogue, and that we were not prisoners of history.

"We also took, in addition, a series of unilateral steps that were public that symbolized this. Then, starting this spring, about concurrently with the visible manifestation of the ping-pong diplomacy, the manifestations having been in a general framework of trying to express a general attitude, both sides moved into a more concrete phase.

"On the other hand, there are a number of really interesting aspects. When you have not been in touch with a country for 25 years, it is amazing how technically difficult it is to simply find out where you should talk, and with whom. That is something that we don't teach in textbooks on diplomacy.

"When you are nursing a rather tenuous dialogue, you don't want to create excessive expectations of how it might go. Even after we knew, for example, that a visit by the American envoy in Peking would be welcome, there still remained a lot to be discussed about how to work it out; what should be discussed; what the objectives should be.

"The President felt that until we know that, it would be best not to raise undue expectations, excessive speculation, for each side to take a public position that it might then regret, and if it turned out that a later moment would be more propitious, we could then do it without embarrassment or without a sense of failure."

Kissinger also addressed the impact of the opening to China on U.S.-Soviet relations, particularly a prospective summit:

"The President's view on a meeting with the Soviet leaders has been frequently stated. It is one that, of course, he has always been, in principle, willing to undertake. It would seem to me that the occasion of a visit to Peking is not the best to also visit Moscow. The issues to be discussed between the two countries are too various. But in principle, we are prepared to meet with the Soviet leaders whenever our negotiations have reached a point where something fruitful can be accomplished.

"Let me make one other point: Nothing that has been done in our relations with the People's Republic of China has any purpose or is in any way directed against any other countries, and especially not against the Soviet Union. We are taking these steps because we cannot imagine a stable, international peace in which a country of 750 million people is kept in isolation. We believe that by improving relations with the People's Republic of China we are contributing to peace in the world, and therefore are contributing to all nations."

Returning to his earlier theme, Kissinger expanded on the two phases in the development of informal relations with the People's Republic of China:

"I was saying that there were two phases in our relationship with the People's Republic of China: One, a period in which a general framework was established, first through a series of communications in various ways on our part that indicated that we were not bound by previous history and that expressed general philosophy. That also was expressed in the President's annual foreign policy report and was expressed in the first public use of the phrase, 'People's Republic of China' last October in a toast of President Nixon to President Ceausescu, and was repeated in February in the President's World Report, even in the middle of the Laotian operation. There was also a series of steps which the Department of State took to indicate a general willingness to open relations as well as public statements by the Secretary of State and others.

"The second phase started in April when we moved from this general framework to a more specific exploration of where we might go from here. Then in April, May, and June this meeting was set up through a series of exchanges and very detailed preparations which were made. The preparations had been somewhat handicapped by the fact that the only senior officials who knew about it were the President, the Secretary of State and myself."

Toward the end of the briefing, Kissinger discussed the opening to China within the context of world affairs:

"We knew that making this decision would hurt some old friends. It is always difficult to break away from a well established pattern, which at least has the advantage that its framework has become very familiar. It forced us to re-think the whole nature of the world in which policy had been conducted more or less as if the People's Republic of China did not exist.

"I don't want to speak for the People's Republic of China, but I don't doubt that for their leaders there were some enormously complex decisions to be made, given their image of the United States and given the fact of this long-time hostility and, indeed, confrontation in so many parts of the world, sometimes physically and always ideologically.

"So it was a complex, and I am frank to say, in many respects a moving occasion to have the privilege of seeing the beginning of this and dealing with what are no doubt very dedicated and very serious

people, and we both recognized that we were engaged on a very difficult path which had many pitfalls and which would take an enormous
sense of restraint and responsibility on both sides." (Library of
Congress, Manuscript Division, Kissinger Papers, Box CL 426, Subject
File, Background Briefings, December 1970–December 1971)

The briefing took place at the Western White House in San
Clemente, California, between 9:15 and 10:10 a.m., Pacific Daylight
Time. White House Press Secretary Ronald Ziegler introduced
Kissinger.

---

94.   Editorial Note

On July 19, 1971, Henry Kissinger met with Soviet Ambassador
Anatoly Dobrynin to "get a feeling for Dobrynin's attitude following
the announcement of the Peking Summit." Kissinger found Dobrynin
concerned that the U.S.-China initiative, in particular a Nixon visit to
China, resulted from the Soviets having been evasive in a recent U.S.
inquiry about the long-discussed U.S.-Soviet Summit. "Dobrynin was at
his oily best," wrote Kissinger in a memorandum of conversation, "and,
for the first time in my experience, totally insecure." With respect to the
question of a U.S.-Soviet summit and its timing in relation to the U.S.-
China meeting, Kissinger spoke bluntly:

"I said that I wanted to be frank with him. Perhaps in the first year
of our Administration we had not always been forthcoming in improving relations with the Soviet Union, but ever since April 1970 we believe
we have made an unending series of overtures. The Soviet response has
been grudging and petty, especially on the Summit Meeting. They simply did not understand the President. The President thought in broad
philosophical terms and had sincerely believed that his meeting with
the Soviet leaders might open new vistas for cooperation around the
world; instead, he found himself confronted with one evasion after
another. As Dobrynin very well knew, I had urged him to have an
answer by July 1st and even then it had taken till July 5th, and he had
then been evasive again, saying that the meeting could take place in
November and December. This was in effect a rejection, because I had
already told him that November and December were highly inconve-
nient. Indeed, I did not know whether Dobrynin was even saying we
should fix a date.

"Dobrynin in reply was almost beside himself with protestations of goodwill. On the contrary, he said, he could tell me strictly off the record that a meeting between his leaders and the President was very much on their minds. What in fact had happened was that September did not seem possible, and now November was the earliest possible date. He was certain the Soviet leaders would be willing to set another date for a Summit, but now they did not know whether our meeting with Peking made it impossible. Would we be willing to come to Moscow before going to Peking?

"I replied that it did not seem to me proper to go to Moscow before having gone to Peking, that we should go in the order in which the announcements were made. He asked whether we would be prepared to announce a meeting before having been in Peking. I said that that was a distinct possibility but that I would have to check this with the President and let him know later in the day.

"[I called Dobrynin at 7:00 that evening after checking with the President and told him that we would be prepared to announce a meeting in Moscow after having set the date of a meeting in Peking but before we had actually visited Peking.]" (Brackets in the source text)

During this meeting, which took place in the Map Room of the White House, Dobrynin also asked Kissinger about his meeting in Peking:

"He asked me whether the Soviet Union had come up. I replied that realistically it was obvious that we could do nothing to help Communist China against the Soviet Union. In any event to us the Soviet Union was a world power, while we recognized that China was primarily significant for Asian settlements. Dobrynin asked whether Chou En-lai had indicated any worry about a Soviet attack. I said there were practically no references to the Soviet Union except an occasional vague allusion, while it seemed to me that the primary fear of Communist China was Japan.

"Dobrynin brightened considerably and said that this was exactly his conviction of Chinese priorities. He asked what there really was to talk about between us and the Chinese? Were we interested in Chinese domination of Southeast Asia? He had always thought that the Soviet interests and ours were much more nearly complementary with respect to the defense of Southeast Asia. I said that I wasn't certain that the Chinese had aggressive tendencies in Southeast Asia but that in any event we would not favor Chinese expansion beyond their borders." (National Archives, Nixon Presidential Materials, NSC Files, Kissinger Office Files, Box 73, Country Files–Europe–U.S.S.R.)

From Kissinger's perspective, Soviet concerns over the U.S. opening to China yielded immediate dividends. He recalled in his memoirs: "Other negotiations deadlocked for months began magically to unfreeze." Such issues as the Berlin discussions and talks to guard against accidental nuclear war "moved rapidly to completion within weeks of the Peking announcement." (Kissinger, *White House Years,* pages 766–767) But Kissinger maintained that the concept of triangular diplomacy was complicated. He recalled:

"It could not be a crude attempt to play off China against the Soviet Union. 'The China card' was not ours to play. Sino-Soviet hostility had followed its own dynamic. We had not generated it; we were, in fact, unaware of its intensity for the better part of a decade. Neither Peking nor Moscow was quarreling with the other to curry favor with us; they were currying favor with us because they were quarreling. We could not 'exploit' that rivalry; it exploited itself." (Ibid., page 763)

---

95.   Press Conference by President Nixon[1]

Washington, August 4, 1971.

[Omitted here is discussion of timing of the President's trip to China.]

Now, as to the effect the visit will have, and the conversations will have, on Vietnam, I will not speculate on that subject. I will only say that as the joint announcement indicated, this will be a wide-ranging discussion of issues concerning both governments. It is not a discussion that is going to lead to instant détente.

What it really is, is moving—as we have moved, I believe, in the situation with regard to the Soviet Union—from an era of confrontation without communication to an era of negotiation with discussion. It does not mean that we go into these meetings on either side with any illusions about the wide differences that we have. Our interests are very different, and both sides recognized this, in the talks that Dr. Kissinger had, the very extended talks he had with Premier Chou En-lai. We do not expect that these talks will settle all of those differences.

What is important is that we will have opened communication to see where our differences are irreconcilable, to see that they can be set-

---

[1] Source: *Public Papers of the Presidents of the United States: Richard Nixon, 1971,* pp. 850–851. The section printed here is from item 2 of the press conference, entitled "The President's Trip to China."

tled peacefully, and to find those areas where the United States, which today is the most powerful nation in the world, can find areas of agreement with the most populous nation in the world which potentially in the future could become the most powerful nation in the world.

As we look at peace in the world for the balance of this century, and for that matter even in the next century, we must recognize that there cannot be world peace on which all the peoples in the world can rely, on which they have such a great stake, unless there is communication between and some negotiation between these two great super powers, the People's Republic and the United States.

I have put this in general terms because that is the understanding of the People's Republic, Premier Chou En-lai, and it is our understanding our agenda will be worked out at a later point; before the trip it will be very carefully worked out so that the discussions will deal with the hard problems as well as the easy ones.

We expect to make some progress, but to speculate about what progress will be made on any particular issue, to speculate, for example, as to what effect this might have on Vietnam, would not serve the interests of constructive talks.

[Omitted here are the remaining items in the press conference.]

---

96.   Memorandum of Conversation[1]

Washington, August 13, 1971, 10:05–11:50 a.m.

SUBJECT

Minutes of NSC Meeting on Defense Strategy

[Omitted here are brief opening comments by the President and Kissinger.]

[Kissinger:] The President asked that the Defense budget be presented in terms of missions, but the most fundamental questions are still unanswered. Substantial work needs to be done to define the purposes of our forces.

---

[1] Source: National Security Council, Nixon NSC Meetings, Minutes—Original, 1971–June 20, 1974. Top Secret. The meeting was held in the Cabinet Room of the White House. (National Archives, Nixon Presidential Materials, White House Central Files, Staff Members and Office Files, Office of Presidential Papers and Archives, Daily Diary)

There has been an extraordinary shift in the strategic balance since the mid-1960's. Until the late 1950's we could win a general war whether we struck first or not. Our general purpose forces could deal with any local conflict—Cuba, for example. But today Soviet strategic forces are far stronger. If a country has superiority, one doesn't have to worry about a disarming first strike. Local situations therefore take on added significance.

Most of our strategic doctrine reflects decisions under the conditions of previous periods. Thus there are some anomalies and questions, that are not yet resolved.

Let me review some of the types of forces and questions we have. This is not intended to be all-inclusive.

First, strategic nuclear forces. What are the missions of these forces? They are: deterrence; second-strike assured destruction; to save American lives; a China ABM against small attacks; some counterforce capability (particularly against Communist China); also strategic interdiction against non-urban targets.

In fact we have no disarming capability against the USSR but we do have some against China. But we cannot use our land-based missiles against China (over USSR); we have to use our bombers and submarines. Thus we must decide whether to dedicate a part of our force. And do we have the intelligence capability to define the targets? As long as we have a disarming capability we can use it to regulate their actions in local situations.

We still confront SIOP problems. We are still targeting silos without a retargeting capability. Thus we risk firing at empty holes. Why should we use bombers to go after missiles that are already fired? The approach of the SIOP hasn't changed much in 10 years. Our strategic forces are inferior in numbers but still carrying functions that are the same as when we had superiority.

As for strategic defensive forces: Our fighters are superior in numbers to theirs, but when we send them they fight their offensive fighters. The question is why would the USSR conduct small air attacks against the U.S. when it can do it with missiles? There are other issues here also—what about Safeguard and SALT?

Then we come to theater nuclear forces: We still don't have a clear doctrine for their use. Thus we can't define how many are needed. Why do we depend on vulnerable short-range artillery to deliver them? How would a war progress after the use of nuclear weapons? We have the same problems in the Pacific. Thus the problem is not resolved as to the types and numbers of forces that we need.

Then come our general purpose forces. Their mission is forward defense in Europe, and elsewhere to maintain a credible posture of defense. In NATO the problem has been to provide a capability of 90 days or more of conventional defense in response to an all-out Warsaw Pact attack. Thus the missions of the three forces—Soviet, U.S., and NATO allies—are different.

We can't get the allies to define what selective use of nuclear weapons means.

I have seen no evidence of how we will get to M+60, let alone M+90 —but our allies' supplies probably won't last that long. The problem is how the three approaches can be taken at the same time.

There is some progress here, but we still have many unsolved problems in NATO.

In other parts of the world, there is less of a problem of having a war-fighting capability; it is more a matter of the political presence of the United States. In Korea, our forces are important to the political context and their withdrawal would have a political impact in Korea and Japan. If our forces in the Pacific drop precipitously, some will see this as a move—misinterpreting the Nixon Doctrine—to withdraw. Air and naval forces are not enough. In the Middle East we have a similar problem. In September 1970, the possible projection of our ground forces was the key.

If the Army goes to 11 divisions, we will be short six divisions for our plans in Europe and will have no strategic reserve. At 13 we are still short of a strategic reserve.

These are some of the issues we are trying to discuss in the DPRC.[2] Some involve our allies, some have an impact that is psychological. If we don't come to grips with them, the consequences will be serious. The Soviets are not building missiles to be nice. Somewhere their umbrella will be translated into political power. Thus we want to continue this study.

The President: The main purpose of our forces is diplomatic wallop. The possibility of nuclear conflict is remote, because the fear of it is so widespread. We can't separate diplomatic power from the ability to deny to the other side an ability to win a war without irreparable losses.

General purpose forces are irrelevant in a nuclear war. Carriers and ground forces have a psychological effect in areas where nations depend on the US. That's the reason for NATO strength in Europe; that's why, if it was only a trip wire, at some point it becomes incredible that the US would support them. Our military plans are probably irrelevant but it is important that our presence be there because people see the US continuing to play a role in the world. This supports our

---

[2] Defense Program Review Committee.

diplomatic posture generally. They know the minimums are political minimums.

While we are negotiating with Soviets and we may negotiate with China, those in Europe and elsewhere who are under the US defense umbrella get nervous. They think we may change the power balance, and they will look elsewhere for their guarantees. Germany and Japan both look to the US guarantees for their defense.

Mel and Dave[3] are well aware that many in the Congress applaud our negotiating for the wrong reasons. They think negotiating means no need for forces. This is clearly the wrong trend. Jackson was attacked by Lowenstein.

We are in a position to have in effect a two-stage policy: To give hope that we are negotiating and maybe in the long-run can reduce our military burden. But at the same time we know we couldn't have come this far without a credible military posture—nor could we bug out in Vietnam. Any possibility for continued progress in the future with the USSR and China—who are continuing to build their military strength— will depend on our military strength.

We have a problem of public relations. Many don't care what position we have. We must explain our attitude and that of the unilateral disarmers. What will the people and the Congress support? We also have economic, budget and balance of payments problems. But I can't accept the argument that these must govern. There is a level beyond which defense can't be reduced—it is most important for diplomatic and psychological purposes.

[Omitted here is a summary of FY 1973 Defense budget considerations presented by Laird, with some discussion.]

Mr. Irwin:[4] You emphasized our concern: the diplomatic and psychological effects of budget reductions. We understand the problem. In strategic forces, sufficiency must be believable to all. In NATO, we also must maintain our commitment. Any Navy cuts should be elsewhere than in the Mediterranean. We have been pursuing the interim Suez agreements and our diplomatic effort must be supported by naval and air power in the region.

In East Asia, the political and psychological factor is the most important. All our friends are concerned about the possible outcome of the war in Vietnam and the effects on them of our China initiative. They see a change in the power balance—our allies are watching us closely.

---

[3] Secretary of Defense Melvin E. Laird and Deputy Secretary of Defense David Packard.

[4] John N. Irwin, II, Under Secretary of State.

Therefore it is essential to maintain our flexibility and our deployments. Under either of Mel's budgets we would be cutting one division in the Pacific. We need to maintain the divisions, the air wings and two carrier task forces; to move any of them would unhinge our allies there. In Japan, they are already nervous; they could be pushed to rearm, even to nuclear armaments.

I don't rule out reductions in the future but not in FY 73. It would be the wrong time. Secretary Rogers called me to emphasize this. This is his strong view.

[Omitted here is additional discussion of FY 1973 Defense budget matters.]

---

97.   Memorandum for the President's File by the President's Assistant for National Security Affairs (Kissinger)[1]

Washington, October 12, 1971.

SUBJECT

President Nixon's Meeting with Congressional Leaders on October 12, 1971, 12 noon–12:54 p.m. in the Cabinet Room. (List of participants is attached.)

The President began the meeting by noting that at that moment the announcement he would shortly be reading out to the Leaders was being simultaneously published in Washington and Moscow. The President said that after reading the announcement he would provide some background and then be open to questions. He looked forward to a good discussion in this small group. The President then read out the announcement concerning his trip to the Soviet Union in May, 1972 (Tab A).[2]

---

[1] Source: Library of Congress, Manuscript Division, Kissinger Papers, Box CL 279, Presidential File, Memoranda of Conversation, October–November 1971. No classification marking. The President, along with Kissinger, Rogers, and two staffers, met with 11 Congressional leaders in the Cabinet Room. (National Archives, Nixon Presidential Materials, White House Central Files, Staff Members and Office Files, Office of Presidential Papers and Archives, Daily Diary) A list of the attendees is attached but not printed.

[2] Not printed. The United States and the Soviet Union jointly announced agreement to hold a Summit meeting in Moscow in late May 1972. The President read the announcement at a news conference on October 12; for text, see *Public Papers of the Presidents of the United States: Richard Nixon, 1971*, p. 1030.

Turning to the background, the President recalled his first press conference in January of 1969 when the question of a summit with the Soviets was raised. At that time he had said that we should not have such a meeting unless something came out of it, otherwise it would be merely cosmetic and there would be a great letdown. This also turned out to be the Soviet view. In April, 1970, the Soviets began exploring the possibility at lower levels. But the President did not think that a meeting at the highest level at that time could serve a useful purpose. There then ensued a period of many discussions at various levels. In the last few weeks the Soviets indicated that they thought the time was ripe and Gromyko brought a formal invitation when he came to Washington.

The President continued that in fact we had made sufficient progress. He cited agreements on biological warfare, the seabeds, the hot line and accidental war. But the most important one was on Berlin. That problem was not solved totally but the United States and the Soviet Union, plus the two other countries involved, were able to reach agreement on an area where our interests clashed.[3] Now the President drew the conclusion that it was possible to go to other areas.

The President then took up the point of why the meeting was set for May rather than, for example, next month. In the first place, he said, the Soviets set the date. In addition, we were having very intensive negotiations on strategic arms. While we were aiming for agreement this year it might not come until next year. The subject was high on the agenda. In this connection, the President referred to recent stories about the huge Soviet arms build-up, particularly on the Soviet side. While SALT had made progress on the defensive side, agreement would not be reached without the offensive side because that was where the Soviets were ahead. We cannot have an agreement based on defensive equality but freezing Soviet offensive advantage. The President was confident that we would have a SALT agreement but it must not freeze us into inferiority.

The President cautioned against euphoria in connection with this Moscow trip. There continued to be great differences: in the Caribbean and Southeast Asia, in Europe and, most fundamentally as regards systems of government. Nevertheless the overwhelming fact was that if there ever was a superpower conflict there would be no victors, only losers. The Soviets know this as well as we do. Neither superpower

---

[3] According to notes of a Cabinet meeting held later that day taken by Assistant to the President Ray Price, Nixon said of these accomplishments: "Any one of them would have been hailed as the second coming if achieved by another President." (National Archives, Nixon Presidential Materials, White House Special Files, President's Office Files, Memos for the President, Box 86, August 22–December 5, 1971)

would let the other get an advantage sufficient to enable it to launch a preemptive strike. Therefore, we should explore areas where we can limit or even perhaps reduce arms.

Apart from arms, there were such problems as Europe and trade. Without listing an agenda, the President said the Moscow talks would deal with all "questions of mutual interest." This included peripheral areas like the Middle East, where we hoped for progress before the summit; Southeast Asia and its future, where we will go forward with our two-track policy and will not wait until May; and the Caribbean.

To sum up, the President said when we look at the future of the world negotiations rather than confrontations were essential. It did not matter if we had a difference with a small country like Bolivia, but in the case of the Soviet Union it could be disastrous. The President then stressed that the two trips he was planning—to Peking and Moscow— were completely separate and independent. We were in the position of pursuing the best relations with both, but not with one at the expense of the other.[4] The President added that we had informed Peking, the European allies and Japan of the Moscow trip, but because of the Soviet passion for secrecy, which they share with other communists, we had to be extremely careful not to risk a leak.

[Omitted here is general discussion among the participants.]

---

[4] Nixon also told the Cabinet, according to Price's notes, that "we are on a very high wire. We are trying to stay there vis-à-vis the Soviet Union and China. We must remember that we are ironically in a position where each rates the other as a greater enemy than the U.S. But the U.S.—to deal with either—must deal evenhandedly, *not* playing off one against the other." (Ibid.)

---

98.   **Editorial Note**

On October 27, 1971, on his return from China, Henry Kissinger held a press conference in the White House Briefing Room. Kissinger was in China October 20–27 to continue planning for the upcoming Presidential trip to China. Unlike the first visit, the second trip was announced publicly beforehand. For Kissinger's account of this trip, see *White House Years*, pages 776–785. When asked during the press conference whether there was any discussion with the Chinese of the upcoming Moscow Summit, Kissinger responded:

"First of all, let me say that I will not comment on any of the sub-stantive discussions. But I do want to take this opportunity to make the following point: Our relations with the People's Republic of China are designed to end the isolation from each other of two great peoples. It is an attempt to settle or to begin the long process of settlement of out-standing issues between two peoples who have had a history of friend-ship.

"It is not directed against any third country. Neither side is going to use the discussions that will come up as an opportunity to discuss the possible settlement of issues that primarily affect third countries. Therefore, we do not feel, nor does the People's Republic require us to give an account of whatever dealings we might have with other coun-tries.

"This, incidentally, this precise rule, will be applied in our relation-ship with Moscow. Whatever differences may or may not exist between the People's Republic of China and the Soviet Union are for them to dis-cuss among themselves. We have a long agenda of bilateral issues to discuss with both of them. This is going to be the exclusive concern of the President when he visits first Peking and then Moscow." (White House Press Release, October 27, 1971; Library of Congress, Manuscript Division, Kissinger Papers, Box CL 426, Subject File, Background Briefings, December 1970–December 1971)

The press conference, which began at 4:16 p.m. and ended at 4:51, was conducted almost entirely "on the record."

99.   Memorandum for the President's File by the President's
        Assistant for National Security Affairs (Kissinger)[1]

Washington, October 30, 1971, 10:05–11:05 a.m.

SUBJECT

  Meeting Between President Nixon and President Tito

PARTICIPANTS

  President Nixon
  Alexander Akalovsky, Department of State

  President Tito
  Miss Lijana Tambaca, Interpreter

[Omitted here is discussion of general subjects.]

First, the President said, he believed that President Tito knew that, while the U.S. had many faults, it was not a threat to the independence of smaller countries. It was certainly not a threat to Yugoslavia, which could have trade and other relations with the U.S. but should not fear any interference on the part of the United States. The U.S. was not saintly, but from the standpoint of its own self-interest—and any country must act on the basis of its self-interest—it believed that its interests would be served by the existence of strong independent nations like Yugoslavia. We realized, however, that Ceausescu, with his big neighbor to the North, and Yugoslavia, which was in the same sphere but somewhat further removed, had a special problem. While he did not know Brezhnev or Kosygin personally, there was no question in his mind that, because of its self-interest, the USSR would continue its efforts to bring its neighbors under increased influence. The independence of Yugoslavia and Romania, regardless of these two countries' internal systems, was consistent with U.S. interests but was not consistent with Soviet interests.

President Tito interjected that there were great differences between Romania and Yugoslavia, with the President commenting that President Tito would still admit that he had been a thorn in the USSR's side, not because he wanted it but because his independent policy was disliked by the Soviets. The problem of the countries in that area was to have good relations with the United States but without going so far as to provoke the Soviets into using their might to stop movement toward independence. In this connection, the President observed that one of the

---

  [1] Source: National Archives, Nixon Presidential Materials, White House Special Files, President's Office Files, B Series Documents, Box 58, Folder 34. Secret; Sensitive; Nodis. The meeting was held in the Oval Office.

major questions to be discussed in Moscow would be the U.S. attitude towards the Eastern bloc. Our position would not be that of liberation; as Hungary had shown, liberation meant suicide. However, the President stressed, his position would be to avoid any kind of understanding with Moscow that would give the Soviets encouragement to fish in troubled waters in Yugoslavia or elsewhere. He felt that he did not have to say more than that.

[Omitted here is discussion of Soviet relations with Yugoslavia and Eastern Europe.]

The President said that another question he wished to discuss with President Tito was our arms talks with the Soviets, because those talks were very important from the standpoint of what other states would do for their defense. Noting that we hoped to reach agreement with the Soviets on limiting both offensive and defensive strategic armaments, the President said that he wished to point out at the same time that if no such agreement was reached he would have to make a decision to increase our armaments. As things stood now, the Soviets were making great efforts to enlarge their arsenal of ICBMs, SS-9s and SLBMs. While we could not object to Soviet efforts to reach parity with the United States, we could not stand by if another nation was gaining superiority. Therefore, if no agreement was reached, we would have to increase our arms spending by $15 to $20 billion, and he, the President, was prepared to do it. President Tito expressed the view that it was important for the U.S. to discuss arms control with the Soviet Union because if agreement was reached in this area, that would make it easier to reach agreement on other issues as well.

The President continued that in certain parts of the world, some seemed to believe that given our winding up some commitments, our Vietnam policy, the Nixon Doctrine, and our moves regarding China and the USSR, he was so concerned about peace that he would make a move for peace even if that should weaken U.S. defenses. This, the President emphasized, was a gross miscalculation. The U.S. was a Pacific power, and it intended to remain such a power because it had interests in the area. If others were to limit their armaments, the U.S. would do the same, but it would not do it unilaterally.

The President recalled the remark in his toast the other night, that President Tito was a man of peace.[2] In a very personal way, he wanted to say that although President Tito's and his own backgrounds were different and his role in history had not been as great as President Tito's, there were also some similarities. Both President Tito and himself had

---

[2] For text of the toast, see *Public Papers of the Presidents of the United States: Richard Nixon, 1971*, p. 1067–1068.

come up the hard way. President Tito was for peace, and he considered himself to be a man of peace too. President Tito was for independence, just as he was a strong believer in independence. He also respected different social systems; President Tito might be a communist and he a capitalist but this did not matter. However, one thing should be clear, and that was that he, President Nixon, was not a soft man. The U.S. was not interested in peace at any cost, and this would be made very clear in the forthcoming discussions with the Chinese and the Soviets. Nor would the U.S. make any arrangement with the Chinese or the Soviets at the expense of third countries. The President continued that it was his firm conviction that a weak United States would be a danger to peace, although some Senators held a different view and called for unilateral disarmament. He did not believe in such disarmament, especially if the other side was building up its armaments. In this connection, the President noted that some leaders on which President Tito had influence might criticize the United States for increasing its military strength, but that he firmly believed that this served the interests of peace. President Tito said that the nations the President was referring to did not criticize the United States for strengthening its defenses but rather for its inadequate participation in their development. Many of those nations were tired of hearing only words about such participation and wanted to see some action.

[Omitted here is discussion of the war in Vietnam.]

---

100.   Address by Secretary of State Rogers[1]

Washington, December 1, 1971.

[Omitted here are introductory comments.]

I think you will agree with me when I say that President Nixon came to office with an experience in foreign affairs matched by few of his predecessors. A review of his public statements shortly before and after he assumed office foreshadowed the major initiatives that this administration has taken. Yet few would have been willing to predict their sweep. They can be broadly stated this way:

---

[1] Source: Department of State *Bulletin*, December 20, 1971, pp. 693–697. Secretary Rogers addressed the 50th anniversary dinner of the Overseas Writers of Washington.

First, maximum practical efforts in every forum to achieve a more peaceful world, as with the SALT [Strategic Arms Limitation Talks],[2] Berlin, and Middle East talks;

Second, concerted action to achieve a better balance of responsibilities to reflect the growing shift in political-economic power in the world; for example, the Nixon doctrine, which has resulted in the reduction of more than 420,000 men from East Asia, and the new economic policy;

Third, intensive diplomatic activity to improve relations throughout the world in order to provide a foundation for a generation of peace, as illustrated by the President's forthcoming trips to Peking and Moscow.

Basic to this third point is a fundamental and often ignored concept in foreign affairs—that nations do not have permanent enemies, only permanent interests.

I will not attempt to cite the various initiatives the President has undertaken to carry out these objectives, because you are all well aware of them.

Rather, tonight I want to speak briefly about the U.S. relationship with Europe—about our permanent interests and, in the true sense of the word, our permanent friends. In each of the permanent interests of United States foreign policy—security, economic well-being, peace—Europe continues to play a central role. Europe's security is indivisible from our own. Europe's economic strength reinforces our own. And as the President has said, "if we are to found a structure of peace on the collaboration of many nations, our ties with Western Europe must be its cornerstone."[3] This statement is fundamental to our foreign policy. We hope it will not be forgotten by our friends in Europe.

It is more than symbolic, then, that the President has scheduled meetings with President Pompidou, Prime Ministers Heath, Trudeau, Caetano, and Chancellor Brandt and that within a few days I will be attending a NATO Foreign Ministers meeting. These consultations are all important aspects of implementing our foreign policy, in which our relations with Western Europe remain of fundamental importance. They will give the President and members of his administration an opportunity to discuss in person the visits he will be making to Peking and Moscow, economic and monetary issues, and other matters of common interest.

---

[2] All brackets in the source text.

[3] The complete text of President Nixon's foreign policy report to the Congress on Feb. 25 appears in the *Bulletin* of Mar. 22, 1971. [Footnote in the source text.]

Europe today is in an important period of transition, a transition embodying two processes. The first, the process toward integration of Western Europe, is progressing rapidly. The second, a process toward reconciliation between countries in Eastern and Western Europe, appears to be beginning.

The United States Government fully supports both of these. Since the days of the Marshall Plan the unity and strength of Western Europe have been central objectives of American foreign policy; we will not cease to be active supporters of these objectives now that they are on the threshold of success. And we are no less determined to participate actively in the process of reducing the political and social barriers which still divide the European Continent.

In the process toward Western European integration, we have always known that, as Western Europeans developed collective policies and a collective identity, their views and ours would not always coincide and transitory differences would develop.

In the economic field this has happened from time to time over the years, but we have resolved our disputes without damaging the underlying strength of our relationship.

We realize that the international aspects of the economic policy announced by President Nixon last August[4] directly affect the interests of Western Europeans. We believe that they understand why we had to take drastic action to correct a balance of payments deficit running at three times the 1970 rate. It is not our intention, of course, to damage the economies of our allies and friends or to impair the system of economic cooperation which has served all of us so well over the past quarter of a century.

Since August 15, we have consulted closely with the principal industrial and financial nations about the measures we have taken. There is a wider measure of agreement among us than is evident from some of the public comment on the subject. There is a recognition that exchange rates had gotten out of line and that a substantial realignment is necessary if the international system is to function effectively. There is understanding that we have unfinished and urgent business of major importance in the area of trade rules and trade practices to insure freer and fairer trade. There is no disagreement that the burden of the common defense should be shared more equitably and that multilateral

---

[4] Reference is to Nixon's so-called "New Economic Policy," which he announced in an address to the nation on August 15. With respect to foreign policy, the address focused on protection of the American dollar as a pillar of monetary stability throughout the world. Text of the address is in *Public Papers of the Presidents of the United States: Richard Nixon, 1971*, pp. 886–890. See also *Foreign Relations*, 1969–1976, vol. III, Documents 164 ff.

efforts must be intensified to accomplish this result. We believe that mutually beneficial solutions can and will be worked out.

U.S.-Western European Interdependence

Moreover, whatever our contemporary economic problems, the broadest interests of Western Europe and of the United States remain inseparable. And neither these nor any other problems will cause us to abandon our support of Western European alliance or our commitment to a strong NATO alliance.

First, there is, of course, no intention on our part—as has been suggested in some quarters—to exploit the economic situation to try to divide Western European countries from each other. We hope Western Europe will continue to speak with unity and cohesion in the economic as in other fields.

Second, while we firmly believe that defense burdens should be shared more equitably, economic differences and problems have not caused us to change our views on the maintenance of U.S. forces in Europe. As President Nixon pledged a year ago: Given a similar approach by our allies, we will maintain and improve those forces and will not reduce them unless there is reciprocal action.[5] The administration's steadfastness of purpose on this point should be clear from the determination and success with which we have continued to oppose attempts in the United States Senate to cut U.S. forces in Europe unilaterally.

Third, we will not withdraw—in the economic field, in the security field, or in the political field—into remoteness or isolation from Western Europe. Rather, in recognition of U.S.-Western European interdependence in all these fields, we will remain committed and involved.

This, then, is the message that the President has asked me to take next week to the NATO Foreign Ministers meeting in Brussels: that America's partnership with Western Europe and America's commitment to its defense are undiminished.

At that meeting the allies will be concerned, too, with the second process I have referred to—the movement toward reconciliation in Europe as a whole. In particular, we will be discussing two elements in that process, the mutual and balanced force reductions (MBFR) and a conference on European security and cooperation.

We hope that it will soon be possible to move into more definitive preparations for a negotiation on force reductions. At the Deputy

---

[5] For a message from President Nixon read by Secretary Rogers before the ministerial meeting of the North Atlantic Council at Brussels on Dec. 3, 1970, see *Bulletin* Jan. 4, 1971, p. 1. [Footnote in the source text.]

Foreign Ministers meeting in October, former NATO Secretary General [Manlio] Brosio was named to explore Soviet views on approaches to negotiation. We regret that the Soviet Government, despite its earlier public assertions of willingness to proceed at once to negotiations, has not agreed to receive Mr. Brosio. We hope it will do so soon.

Concern has been expressed in certain quarters in Western Europe that the United States Government may consider the discussion on force reductions as little more than a cover for American troop withdrawals. This concern is without any foundation. We have no interest in an agreement which would alter the conventional-force balance in Europe to the West's disadvantage. Only reciprocal withdrawals which are carefully balanced could be contemplated. Only such withdrawals can contribute to the overall process of East-West reconciliation to which we and our allies are committed. Together with our allies we must make certain that all proposals for force reductions are carefully examined for their security implications.

Conference on European Security

Another step in the process of reconciliation which will receive active consideration at the coming NATO meeting is a conference on European security and cooperation.

NATO has made clear that it would not engage in preparations for such a conference until the Berlin negotiations were successfully concluded. The first phase of the Berlin agreement was signed by the United States, the Soviet Union, the United Kingdom, and France in September. The second phase, the talks between East and West Germany, has now reached the point of decision. If those talks succeed—and there is now every reason to believe they will—the four powers would subsequently proceed toward the signing of a final protocol bringing the entire Berlin agreement into effect. When this would occur is uncertain at the present time because of the Soviet Union's insistence that it will not sign the protocol until the time of the ratification of the treaty between the Soviet Union and the Federal Republic of Germany. They insist that it be done simultaneously. The United States, for its part, would be prepared to sign the final protocol as soon as the results of the German negotiations have been found acceptable. And we expect this to occur very soon.

However, when the protocol is signed—so that a satisfactory solution to the question of Berlin is an accomplished fact—the way will be open for concrete preparations during the coming year for a conference. In this connection we would be prepared to support the convening of a special NATO Deputy Foreign Ministers meeting to consider ways to proceed.

Let me outline the basic United States approach to such a conference.

In the first place, we believe that a conference should emphasize substance over atmosphere. It must attempt to mitigate the underlying causes of tension, not merely its superficial manifestations. It should therefore deal with any security issues on the agenda in a concrete way.

In the second place, we believe that the discussions could usefully address the basic principles that should govern relations among states. A conference should encourage the reconciliation of sovereign European states, not confirm their division. The conference could help make this clear by affirming—as President Nixon and President Tito affirmed in October—the independence and equality of sovereign states, whether their political or social systems are different or similar.

In the third place, we believe that a conference should give major emphasis to issues of cooperation on which East-West progress is attainable. While a conference might contribute to enhanced security, the progress achieved on Berlin and in the SALT talks suggests that detailed negotiation of individual security issues is more likely to be handled in less general and less highly visible forums.

A conference could, however, stimulate cooperation in Europe toward increased East-West trade, toward more frequent and more useful exchanges of science and technology, and toward common efforts to preserve the human environment.

In the fourth place, we believe that a conference should go beyond the traditional pattern of cultural exchanges between East and West. It should take specific steps to encourage the freer movement of people, ideas, and information.

In general, we would view a conference on European security and cooperation in dynamic rather than static terms. We would firmly oppose any attempt to use it to perpetuate the political and social division of Europe. We would see a conference not as a ratification of the existing divisions but as a step on the long road to a new situation—a situation in which the causes of tension are fewer, contacts are greater, and the continent could once more be thought of as Europe rather than as two parts.

Improving Relations With Eastern Europe

I have spoken of our efforts with our allies to lessen tensions and improve relations with the peoples and states of Eastern Europe. In our bilateral efforts as well, we are seeking the same objectives and making progress. As you know, we have been making progress in the SALT talks. The success of Secretary [of Commerce Maurice H.] Stans' visit to the Soviet Union underscores the progress we are making in our relations. You know, for example, the progress that has been made in trade recently.

In May President Nixon will become the first American President to visit the Soviet Union in 27 years. As the official announcement of the trip made clear, both we and the Soviets had agreed that a summit meeting "would be desirable once sufficient progress had been made in negotiations at lower levels."[6] We are pleased that such progress is taking place.

The objectives of the President's visit—to improve bilateral relations and enhance the prospects for peace—cannot be attained, nor will they be sought, at the expense of the other countries of Europe, Eastern or Western. Indeed, we are prepared to improve and expand our relations with the Eastern European states at whatever pace they are willing to maintain. Good beginnings have been made. In bilateral trade, the area in which the Soviet Union's allies have shown the greatest interest, the total is expected to reach $415 million this year; although still small, it is an increase of more than 50 percent since 1967. We hope to increase it substantially in years to come.

We welcome the authority President Nixon was given by Congress to approve Export-Import Bank financing of trade with Eastern Europe. Yesterday, as you know, the President notified Congress of his intention to apply this authority to Romania, and we have some possibilities under active consideration now to carry out in practice that authority.

Other Eastern European countries, notably Poland and Hungary, have also shown a desire for improvement in their relations with us. We reciprocate this desire and are responding to it. With Poland, for example, our overall trade already approaches in volume our trade with the Soviet Union, and we hope further steps will soon be possible to increase it.

Our approach in Eastern Europe, as elsewhere, corresponds to the words of President Nixon's inaugural address in 1969: "We seek an open world—open to ideas, open to the exchange of goods and people—a world in which no people, great or small, will live in angry isolation."

There are voices in this country calling for United States withdrawal from the affairs of Europe. Such withdrawal would be folly. It would not be in the interests of our allies. It would not be in the interests of a more peaceful and more open European Continent. It would not be in the permanent interests of the United States.

---

[6] For background, see *Bulletin* Nov. 1, 1971, p. 473. [Footnote in the source text.]

Therefore we will work to strengthen our partnership with our allies in Western Europe. We will work to improve our relations with the states of Eastern Europe. And we will work to help clear the way for more stable and cooperative relationships within the whole of Europe.

[Omitted here are questions and answers.]

101.   Memorandum of Conversation[1]

Washington, December 1, 1971, 9:30 p.m.

PARTICIPANTS

Meeting with the Business Council (list attached)
Henry A. Kissinger

[Omitted here are Kissinger's introductory comments and a passing reference to the war in Vietnam.]

When this Administration came to power at the beginning of 1969, we found ourselves in a period with the foreign policy capital of the post-war era virtually exhausted. That era was one in which the United States was the sole nation of the non-Communist world with power sufficient to run foreign affairs. Following the Second World War the traditional powers were shattered economically and had domestic structures that would not sustain the active conduct of foreign policy. At the same time the emerging nations were still looking for power. They had not achieved it. During that era, throughout the non-Communist world questions of security and progress depended on answers from the United States. It came to be the view of the other nations that their security and progress was of more interest to the United States than it was to them themselves. As a reflection of that, foreign affairs for them came to be little more than lobbying efforts in the United States for action by our government. This situation, of course, simply could not last.

In the subsequent period we have seen Europe and Japan both grow enormously in their economic and military potential. Japan by

---

[1] Source: Library of Congress, Manuscript Division, Kissinger Papers, Box CL 270, Memoranda of Conversations, September 1971–November 1972. Administratively Confidential. There is no drafting information on the memorandum. The meeting was held in the Chinese Room of the Mayflower Hotel. A list of the Business Council participants is attached but not printed.

now has one of the largest economies in the world. During that same period we have seen the Communist world split; and now, surprisingly enough, the most significant political split in the world is not between the Communists and the non-Communists, but within the Communist world between Russia and China. So the whole international balance had changed by the time this Administration came into power: first, due to the growth of the power of our friends, and second, due to the growth of the power of our enemies.

As an example, in 1962 during the Cuban missile crisis, President Kennedy's supporters were proud to say that the President had gone to the edge of cataclysm to prevent intrusion in the Western Hemisphere. At that time, the Russians had some 70 intercontinental ballistic missiles: all were standing in the open, and required ten hours to fuel. By the time this Administration came into power in 1969, the Russians had 1200 missiles, all in hard sites, and they had a constantly growing fleet of missile-armed submarines. So during this era, decisions about peace and war in the international area have been taken under circumstances drastically different from those which prevailed in the 1960's.

The Europeans, most of all, have been slowly recognizing the changes in the international order. On the other side of the iron curtain, of course, there have also been significant changes. Russia was torn between her revolutionary ideology and the management of her national bureaucracy. And the Russians found themselves in a situation where their national economy could not continue to support revolutionary foreign policy. Interestingly enough also, Russia's main enemy turned out to lie in Asia, and to be Communist (that is to say China) and not to be as traditionally though, in Western Europe. And this, of course, was not long after the Russians were wont to celebrate the Communist feats of the Chinese. As a further shock to Russia the Chinese have chosen to deal now with the least dangerous of the four major powers that it sees in the world—the United States. In any case this is the situation that we faced in 1969, and to which we have tried to adjust.

Among the requirements of this new adjustment was to leave behind an attitude from the post-war foreign policy era that engagement itself was an end to be sought. Such engagements throughout the world have become beyond our resources, not only physically but also psychologically.

I have been asked not infrequently what I have learned from this job. In attempting to answer that, let me say that humility is not one of my strongest virtues. Later, after I leave this job, I may have a better perspective on what I have learned. But I will say that working outside the government the toughest problem I found was to identify issues. Once I had identified an issue, I could work to the best of my ability in reaching whatever solution seemed appropriate. Here in the government I find that there is no problem about getting the issues: they pile up in my "In-Box" every day. The problem here is how to get time to deal with them.

You all probably know that a large number of articles exist on the subject of policy planning. In fact, I myself have authored some scholarly (if not learned) articles of that nature. But I will tell you gentlemen tonight that concepts about policy planning are entirely esoteric if the issues involved cannot get to the policy-makers in the limit with which we realistically have to deal. If we were to try to take on the entire world in our foreign policy, the mere quantity of work that would be produced would just simply be too great to be handled by our top decision-makers. The greater our involvement in the world, the more the railroad train which always seems to be coming down the track toward you is likely to hit you. And while the chance that the train will hit you is growing enormously, your ability to deal thoughtfully with issues is of course declining.

The policy of this Administration is not to withdraw from the world; it is to maintain an involvement in the world—an involvement under a policy that we are capable of maintaining. In the non-Communist world this is the Nixon Doctrine. The basic premise of this doctrine is that we cannot expect to defend others beyond the point where they cannot defend themselves. Intellectually, organizationally, they must take the lead. Key here are psychological factors. We want the top policy-makers around the world to think for themselves, to organize regionally on their own, not to come automatically to the United States for answers to their problems. We are not going to withdraw from the world; this is surely evidenced by our continuing fight against amendments to limit our capacities around the world attached to the appropriation bills in Congress. We are going to demand more from the other nations of the world community.

Now let me turn for a moment to address our adversaries. We face two entirely different situations. The Soviet Union is a highly developed Communist society. The Chinese have a society which is in infancy. There is a peculiar nostalgia that leads Americans to believe that all the peoples of the world are secretly Americans. I have often said that the Americans hold the view that if you caught a Britisher off guard, when he didn't know you were listening, for instance, at 4 a.m. in the morning, he would drop that phony British accent and talk like an American. (Laughter) This nostalgia is reflected in the traditional view that our differences with the Russians must be reflections of mere personal misunderstandings and that the remedy for national differences is the development of interpersonal good will. The theory was that if we could only show the Russians we are regular guys, our problems would be resolved.

Now this theory is one that the Russians have gone along with when it has been convenient for them. This has led us to a history of brief periods of détente followed inevitably by periods of increased tensions. The inevitability of these increased tensions is evidenced by the fact that they have regularly reappeared over the last fifty years of relationship with the Russians. They must have some basis in fact other than personal misunderstandings.

The policy of this Administration, and it was reflected in the President's first press conference, has been not to talk about tensions with the Russians. We are not going to confuse foreign policy with psychotherapy. What we want to do is deal with concrete issues in our relationships, and we must avoid giving the Russians the impression that realities can be affected by changes in the atmospherics and personal relationships; otherwise, they would have no incentive to settle the real problems that exist between us.

An example of what I am talking about occurred early in the Administration. We had a problem about businessmen wanting licenses to deal with Russia. Businessmen kept coming to the White House with threats that they were going to do grave things when they got back to their Board of Directors if we didn't "okay" new trade with Russia. President Nixon's first press conference outlined the Administration policy of viewing all foreign problems as inter-related. This is a policy sometimes called "linkage"—a policy we deny in words but carry out in actions.

In the fall of 1970 there was surely evidence to the Russians that we were serious about dealing on concrete issues. There was the Middle East crisis, the frustration of trying to reach progress on the German question, the Cuban problem, and our firm position on the Polish uprising. Subsequent to that, we have seen dramatic progress in SALT negotiations, in Berlin (an area that brought the world four times in the postwar era to the brink of war), and in other areas. In addition, we have seen an opening of trade. The period immediately following this one may not be one of an expanding trade, at least prior to the consolidation of political advances commensurate with already expanded trade. But I do predict, gentlemen, that if those political advances continue we will see a tremendous growth in trade with the Russians.

Let me say (and by the way let me take this opportunity to confirm that my remarks this evening are totally off-the-record), that one might say that the Russians can be characterized as slightly thuggish bureaucrats, whereas the Chinese are more like fanatical monks. As we confront the Chinese, we confront a young society which has been totally isolated from us for some 22 years. China is a nation that does not impinge upon us except in our relations with Taiwan. The Russians are in a different situation. With them we have numerous, precise issues and conflicts.

In China our problem is in setting a basic direction of foreign affairs. What we must identify is a long-range direction, and I mean a direction for the next five to ten years. We must use our opening to identify those areas in which we have conflicting interests and those areas in which there is no such conflict (and cooperation is possible). Our meeting with the Russians will likely result in specific objective agreements; but at the Chinese summit the communiqué which results will not be the key to the understanding reached there. Most important will be a philosophical, intangible understanding of motives and of the basic direction of our relationship.

As we deal with the Chinese we have no illusions about the depth of their ideological hostility to us. But my experience with the Chinese to this point leads me to reflect that they have an extraordinary depth of understanding about the world situation. They demonstrate considerably greater flexibility than the Russians in dealing with us. In the interim phase with the Chinese our big task is going to be to show them that we are serious enough to be dealt with.

As the Chinese approach relations with the United States, they have two basic alternatives. First, they can deal with us in a revolutionary manner by stirring up anti-government sentiment domestically. Second, they can deal directly with the government of the United States. They have chosen the second route, and we think that is a desirable route, and in the interest of world peace. Of course, if that choice proves not to be fruitful, they could revert to the revolutionary anti-government alternative. This gives you the general direction that we are headed vis-à-vis the Communist world.

Let me say this Administration hopes that when the passions have cooled, and history looks back on this period of foreign affairs, it will not be remembered as the Administration which settled the Vietnam war (though we certainly do intend to have the Vietnam war settled), but rather as the Administration that set a new direction in foreign policy—a direction desirable without regard to party affiliation—a new direction which would contribute not only to the likelihood of international peace, but also to the unity of the American nation. You know, one of the most serious things that we have faced in this Administration has been the loss of moral support from the American Establishment. By the loss of moral support I do not mean the lack of agreement on individual issues, but rather the absence of a feeling in foreign affairs that the nation is a unified and functioning entity.

These, then, are the foreign policy goals that this Administration seeks internationally, and domestically (regarding the reintegration of American society).

[Omitted here are concluding remarks and questions and answers.]

---

102.   **Memorandum for the President's File by the President's Assistant for National Security Affairs (Kissinger)**[1]

Bermuda, December 20, 1971, 1:30–5 p.m.

SUBJECT

The President's Private Meeting with British Prime Minister Edward Heath

PARTICIPANTS

The President
Prime Minister Heath
Henry A. Kissinger
Sir Burke Trend, Secretary to the Cabinet

[Omitted here is discussion of bilateral and European political issues.]

The President then made an eloquent statement of his personal world view: "The Establishment has a guilt complex. They can't stand the fact that I, their political opponent, am rectifying their mistakes. In addition, the Establishment has this growing obsession with domestic problems. The intellectual establishment is confused and frustrated by their own role, and by the United States' role. They have never believed that there was any real danger from the Left. They are turning inward. They have made it a problem whether we are going to continue our involvement in the world. The point of this too-long discourse is this: I know the issue; I'll see it through; we will have a world role. You'll wake up day after day wondering what's happening to us. Our initiatives are necessary to give our people hope. A political leader must constantly feed hope—but he must constantly know what he is doing, without illusion. One reason these present visits are so helpful is because the Right has become worried about our actions' impact on our

---

[1] Source: National Archives, Nixon Presidential Materials, White House Special Files, President's Office Files, B Series Documents, Box 58, Folder 39. Top Secret; Sensitive; Exclusively Eyes Only. The meeting was held in the Sitting Room of Government House.

friends. Our answer is that we will not sacrifice our friends to détente. We must do it to keep our negotiating partners."

After some remarks on China policy by Dr. Kissinger, the President emphasized to Prime Minister Heath that "We feel that you should take an active role in world affairs. We must have better communications. We should reach some sort of agreement on general objectives. As for China, when you have two enemies, we want to tilt towards the weaker, not towards the stronger—though not in a way that we can be caught at it." The President went on to discuss why we had to keep the bureaucracy in the dark as we went about setting up the first Kissinger trip. "We'd like to keep you informed on a personal basis," he stressed to the Prime Minister. Dr. Kissinger explained why it was not possible to inform allied governments any sooner before the July 15 announcement. The ROC had a better claim to advance notice than the Japanese had, but they would have leaked it. The Japanese themselves have the leakiest government in the world, so we couldn't afford to give them advance word.

The President said, "The Japanese are all over Asia like a bunch of lice. Let's look at Japan and Germany: Both have a sense of frustration and a memory of defeat. What must be done is to make sure we have a home for them. Maybe NATO is no longer relevant. Japan is today denied a nuclear capability; in terms of security, if our nuclear umbrella should become less credible, the effect on Japan would be a catastrophe. The biggest reason for our holding on in Vietnam is Japan. (An example of that is the impact the end of the bombing had on the Japanese.) We have to reassure the Asians that the Nixon Doctrine is not a way for us to get out of Asia but a way for us to stay in. They must see that the China trip is not taken at their expense. The August 15 thing was agony to me; I'm very glad that Connally and Barber worked things out, because it was vital also for Japan. Sato, you know, wanted to come to Hawaii."

[less than 1 line of source text not declassified] the Prime Minister noted. "We ought to tie them in." The President agreed: "We mustn't leave Japan completely isolated. We give aid stupidly; the Japanese give aid too selfishly. We shouldn't resent that if the Japanese play a constructive role ultimately; it won't necessarily be the same kind of role as ours."

[Omitted here is brief discussion of South Asia.]

The Prime Minister then posed a philosophical question. "We are moving more and more into a state of world affairs in which effective action is no longer possible. How much can you do?" The President replied, "The Soviets have tested us to see if they could control events. Of course you have to consider the much bigger stakes in the Middle

East and Europe. Part of the reason for conducting our Vietnam withdrawal so slowly is to give some message that we are not prepared to pay *any* price for ending a war; we must now ask ourselves what we are willing to pay to avert war. If we are not, we have tough days ahead." [Omitted here are very brief comments on South Asia.]

103.   Editorial Note

On January 6, 1972, President Nixon received Japanese Prime Minister Eisaku Sato and Ambassador Nobuhiko Ushiba in San Clemente, California. According to a memorandum of conversation prepared by John H. Holdridge, Nixon presented a multi-faceted analysis of the relationship among Japan, Europe, and the United States, and its global economic impact:

"The President noted that the United States relationship with Europe differed from its relationships in the Pacific. He said that he made the point with each of the leaders he met (Pompidou, Heath, and Brandt) that while we have a responsibility to maintain the closest consultations between the United States and the major European powers we must also work closely with Japan. The reason he believes this important is that in viewing the Free World, the great economic powers, the United States, Japan, Germany, Britain, France, and possibly Canada must consult closely if we are to build a stable and productive Free World economy with trade and monetary stability. In a geopolitical sense also we cannot view it in global terms. England, France, and Germany no longer maintain a significant military presence in Asia, where Japan is the major Free World nation. Therefore, he believed that the development of a 5-power consultative process (adding Italy, perhaps, and Canada) would not only serve the economic needs of the entire Free World, but would also contribute to the development of cohesion in policy for handling all the difficult political and security problems that arise."

Nixon then elaborated on the demands of global security:

"The United States, the President added, is in a unique position, having separate security treaties with Japan and the Western European nations, but since its policy must be global the United States cannot separate the two."

Following a mention of European isolationism, Nixon concluded by speaking of his larger world view:

"The President stressed his belief that we all must inevitably compete, which is good, but we must do so on fair terms. Therefore, he believed it important to get the Europeans to think as we do in the United States, that is, view the world as a whole, and to recognize that Japan must be an important part of the Free World community." (Memoranda from Holdridge of the NSC Staff to Kissinger, January 21, 1972; National Archives, Nixon Presidential Materials, NSC Files, Box 925, VIP Visits, Japan, January 1972, Sato (San Clemente))

---

104.   **Third Annual Report on U.S. Foreign Policy**[1]

Washington, February 9, 1972.

[Omitted here is a table of contents.]

PART I: 1971—THE WATERSHED YEAR—AN OVERVIEW

This is the third Report of this kind which I have made to the Congress. It comes after a year of dramatic developments. The earlier Reports set forth fully this Administration's analysis of the world situation. They expressed the conviction that new conditions required fundamental changes in America's world role. They expounded our conception of what that role should be.

In short, they foreshadowed a transformation of American foreign relations with both our friends and our adversaries.

For three years, our policies have been designed to move steadily, and with increasing momentum, toward that transformation.

1971 was the watershed year. The foundation laid and the cumulative effect of the actions taken earlier enabled us to achieve, during the past year, changes in our foreign policy of historic scope and significance:

—An opening to the People's Republic of China;

—The beginning of a new relationship with the Soviet Union;

---

[1] Source: *Public Papers of the Presidents of the United States: Richard Nixon, 1972*, pp. 195–196, 345–346. The report, as issued by the White House, was entitled "U.S. Foreign Policy for the 1970s: The Emerging Structure of Peace; A Report to the Congress by Richard Nixon, President of the United States, February 9, 1972." The full text of the report is ibid., pp. 194–346.

—The laying of a foundation for a healthier and more sustainable relationship with our European allies and Japan;

—The creation of a new environment for the world's monetary and trade activities.

This Report is addressed to those and other developments. It is, however, a companion piece to the two earlier Reports, for without an understanding of the philosophical conception upon which specific actions were based, the actions themselves can neither be adequately understood nor fairly judged. This account of a year of intense action, therefore, properly begins with a brief review of the intellectual foundation on which those actions rest.

A Changed World

In the first two Reports, I stressed the fact that the postwar period of international relations had ended, and that it was the task of this Administration to shape a new foreign policy to meet the requirements of a new era. I set forth at some length the changes in the world which made a new policy not only desirable, but necessary.

1. The recovery of economic strength and political vitality by Western Europe and Japan, with the inexorable result that both their role and ours in the world must be adjusted to reflect their regained vigor and self-assurance.

2. The increasing self-reliance of the states created by the dissolution of the colonial empires, and the growth of both their ability and determination to see to their own security and well-being.

3. The breakdown in the unity of the Communist Bloc, with all that implies for the shift of energies and resources to purposes other than a single-minded challenge to the United States and its friends, and for a higher priority in at least some Communist countries to the pursuit of national interests rather than their subordination to the requirements of world revolution.

4. The end of an indisputable U.S. superiority in strategic strength, and its replacement by a strategic balance in which the U.S. and Soviet nuclear forces are comparable.

5. The growth among the American people of the conviction that the time had come for other nations to share a greater portion of the burden of world leadership; and its corollary that the assured continuity of our long term involvement required a responsible, but more restrained American role.

The Philosophy of a New American Foreign Policy

The earlier Reports also set forth the philosophical convictions upon which this Administration was proceeding to reshape American policies to the requirements of the new realities. The core principles of this philosophy are:

—A leading American role in world affairs continues to be indispensable to the kind of world our own well-being requires.

—The end of the bipolar postwar world opens to this generation a unique opportunity to create a new and lasting structure of peace.

—The end of bipolarity requires that the structure must be built with the resources and concepts of many nations—for only when nations participate in creating an international system do they contribute to its vitality and accept its validity.

—Our friendships are constant, but the means by which they are mutually expressed must be adjusted as world conditions change. The continuity and vigor of our alliances require that our friends assume greater responsibilities for our common endeavors.

—Our enmities are not immutable, and we must be prepared realistically to recognize and deal with their cause.

—This requires mutual self-restraint and a willingness to accommodate conflicting national interests through negotiation rather than confrontation.

—Agreements are not, however, an end in themselves. They have permanent significance only when they contribute to a stable structure of peace which all countries wish to preserve because all countries share its benefits.

—The unprecedented advances in science and technology have created a new dimension of international life. The global community faces a series of urgent problems and opportunities which transcend all geographic and ideological borders. It is the distinguishing characteristic of these issues that their solution requires international cooperation on the broadest scale.

—We must, therefore, be willing to work with all countries—adversaries as well as friends—toward a structure of peace to which all nations contribute and in which all nations have a stake.

[Omitted here are the remainder of Part I, discussing accomplishments, disappointments, and goals, and Parts II–VII.]

PART VIII: CONCLUSION

I have stated many times that we seek a generation of peace. That is the goal of this Administration, and it is against that standard that the initiatives of 1971 should be judged.

In the last analysis, only the future will tell whether or not the developments of the past year have truly brought us closer to that goal. All we can say with certainty now is that a generation of peace is a more credible goal at the end of 1971 than it appeared to be at its beginning. It may still appear to be distant. It does not, however, still appear fanciful and utopian.

That fact in itself is important. Both this country and the world need a brighter vision than managing crises and aiming only at staving off the ultimate conflagration. The influence which history and our own efforts have given this Nation can—and must—be used for something more than an organization of world affairs which aims merely at keeping international animosities in some sort of tenuous, fragile and constantly endangered balance. The containment of enmity is better than its release. But it is not enough as a permanent goal.

For too long, American policy consisted of reacting to events. We had a sense of mission, but rarely a clear definition of our purpose. We were drawn into situations, responding tactically, without a clear perception of where we would end up. When we were not forced by events, we seldom struck out along new paths because we had no positive conception of where we wanted to go.

Our times demand more. A durable peace is a set of conditions and requires a conscious effort to create those conditions. Peace will not come about by itself, with us passively looking on or striking moralistic poses. Nor will it come about automatically with the ending of a war. How many wars in this century have ended without bringing a lasting peace because statesmen failed to shape a durable peace out of the conditions which emerged from the conflict? This is why it makes a difference *how* we liquidate the vestiges of an earlier era as we move into the new. The future of peace—in Asia, in the Middle East, in Europe— depends in large measure upon the steadfastness and purposefulness of American policy all around the world.

Today the United States is once again acting with assurance and purpose on the world stage.

Vietnam no longer distracts our attention from the fundamental issues of global diplomacy or diverts our energies from priorities at home.

Our dramatic departures of the past year—the fruits of our planning and policies over three years—reflect the historical conditions we see today and the historic possibilities we see for tomorrow. They were momentous steps, accelerating the very process of change which they addressed. The world—and we ourselves—are still in the process of adjusting to the developments we have set in train. But we know where we are going. We are moving with history, and moving history ourselves.

There will always be conflict in the world, and turbulent change and international rivalries. But we can seek a new structure of global relationships in which all nations, friend and adversary, participate and have a stake. We can seek to build this into a world in which all nations, great and small, can live without fear that their security and survival are in danger, and without fear that every conflict contains for them the potential for Armageddon. In such a structure of peace, habits of moderation and compromise can be nurtured, and peoples and nations will find their fullest opportunities for social progress, justice, and freedom.

This is what we mean by a generation of peace.

---

105.   Editorial Note

Three days before his trip to the People's Republic of China, on February 14, 1972, President Nixon spoke about his trip with Henry Kissinger in the Oval Office following a meeting with André Malraux, former Minister of Culture of France. (A memorandum of the conversation with Malraux is in the National Archives, Nixon Presidential Materials, White House Special Files, President's Office Files, Memoranda for the President.) During the President's conversation with Kissinger, which was recorded on tape, Kissinger briefly compared the Chinese and Russians from a national perspective:

"Kissinger: Now, you have a tendency, if I may say so, Mr. President, to lump them [the Chinese] and the Russians; they're a different phenomenon.

"Nixon: Oh, I know.

"Kissinger: They're just as dangerous, in fact they're more dangerous over an historical period. But the Russians don't think they're lovable, and the Russians don't think they have inward security. The Russians are physical and they want to dominate physically. And what they can't dominate, they don't really know how to handle. The Chinese are much surer of themselves because they've been a great power all their history. And, being Confucians, they really believe that virtue is power."

Kissinger then discussed how he saw the role of the United States with respect to the Soviet Union and China: "For the next 15 years we have to lean toward the Chinese against the Russians. We have to play this balance of power game totally unemotionally. Right now, we need the Chinese to correct the Russians, and to discipline the Russians."

Shortly thereafter, Kissinger continued in this vein:

"Kissinger: Our concern with China right now, in my view Mr. President, is to use it as a counterweight to Russia, not for its local policy.

"Nixon: I agree.

"Kissinger: As a conduit, to keep it in play on the subcontinent for the time being, but above all as a counterweight to Russia. The fact that it doesn't have a global policy is an asset to us, the fact that it doesn't have global strength yet—and to prevent Russia from gobbling it up. If Russia dominates China, that would be a fact of such tremendous significance." (Conversation Between President Nixon and Henry Kissinger, February 14, 1972, 4:09–6:19 p.m.; ibid., White House Tapes, Oval Office, OVAL 671–1)

This transcript was prepared in the Office of the Historian for use in this *Foreign Relations* volume. A more complete transcript of this conversation is scheduled for publication in *Foreign Relations, 1969–1976, China, 1969–1972*.

---

106.   Editorial Note

President Nixon met with Chairman Mao Tse-tung on February 21, 1972, at the beginning of his visit to China. The meeting took place at the Chairman's residence. In a one-hour discussion that touched broadly on U.S.-China bilateral relations, Nixon spoke of the future: "Because only if we see the whole picture of the world and the great forces that move the world will we be able to make the right decisions about the immediate and urgent problems that always completely dominate our vision." (Memorandum of conversation, February 21, 1972; National Archives, Nixon Presidential Materials, White House Special Files, President's Office Files, Memos for the President, Classified Material, Box 3)

Later in the discussion, the President shared his view of the relative position of the United States and China with respect to each other within the international community:

"Mr. Chairman, I am aware of the fact that over a period of years my position with regard to the People's Republic was one that the Chairman and Prime Minister totally disagreed with. What brings us together is a recognition of a new situation in the world and a recognition on our part that what is important is not a nation's internal political philosophy. What is important is its policy toward the rest of the world and toward us. That is why—this point I think can be said to be honest—we have differences. The Prime Minister and Dr. Kissinger discussed these differences.

"It also should be said—looking at the two great powers, the United States and China—we know China doesn't threaten the territory of the United States; I think you know the United States has no territorial designs on China. We know China doesn't want to dominate the United States. We believe you too realize the United States doesn't want to dominate the world. Also—maybe you don't believe this, but I do—neither China nor the United States, both great nations, want to dominate the world. Because our attitudes are the same on these two issues, we don't threaten each other's territories.

"Therefore, we can find common ground, despite our differences, to build a world structure in which both can be safe to develop in our own ways on our own roads. That cannot be said about some other nations in the world."

In his concluding comment, Nixon attempted to establish a positive atmosphere for the talks:

"Mr. Chairman, we know you and the Prime Minister have taken great risks in inviting us here. For us also it was a difficult decision. But having read some of the Chairman's statements, I know he is one who sees when an opportunity comes, that you must seize the hour and seize the day.

"I would also like to say in a personal sense—and this to you Mr. Prime Minister—you do not know me. Since you do not know me, you shouldn't trust me. You will find I never say something I cannot do. And I always will do more than I can say. On this basis I want to have frank talks with the Chairman and, of course, with the Prime Minister."

The following afternoon, in an extended meeting with Prime Minister Chou En-lai, Nixon discussed at length his view of U.S.-China relations within the context of the world stage:

"Now, I come to a point where I find I am in disagreement with the Prime Minister's analysis of what America's role in the world should be. Let me say that in terms of pure ideology, if I were in the Prime Minister's position, as one who deeply believed in the socialist revolution, I would take the same position he took with regard to the United States in his talks with Dr. Kissinger. And publicly I think that the Prime Minister and Chairman Mao have to take that position, that is, the U.S. is a great capitalist imperialist power reaching out its hands and it should go home from Asia, home from Europe, and let the democratic forces and liberation forces develop in their own way.

"There are some of my advisers who tell me I could win the next election in a landslide if I advocated such a policy, because the American people did not seek this position of a world power and they would like to be relieved of maintaining forces in Europe and the burden of maintaining guarantees to various other nations in the world. And some would say why not cut the American defense budget from $80 billion to $40 billion and then we could use the money for domestic purposes to help the poor, rebuild the cities, and all that sort of thing.

"I have resisted that—it is what we call the new isolationism for the U.S.—and have barely been able to get a majority on some key votes. I am in an ironic position because I am not a militarist. I don't want the U.S. to be engaged in conquest around the world, but because as I analyze the situation around the world I see we would be in great danger if we didn't maintain certain levels of defense, I have had to come down hard for those levels of defense.

"Now let me come to the point. I believe the interests of China as well as the interests of the U.S. urgently require that the U.S. maintains its military establishment at approximately its present levels and that the U.S., with certain exceptions which we can discuss later, should maintain a military presence in Europe, in Japan, and of course our naval forces in the Pacific. I believe the interests of China are just as great as those of the U.S. on that point.

"Let me make now what I trust will not be taken as an invidious comparison. By religion I am a Quaker, although not a very good one, and I believe in peace. All of my instincts are against a big military establishment and also against military adventures. As I indicated a moment ago, the Prime Minister is one of the world's leading spokesman for his philosophy and has to be opposed to powers such as the U.S. maintaining huge military establishments. But each of us had to put the survival of his nation first, and if the U.S. were to reduce its military strength, and if the U.S. were to withdraw from the areas I have described in the world, the dangers to the U.S. would be great—and the dangers to China would be greater.

"I do not impute any motives of the present leaders of the Soviet Union. I have to respect what they say, but I must make policy on the basis of what they do. And in terms of the nuclear power balance, the Soviet Union has been moving ahead at a very alarming rate over the past four years. I have determined that the U.S. must not fall behind, or our shield of protection for Europe, or for some of the nations of the Pacific with which we have treaties, would be worthless.

"Then, as I look at the situation with respect to China, as we mentioned yesterday, the Soviet Union has more forces on the Sino-Soviet borders than it has arrayed against the Western Alliance. [4 lines of *source text not declassified*] I suggest that if the Prime Minister could designate, in addition to people on the civilian side, someone such as the Vice Chairman for Military Affairs, (note: Yeh Chien-ying, Vice Chairman of the Military Affairs Mission of the CCP) I believe it would be extremely interesting for him. The meeting place should be highly secret, however, if this could be arranged.

"Dr. Kissinger: We have.

"President Nixon: O.K.

"Now as I see China, and as I look at China's neighbors, this is what would concern me. I believe Chairman Mao and the Prime Minister when they say that China does not seek to reach out its hands, and that while it will support forces of liberation, it does not seek territory around the world. However, turning to what others may do, and looking to the south, as far as India is concerned, China could probably handle India in a month in the event they went to war. India is no threat to China, but India supported by the Soviet Union is a very present threat to China because China's ability to move, to deal with respect to India and to take military action would be seriously in question if the Soviet Union, its northern neighbor, was supporting India.

"That was why in the recent crisis that was one of the reasons we felt it was very important to call the hand of India in moving against West Pakistan—and we had conclusive evidence that the Prime Minister of India was embarked on such a course—why we had to call their hand and prevent that from happening. In other words, when we took a hard line against India and for Pakistan, we were speaking not just to India or Pakistan but also—and we made them well aware of it— to the Soviet Union.

"That brings us back again, to my major premise: if the U.S. were in a position of weakness vis-à-vis the Soviet Union, whatever policy the U.S. followed would have much less credence with the Soviet Union. For the U.S. to be able to inhibit the Soviets in areas like the subcontinent, the U.S. must at least be in a position of equality with the Soviet Union.

"We took a lot of heat on this policy because, again, we had a unholy alliance against us (Chou laughs)—the pro-Soviet group, and the pro-India group which has an enormous propaganda organization in the U.S., and also what you could call the anti-Pakistan group because they didn't like the form of government in Pakistan. They charged we were sacrificing India, the second biggest country in the world, because of our desire to go forward with the China initiative. That's to a certain extent true, because I believe Mr. Prime Minister, it is very important that our policies—and this is one area I think we can agree—that our policies in the subcontinent go together. I do not mean in collusion, but I mean we don't want to make movement with respect to India and Pakistan unless you are fully informed, because we believe your interest here is greater than ours. We face a problem here because the question of resuming aid to India, economic aid, will soon arise when I return. A case can be made against this on the grounds that they will be able to release funds from buying arms from the Soviet Union which can then be manufactured in India.

"But a very critical question which we have to ask ourselves, the Prime Minister and I, is would it be better for the U.S. to have some relation with India, some influence in India or should we leave the field for the Soviet Union?

"Let me use one other example to bear out my argument that a U.S. presence in Asia is in the interest of not just the U.S. but in the interest of China. I think that the Prime Minister in terms of his philosophy has taken exactly the correct position with respect to Japan, for example the U.S. should withdraw its troops, the Treaty between Japan and the U.S. should be abrogated, and Japan should be left to become a neutral country that is unarmed. I think that the Prime Minister has to continue to say that. But I want him to understand why I think strongly that our policy with respect to Japan is in the security interest of his country even though it is opposed to the philosophic doctrine which he espouses.

"The U.S. can get out of Japanese waters, but others will fish there. And both China and the U.S. have had very difficult experiences with Japanese militarism. We hope that the situation is changed permanently away from the militarism that has characterized Japanese government in the past. On the other hand, we cannot guarantee it and consequently we feel that if the U.S. were to leave Japan naked, one of two things would happen, both of them bad for China. The Japanese, with their enormously productive economy, their great natural drive and their memories of the war they lost, could well turn toward building their own defenses in the event that the U.S. guarantee were removed. That's why I say that where Taiwan is concerned, and I would add where Korea is concerned, the U.S. policy is opposed to Japan moving in as the U.S. moves out, but we cannot guarantee that. And if we had no defense arrangement with Japan, we would have no influence where that is concerned.

"On the other hand, Japan has the option of moving toward China and it also has the option of moving toward the Soviet Union.

"So the point I would summarize on is this. I can say, and I think the Prime Minister will believe me, that the U.S. has no designs on China, that the U.S. will use its influence with Japan and those other countries where we have a defense relationship or provide economic assistance, to discourage policies which would be detrimental to China. But if the U.S. is gone from Asia, gone from Japan, our protests, no matter how loud, would be like—to use the Prime Minister's phrase—firing an empty cannon; we would have no rallying effect because fifteen thousand miles away is just too far to be heard.

"Now I realize that I have painted here a picture which makes me sound like an old cold warrior (Prime Minister Chou laughs). But it is the world as I see it, and when we analyze it, it is what brings us, China and America, together; not in terms of philosophy, not in terms of friendship—although I believe that is important—but because of national security I believe our interests are in common in the respects I have mentioned.

"I will just close by saying that after this analysis I would not want to leave the impression that the U.S. is not going to try to go to the source of the trouble, the Soviet Union, and try to make any agreements that will reduce the common danger. Our policy will be completely open and frank with China. Since Dr. Kissinger's visit, we have informed his (Prime Minister Chou's) government completely with respect to the contacts we have had with the Soviets. When we have had my meeting in Moscow, if the Prime Minister agrees, I would like to have Dr. Kissinger come and report personally to the Prime Minister on what we have discussed and what agreements we reached in Moscow. We are going to try, for example, to get an arms limitation agreement and also make progress on the Middle East if that subject is still before us.

"But the most important fact to bear in mind is that as far as China and the U.S. are concerned, if the U.S. were to follow a course of weakening its defense, of withdrawing totally or almost exclusively into the U.S., the world would be much more dangerous in my view. The U.S. has no aggressive intent against any other country; we have made our mistakes in the past. And I do not charge that the Soviet Union has any aggressive interests against any other country in the world, but in terms of the safety of these nations which are not superpowers in the world, they will be much safer if there are two superpowers, rather than just one." (Memorandum of conversation, February 22, 1972; ibid., Box 87, February 20, 1972)

The President returned to a discussion of his broader world view in a meeting with Chou En-lai the following afternoon: "I believe it is very useful to think in philosophical terms. Too often we look at problems of the world from the point of view of tactics." He continued: "It is essential to look at the world not just in terms of immediate diplomatic battles and decisions but the great forces that move the world. Maybe we have some disagreements, but we know there will be changes, and we know that there can be a better, and I trust safer, world for our two peoples regardless of differences if we can find common ground. As the Prime Minister and I both have emphasized in our public toasts and in our private meetings, the world can be a better and more peaceful place." (Memorandum of conversation, February 23, 1972; ibid.)

The full records of these conversations are scheduled for publication in *Foreign Relations, 1969–1976, China, 1969–1972.*

---

107. Editorial Note

During the course of a long meeting between President Nixon and Premier Chou En-lai on February 23, 1972, the President raised the issue of a triangular relationship among the United States, China, and the Soviet Union for the purpose of assuring the Prime Minister that the United States did not intend to promote discord between China and the Soviet Union:

"I am sure the Prime Minister, who follows our press very closely has noted that some rather cynical observers have implied that it would be in our interests to have the two great socialist superpowers—the USSR is one, and China could be one—be in conflict because this would make things safer for us. Some have written this. The Prime Minister probably didn't notice this, but I was asked in one of my press conferences a year ago about this, and I categorically said that it was not in the interest of the United States to have war between the Soviet Union and China. War between major powers can never be contained, and the whole world would become involved.

"Prime Minister Chou: Because everything is linked.

"President Nixon: Now to the assurance that I give the Prime Minister.

"Prime Minister Chou: Yes, I also read your press conference.

"President Nixon: To the assurances I already gave the Prime Minister I add this. In December, when the situation was getting very sensitive in the subcontinent—I'm using understatement—I was prepared to warn the Soviet Union against undertaking an attack on China. A warning, of course, means nothing unless the individual being warned realizes you may have the will to carry it out. Insofar as Japan is concerned and India, there is no question about where our influence will be used. With regard to the Soviet Union, I can also give assurances that the U.S. would oppose any attempt by the Soviet Union to engage in an aggressive action against China. This we would do because we believe it is in our interest, and in the interest of preserving peace as well, world peace." (Memorandum of conversation, February 23, 1972; National Archives, Nixon Presidential Materials, White House Special Files, President's Office Files, Memos for the President, Classified Material, Box 3)

The President raised the subject again in a meeting with Chou En-lai on February 25, speaking of the Soviet Union:

"I think they apparently welcomed an antagonistic relationship between the United States and the People's Republic of China. That is why they reacted when we showed we had changed our attitude. They did not want us to have more normal relations.

"I would not try to judge motives, but based on their conduct they apparently want the People's Republic and the United States to be at odds. However, our policy is not, as I said to the Prime Minister, to have the People's Republic and the Soviet Union at odds. As I told the Prime Minister, I reject the proposition that it is in the interest of the United States to have the Soviet Union and China in a state of belligerency.

"In a sentence, we want good relations with the People's Republic and we want good relations with the Soviet Union. And we would welcome better relations between the Soviet Union and the People's Republic of China. That, however, is something the Soviet Union and the People's Republic will have to work out.

"As I said when I was in Romania and Yugoslavia, my principle is any nation can be a friend of the United States without being someone else's enemy. That is my view.

"I realize that is sometimes very difficult to achieve, because there is a tendency for some nations to gang up against other nations. But in the very delicate power balances in the world we in the United States would not gain in the long run by trying to stir up trouble between other nations. We, the United States, would not gain by trying to stimulate conflict between the Soviet Union and the People's Republic. The People's Republic would not gain, the Soviet Union would not gain, and we would not gain by trying to stimulate conflict between the others.

"That is the idea, but in practicality we realize that the real world is very different than the ideal, and that is what we are concerned about, the real world." (Memorandum of conversation, February 25, 1972; ibid.)

The full text of the conversation is scheduled for publication in *Foreign Relations, 1969–1976,* China, 1969–1972.

108.   Editorial Note

On February 29, 1972, President Nixon met with the bipartisan Congressional leadership in the Cabinet Room of the White House to discuss his trip to China. During the course of his comments, which were summarized in a memorandum for the President's file prepared by Tom C. Korologos of the White House Staff, Nixon considered the possible long-term results of the unprecedented visit:

"He then turned to long-term results which he classed as most important. He said that he hopes that we will conduct our policy in Asia without threat or use of force, and he hoped the Chinese would do the same. He said neither the United States or China seek to dominate Asia, and both oppose the other nation's domination in the future. He said that we shall speak of a common interest and normalization of relations.

"He touched upon a 'naive' reporter's analysis that what finally got us together was that both the PRC and the United States had found that their philosophies were not that far apart. The President said that this was not at all true. All we are trying to do is get to know each other better, and now I know them and they know us. We wanted to help eliminate the inevitable road of suspicion over the past 25 years. He said this road is the one which may lead to war.

"The President pointed out that had this meeting occurred 25 years ago, Korea might have been avoided. He said neither side changed its beliefs. 'They are dedicated Communists and I am a dedicated American.'

"The simple thing that brought us together was a common interest, the President said. We want to maintain our integrity and independence as they do, and we both want to build a structure of peace in the Pacific and in the World. If we do not find a way, we will be on a collision course.

"The President pointed to two more or less guidelines for the future. First, they are the first to say that they are not a super power. Inevitably, however, the President pointed out 750 million Chinese Communists are something to be reckoned with. Consequently, they are destined to become a major force.

"Second, the President said the relationship between the United States and China is a very delicate one. The President then quoted Ayub Khan, who said that relationships between nations are based on trust, no matter what their beliefs are. He said that Khan said trust is a very thin thread. If it is broken, it is important to put it back together. We have started to put it back together. We are reliable, we are strong and we will continue to build for the future.

"Our part is much greater than theirs. They read everything said in the Senate and House and they read the newspaper editorials and columns. They think that whenever a columnist speaks that that is the United States speaking, the President said.

"While we have made a beginning in certain areas, we are far apart in other areas, such as in Africa, the Middle East, etc., the President said.

"The President said that in the future, we must expect the Chinese at the United Nations to express their views vociferously, but not to worry about it. It would not mean our relationship is ended when they blast us.

"We must assume they are still as dedicated to their philosophies as we are to ours. The President said, 'I am glad I went. I am impressed with what I saw and I am glad to be home. I have a new realization for us not to become one of them, and to realize that when you get people as dedicated as they are, that a soft and flabby or weak United States will not long survive in the world. We need certain dedication and belief in our country. So, we must continue our debates, but we must recognize that we must not lose dedication, determination or our love of country.'

"He said that if the United States would withdraw and live as an island, then others who may want to dominate the world would have a free hand to do so. Consequently, we need to keep America strong with strong commitments around the world. The most important thing to remember is that they constantly are reinvigorating their people and we must reinspire our people." (Memorandum for the President's File, February 29, 1972; National Archives, Nixon Presidential Materials, White House Special Files, President's Office Files, Memos for the President, Box 88, February 27–May 28, 1972)

The meeting took place between 10:07 and 11:45 a.m. (Ibid., White House Central Files, Staff Members and Office Files, Office of Presidential Papers and Archives, Daily Diary)

---

109.   **Editorial Note**

On March 30, 1972, North Vietnam initiated a major offensive against the South. The offensive was supplied in large measure by the Soviet Union, which continued to be the principal support for Hanoi.

With the planned U.S.-Soviet Moscow Summit less than 2 months away, the latest North Vietnamese offensive put to the test the Nixon administration's long-standing concept of linkage, where progress with the Soviet Union in some aspects of U.S.-Soviet relations must be accompanied by progress in other, more difficult areas. While at the Pentagon on April 9, Henry Kissinger called to confer with the President, who was in Key Biscayne. According to the Nixon Diary, the telephone call was placed at 10:47 a.m. and concluded at 11:10 a.m. (National Archives, Nixon Presidential Materials, White House Central Files, Staff Members and Office Files, Office of Presidential Papers and Archives, Daily Diary) "We are coming to the point," Nixon said, when "knocking off of the Soviet Summit becomes more and more a possibility." The conversation continued:

"K: I am afraid so. I do not have another view. I do not think we can survive a Soviet Summit as a country if we are humiliated in Vietnam. Unless they accept rules of conduct, we may have to confront them. It is easy for me to say. But if one looks at an election on that platform . . .

"P: The country would be done then.

"K: I think our bargaining position in Moscow, if it came out of a position of total weakness, would be hopeless.

"P: I have been arguing for sending more carriers, planes, etc. and taking the heat on it because I realize everything rides on this. If we lose this one, the other stuff won't hold up. Our great China initiative—we at least opened the door, and handle ourselves as gracefully as we can—and quietly leave the scene."

The President declared that "We have to look closely at our whole American purpose as to whether or not it is possible for one [sic] [non-Communist] country to defend itself and leave. We know it is possible for a Communist country to do that. I am not sure. We shall see." Nixon ordered Kissinger to "call Dobrynin in" and relate the current U.S. thinking. "Tell him the Summit is on the line now," the President said. "I think he has to know with this going on as it is that we are under enormous pressure. The whole Summit is being jeopardized. Our hole card is to play more with the Chinese."

After brief discussion, the President concluded: "We both agree to go ahead under those circumstances. . . . In the meantime, we will keep kicking them in the balls. I made a decision no Summit if this thing goes. We have no other choices now. We can't be put in a position of letting our whole policy be hostage to a couple of summits." (Transcript of telephone conversation between President Nixon and Kissinger; Library of Congress, Manuscript Division, Kissinger Papers, Box 371, Telephone Conversations, Chronological File)

110.   Telegram From President Nixon to the President's Assistant for National Security Affairs (Kissinger) in Moscow[1]

Washington, April 23, 1972, 1945Z.

CPD–203–72.

Memorandum for Henry Kissinger From the President

I am dictating this message personally to you rather than transmitting through Haig so that you can directly sense my views with regard to the state of play in your historic journey.

First, there is no question whatever among any of us here about the skill, resourcefulness and determination you have displayed in conducting your talks to date. I have read each one of your messages carefully and have been enormously impressed with how you have had exactly the right combination of sweet and sour in dealing with them.

Second, as Haig has already indicated, I have no objection to your staying until 1500 Moscow time or even until 1700 or 1800 Moscow time, provided that you determine that your staying on may make some contribution on Vietnam. It is important for you to arrive at Camp David before midnight on Monday[2] so that we can go back to Washington and thereby maintain our cover and have time to prepare the announcement for Tuesday noon and Tuesday evening, as well as getting your recommendations with regard to what I should say on Wednesday or Thursday. As I am sure it has occurred to you, your hosts have already gained one of their goals—that of having you stay longer in Moscow on your first visit than you stayed in Peking. Of course, this is of very little concern to us and a few more hours makes no difference on that score.

It was predictable that they would give no ground on Vietnam although it seems to me that their primary purpose of getting you to Moscow to discuss the Summit has now been served while our purpose of getting some progress on Vietnam has not been served, except, of course, in the very important, intangible ways you have pointed out—

---

[1] Source: National Archives, Nixon Presidential Materials, NSC Files, Kissinger Office Files, HAK Trip Files, HAK's Secret Moscow Trip, TOHAK/HAKTO, April 1972 (Part 1), Box 21. Top Secret; Sensitive; Eyes Only. Kissinger made a secret trip to Moscow between April 20 and 24, 1972, ostensibly to discuss the situation in Vietnam, as well as many other bilateral and international issues, in preparation for the U.S.-Soviet Summit planned for the next month. Documentation on this visit and the Summit is scheduled for publication in *Foreign Relations*, 1969–1976, Moscow Summit.

[2] April 24.

the effect on Hanoi of Moscow receiving you three days after we bombed Hanoi–Haiphong, of course, the obvious result of keeping Peking balanced vis-à-vis Moscow.

As far as what they have agreed to—sending messages to Hanoi, I suppose that in the long run this might have some beneficial effect. At least it enlists them in the diplomatic game in a way that they have refused to become enlisted before. However, we cannot be oblivious to the fact that while they have agreed to send messages, secretly, they will be continuing to send arms, publicly, and the latter fact will be the one our critics at home on both the left and the right will eventually seize upon.

Whether your hosts were in collusion with Hanoi is, of course, a question none of us can answer without knowing their innermost thoughts. But as far as the observers who will be trying to appraise the success or failure of your trip and later the Summit, if it comes off, there is one hard fact that stands out—anyone who gives a murder weapon to someone he knows is going to kill with it is equally responsible for the crime. You and I might have reason to believe that both Peking and Moscow would like to de-fuse the situation in Southeast Asia but cannot do so for reasons of which we are aware. On the other hand, in dealing with our own opinion at home, this sophisticated analysis makes no dent whatever.

[Omitted here are comments on domestic issues.]

After the first shock of the announcement of your trip wears off—by the end of the week a chorus will arise from both the doves and the hawks raising two questions: First, what did Kissinger discuss with the Russians? (and here there will be insistence that you inform the Foreign Relations Committee and all others on this score) and (2) what did the Kissinger trip accomplish in terms of getting progress on Vietnam?

You and I know that it has to have accomplished a considerable amount indirectly by the message it sends to Hanoi and also that it may open the door for future progress on Vietnam where the Soviet Union may play a more helpful role. On the other hand, we must batten down the hatches for what will be a rising chorus of criticism from our political opponents on the left and from our hawk friends on the right for going to Moscow and failing to get progress on the major issue.

I have deliberately painted this picture at its worst because, of course, we must prepare for the worst and hope for the best. Haig makes the point, and I share it to an extent, that Hanoi will be under enormous heat to be more forthcoming in their private meeting with you on May 2nd. On the other hand, they may hold firm. It is then that we will have to make the really tough decision. It is my view that if they give no more than they have given on the twelve previous meetings they have had with you—and I believe those meetings were constructive of course but not on the decisive issue—then we will have to go all-out on the bombing front.

That is why it is vitally important that your hosts know that all options—repeat—all options as far as actions against the North are open in the event that the meeting of May 2 turns out to be as non-productive on the really critical issues as have the previous meetings you have had with the North Vietnamese.

Going back to our major goals, I could not agree with you more that the Summit in terms of long-term interests of the US is vitally important. However, no matter how good a deal we get out of the Summit on SALT and on the other issues, we must realize that now the Soviet Summit, far more than the Chinese Summit, due to the fact that your trip directly dealt with Vietnam, will be judged as a success or failure depending upon whether we get some progress on Vietnam. My feeling about the necessity for resuming attacks on the Hanoi–Haiphong complex in the event that the May 2 meeting is a dud is as you can recognize quite different from the decision I made with regard to activities we would undertake prior to, during and after the China visit. For four weeks before we went to China, for the two weeks that we were there or on the way and for three weeks after we were there we made a decision, which I think was right, not to be provocative in our bombing of targets north of the DMZ even though we knew from all intelligence reports that an enemy build-up was going forward. I think that decision was right at that time.

However, I am convinced that we cannot pay that kind of price for the Soviet Summit—much as I recognize substantively that the Soviet Summit is of course going to be infinitely more productive than the Chinese Summit.

[Omitted here are brief comments, mainly concerning SALT.]

We have painted ourselves into this corner—quite deliberately—and I only hope that developments will justify the course we have followed.

In sum, we risked the Summit by hitting Hanoi and Haiphong. After we have gone through your meeting of May 2, we may be faced with the hard decision to risk it again and probably damage it irreparably because we may have no other choice if that meeting turns out to be a failure.

I cannot emphasize too strongly that except for a few sophisticated foreign policy observers, interest in what we are able to get on a SALT agreement, trade, a better communiqué than the French got, etc., will not save the Summit unless one way or another we are able to point to some progress on Vietnam. Of course, I am aware of the fact that if your hosts still want to go forward with the Summit, despite the actions we may have had to take after May 2, we will do so because we know that the substantive agreements that we will reach at the Summit are in and of themselves substantively very important even without progress on Vietnam. What I am trying to emphasize is that we must face the hard fact that we have now convinced the country that Soviet arms and Soviet tanks have fueled this massive invasion of South Vietnam by the North. Having done so, it is only logical that our critics on both right and left will hammer us hard if we sit down and meet with the Soviets, drink toasts, sign communiqués, etc., without getting progress on Vietnam.

However it all comes out, just remember we all know we couldn't have a better man in Moscow at this time than Kissinger. Rebozo joins us in sending our regards.

---

111.   Memorandum of Conversation[1]

New York, May 5, 1972.

PARTICIPANTS

List Attached[2]

Following the introduction of members of the head table, Dr. Kissinger was introduced and received a standing ovation.[3]

[Omitted here are introductory comments.]

We took over essentially a post-war foreign policy. Complete attitudes had to be changed. We took office when the American pre-eminence to wage war had begun to wane. Much of our policy was based on previous successes. The principal problem was to adjust to the new realities.

When America adopted the post-war policies, the United States was the only country capable of having a global foreign policy. We had a history of uninterrupted success. We could invite challenge anywhere in the world.

---

[1] Source: National Archives, Nixon Presidential Materials, NSC Files, Box 1026, Presidential/HAK Memcons. Administratively Confidential. There is no drafting information on the memorandum.

[2] Not printed.

[3] Kissinger was addressing a dinner of the Asian Society in the Plaza Hotel.

Our task was how to define a role for the United States where we could have a constructive and permanent relationship with other nations. The Nixon Doctrine gives other countries a bigger role. Some call it a retreat. It has led to our now evolving relationships with the People's Republic of China and the Soviet Union. It is sometimes called the balance of power approach.

The first concern of any leader must be the basic security of the country. It cannot base decisions on circumstances elsewhere. Each country wants independent relations with the other nations. We have been lucky in the past because of geographic considerations. Vast oceans lay between ourselves and possible enemies. Technology has changed all this, requiring us now to develop careful relationships with other countries. It is important that we establish relationships with other countries even where painful to our traditional friends, who are seeing us establish relationships with previously rejected countries. We no longer have a black and white foreign policy. All nations have a stake. We could not overlook the 800 million people in the People's Republic of China.

Our relations with China started in a curious way. The President asked us to explore contacts. It is amazing how difficult it is to establish ties to a nation after 22 years of an isolationist policy. It is difficult to find an intermediary and even to do simple things like drafting messages acceptable to both sides. It is an interesting analysis for a good student in foreign relations. Once contact was established, problems arose because so many nations were looking at our China policy. They were looking at specific details and were concerned we might be shifting our weight.

The essence of our China policy is that we do not impinge on Chinese interests very much. Our effort was basically in three levels. First was what specific arrangement could be made in Shanghai. Second was to make inroads bilaterally which, if acceptable, would prove significant. And third was the impact of Americans on Chinese society, and vice versa.

In our discussions with the Chinese our vast cultural differences became apparent. Where Americans are pragmatic, the Chinese concentrate on principle. They want to distill things into absolute terms. We talk about peace. The Chinese talk about justice and they are dedicated to the proposition that without justice, peace is meaningless. We talk about compromise. They talk about truth. It is interesting to observe what happens. The Chinese have many of the rules my former students thought they would like to have, but with the Chinese we are making no great deals. There is no counter-Soviet strategy or shifting of weight from Tokyo to Peking.

With Japan we have concrete problems. In China we are making a policy framework, results of which will not be known for four to five years. Our Japanese experience has been considerably different than the Chinese. After the war, the Japanese concentrated on economic matters and left foreign policy and security in American hands. This relationship could not continue. Japan must play a more significant role without nationalism and without all their weight with one major power.

Our objective in the Soviet summit is to try to create vested interests for both parties in many areas so that when crises occur, there will be a group within the Soviet Union with a vested interest wanting a steady course resulting in negotiation.

Now, about Southeast Asia. Our major concern is that a new international order must be built. This is complicated by a disaster which has lasted ten years. The debate is so strong that I cannot bridge the valley. The problem we face is how to act in a situation where success for the opponent would mean the capture of an additional 60,000 Americans. The only alternative given us is to impose a Communist government on the South. This we refuse to do. We will not join our enemies to defeat our friends. This is the only obstacle. This is a very painful problem and painful decisions have to be made.

I am not here to talk about Vietnam but Asian policy, but the discussion must include Vietnam. After the elections, we will find we have had great successes but also some regrets. We want to help other nations become participants in world order. [applause][4]

[Omitted here is a non-substantive explanatory comment by the notetaker.]

---

[4] Brackets in the source text.

112.   Address by President Nixon to the Nation[1]

Washington, May 8, 1972.

Good evening:

Five weeks ago, on Easter weekend, the Communist armies of North Vietnam launched a massive invasion of South Vietnam, an invasion that was made possible by tanks, artillery, and other advanced offensive weapons supplied to Hanoi by the Soviet Union and other Communist nations.

The South Vietnamese have fought bravely to repel this brutal assault. Casualties on both sides have been very high. Most tragically, there have been over 20,000 civilian casualties, including women and children, in the cities which the North Vietnamese have shelled in wanton disregard of human life.

As I announced in my report to the Nation 12 days ago, the role of the United States in resisting this invasion has been limited to air and naval strikes on military targets in North and South Vietnam. As I also pointed out in that report, we have responded to North Vietnam's massive military offensive by undertaking wide-ranging new peace efforts aimed at ending the war through negotiation.

On April 20, I sent Dr. Kissinger to Moscow for 4 days of meetings with General Secretary Brezhnev and other Soviet leaders. I instructed him to emphasize our desire for a rapid solution to the war and our willingness to look at all possible approaches. At that time, the Soviet leaders showed an interest in bringing the war to an end on a basis just to both sides. They urged resumption of negotiations in Paris, and they indicated they would use their constructive influence.

I authorized Dr. Kissinger to meet privately with the top North Vietnamese negotiator, Le Duc Tho, on Tuesday, May 2, in Paris. Ambassador Porter, as you know, resumed the public peace negotiations in Paris on April 27 and again on May 4. At those meetings, both public and private, all we heard from the enemy was bombastic rhetoric and a replaying of their demands for surrender. For example, at the May 2 secret meeting, I authorized Dr. Kissinger to talk about every conceivable avenue toward peace. The North Vietnamese flatly refused to consider any of these approaches. They refused to offer any new

---

[1] Source: *Public Papers of the Presidents of the United States: Richard Nixon, 1972,* pp. 583–587. The President spoke at 9 p.m. from the Oval Office at the White House. His address was broadcast live on radio and television.

approach of their own. Instead, they simply read verbatim their previous public demands.

Here is what over 3 years of public and private negotiations with Hanoi has come down to: The United States, with the full concurrence of our South Vietnamese allies, has offered the maximum of what any President of the United States could offer.

We have offered a deescalation of the fighting. We have offered a cease-fire with a deadline for withdrawal of all American forces. We have offered new elections which would be internationally supervised with the Communists participating both in the supervisory body and in the elections themselves.

President Thieu has offered to resign one month before the elections. We have offered an exchange of prisoners of war in a ratio of 10 North Vietnamese prisoners for every one American prisoner that they release. And North Vietnam has met each of these offers with insolence and insult. They have flatly and arrogantly refused to negotiate an end to the war and bring peace. Their answer to every peace offer we have made has been to escalate the war.

In the 2 weeks alone since I offered to resume negotiations, Hanoi has launched three new military offensives in South Vietnam. In those 2 weeks the risk that a Communist government may be imposed on the 17 million people of South Vietnam has increased, and the Communist offensive has now reached the point that it gravely threatens the lives of 60,000 American troops who are still in Vietnam.

There are only two issues left for us in this war. First, in the face of a massive invasion do we stand by, jeopardize the lives of 60,000 Americans, and leave the South Vietnamese to a long night of terror? This will not happen. We shall do whatever is required to safeguard American lives and American honor.

Second, in the face of complete intransigence at the conference table do we join with our enemy to install a Communist government in South Vietnam? This, too, will not happen. We will not cross the line from generosity to treachery.

We now have a clear, hard choice among three courses of action: Immediate withdrawal of all American forces, continued attempts at negotiation, or decisive military action to end the war.

I know that many Americans favor the first course of action, immediate withdrawal. They believe the way to end the war is for the United States to get out, and to remove the threat to our remaining forces by simply withdrawing them.

From a political standpoint, this would be a very easy choice for me to accept. After all, I did not send over one-half million Americans to Vietnam. I have brought 500,000 men home from Vietnam since I took office. But, abandoning our commitment in Vietnam here and now would mean turning 17 million South Vietnamese over to Communist tyranny and terror. It would mean leaving hundreds of American prisoners in Communist hands with no bargaining leverage to get them released.

An American defeat in Vietnam would encourage this kind of aggression all over the world, aggression in which smaller nations armed by their major allies, could be tempted to attack neighboring nations at will in the Mideast, in Europe, and other areas. World peace would be in grave jeopardy.

The second course of action is to keep on trying to negotiate a settlement. Now this is the course we have preferred from the beginning and we shall continue to pursue it. We want to negotiate, but we have made every reasonable offer and tried every possible path for ending this war at the conference table.

The problem is, as you all know, it takes two to negotiate and now, as throughout the past 4 years, the North Vietnamese arrogantly refuse to negotiate anything but an imposition, an ultimatum that the United States impose a Communist regime on 17 million people in South Vietnam who do not want a Communist government.

It is plain then that what appears to be a choice among three courses of action for the United States is really no choice at all. The killing in this tragic war must stop. By simply getting out, we would only worsen the bloodshed. By relying solely on negotiations, we would give an intransigent enemy the time he needs to press his aggression on the battlefield.

There is only one way to stop the killing. That is to keep the weapons of war out of the hands of the international outlaws of North Vietnam.

Throughout the war in Vietnam, the United States has exercised a degree of restraint unprecedented in the annals of war. That was our responsibility as a great Nation, a Nation which is interested—and we can be proud of this as Americans—as America has always been, in peace not conquest.

However, when the enemy abandons all restraint, throws its whole army into battle in the territory of its neighbor, refuses to negotiate, we simply face a new situation.

In these circumstances, with 60,000 Americans threatened, any President who failed to act decisively would have betrayed the trust of his country and frayed the cause of world peace.

I therefore concluded that Hanoi must be denied the weapons and supplies it needs to continue the aggression. In full coordination with the Republic of Vietnam, I have ordered the following measures which are being implemented as I am speaking to you.

All entrances to North Vietnamese ports will be mined to prevent access to these ports and North Vietnamese naval operations from these ports. United States forces have been directed to take appropriate measures within the internal and claimed territorial waters of North Vietnam to interdict the delivery of any supplies. Rail and all other communications will be cut off to the maximum extent possible. Air and naval strikes against military targets in North Vietnam will continue.

These actions are not directed against any other nation. Countries with ships presently in North Vietnamese ports have already been notified that their ships will have three daylight periods to leave in safety. After that time, the mines will become active and any ships attempting to leave or enter these ports will do so at their own risk.

These actions I have ordered will cease when the following conditions are met:

First, all American prisoners of war must be returned.

Second, there must be an internationally supervised cease-fire throughout Indochina.

Once prisoners of war are released, once the internationally supervised cease-fire has begun, we will stop all acts of force throughout Indochina and at that time we will proceed with a complete withdrawal of all American forces from Vietnam within 4 months.

Now, these terms are generous terms. They are terms which would not require surrender and humiliation on the part of anybody. They would permit the United States to withdraw with honor. They would end the killing. They would bring our POW's home. They would allow negotiations on a political settlement between the Vietnamese themselves. They would permit all the nations which have suffered in this long war—Cambodia, Laos, North Vietnam, South Vietnam—to turn at last to the urgent works of healing and of peace. They deserve immediate acceptance by North Vietnam.

It is appropriate to conclude my remarks tonight with some comments directed individually to each of the major parties involved in the continuing tragedy of the Vietnam war.

First, to the leaders of Hanoi, your people have already suffered too much in your pursuit of conquest. Do not compound their agony with continued arrogance; choose instead the path of a peace that redeems your sacrifices, guarantees true independence for your country, and ushers in an era of reconciliation.

To the people of South Vietnam, you shall continue to have our firm support in your resistance against aggression. It is your spirit that will determine the outcome of the battle. It is your will that will shape the future of your country.

To other nations, especially those which are allied with North Vietnam, the actions I have announced tonight are not directed against you. Their sole purpose is to protect the lives of 60,000 Americans, who would be gravely endangered in the event that the Communist offensive continues to roll forward, and to prevent the imposition of a Communist government by brutal aggression upon 17 million people.

I particularly direct my comments tonight to the Soviet Union. We respect the Soviet Union as a great power. We recognize the right of the Soviet Union to defend its interests when they are threatened. The Soviet Union in turn must recognize our right to defend our interests.

No Soviet soldiers are threatened in Vietnam. Sixty thousand Americans are threatened. We expect you to help your allies, and you cannot expect us to do other than to continue to help our allies, but let us, and let all great powers, help our allies only for the purpose of their defense, not for the purpose of launching invasions against their neighbors.

Otherwise the cause of peace, the cause in which we both have so great a stake, will be seriously jeopardized.

Our two nations have made significant progress in our negotiations in recent months. We are near major agreements on nuclear arms limitation, on trade, on a host of other issues.

Let us not slide back toward the dark shadows of a previous age. We do not ask you to sacrifice your principles, or your friends, but neither should you permit Hanoi's intransigence to blot out the prospects we together have so patiently prepared.

We, the United States and the Soviet Union, are on the threshold of a new relationship that can serve not only the interests of our two countries, but the cause of world peace. We are prepared to continue to build this relationship. The responsibility is yours if we fail to do so.

And finally, may I say to the American people, I ask you for the same strong support you have always given your President in difficult moments. It is you most of all that the world will be watching.

I know how much you want to end this war. I know how much you want to bring our men home. And I think you know from all that I have said and done these past 3-1/2 years how much I, too, want to end the war to bring our men home.

You want peace. I want peace. But, you also want honor and not defeat. You want a genuine peace, not a peace that is merely a prelude to another war.

At this moment, we must stand together in purpose and resolve. As so often in the past, we Americans did not choose to resort to war. It has been forced upon us by an enemy that has shown utter contempt toward every overture we have made for peace. And that is why, my fellow Americans, tonight I ask for your support of this decision, a decision which has only one purpose, not to expand the war, not to escalate the war, but to end this war and to win the kind of peace that will last.

With God's help, with your support, we will accomplish that great goal.

Thank you and good night.

---

113.   Editorial Note

On May 8, 1972, immediately following the President's address on the situation in South Vietnam (see Document 112), Nixon spoke to the Cabinet and selected senior White House staff in the Cabinet Room. According to the notes of the President's Assistant, Raymond K. Price, Jr., the President discussed the possible risk to the Moscow Summit that could result from his decision to mine Haiphong harbor:

"'We're aware of the risks. We also must realize that an American President couldn't be in Moscow when Soviet tanks were rumbling through the streets of Hue—unless he could do something about it.'

"He added that we have put the proposition to the Soviets very directly: we are prepared to go forward and negotiate on SALT, etc., and even with the Summit—so the responsibility is theirs as to whether it goes forward or is postponed." (Memorandum for the President's File, May 8, 1972; National Archives, Nixon Presidential Materials, White House Special Files, President's Office Files, Memos for the President, Box 88, February 27–May 28, 1972)

The next day, May 9, Henry Kissinger told a group of reporters at a news conference:

"For 2 years we have been engaged in negotiations on a broad range of issues with the Soviet Union. We are on the verge not just of success in this or that negotiation, but of what could be a new relationship of benefit to all of mankind, a new relationship in which, on both sides, whenever there is a danger of crisis, there will be enough people who have a commitment to constructive programs so that they could exercise restraining influences. But in order for such a policy to succeed, it cannot be accepted that one country can be oblivious to the impact on another of the actions of its friends, particularly when those friends are armed with the weapons of this country." (*Weekly Compilation of Presidential Documents*, Volume 8, May 15, 1972, page 844)

---

114. Memorandum for the President's File by the President's Special Consultant (Scali)[1]

Washington, May 19, 1972, 4 p.m.

President's Pre-Moscow Summit

Briefing of Congressional Leaders

[Omitted here are comments by Nixon relating to background matters and some specific issues for negotiation.]

Let me talk to you a moment about summitry. I've expressed some very direct views about this. Previous summits have generated a spirit of Vienna, Geneva, Camp David and Glassboro, but we wound up with flat beer as far as agreements were concerned. I wanted the summit prepared not for cosmetics which raise great hopes, which are then dashed, but to cover substance. This is why we have taken so much time to arrange this meeting—to prepare for probable agreements in certain areas.[2] I would say it is probably difficult to find any meeting of powerful heads of state where there has been more meticulous groundwork laid. We have discussed in detail the key areas—commerce, space, SALT, etc. Also Kissinger's trip to Moscow and discussions with Soviet leaders have been helpful in spotlighting further opportunities and difficulties.

---

[1] Source: National Archives, Nixon Presidential Materials, White House Special Files, President's Office Files, Memos for the President, Box 88, February 27–May 28, 1972. No classification marking. Prepared on June 7. According to the President's Daily Diary, Nixon met with the bipartisan Congressional leadership in the Cabinet Room of the White House at 4:13 p.m. on May 19. Members of the press later joined the group before the session adjourned at 5:23 p.m. (Ibid., White House Central Files, Staff Members and Office Files, Office of Presidential Papers and Archives, Daily Diary)

[2] Shortly after this meeting, Nixon covered much the same ground in remarks to members of the press at a White House reception for those accompanying the President on his trip. For text of Nixon's remarks, see *Public Papers of the Presidents of the United States: Richard Nixon, 1972*, p. 603.

I saw Ambassador Dobrynin yesterday, who brought me a personal message from Brezhnev.[3] I can tell you there is no question of the amount of good will and good intentions on our side and on their side. We both want a successful meeting. But this meeting must be one which is not detrimental to each other's vital security interests. It promises to be a very difficult trip with many long and arduous meetings.

[Omitted here is brief commentary on logistics and on Brezhnev.]

Vietnam will be on the agenda and will be discussed, but it is best not to speculate on this and put us or the Russians on the spot. Another quite difficult area that we will discuss is the Middle East where we are very, very far apart. Perhaps we can narrow the differences by the time we leave so that each will know more accurately what the other's position is.

The fact that this summit is going forward has great significance. Both sides are recognizing the fundamental principle that their own security interests must take precedence over certain matters and issues which are peripheral and collateral, Vietnam and the Middle East, for example. It is important to find areas where we can cooperate. Neither side believes that just getting to know one another better will change the actual conditions. There are some very pragmatic considerations. Confrontation is not in their interest or in ours. We must both avoid being dragged into major conflicts in outlying areas where it is not to either side's interests. I look forward to hard bargaining without propaganda. But let's not raise our hopes too high or too low.

The President then asked Secretary Rogers to speak. Rogers said he wanted to underscore two points. The preparation for this summit has been excellent and that a large number of government departments and agencies have been involved. The Soviet attitude thus far has been constructive and in preliminary talks the Soviets have made some concessions. In the final analysis, however, nothing comes into play because a lot of these agreements are interrelated.

The President interjected to say "linked" and that we have some reason to believe that they will be linked successfully because no nation has ever been better prepared for a meeting. The President then asked Kissinger to speak.

---

[3] Reference is to a meeting at Camp David on May 18. The Brezhnev message may have been delivered orally as no written message was found, nor was it mentioned in the written record of the Nixon–Dobrynin discussion. (Memorandum of conversation, May 18; National Archives, Nixon Presidential Materials, NSC Files, Box 494, President's Trip Files, Dobrynin/Kissinger, 1972, Vol. 12 [Part 2])

Kissinger opened by saying he had a few general observations. The fact that the summit is going forward underlines the point that if both sides did not believe there would be progress possible at the session then it would have been canceled. There has been an understanding, a recognition of the pressures on both of us. In advance of the meeting, the President wanted precise, concrete negotiations. On the Russian side the leadership has many pressures upon it. The leaders understand the impact that a nuclear war could have on the Soviets. In addition, they have a very complex economy which needs assistance and a resulting pressure from the Soviet people. One comes away from all of this with the belief that the Soviets have a stake in improving relations with the United States. It is not inconceivable that the Soviet leadership is interested in a period of détente for the purpose of softening up the United States and then pushing us out of Europe. But whatever their motive, we should not be afraid. Our strategy will be to create vested interests for peace within the Soviet structure which would help encourage restraint on their actions.

In China, as a result of our visit, we set up a framework for a new relationship. In Moscow, we hope to get concrete agreements which can lead to mutual restraints on our policies. We also hope to nail down plans for mutual cooperation in space and in other areas where we can work together. We have an historic opportunity, but what will happen will depend on what the President and the Secretary of State and others can negotiate.

The President interjected to say that it is very important that we not picture the meeting as an effort to set up a Soviet-United States condominium.

Kissinger said, yes, this was so, or to portray the meeting as one which is going forward at the expense of the allies of both sides.

The President added, perhaps the greatest consideration that one should recognize as this meeting is about to get underway is the fact that the Soviets have now achieved nuclear parity. We have MIRV, but they have more missiles. If either President Eisenhower or President Kennedy had gone to Moscow they both would have gone in a position where they were looking down the throat of the Soviets. But the situation has now changed.

In this circumstance, the President said, you don't have to tote up who won or who lost as a result of this meeting. You can be sure that I, Bill, and Kissinger will make sure that the United States' interests will be protected. But if the two super-powers meet and then either one begins to say that I won and you lost, perhaps we will have done more harm than good. The whole business is one of mutuality. The Russians are extremely sensitive. They want to be accepted on an equal basis.

They remember all too well the strategic military situation during the Cuban missile crisis. We both expect to bargain very hard, very tough. But when both sides realize they have a mutual interest in keeping a deal, that's when it will mean something.

[Omitted here are comments and discussion of specific issues.]

115. Editorial Note

President Nixon and senior U.S. officials visited the Soviet Union May 22–29, 1972, for Summit meetings. During the first plenary session held in St. Catherine's Hall, Grand Kremlin Palace on May 23, Nixon expounded on détente:

"The President said he would like to think that each person at the table is a sentimental man to a certain degree, but we are meeting here not because of sentiment, but because we are pragmatic men. As practical and honest men we recognize that our systems are different and that in many parts of the world our interests conflict. But as practical men, we have learned the lessons of history and will not allow ourselves to be dragged into conflict in areas peripheral to our interests. These problems may seem important at the time, but cannot compare in importance with the need to have good relations between the two most powerful countries in the world.

"So we see that the time has come when our two nations have an opportunity which perhaps has not come to nations in history up to this point. That time means that we must find ways to work together to limit arms, to expand our economic relations for our mutual benefit and also to work together in other fields such as improvement of the environment, cooperation in outer space and others. We would continue to compete, but it can be a friendly competition in which each side would gain rather than lose, and we can both work for the mutual good.

"This does not mean that settlement of differences will always be easy. Differences are settled easily only under the dictation of the strong to the weak. We had reached the stage in our relations—and the President believes this was fortunate—where we consider ourselves to be equally strong. Therefore, we feel this opportunity is one which is unique, not only because of what we do here on these agreements which are important in themselves, but even more so because of the way we view the future.

"Good relations between the Soviet Union and the United States can have an enormous effect for the good of the people of the whole world and above all for the good of the people of our two countries. It is his hope that this week the personal relationships between us will become better. We can begin the process of exploring future progress which could make these agreements seem small in terms of what can be accomplished in the future.

"The President said he wished to close his remarks by saying what his Soviet friends may be too polite to say. He said his reputation is of being very hard-line and cold-war oriented.

"Kosygin remarked that he had heard this sometime back.

"The President said that he has a strong belief in our system but at the same time he respects those who believe just as strongly in their system. There must be room in this world for two great nations with different systems to live together and work together. We cannot do this however, by mushy sentimentality or by glossing over differences which exist. We can do it only by working out real problems in a concrete fashion, determined to place our common interests above our differences." (Memorandum of conversation between President Nixon and General Secretary Brezhnev, May 23, 1972; National Archives, Nixon Presidential Materials, NSC Files, Box 487, President's Trip Files, The President's Conversations in Salzburg, Moscow, Tehran and Warsaw, May 1972, Part 1)

At the final plenary session, held at St. Catherine's Hall on May 29, the President returned to the theme of détente:

"The President said he was grateful for the boundless hospitality of his hosts, and, more important, that he was grateful for the frank talks. The results were significant because of the preparatory work by the experts both in Moscow and in the United States. We recognized at the outset that most summit conferences had been failures; since the end of World War II they had raised hopes and then failed. These meetings, on the other hand, had been successful because they were well prepared, and also because—and this was important but quite difficult to measure—because of an acceptance of mutual responsibility to respect the other side's viewpoint, and its right to disagree strongly, and, while respecting the equal strength of each side, finally to find a way to reach agreement on fundamental matters.

"The President continued by noting that superficial observers, sometimes in the press, would judge the meeting only by the agreements signed. These are important, but as pointed out by the Soviet side the results will be determined more by how the agreements are implemented. By establishing a process for progress in all areas, this enabled us to reach agreement.

"The President said that on the part of the United States he could assure the Soviet leaders that on all levels of the US Government there would be an intention to take a forthcoming attitude in working out problems that might arise. For example, there is the question of trade. The President noted that he had pointed out the great possibilities in this field. Even though we had not made the progress we would have liked, our differences were narrowed and we could be confident that we would see a blossoming of trade and a new relationship of enormous benefit to our peoples. The key to this, as well as other difficult issues, will be the continuation of frank contacts at all levels, including ambassadors and ministers, and, of course, at the summit level where that is the best way to break an impasse.

"The President said he wanted to conclude his remarks by saying that history had been made by what had been signed, but the real test is what happens in the future. Now that we all know and respect each other, we have an opportunity to make even greater history for future generations." (Memorandum of conversation between President Nixon and General Secretary Brezhnev, May 29, 1972; ibid., Part 2)

116.   **Paper Agreed Upon by the United States and the Soviet Union**[1]

Moscow, May 29, 1972.

BASIC PRINCIPLES OF RELATIONS BETWEEN THE
UNITED STATES OF AMERICA AND THE UNION OF
SOVIET SOCIALIST REPUBLICS

The United States of America and the Union of Soviet Socialist Republics,

Guided by their obligations under the Charter of the United Nations and by a desire to strengthen peaceful relations with each other and to place these relations on the firmest possible basis,

Aware of the need to make every effort to remove the threat of war and to create conditions which promote the reduction of tensions in the world and the strengthening of universal security and international cooperation,

Believing that the improvement of US-Soviet relations and their mutually advantageous development in such areas as economics, science and culture, will meet these objectives and contribute to better mutual understanding and business-like cooperation, without in any way prejudicing the interests of third countries,

Conscious that these objectives reflect the interests of the peoples of both countries,

Have agreed as follows:

First. They will proceed from the common determination that in the nuclear age there is no alternative to conducting their mutual relations on the basis of peaceful coexistence. Differences in ideology and in the social systems of the USA and the USSR are not obstacles to the bilater-

---

[1] Source: *Public Papers of the Presidents of the United States: Richard Nixon, 1972,* pp. 633–634. The text was signed by President Nixon and General Secretary Brezhnev. Following the signing, Kissinger briefed the press. Speaking of the text of the "Basic Principles," Kissinger stated in part:

"As in every document, this document indicates an aspiration and an attitude, and if either the aspiration or the attitude changes, then, of course, as sovereign countries, either side can change its course. Nothing in this document entitles us to give up our alliances or would justify lowering the efforts that have brought us to this point; but at the same time, it is an event of considerable significance that the countries whose seemingly irreconcilable hostility has characterized the entire postwar period, and the two countries which, between themselves or, indeed, individually have the capacity to destroy humanity are making an effort which would state some principles which would reduce the dangers of war and which would enable them to promote a more stable international system." (*Weekly Compilation of Presidential Documents,* Vol. 8, June 5, 1972, p. 952)

al development of normal relations based on the principles of sovereignty, equality, non-interference in internal affairs and mutual advantage.

Second. The USA and the USSR attach major importance to preventing the development of situations capable of causing a dangerous exacerbation of their relations. Therefore, they will do their utmost to avoid military confrontations and to prevent the outbreak of nuclear war. They will always exercise restraint in their mutual relations, and will be prepared to negotiate and settle differences by peaceful means. Discussions and negotiations on outstanding issues will be conducted in a spirit of reciprocity, mutual accommodation and mutual benefit.

Both sides recognize that efforts to obtain unilateral advantage at the expense of the other, directly or indirectly, are inconsistent with these objectives. The prerequisites for maintaining and strengthening peaceful relations between the USA and the USSR are the recognition of the security interests of the Parties based on the principle of equality and the renunciation of the use or threat of force.

Third. The USA and the USSR have a special responsibility, as do other countries which are permanent members of the United Nations Security Council, to do everything in their power so that conflicts or situations will not arise which would serve to increase international tensions. Accordingly, they will seek to promote conditions in which all countries will live in peace and security and will not be subject to outside interference in their internal affairs.

Fourth. The USA and the USSR intend to widen the juridical basis of their mutual relations and to exert the necessary efforts so that bilateral agreements which they have concluded and multilateral treaties and agreements to which they are jointly parties are faithfully implemented.

Fifth. The USA and the USSR reaffirm their readiness to continue the practice of exchanging views on problems of mutual interest and, when necessary, to conduct such exchanges at the highest level, including meetings between leaders of the two countries.

The two governments welcome and will facilitate an increase in productive contacts between representatives of the legislative bodies of the two countries.

Sixth. The Parties will continue their efforts to limit armaments on a bilateral as well as on a multilateral basis. They will continue to make special efforts to limit strategic armaments. Whenever possible, they will conclude concrete agreements aimed at achieving these purposes.

The USA and the USSR regard as the ultimate objective of their efforts the achievement of general and complete disarmament and the establishment of an effective system of international security in accordance with the purposes and principles of the United Nations.

Seventh. The USA and the USSR regard commercial and economic ties as an important and necessary element in the strengthening of their bilateral relations and thus will actively promote the growth of such ties. They will facilitate cooperation between the relevant organizations and enterprises of the two countries and the conclusion of appropriate agreements and contracts, including long-term ones.

The two countries will contribute to the improvement of maritime and air communications between them.

Eighth. The two sides consider it timely and useful to develop mutual contacts and cooperation in the fields of science and technology. Where suitable, the USA and the USSR will conclude appropriate agreements dealing with concrete cooperation in these fields.

Ninth. The two sides reaffirm their intention to deepen cultural ties with one another and to encourage fuller familiarization with each other's cultural values. They will promote improved conditions for cultural exchanges and tourism.

Tenth. The USA and the USSR will seek to ensure that their ties and cooperation in all the above-mentioned fields and in any others in their mutual interest are built on a firm and long-term basis. To give a permanent character to these efforts, they will establish in all fields where this is feasible joint commissions or other joint bodies.

Eleventh. The USA and the USSR make no claim for themselves and would not recognize the claims of anyone else to any special rights or advantages in world affairs. They recognize the sovereign equality of all states.

The development of US-Soviet relations is not directed against third countries and their interests.

Twelfth. The basic principles set forth in this document do not affect any obligations with respect to other countries earlier assumed by the USA and the USSR.

117.   Address by President Nixon to a Joint Session of the Congress[1]

Washington, June 1, 1972.

Mr. Speaker, Mr. President, Members of the Congress, our distinguished guests, my fellow Americans:

Your welcome in this great Chamber tonight has a very special meaning to Mrs. Nixon and to me. We feel fortunate to have traveled abroad so often representing the United States of America. But we both agree after each journey that the best part of any trip abroad is coming home to America again.

During the past 13 days we have flown more than 16,000 miles and we visited four countries. Everywhere we went—to Austria, the Soviet Union, Iran, Poland—we could feel the quickening pace of change in old international relationships and the peoples' genuine desire for friendship for the American people. Everywhere new hopes are rising for a world no longer shadowed by fear and want and war, and as Americans we can be proud that we now have an historic opportunity to play a great role in helping to achieve man's oldest dream—a world in which all nations can enjoy the blessings of peace.

On this journey we saw many memorable sights, but one picture will always remain indelible in our memory—the flag of the United States of America flying high in the spring breeze above Moscow's ancient Kremlin fortress.

To millions of Americans for the past quarter century the Kremlin has stood for implacable hostility toward all that we cherish, and to millions of Russians the American flag has long been held up as a symbol of evil. No one would have believed, even a short time ago, that these two apparently irreconcilable symbols would be seen together as we saw them for those few days.

But this does not mean that we bring back from Moscow the promise of instant peace, but we do bring the beginning of a process that can lead to a lasting peace. And that is why I have taken the extraordinary action of requesting this special joint session of the Congress because we have before us an extraordinary opportunity.

---

[1] Source: *Public Papers of the Presidents of the United States: Richard Nixon, 1972*, pp. 660–666. The President spoke at 9:40 p.m. in the House Chamber at the Capitol. The address, presented upon the President's return from the Moscow Summit, as well as visits to Austria, Iran, and Poland, was broadcast live on radio and television.

I have not come here this evening to make new announcements in a dramatic setting. This summit has already made its news. It has barely begun, however, to make its mark on our world, and I ask you to join me tonight—while events are fresh, while the iron is hot—in starting to consider how we can help to make that mark what we want it to be.

The foundation has been laid for a new relationship between the two most powerful nations in the world. Now it is up to us—to all of us here in this Chamber, to all of us across America—to join with other nations in building a new house upon that foundation, one that can be a home for the hopes of mankind and a shelter against the storms of conflict.

As a preliminary, therefore, to requesting your concurrence in some of the agreements we reached and your approval of funds to carry out others, and also as a keynote for the unity in which this Government and this Nation must go forward from here, I am rendering this immediate report to the Congress on the results of the Moscow summit.

The pattern of U.S.-Soviet summit diplomacy in the cold war era is well known to all those in this Chamber. One meeting after another produced a brief euphoric mood—the spirit of Geneva, the spirit of Camp David, the spirit of Vienna, the spirit of Glassboro—but without producing significant progress on the really difficult issues.

And so early in this Administration I stated that the prospect of concrete results, not atmospherics, would be our criterion for meeting at the highest level. I also announced our intention to pursue negotiations with the Soviet Union across a broad front of related issues, with the purpose of creating a momentum of achievement in which progress in one area could contribute to progress in others.

This is the basis on which we prepared for and conducted last week's talks. This was a working summit. We sought to establish not a superficial spirit of Moscow, but a solid record of progress on solving the difficult issues which for so long have divided our two nations and also have divided the world. Reviewing the number and the scope of agreements that emerged, I think we have accomplished that goal.

Recognizing the responsibility of the advanced industrial nations to set an example in combatting mankind's common enemies, the United States and the Soviet Union have agreed to cooperate in efforts to reduce pollution and enhance environmental quality. We have agreed to work together in the field of medical science and public health, particularly in the conquest of cancer and heart disease.

Recognizing that the quest for useful knowledge transcends differences between ideologies and social systems, we have agreed to expand United States and Soviet cooperation in many areas of science and technology.

We have joined in plans for an exciting new adventure, a new adventure in the cooperative exploration of space, which will begin—subject to Congressional approval of funding—with a joint orbital mission of an Apollo vehicle and a Soviet spacecraft in 1975.

By forming habits of cooperation and strengthening institutional ties in areas of peaceful enterprise, these four agreements, to which I have referred, will create on both sides a steadily growing vested interest in the maintenance of good relations between our two countries.

Expanded United States-Soviet trade will also yield advantages to both of our nations. When the two largest economies in the world start trading with each other on a much larger scale, living standards in both nations will rise, and the stake which both have in peace will increase.

Progress in this area is proceeding on schedule. At the summit, we established a joint Commercial Commission which will complete the negotiations for a comprehensive trade agreement between the United States and the U.S.S.R. And we expect the final terms of this agreement to be settled later this year.

Two further accords which were reached last week have a much more direct bearing on the search for peace and security in the world.

One is the agreement between the American and Soviet navies aimed at significantly reducing the chances of dangerous incidents between our ships and aircraft at sea.

And second, and most important, there is the treaty and the related executive agreement which will limit, for the first time, both offensive and defensive strategic nuclear weapons in the arsenals of the United States and the Soviet Union.

Three-fifths of all the people alive in the world today have spent their whole lifetimes under the shadow of a nuclear war which could be touched off by the arms race among the great powers. Last Friday in Moscow we witnessed the beginning of the end of that era which began in 1945. We took the first step toward a new era of mutually agreed restraint and arms limitation between the two principal nuclear powers.

With this step we have enhanced the security of both nations. We have begun to check the wasteful and dangerous spiral of nuclear arms which has dominated relations between our two countries for a generation. We have begun to reduce the level of fear by reducing the causes of fear, for our two peoples and for all peoples in the world.

The ABM Treaty will be submitted promptly for the Senate's advice and consent to ratification and the interim agreement limiting certain offensive weapons will be submitted to both Houses for concurrence, because we can undertake agreements as important as these only on a basis of full partnership between the executive and legislative branches of our Government.

I ask from this Congress and I ask from the Nation the fullest scrutiny of these accords. I am confident such examination will underscore the truth of what I told the Soviet people on television just a few nights ago—that this is an agreement in the interest of both nations. From the standpoint of the United States, when we consider what the strategic balance would have looked like later in the seventies, if there had been no arms limitation, it is clear that the agreements forestall a major spiraling of the arms race—one which would have worked to our disadvantage, since we have no current building programs for the categories of weapons which have been frozen, and since no new building program could have produced any new weapons in those categories during the period of the freeze.

My colleagues in the Congress, I have studied the strategic balance in great detail with my senior advisers for more than 3 years. I can assure you, the Members of the Congress, and the American people tonight that the present and planned strategic forces of the United States are without question sufficient for the maintenance of our security and the protection of our vital interests.

No power on earth is stronger than the United States of America today. And none will be stronger than the United States of America in the future.

This is the only national defense posture which can ever be acceptable to the United States. This is the posture I ask the Senate and the Congress to protect by approving the arms limitation agreements to which I have referred. This is the posture which, with the responsible cooperation of the Congress, I will take all necessary steps to maintain in our future defense programs.

In addition to the talks which led to the specific agreements I have listed, I also had full, very frank, and extensive discussions with General Secretary Brezhnev and his colleagues about several parts of the world where American and Soviet interests have come in conflict.

With regard to the reduction of tensions in Europe, we recorded our intention of proceeding later this year with multilateral consultations looking toward a conference on security and cooperation in all of Europe. We have also jointly agreed to move forward with negotiations on mutual and balanced force reductions in central Europe.

The problem of ending the Vietnam war, which engages the hopes of all Americans, was one of the most extensively discussed subjects on our agenda. It would only jeopardize the search for peace if I were to review here all that was said on that subject. I will simply say this: Each side obviously has its own point of view and its own approach to this very difficult issue. But at the same time, both the United States and the Soviet Union share an overriding desire to achieve a more stable peace in the world. I emphasize to you once again that this Administration has no higher goal, a goal that I know all of you share, than bringing the Vietnam war to an early and honorable end. We are ending the war in Vietnam, but we shall end it in a way which will not betray our friends, risk the lives of the courageous Americans still serving in Vietnam, break faith with those held prisoners by the enemy, or stain the honor of the United States of America.

Another area where we had very full, frank, and extensive discussions was the Middle East. I reiterated the American people's commitment to the survival of the state of Israel and to a settlement just to all the countries in the area. Both sides stated in the communiqué their intention to support the Jarring peace mission and other appropriate efforts to achieve this objective.

The final achievement of the Moscow conference was the signing of a landmark declaration entitled "Basic Principles of Mutual Relations Between the United States and the U.S.S.R."[2] As these 12 basic principles are put into practice, they can provide a solid framework for the future development of better American-Soviet relations.

They begin with the recognition that two nuclear nations, each of which has the power to destroy humanity, have no alternative but to coexist peacefully, because in a nuclear war there would be no winners, only losers.

The basic principles commit both sides to avoid direct military confrontation and to exercise constructive leadership and restraint with respect to smaller conflicts in other parts of the world which could drag the major powers into war.

They disavow any intention to create spheres of influence or to conspire against the interests of any other nation—a point I would underscore by saying once again tonight that America values its ties with all nations, from our oldest allies in Europe and Asia, as I emphasized by my visit to Iran, to our good friends in the third world, and to our new relationship with the People's Republic of China.

The improvement of relations depends not only, of course, on words, but far more on actions. The principles to which we agreed in Moscow are like a road map. Now that the map has been laid out, it is up to each country to follow it. The United States intends to adhere to these principles. The leaders of the Soviet Union have indicated a similar intention.

However, we must remember that Soviet ideology still proclaims hostility to some of America's most basic values. The Soviet leaders

---

[2] Document 116.

remain committed to that ideology. Like the nation they lead, they are and they will continue to be totally dedicated competitors of the United States of America.

As we shape our policies for the period ahead, therefore, we must maintain our defenses at an adequate level until there is mutual agreement to limit forces. The time-tested policies of vigilance and firmness which have brought us to this summit are the only ones that can safely carry us forward to further progress in reaching agreements to reduce the danger of war.

Our successes in the strategic arms talks and in the Berlin negotiations, which opened the road to Moscow, came about because over the past 3 years we have consistently refused proposals for unilaterally abandoning the ABM, unilaterally pulling back our forces from Europe, and drastically cutting the defense budget. The Congress deserves the appreciation of the American people for having the courage to vote such proposals down and to maintain the strength America needs to protect its interests.

As we continue the strategic arms talks, seeking a permanent offensive weapons treaty, we must bear the lessons of the earlier talks well in mind.[3]

By the same token, we must stand steadfastly with our NATO partners if negotiations leading to a new détente and a mutual reduction of forces in Europe are to be productive. Maintaining the strength, integrity, and steadfastness of our free world alliances is the foundation on which all of our other initiatives for peace and security in the world must rest. As we seek better relations with those who have been our adversaries, we will not let down our friends and allies around the world.

And in this period we must keep our economy vigorous and competitive if the opening for greater East-West trade is to mean anything at all, and if we do not wish to be shouldered aside in world markets by the growing potential of the economies of Japan, Western Europe, the Soviet Union, the People's Republic of China. For America to continue its role of helping to build a more peaceful world, we must keep America number one economically in the world.

We must maintain our own momentum of domestic innovation, growth, and reform if the opportunities for joint action with the Soviets are to fulfill their promise. As we seek agreements to build peace abroad, we must keep America moving forward at home.

---

[3] Documentation on the planning, negotiations, and agreements on SALT is scheduled for publication in a forthcoming *Foreign Relations* volume.

Most importantly, if the new age we seek is ever to become a reality, we must keep America strong in spirit—a nation proud of its greatness as a free society, confident of its mission in the world. Let us be committed to our way of life as wholeheartedly as the Communist leaders with whom we seek a new relationship are committed to their system. Let us always be proud to show in our words and actions what we know in our hearts—that we believe in America.

These are just some of the challenges of peace. They are in some ways even more difficult than the challenges of war. But we are equal to them. As we meet them, we will be able to go forward and explore the sweeping possibilities for peace which this season of summits has now opened up for the world.

For decades, America has been locked in hostile confrontation with the two great Communist powers, the Soviet Union and the People's Republic of China. We were engaged with the one at many points and almost totally isolated from the other, but our relationships with both had reached a deadly impasse. All three countries were victims of the kind of bondage about which George Washington long ago warned in these words: "The nation which indulges toward another an habitual hatred . . . is a slave to its own animosity."

But now in the brief space of 4 months, these journeys to Peking and to Moscow have begun to free us from perpetual confrontation. We have moved toward better understanding, mutual respect, point-by-point settlement of differences with both the major Communist powers.

This one series of meetings has not rendered an imperfect world suddenly perfect. There still are deep philosophical differences; there still are parts of the world in which age-old hatreds persist. The threat of war has not been eliminated—it has been reduced. We are making progress toward a world in which leaders of nations will settle their differences by negotiation, not by force, and in which they learn to live with their differences so that their sons will not have to die for those differences.

It was particularly fitting that this trip, aimed at building such a world, should have concluded in Poland.

No country in the world has suffered more from war than Poland—and no country has more to gain from peace. The faces of the people who gave us such a heartwarming welcome in Warsaw yesterday, and then again this morning and this afternoon, told an eloquent story of suffering from war in the past and of hope for peace in the future. One could see it in their faces. It made me more determined than ever that America must do all in its power to help that hope for peace come true for all people in the world.

As we continue that effort, our unity of purpose and action will be all-important.

For the summits of 1972 have not belonged just to one person or to one party or to one branch of our Government alone. Rather they are part of a great national journey for peace. Every American can claim a share in the credit for the success of that journey so far, and every American has a major stake in its success for the future.

An unparalleled opportunity has been placed in America's hands. Never has there been a time when hope was more justified or when complacency was more dangerous. We have made a good beginning. And because we have begun, history now lays upon us a special obligation to see it through. We can seize this moment or we can lose it; we can make good this opportunity to build a new structure of peace in the world or we can let it slip away. Together, therefore, let us seize the moment so that our children and the world's children can live free of the fears and free of the hatreds that have been the lot of mankind through the centuries.

Then the historians of some future age will write of the year 1972, not that this was the year America went up to the summit and then down to the depths of the valley again, but that this was the year when America helped to lead the world up out of the lowlands of constant war, and onto the high plateau of lasting peace.

118.   Briefing by the President's Assistant for National Security
        Affairs (Kissinger) for the Senate Foreign Relations
        Committee[1]

Washington, June 15, 1972.

[Omitted here is a very brief introductory comment by Kissinger.]

In considering the two agreements before the Congress, the treaty on the limitation of antiballistic missile systems and the interim agreement on the limitation of offensive arms,[2] the overriding questions are these: Do these agreements permit the United States to maintain a defense posture that guarantees our security and protects our vital interests? Second, will they lead to a more enduring structure of peace?

In the course of the formal hearings over the coming days and weeks, the Administration will demonstrate conclusively that they serve both of these ends. I will begin that process this morning by offering some general remarks on the agreement, after which I will be happy to take your questions.

U.S.-Soviet Relations in the 1970's

The first part of my remarks will deal with U.S.-Soviet relations as they affect these agreements. The agreement which was signed 46 minutes before midnight in Moscow on the evening of May 26th by President Nixon and General Secretary Brezhnev is without precedent in the nuclear age; indeed, in all relevant modern history.

Never before have the world's two most powerful nations, divided by ideology, history and conflicting interests, placed their central armaments under formally agreed limitation and restraint. It is fair to ask: What new conditions now prevail to have made this step commend itself to the calculated self-interests of both of the so-called superpowers, as it so clearly must have done for both willingly to undertake it?

Let me start, therefore, with a sketch of the broad design of what the President has been trying to achieve in this country's relations with the Soviet Union, since at each important turning point in the SALT negotiations we were guided not so much by the tactical solution that seemed most equitable or prudent, important as it was, but by an

---

[1] Source: *Strategic Arms Limitations Agreements: Hearings Before the Committee on Foreign Relations, United States Senate, Ninety-second Congress, Second Session* (Washington, 1972), pp. 393–398, 400–402.

[2] The Strategic Arms Limitation Treaties (SALT) were signed by President Nixon and General Secretary Brezhnev in Moscow on May 26. The signing was a major highlight of the Moscow Summit meeting.

underlying philosophy and a specific perception of international reality.

The international situation has been undergoing a profound structural change since at least the mid-1960s. The post-World War II pattern of relations among the great powers had been altered to the point that when this Administration took office, a major reassessment was clearly in order.

The nations that had been prostrate in 1945 had regained their economic strength and their political vitality. The Communist bloc was divided into contending factions, and nationalistic forces and social and economic pressures were reasserting themselves within the individual Communist states.

Perhaps most important for the United States, our undisputed strategic predominance was declining just at a time when there was rising domestic resistance to military programs, and impatience for redistribution of resources from national defense to social demands.

Amidst all of this profound change, however, there was one important constant—the continuing dependence of most of the world's hopes for stability and peace upon the ability to reduce the tensions between the United States and the Soviet Union.

The factors which perpetuated that rivalry remain real and deep.

We are ideological adversaries, and we will in all likelihood remain so for the foreseeable future.

We are political and military competitors, and neither can be indifferent to advances by the other in either of these fields.

We each have allies whose association we value and whose interests and activities of each impinge on those of the other at numerous points.

We each possess an awesome nuclear force created and designed to meet the threat implicit in the other's strength and aims.

Each of us has thus come into possession of power singlehandedly capable of exterminating the human race. Paradoxically, this very fact, and the global interest of both sides, create a certain commonality of outlook, a sort of interdependence for survival between the two of us.

Although we compete, the conflict will not admit of resolution by victory in the classical sense. We are compelled to coexist. We have an inescapable obligation to build jointly a structure for peace. Recognition of this reality is the beginning of wisdom for a sane and effective foreign policy today.

President Nixon has made it the starting point of the United States policy since 1969. This Administration's policy is occasionally characterized as being based on the principles of the classical balance of power. To the extent that that term implies a belief that security requires a measure of equilibrium, it has a certain validity. No national leader has the right to mortgage the survival of his people to the good will of another state. We must seek firmer restraints on the actions of potentially hostile states than a sanguine appeal to their good nature.

But to the extent that balance of power means constant jockeying for marginal advantages over an opponent, it no longer applies. The reason is that the determination of national power has changed fundamentally in the nuclear age. Throughout history, the primary concern of most national leaders has been to accumulate geopolitical and military power. It would have seemed inconceivable even a generation ago that such power once gained could not be translated directly into advantage over one's opponent. But now both we and the Soviet Union have begun to find that each increment of power does not necessarily represent an increment of usable political strength.

With modern weapons, a potentially decisive advantage requires a change of such magnitude that the mere effort to obtain it can produce disaster. The simple tit-for-tat reaction to each other's programs of a decade ago is in danger of being overtaken by a more or less simultaneous and continuous process of technological advance, which opens more and more temptations for seeking decisive advantage.

A premium is put on striking first and on creating a defense to blunt the other side's retaliatory capability. In other words, marginal additions of power cannot be decisive. Potentially decisive additions are extremely dangerous, and the quest for them are destabilizing. The argument that arms races produce war has often been exaggerated. The nuclear age is overshadowed by its peril.

All of this was in the President's mind as he mapped the new directions of American policy at the outset of this Administration. There was reason to believe that the Soviet leadership might also be thinking along similar lines as the repeated failure of their attempts to gain marginal advantage in local crises or in military competition underlined the limitation of old policy approaches.

The President, therefore, decided that the United States should work to create a set of circumstances which would offer the Soviet leaders an opportunity to move away from confrontation through carefully prepared negotiations. From the first, we rejected the notion that what was lacking was a cordial climate for conducting negotiations.

Past experience has amply shown that much heralded changes in atmospherics, but not buttressed by concrete progress, will revert to previous patterns at the first subsequent clash of interests.

We have, instead, sought to move forward across a broad range of issues so that progress in one area would add momentum to the progress of other areas.

We hoped that the Soviet Union would acquire a stake in a wide spectrum of negotiations and that it would become convinced that its interests would be best served if the entire process unfolded. We have sought, in short, to create a vested interest in mutual restraint.

At the same time, we were acutely conscious of the contradictory tendencies at work in Soviet policy. Some factors—such as the fear of nuclear war; the emerging consumer economy, and the increased pressures of a technological, administrative society—have encouraged the Soviet leaders to seek a more stable relationship with the United States. Other factors—such as ideology, bureaucratic inertia, and the catalytic effect of turmoil in peripheral areas—have prompted pressures for tactical gains.

The President has met each of these manifestations on its own terms, demonstrating receptivity to constructive Soviet initiatives and firmness in the face of provocations or adventurism. He has kept open a private channel through which the two sides could communicate candidly and settle matters rapidly. The President was convinced that agreements dealing with questions of armaments in isolation do not, in fact, produce lasting inhibitions on military competition because they contribute little to the kind of stability that makes crises less likely. In recent months, major progress was achieved in moving toward a broadly-based accommodation of interests with the USSR, in which an arms limitation agreement could be a central element.

This approach was called linkage, not by the Administration, and became the object of considerable debate in 1969. Now, three years later, the SALT agreement does not stand alone, isolated and incongruous in the relationship of hostility, vulnerable at any moment to the shock of some sudden crisis. It stands, rather, linked organically, to a chain of agreements and to a broad understanding about international conduct appropriate to the dangers of the nuclear age.

The agreements on the limitation of strategic arms is, thus, not merely a technical accomplishment, although it is that in part, but it must be seen as political event of some magnitude. This is relevant to the question of whether the agreements will be easily breached or circumvented. Given the past, no one can answer the question with certainty, but it can be said with some assurance that any country which contemplates a rupture of the agreement or a circumvention of its letter and spirit must now face the fact that it will be placing in jeopardy not only a limited arms control agreement, but a broad political relationship.

[Omitted here is a review of the preparation for the arms talks and the provisions of the SALT agreements.]

What Do the Agreements Mean?

Taking the longer perspective, what can we say has been accomplished?

First, it is clear that the agreement will enhance the security of both sides. No agreement which fails to do so could have been signed in the first place or stood any chance of lasting after it was signed. An attempt to gain a unilateral advantage in the strategic field must be self-defeating.

The President has given the most careful consideration to the final terms. He has asked me to reiterate most emphatically this morning his conviction that the agreements fully protect our national security and our vital interests.

Secondly, the President is determined that our security and vital interests shall remain fully protected. If the Senate consents to ratification of the treaty and if the Congress approves the interim agreement, the Administration will, therefore, pursue two parallel courses.

On the one hand, we shall push the next phase of the Strategic Arms Limitation Talks with the same energy and conviction that have produced these initial agreements.

On the other hand, until further arms limits are negotiated, we shall push research and development and the production capacity to remain in a fully protected strategic posture should follow-on agreements prove unattainable and so as to avoid giving the other side a temptation to break out of the agreement.

Third, the President believes that these agreements, embedded as they are in the fabric of an emerging new relationship, can hold tremendous political and historical significance in the coming decades. For the first time, two great powers, deeply divided by their divergent values, philosophies, and social systems, have agreed to restrain the very armaments on which their national survival depends. No decision of this magnitude could have been taken unless it had been part of a larger decision to place relations on a new foundation of restraint, cooperation and steadily evolving confidence. A spectrum of agreements on joint effort with regard to the environment, space, health, and promising negotiations on economic relations provides a prospect for avoiding the failure of the Washington Naval Treaty and the Kellogg–Briand pact outlawing war which collapsed in part for lack of an adequate political foundation.

The final verdict must wait on events, but there is at least reason to hope that these accords represent a major break in the pattern of suspicion, hostility, and confrontation which has dominated U.S.-Soviet relations for a generation. The two great nuclear powers must not let this opportunity slip away by jockeying for marginal advantages.

Inevitably an agreement of such consequence raises serious questions on the part of concerned individuals of quite different persuasions. I cannot do justice to all of them here. Let me deal with some of the most frequently asked since the agreements were signed three weeks ago.

Who won?

The President has already answered this question. He has stressed that it is inappropriate to pose the question in terms of victory or defeat. In an agreement of this kind, either both sides win or both sides lose. This will either be a serious attempt to turn the world away from time-worn practices of jockeying for power, or there will be endless, wasteful and purposeless competition in the acquisition of armaments.

Does the agreement perpetuate a U.S. strategic disadvantage?

We reject the premise of that question on two grounds. First, the present situation is on balance advantageous to the United States. Second, the Interim Agreement perpetuates nothing which did not already exist in fact and which could only have gotten worse without an agreement.

Our present strategic military situation is sound. Much of the criticism has focused on the imbalance in number of missiles between the U.S. and the Soviet Union. But, this only examines one aspect of the problem. To assess the overall balance it is necessary to consider those forces not in the agreement; our bomber force which is substantially larger and more effective than the Soviet bomber force, and our forward base systems.

The quality of the weapons must also be weighed. We are confident we have major advantage in nuclear weapons technology and in warhead accuracy. Also, with our MIRV's we have a two-to-one lead today in numbers of warheads and this lead will be maintained during the period of the agreement, even if the Soviets develop and deploy MIRV's of their own.

Then there are such factors as deployment characteristics. For example, because of the difference in geography and basing, it has been estimated that the Soviet Union requires three submarines for two of ours to be able to keep an equal number on station.

When the total picture is viewed, our strategic forces are seen to be completely sufficient.

The Soviets have more missile launchers, but when other relevant systems such as bombers are counted there are roughly the same number of launchers on each side. We have a big advantage on warheads. The Soviets have an advantage on megatonnage.

What is disadvantageous to us, though, is the trend of new weapons deployment by the Soviet Union and the projected imbalance five years hence based on that trend. The relevant question to ask, therefore, is what the freeze prevents; where would we be by 1977 without a freeze? Considering the current momentum by the Soviet Union, in both ICBM's and submarine launched ballistic missiles, the ceiling set in the Interim Agreement can only be interpreted as a sound arrangement that makes a major contribution to our national security.

Does the agreement jeopardize our security in the future?

The current arms race compounds numbers by technology. The Soviet Union has proved that it can best compete in sheer numbers. This is the area which is limited by the agreement.

Thus the agreement confines the competition with the Soviets to the area of technology. And, heretofore, we have had a significant advantage.

The follow-on negotiations will attempt to bring the technological race under control. Until these negotiations succeed, we must take care not to anticipate their outcome by unilateral decisions.

Can we trust the Soviets?

The possibility always exists that the Soviets will treat the Moscow agreements as they have sometimes treated earlier ones, as just another tactical opportunity in the protracted conflict. If this happens, the United States will have to respond. This we shall plan to prepare to do psychologically and strategically and provided the Congress accepts the strategic programs on which the acceptance of the agreements was predicated.

I have said enough to indicate we advocate these agreements not on the basis of trust, but on the basis of the enlightened self-interests of both sides. This self-interest is reinforced by the carefully drafted verification provisions in the agreement. Beyond the legal obligations, both sides have a stake in all of the agreements that have been signed, and a large stake in the broad process of improvement in relations that has begun. The Soviet leaders are serious men, and we are confident that they will not lightly abandon the course that has led to the summit meeting and to these initial agreements. For our own part, we will not abandon this course without major provocation, because it is in the interest of this country and in the interest of mankind to pursue it.

Prospects for the Future

At the conclusion of the Moscow summit, the President and General Secretary signed a Declaration of Principles to govern the future relationship between the United States and the Soviet Union.[3] These principles state that there is no alternative to peaceful coexistence

---

[3] Document 116.

in the nuclear age. They commit both sides to avoid direct armed confrontation, to use restraint in local conflicts, to assert no special claims in derogation of the sovereign equality of all nations, to stress cooperation and negotiation at all points of our relationship.

At this point, these principles reflect an aspiration and an attitude. This Administration will spare no effort to translate the aspiration into reality. We shall strive with determination to overcome further the miasma of suspicion and self-confirming preemptive actions which have characterized the Cold War.

Of course the temptation is to continue along well worn paths. The status quo has the advantage of reality, but history is strewn with the wreckage of nations which sought their future in their past. Catastrophe has resulted far less often from conscious decisions than from the fear of breaking loose from established patterns through the inexorable march towards cataclysm because nobody knew what else to do. The paralysis of policy which destroyed Europe in 1914 would surely destroy the world if we let it happen again in the nuclear age.

Thus the deepest question we ask is not whether we can trust the Soviets, but whether we can trust ourselves. Some have expressed concern about the agreements not because they object to their terms, but because they are afraid of the euphoria that these agreements might produce.

But surely we cannot be asked to maintain unavoidable tension just to carry out programs which our national survival should dictate in any event. We must not develop a national psychology by which we can act only on the basis of what we are against and not on what we are for.

Our challenges then are: Can we chart a new course with hope but without illusion, with large purposes but without sentimentality? Can we be both generous and strong? It is not often that a country has the opportunity to answer such questions meaningfully. We are now at such a juncture where peace and progress depend on our faith and our fortitude.

[Omitted here is a brief concluding comment by Kissinger.]

119. Memorandum for the President's File by the President's Special Assistant (Price)[1]

Washington, June 16, 1972.

[Omitted here is commentary on domestic politics.]

As we look at what happened with the Chinese and Soviets, the reason China and the U.S. finally got together is not because we or they finally reached the conclusion that we had been mistaken. It was because at this juncture in history there were very fundamental shifts in the world balance of power that made it imperative that they look elsewhere, and useful to us to have better relations with them.

The leaders of the Chinese government are more dedicated to Communism as an ideology than the Soviets, because they are in an earlier stage. Also, they are more dedicated to supporting the "third world." They consider themselves weak. When it comes to Africa, to Southeast Asia, to the Middle East—the Chinese speak out strongly to those nations. Also, for another reason—not because they love all those people, but also because the overriding Chinese and Russian concern is the fact that both are in competition for the leadership of the Communist world. When the Russians are trying to make an accommodation with the major powers, the Chinese see this as an opportunity to make gains with minor powers around the world. This hasn't worked very well.

The fundamental point, however, is why the Chinese felt it was in their interest. Put yourself in the position of the Chinese leaders—with 800 million people, on one border they see the Russians, with more men there than against Western Europe. To the south, there is India. The Chinese have contempt for the Indians, after the 1962 war. But it gives them pause to see what India could do with the support of the Soviets against China's friend, Pakistan. To the northeast, they see Japan. They have no reason to fear Japan, because Japan has no nuclear weapons. But they have enormous respect for Japan, which has invaded and occupied China. Also, Japan is now the third and will soon be the second economic power in the world, and they could well develop nuclear weapons soon on the industrial base that they have.

---

[1] Source: National Archives, Nixon Presidential Materials, White House Special Files, President's Office Files, B Series Documents, Box 7 ("B" Box 59, Folder 14). Confidential. The President addressed the Cabinet and selected members of the White House staff in the Cabinet Room. According to the Daily Diary, the meeting convened at 8:37 and ended at 10:17 a.m. (Ibid., White House Central Files, Staff Members and Office Files, Office of Presidential Papers and Archives, Daily Diary)

Then there's the U.S. As far as our system is concerned, we are much more antagonistic toward them than anyone else. Mao and Chou make no decisions on a personal basis—only on cold calculation—which is true of most world leaders.

So, if you were the Chinese—you would welcome better relations with the U.S.—given on one flank not an enemy at the very least, and also a nation that because of its interest might restrain some of China's neighbors.

One of the major Chinese doctrines is that Japan must never rearm. Also they say that the U.S. and Japan should dissolve our defense arrangement. But they don't *want* this. Japan, unprotected, facing Russia and China with its enormous economic capacity is not going to be neutral—it will either go with one of the others or rearm. The Chinese know that.

These clowns who write for the media do not understand this. They see it all in terms of their own prejudices from the past.

Now look at the Soviet Union—why is the Soviet Union interested in talking to the U.S. in a number of fields? While they of course jump through the ceiling if you talk about linkage, they link everything.

What are the Soviet Union's problems? They look at China—they know they have nothing to fear now from China, but they also know what they themselves have done economically in 50 years in a relatively backward country. They respect the Chinese people. They know that a billion Chinese in 25 years could be an enormous threat in the future.

The Soviets' major purpose with the U.S. is to weaken the European alliance, and to erase the idea that the Soviets pose any threat to NATO.

As they look to the future, they realize their interests at this time would not be served by allowing the U.S.-Chinese opening to ripen into, not friendship, but a possible accommodation which down the road might threaten them.

So—did we go to China to play against the Soviets, and vice versa? We have to say no. If we ever said yes, they'd have to react the other way. But put yourself in their position.

On arms control, there would have been no agreement whatever if we hadn't had ABM. And we won that by only one vote in the Senate.

The Soviets are no more interested in peace as an end in itself than the Fascists were. They prefer it. Their people don't want war. But the leaders—their goals, while not as violently expressed as the Chinese, have not changed. They still want Communism to spread to other countries, by subversion perhaps. They play it down. No Soviet soldier has been lost since World War II. But, because they have avoided a military confrontation with the U.S., this does not mean that the Soviet leaders have abandoned their ultimate goal—the victory of Communism in other areas of the world.

Every one of the Eastern European countries is a potential problem for the Soviet Union except for perhaps Bulgaria.

These countries are pulled toward Western Europe. They have differences with the Russians. Communism hasn't sunk in there. So the Russians have Eastern Europe on one side, China on the other—and also internal problems.

Anyone who has gone to the Soviet Union 12 years ago, and again now, has to be impressed by the changes. But theirs is still a very primitive society by our standards. They want more consumer goods. So—where's the logical place to turn? France and England don't matter any more. The Soviet and Chinese leaders are total pragmatists. They know where the power is.

Unless the U.S. has not only military strength, but also leadership that makes us respected and credible, they wouldn't be interested in talking to us.

That's why I took the action I did in mining Haiphong.[2] If we were to lose in Vietnam, it would have pleased the Soviets and the Chinese, but there would have been no respect for the American President, no matter who he was—because we had power and didn't use it. When U.S. does become involved, we must be credible. We must stand by our commitments, our allies, our friends.

So the Soviets look at the situation—the arms race—in major categories, they have caught us. They do respect our enormous economic power, and they believe if they get into a race with us on the military side, they cannot hope to gain an advantage and win it.

Therefore, we have reached these agreements.

[Omitted here is commentary relating to defense issues.]

I'm convinced that as a result of what we have done, the chances of having a more peaceful world 50 years from now are substantially increased. But this would not have been done with woolly-headed idealism. If we've come this far, it is because we have not been belligerent, we have avoided exacerbating the problem by engaging in a shouting match. Our personal relationship is as good as it can be. I never believe in letting personal relationships make difficult decisions more difficult. But—you've got to put yourself in their position—how are they going to evaluate us? If they think we are weak, they are going to pounce on us. If they think we are strong, they are going to deal with us.

---

[2] See Document 113.

[Omitted here is brief discussion on defense matters and domestic politics.]

---

120.   **Memorandum for the President's File by the President's Assistant (Flanigan)**[1]

Washington, September 11, 1972.

[Omitted here is discussion on general economic matters and domestic issues relating to trade.]

The President said that eventually we have to look to the longer term aspects of our relations in broader focus. For the present, we have a tough line. For example, his speech to the IMF meeting[2] will not be forthcoming on trade matters. However, we should understand that more is involved here than just questions of "horse-trading between soybeans and cheese."

The real question was what do the Europeans want their position vis-à-vis the U.S. and the Soviet Union to be? Does Europe want to go the route of a "Finlandization" of Europe? If they adopt an anti-U.S. trade policy, resulting in "an unenthusiastic" attitude in the U.S. about Europe, they must be made to understand that it will carry over into the political area. NATO could blow apart. The idea that the Europeans can defend themselves without us is "bull." If NATO comes apart, they will be in a position of being economic giants and military pygmies. Cutting themselves off from the U.S. risks a more subtle form of invasion by the Soviet Union than in the conventional military sense.

European leaders, he said, are "terrified" at that prospect. However, "the economic guys over there just want to screw us and our economic guys should want to do the same. There ought to be a lot of screwing going on."

---

[1] Source: National Archives, Nixon Presidential Materials, White House Special Files, President's Office Files, Memos for the President, Box 89, June 4–September 17, 1972. Secret. The memorandum is a record of the President's meeting with the Council on International Economic Policy (CIEP). The meeting took place in the Cabinet Room between 10:06 and 11:06 a.m. (Ibid., White House Central Files, Staff Members and Office Files, Office of Presidential Papers and Archives, Daily Diary) Another account of this meeting is printed in *Foreign Relations, 1969–1976*, vol. III, Document 100.

[2] Document 121.

Nevertheless, the political aspects of our relations should be overriding for both sides. Between now and the elections, we should say nothing, but we should be giving careful thought about how trade relations fit into the context of our overall relations. We need to examine the trade prices which both we and they will have to pay for the continued strength of our overall relations. "We cannot allow the umbilical cord to be cut and Europe to be nibbled away by the Soviets." We need to strengthen the bonds of trade, monetary relations, parliamentary exchanges, etc.

To illustrate his point, the President recalled that, in watching the 100 meter race of the Olympics, he was struck by the remarks of the Soviet winner. Borzov said that the "race marked the end of an era and now the *Europeans* are the best." This was an example of the new style, according to which the Soviets are trying to identify themselves with the Europeans and against the U.S. Basically this example was just white racism (since our runners were black), but the idea of *Europe* versus the U.S. is a Soviet line. Brezhnev and Kosygin say almost the same thing.

Free Europeans know they would be out of their minds to come under this influence. They know we have the divisions and the nuclear weapons. It is easy to say we will take them out of Europe, but it is definitely not in our interest to do so. Nevertheless, there is a growing sentiment in the U.S. to the effect of "damn the Europeans" and "the foreigners are doing us in."

It is true that the foreigners are treating us badly and understandable that we should want to do them in too. However, he urged that we be under no illusions. We cannot turn isolationist in the broader context. If we were only looking at trade, we could get along without the Europeans or the rest of the world, since trade is much less important to our GNP than it is to others. Trade is "the froth on top of the beer" but "beer without froth does not taste too bad."

However, trade is part of a bigger package. For instance, we have to treat Japan with "tender loving care" since, what Europe could become to the Soviets, Japan to China would be even more. Trade is important politically, and good trade relations can contribute to good overall relations. We must realize that our interests can be served by being as tough as we can without going over the line where anti-U.S. sentiment will cause them to turn against us and break with us. The Europeans recognize that they do not matter in the world anymore, and thus they concentrate on economic issues which are more important to them. That means that we may have to give more than our trade interest, strictly construed, would require. However, for the moment, we should let them know that a lot of Americans would welcome a trade split with Europe. We should stress that the Administration is fighting against this, but the Europeans should realize why we are doing it. It is not because our economic survival is at stake but rather that we value our overall relations very highly, in the interest of world peace.

At the same time, they must understand that our economic relations affect our leadership position in the world. In the future, our relations will have a larger economic content and this will require more subtlety in the way we conduct our overall relations. We are best at this game because we are strongest.

This is not the time to fix on a major strategy. After the elections is the time to do this. Then we can do what we have to do. It is going to be very hard to sell trade liberalization to the Congress. We will be prepared to do it because we know that more is at stake than just trade. But for now we should not talk in public about the political-commercial trade-off.

Secretary Peterson asked what the possibilities looked like for a longer term political-security-trade linkage in our relations with Europe, and the prospects of selling liberalization bill to Congress.

The President said that if we do well in the elections, for a few months we can get quite a lot from the Congress. This does not mean we need a landslide but just a good majority. With that, we can make a major move to propose what is best for the country and to educate the country so that it sees the issues in the broader context.

We have to be able to show the country that there is a major shift in the world balance of power, particularly as among ourselves, the Russians, the Chinese and the Japanese. As regards Europe, the Europeans "will have one hell of a time acting as a bloc." They do not get along with each other and it will be some time before they can learn to act as a group. This means we have to work with the heads of government in the various countries and not "that jackass" in the European Commission in Brussels.[3]

The President said that it is important that, after the elections, we look at the long-range relations. We have to tie this in with the whole political problem of what we want our relations with Europe to be. "We have to think internationally—we're it in the Free World." We would miss a great opportunity if we do not see these relations in broader terms and be guided by the broader picture. Then we can move to educate the public as to how it is in their own self-interest. However, we may also be able to get something in the economic area by using our political-security leverage.

---

[3] Presumably a reference to European Commission President Sicco Mansholt.

[Omitted here is a concluding comment by Nixon relating mainly to political concerns.]

---

121.   Remarks by President Nixon[1]

Washington, September 25, 1972.

[Omitted here are brief introductory comments.]

I am convinced, on the basis of the evidence of the past year, that we are not only participating today in a great moment in history, but that we are witnessing and helping to create a profound movement in history.

That movement is away from the resolution of potential conflict by war, and toward its resolution through peaceful means. The experienced people gathered in this room are not so naive as to expect the smoothing out of all differences between peoples and between nations. We anticipate that the potential for conflict will exist as long as men and nations have different interests, different approaches, different ideals.

Therefore, we must come to grips with the paradoxes of peace. As the danger of armed conflict between major powers is reduced, the potential for economic conflict increases. As the possibility of peace grows stronger, some of the original ties that first bound our postwar alliances together grow weaker. As nations around the world gain new economic strength, the points of commercial contact multiply along with the possibilities of disagreements.

There is another irony that we should recognize on this occasion. With one exception, the nations gathered here whose domestic economies are growing so strongly today can trace much of their postwar growth to the expansion of international trade. The one exception is the United States—the industrial nation with by far the smallest percentage of its gross national product in world trade.

---

[1] Source: *Public Papers of the Presidents of the United States: Richard Nixon, 1972*, pp. 907–908. The President spoke at 11:18 a.m. in the Ballroom of the Sheraton Park Hotel at the opening session of the annual meeting of the Boards of Governors of the International Monetary Fund and the International Bank for Reconstruction and Development.

Why, then, is the United States—seemingly with the least at stake—in the forefront of those working for prompt and thoroughgoing reform of the international monetary system, with all that will mean for the expansion of trade now and in the future?

One reason, of course, is our national self-interest. We want our working men and women, our business men and women, to have a fair chance to compete for their share of the expanding trade between nations. A generation ago, at the end of World War II, we deliberately set out to help our former enemies as well as our weakened allies, so that they would inevitably gain the economic strength which would enable them to compete with us in world markets. And now we expect our trading partners to help bring about equal and fair competition.

There is another reason, more far-reaching and fundamental, that motivates the United States in pressing for economic and monetary reform.

Working together, we must set in place an economic structure that will help and not hinder the world's historic movement toward peace.

We must make certain that international commerce becomes a source of stability and harmony, rather than a cause of friction and animosity.

Potential conflict must be channeled into cooperative competition. That is why the structure of the international monetary system and the future system of world trade are so central to our concerns today. The time has come for action across the entire front of international economic problems. Recurring monetary crises such as we have experienced all too often in the past decade, unfair currency alignments and trading agreements which put the workers of one nation at a disadvantage with workers of another nation, great disparities in development that breed resentment, a monetary system that makes no provision for the realities of the present and the needs of the future—all these not only injure our economies, they also create political tensions that subvert the cause of peace.

There must be a thoroughgoing reform of the world monetary system to clear the path for the healthy economic competition of the future.

We must see monetary reform as one part of a total reform of international economic affairs encompassing trade and investment opportunity for all.

We must create a realistic code of economic conduct to guide our mutual relations—a code which allows governments freedom to pursue legitimate domestic objectives, but which also gives them good reason to abide by agreed principles of international behavior.

Each nation must exercise the power of its example in the realistic and orderly conduct of internal economic affairs so that each nation exports its products and not its problems.

[Omitted here are comments relating to domestic economic matters and to recently concluded agreements with the Soviet Union.]

We recognize that the issues that divide us are many and they are very serious and infinitely complex and difficult. But the impetus that will make this negotiation successful is the force that unites us all, all the 124 nations represented here today: that is a common need to establish a sound and abiding foundation for commerce, leading to a better way of life for all the citizens of all the nations here and all the citizens of the world.

That common need, let us call it the world interest, demands a new freedom of world trade, a new fairness in international economic conduct.

It is a mark of our maturity that we now see that an unfair advantage gained in an agreement today only sabotages that agreement tomorrow.

I well remember when I was a first-year law student, 32 years ago, what the professor of contracts said as he opened the course. He said, "A contract is only as good as the will of the parties to keep it."

The only system that can work is one that each nation has an active interest in making work. The need is self-evident. The will to reform the monetary system is here in this room, and, in a proverb that has its counterpart in almost every language here, where there is a will there is a way.

We are gathered to create a responsible monetary system, responsive to the need for stability and openness, and responsive to the need of each country to reflect its unique character.

In this way we bring to bear one of the great lessons of federalism: that often the best way to enforce an agreed-upon discipline is to let each member take action to adhere to it in the way that is best suited to its local character, its stage of development, its economic structure.

For its part, I can assure you, the United States will continue to rise to its world responsibilities, joining with other nations to create and participate in a modern world economic order.

We are secure enough in our independence to freely assert our interdependence.

These are the principles that I profoundly believe should and will guide the United States in its international economic conduct now and in the years ahead.

We shall press for a more equitable and a more open world of trade. We shall meet competition rather than run away from it.

We shall be a stimulating trading partner, a straightforward bargainer.

We shall not turn inward and isolationist.

In turn we shall look to our friends for evidence of similar rejection of isolationism in economic and political affairs.

Let us all resolve to look at the ledgers of international commerce today with new eyes—to see that there is no heroism in a temporary surplus nor villainy in a temporary deficit, but to see that progress is possible only in the framework of long-term equilibrium. In this regard we must take bold action toward a more equitable and a more open world trading order.

Like every leader of the nations represented here, I want to see new jobs created all over the world, but I cannot condone the export of jobs out of the United States caused by any unfairness built into the world's trading system.

Let all nations in the more advanced stages of industrial development share the responsibility of helping those countries whose major development lies ahead, and let the great industrial nations, in offering that help, in providing it, forgo the temptation to use that help as an instrument of domination, discrimination, or rivalry.

Far more is at stake here than the mechanics of commerce and finance. At stake is the chance to add genuine opportunity to the lives of people, hundreds of millions of people in all nations, the chance to add stability and security to the savings and earnings of hundreds of millions of people in all of our nations, the chance to add economic muscle to the sinews of peace.

I have spoken this morning in general terms about how we can advance our economic interdependence. Later this week, Secretary Shultz will outline a number of proposals which represent the best thinking of my top economic advisers. I commend those proposals to you for your careful consideration.[2]

The word "economics," traced to its Greek root, means "the law of the house."

This house we live in—this community of nations—needs far better laws to guide our future economic conduct. Every nation can prosper and benefit working within a modern world economic order that it has a stake in preserving.

---

[2] See Document 122.

Now, very little of what is done in these negotiations will be widely understood in this country or in any of your countries as well. And very little of it will be generally appreciated.

But history will record the vital nature of the challenge before us. I am confident that the men and the nations gathered here will seize the opportunity to create a monetary and trading system that will work for the coming generation—and will help to shape the years ahead into a generation of peace for all nations in the world.

---

122.   Statement by Secretary of the Treasury Shultz[1]

Washington, September 26, 1972.

The nations gathered here have it in their power to strike a new balance in international economic affairs

The new balance of which I speak does not confine itself to the concepts of a balance of trade or a balance of payments. The world needs a new balance between flexibility and stability in its basic approach to doing business. The world needs a new balance between a unity of purpose and a diversity of execution that will permit nations to cooperate closely without losing their individuality or sovereignty.

We lack that balance today. Success in the negotiations in which we are engaged will be measured in terms of how well we are able to achieve that balance in the future.

I anticipate working closely and intensively with you to that end, shaping and reshaping the best of our thinking as we proceed in full recognition that the legitimate requirements of each nation must be meshed into a harmonious whole.

In that spirit, President Nixon has asked me to put certain ideas before you.

[Omitted here are brief general remarks on economic policy matters.]

---

[1] Source: Department of State *Bulletin,* October 23, 1972, pp. 460–462, 465–466. Secretary Shultz made his statement before the combined IMF–IBRD Boards of Governors. He was U.S. Governor of the Fund and the Bank.

Principles Underlying Monetary Reform

Drawing from this interchange of views, and building upon the Smithsonian agreement,[2] we can now seek a firm consensus for new monetary arrangements that will serve us all in the decades ahead. Indeed, I believe certain principles underlying monetary reform already command widespread support.

First is our mutual interest in encouraging freer trade in goods and services and the flow of capital to the places where it can contribute most to economic growth. We must avoid a breakup of the world into antagonistic blocs. We must not seek a refuge from our problems behind walls of protectionism.

The pursuit of the common welfare through more open trade is threatened by an ancient and recurring fallacy: Surpluses in payments are too often regarded as a symbol of success and of good management rather than as a measure of the goods and services provided from a nation's output without current return.

We must recognize, of course, that freer trade must be reconciled with the need for each country to avoid abrupt change involving serious disruptions of production and employment. We must aim to expand productive employment in all countries—and not at one another's expense.

A second fundamental is the need to develop a common code of conduct to protect and strengthen the fabric of a free and open international economic order.

Such basic rules as "no competitive devaluation" and "most-favored-nation treatment" have served us well, but they and others need to be reaffirmed, supplemented, and made applicable to today's conditions. Without such rules to guide us, close and fruitful cooperation on a day-to-day basis would not be possible.

Third, in shaping these rules we must recognize the need for clear disciplines and standards of behavior to guide the international adjustment process—a crucial gap in the Bretton Woods system. Amid the debate about the contributing causes of past imbalances and the responsibility for initiative toward correction, sight has too often been lost of the fact that adjustment is inherently a two-sided process—that for the world as a whole, every surplus is matched by a deficit.

Resistance of surplus countries to loss of their surpluses defeats the objective of monetary order as surely as failure of deficit countries to attack the source of their deficits. Any effort to develop a balanced and

---

[2] For background, see *Bulletin* of Jan. 10, 1972, p. 32. [Footnote in the source text. See also *Foreign Relations, 1969–1976*, vol. III, Document 221.]

equitable monetary system must recognize that simple fact; effective and symmetrical incentives for adjustment are essential to a lasting system.

Fourth, while insisting on the need for adjustment, we can and should leave considerable flexibility to national governments in their choice among adjustment instruments. In a diverse world, equal responsibility and equal opportunity need not mean rigid uniformity in particular practices. But they do mean a common commitment to agreed international objectives. The belief is widespread—and we share it—that the exchange rate system must be more flexible. However, important as they are, exchange rates are not the only instrument of adjustment policy available; nor in specific instances will they necessarily be the most desirable.

Fifth, our monetary and trading systems are an interrelated complex. As we seek to reform monetary rules, we must at the same time seek to build in incentives for trade liberalization. Certainly, as we look ahead, ways must be found to integrate better the work of the GATT and the IMF. Simultaneously we should insure that there are pressures which move us toward adequate development assistance and away from controls which stifle the free flow of investment.

Finally, and perhaps most fundamental, any stable and well-functioning international monetary system must rest upon sound policies to promote domestic growth and price stability in the major countries. These are imperative national goals for my government—and for yours. And no matter how well we design an international system, its prospects for survival will be doubtful without effective discharge of those responsibilities.

[Omitted here are policy details.]

Cooperation for Equilibrium

I am fully aware that the United States as well as other countries cannot leap into new monetary and trading arrangements without a transitional period. I can state, however, that after such transitional period the United States would be prepared to undertake an obligation to convert official foreign dollar holdings into other reserve assets as a part of a satisfactory system such as I have suggested—a system assuring effective and equitable operation of the adjustment process. That decision will of course need to rest on our reaching a demonstrated capacity during the transitional period to meet the obligation in terms of our reserve and balance of payments position.

We fully recognize that we have not yet reached the strength we need in our external accounts. In the end, there can be no substitute for such strength in providing the underpinning for a stable dollar and a stable monetary system.

An acceptable monetary system requires a willingness on the part of all of us to contribute to the common goal of full international equilibrium. Lacking such equilibrium, no system will work. The equilibrium cannot be achieved by any one country acting alone.

We engage in discussions on trade and financial matters with a full realization of the necessity to continue our own efforts on a broad front to restore our balance of payments. I must add, in all candor, that our efforts to improve our position have in more than one instance been thwarted by the reluctance of others to give up an unjustified preferential and highly protected market position. Yet without success in our endeavor, we cannot maintain our desired share in the provision of aid and reduce our official debt to foreign monetary authorities.

We take considerable pride in our progress toward price stability, improved productivity, and more rapid growth during the past year. Sustained into the future, as it must be, that record will be the best possible medicine not only for our domestic prosperity but for the effective functioning of the international financial system.

[Omitted here are brief concluding comments.]

---

123.   Address by President Nixon[1]

Washington, November 4, 1972.

Good afternoon:

Through the long years of America's involvement in Vietnam, our people's yearning for peace has largely been focused on winning an end to that difficult war. As a result, there has often been a tendency to lose sight of the larger prospects for peace in the rest of the world. As peace in Vietnam comes closer, we can look to the larger world and the long-term future with hope and satisfaction.

Four years ago I promised that we would move from an era of confrontation to an era of negotiation. I also said that we would maintain

---

[1] Source: *Public Papers of the Presidents of the United States: Richard Nixon, 1972*, pp. 1110–1114. The President's address was recorded at the White House for broadcast at 12:07 p.m. on nationwide radio.

our own strength and work to restore that of our alliances, because the way to make real progress toward peace is to negotiate from strength and not from weakness. Because we have done so, the world today is more peaceful by far than it was 4 years ago. The prospects for a full generation of peace are brighter than at any time since the end of World War II.

In the past 4 years, we have concluded more—and more significant—agreements with the Soviets than in all the previous years since World War II. We have ended nearly a quarter century of mutual isolation between the United States and the People's Republic of China. All over the world, the tide toward negotiation is moving. North and South Korea are negotiating with one another. East and West Germany are negotiating with one another. A cease-fire has been in effect for more than 2 years in the Middle East. The leaders of India and Pakistan are talking with one another. The nations of Europe, of NATO, and of the Warsaw Pact are preparing to meet next year in a European Security Conference, and preparations are underway for negotiations on mutual and balanced reduction of armed forces in Central Europe.

All this is evidence of solid progress toward a world in which we can talk about our differences rather than fight about them.

Nineteen hundred seventy-two has been a year of more achievement for peace than any year since the end of World War II. This progress did not just happen by itself.

In my Inaugural Address nearly 4 years ago, I said that the greatest honor history can bestow is the title of peacemaker, but I also pointed out that peace does not come through wishing for it, that there is no substitute for days and even years of patient and prolonged diplomacy.

For the past 4 years this Nation has engaged in patient and prolonged diplomacy in every corner of the world, and we have also maintained the strength that has made our diplomacy credible and peace possible. As a result, we are well on the way toward erecting what I have often referred to as a structure of peace, a structure that rests on the hard concrete of common interests and mutual agreements, and not on the shifting sands of naive sentimentality.

That term, "a structure of peace," speaks an important truth about the nature of peace in today's world. Peace cannot be wished into being. It has to be carefully and painstakingly built in many ways and on many fronts, through networks of alliances, through respect for commitments, through patient negotiations, through balancing military forces and expanding economic interdependence, through reaching one agreement that opens the way to others, through developing patterns of international behavior that will be accepted by other powers. Most important of all, the structure of peace has to be built in such a way that all those who might be tempted to destroy it will instead have a stake in preserving it.

In the past 4 years, my efforts to build that structure of peace have taken me to 22 countries, including four world capitals never visited by an American President before—Peking, Moscow, Warsaw, and Bucharest. Everywhere I have traveled I have seen evidence that the times are on the side of peace, if America maintains its strength and continues on course. For example, ever since World War II, the world's people and its statesmen have dreamed of putting the nuclear genie back in the bottle, of controlling the dreaded nuclear arms race, but always that race remained unchecked until this year.

In Moscow last May, we and the Soviet Union reached the first agreement ever for limiting strategic nuclear arms. We signed that agreement last month in Washington. This was an historic beginning. It moved back the frontiers of fear. It helped check the dangerous spiral of nuclear weapons. It opened the way to further negotiations on further limitations on nuclear arsenals which will soon begin.

As we pursue these negotiations, however, let us remember that no country will pay a price for something that another country will give up for nothing. If we had scrapped the ABM missile system, as many advocated, we would never have achieved the first arms agreement with the Soviets. If we unilaterally slashed our defenses now as our opponents in this election advocate, the Soviets would have no incentive to negotiate further arms limitations.

Or take another example. After 10 years of recurring international monetary crises, we took bold actions a year ago to strengthen the dollar and to bring about a reformed international monetary system that would be fair to the United States and fair to the world. The result of these actions has been a solid and substantial beginning on just such a system, and the stage is now set for an international effort to achieve some of the most important monetary and trade reforms in history. As we complete these reforms in the years ahead, we can usher in a new age of world prosperity, a prosperity made even greater by the rapid expansion of peaceful trade that is now taking place, not only with our traditional trading partners but also with nations that have been our adversaries.

I cite these simply as examples of the broad, unfinished agenda of peace that now lies before us, the agenda of new starts made, of negotiations begun, of new relationships established, which now we must build on with the same initiative and imagination that achieved the initial breakthroughs. As we move forward on this agenda, we can see vast areas of peaceful cooperation to be explored.

We agreed in Peking to pursue cultural, journalistic, educational, and other exchanges, so that the world's most prosperous nation and its most populous nation can get to know one another again.

We agreed in Moscow to cooperate in protecting the environment, explore in space, fight disease. This means the day is fast approaching when a Russian cosmonaut and an American astronaut will shake hands in space, when a Russian chemist and an American biologist will work side by side to find a cure for cancer. And each time our nations join hands in the works of peace, we advance the day when nations will no longer raise their hands in warfare.

Throughout the world today America is respected. This is partly because we have entered a new era of initiative in American foreign policy, and the world's leaders and its people have seen the results. But it is also because the world has come to know America. It knows we are a nation of peaceful intentions, of honorable purposes, true to our commitments. We are respected because for a third of a century under six Presidents we have met the responsibilities of a great and free nation. We have not retreated from the world. We have not betrayed our allies. We have not fallen into the foolish illusion that we could somehow build a wall around America, here to enjoy our comforts, oblivious to the cries or the threats of others. We have maintained our strength.

There are those today who condemn as a relic of a cold war mentality the idea that peace requires strength. There are those who ridicule military expenditures as wasteful and immoral. Our opponents in this campaign have even described the great bipartisan tradition of negotiating from strength as one of the most damaging and costly clichés in the American vocabulary. If the day ever comes when the President of the United States has to negotiate from weakness, that will be a dangerous day, not only for America but for the whole world.

Those who scoff at balance of power diplomacy should recognize that the only alternative to a balance of power is an imbalance of power, and history shows that nothing so drastically escalates the danger of war as such an imbalance. It is precisely the fact that the elements of balance now exist that gives us a rare opportunity to create a system of stability that can maintain the peace, not just for a decade but for a generation and more.

The years ahead will not be easy. The choices will not be simple. They will require an extra measure of care in distinguishing between rhetoric and reality, between the easy temptation and the hard necessity. We will be told that all the things we want to do at home could be painlessly financed if we slashed our military spending. We will be told that we can have peace merely by asking for it, that if we simply demonstrate good will and good faith, our adversaries will do likewise, and that we need do no more. This is dangerous nonsense.

A heavy responsibility lies on the shoulders of those who hold or seek power in today's world, a responsibility not to court the public favor by fostering illusions that peace can be either achieved or kept without maintaining our strength and meeting our responsibilities.

As we approach the end of the war in Vietnam, the great question is whether the end of that war will be only an interlude between wars or the beginning of a generation of peace for the world.

Five months ago, I delivered the first television address to the Soviet people ever made by an American President. I tried to tell them something about America, about the people of America, about our hopes, our desire for peace and progress, not only for ourselves but for all the people of the world. In that talk, I repeated an old story told in Russia about a traveler who was walking to another village, who stopped and asked a woodsman how long it would take him to get there. The woodsman replied he did not know. The traveler was angry, because he was sure the woodsman lived in the village and knew how far it was. But then as soon as he had gone a few steps further down the road, the woodsman called out to him to stop. "It will take you 15 minutes," the woodsman said. "Why didn't you tell me that in the first place?" the traveler demanded. And the woodsman answered, "Because then I didn't know the length of your stride."

In these past 4 years, we and the other nations of the world have had a chance to measure the length of our strides. At last we are traveling in the same direction toward a world of peace, toward an era of negotiation, and of expanding cooperation. In the next 4 years, the President of the United States, whoever he is, will negotiate with the leaders of many nations on a broad range of issues vital to America, vital to the world. As we cast our ballots next Tuesday, the world will see whether we have changed the length of our stride.

If you approve the beginnings we have made, then your vote on election day to support those policies will be a message to the leaders of all other nations that the American people are not going to retreat, are not going to surrender. It will strengthen the President's hand immensely as we continue to move from confrontation to negotiation to cooperation all around the world as we build toward a generation of peace.

Index

ISBN 0-16-051282-4